PRAISE FOR *THE EMPIRE OF NECESSITY*

'*The Empire of Necessity* is scholarship at its best. Greg Grandin's deft penetration into the marrow of the slave industry is compelling, brilliant, and necessary.'

Toni Morrison

'[Grandin] writes with the skills of a fine novelist. With herculean archival research, he traces the backstory of each of the main participants... the owner of the slaves, the Spanish captain, the Yankee captain, and those slaves whose paths to the fateful revolt can be tracked or at least surmised. Then Grandin extends their stories beyond the revolt to the ends of their lives. Each life story leads through the explosive contradictions of the Age of Revolution... Inventive, audacious, passionate.'

Los Angeles Review of Books

'Grandin's pen is exquisite, the descriptions are lively and sensuous. But he is also deeply reflective. The book has import that extends beyond the interest of the story. He is, as scholars often say, making an intervention, challenging how we see the world and its history... Exciting and illuminating.'

San Francisco Chronicle

'Greg Grandin is one of the best of a new generation of historians who have rediscovered the art of writing for both serious scholars and general readers. This may be his best book yet... a work of astonishing power, eloquence and suspense, a genuine tour de force.'

Debby Applegate, Pulitzer Prize-winning author of *The Most Famous Man in America: The Biography of Henry Ward Beecher*

'Engrossing, well researched, and beautifully written... A rigorously sourced work of scholarship with a suspenseful narrative structure that boomerangs back and forth through time. Grandin has delivered a page-turner. You read it as if it were a thriller novel by Scott Turow or Lee Child.'

Chicago Tribune

'Fascinating and engaging.'

Seattle Times

'Rooted in an event known primarily through the genius of Herman Melville's transcendent Benito Cereno, *The Empire of Necessity* is a stunning work of research done all over the rims of two oceans, as well as beautiful, withering storytelling. This is a harrowing story of Muslim Africans trekking across South America, and ultimately a unique window on to the nature of the slave trade, the maritime worlds of the early nineteenth century, the lives lived in-between slavery and freedom all over the Americas, and even the ocean-inspired imagination of Melville. Grandin is a master of grand history with new insights.'

David W. Blight, author of *A Slave No More*

'As well as correcting the factual errors in Melville's book, Mr Grandin uses Captain Delano's account of this and other incidents to explore the complexities and ambiguities of the Atlantic slave trade.'

The Economist

'Grandin tracks backwards… like a sleuth, unearthing the motivations and machinations… It's a testament to Grandin's power as a writer that [seal hunter] Delano's hardships and failings generate sympathy – even when compared with the stuff the Africans faced… I can't say enough good things about *The Empire of Necessity*. It's one of the best books I've read in a decade.'

Victor Lavalle, *Bookforum*

'A splendid account… deeply researched and well-written.'

Dallas Morning News

'A great and moving story.'

Washington Post

ALSO BY GREG GRANDIN

Fordlandia: The Rise and Fall of Henry Ford's
Forgotten Jungle City

Empire's Workshop: Latin America, the United States,
and the Rise of the New Imperialism

The Last Colonial Massacre: Latin America in the Cold War

The Blood of Guatemala: A History of Race and Nation

THE EMPIRE OF NECESSITY

THE EMPIRE OF
NECESSITY

THE UNTOLD HISTORY OF A SLAVE REBELLION
IN THE AGE OF LIBERTY

GREG GRANDIN

ONEWORLD

A ONEWORLD BOOK

First published in Great Britain and Australia
by Oneworld Publications in 2014

Originally published in the United States of America by Metropolitan Books,
an imprint of Henry Holt and Company, LLC,
175 Fifth Avenue, New York, New York 10010, USA

Hardback ISBN: 978-1-78074-410-0
Ebook ISBN: 978-1-78074-411-7

Maps by Jeffrey L. Ward
Designed by Kelly S. Too
Printed by TJ International Ltd, Padstow, UK

Oneworld Publications
10 Bloomsbury Street, London WC1B 3SR

For Eleanor

Seeking to conquer a larger liberty, man but extends the empire of necessity.

Author unknown. Used as epigraph to Herman Melville's 'The Bell-Tower.'

CONTENTS

THE EMPIRE OF NECESSITY

INTRODUCTION

Wednesday, February 20, 1805,
shortly after sunrise, in the South Pacific

Captain Amasa Delano was lying awake in his cot when his deck officer came to tell him that a vessel had been spotted coming round the southern head of Santa María, a small, uninhabited island off the coast of Chile. By the time Delano had dressed and come topside the 'strange ship,' as he later described it, had slackened its sails and was now drifting with the wind toward an underwater ledge. To his puzzlement, it flew no flag. It looked to be in want and, if it drew closer to the shallows, in danger. Delano hastily had water, pumpkins, and fresh fish loaded in a boat. He then ordered it hoisted down and went on board.

The weather that morning was thick and breezy but the sun rose to reveal a calm bay. The other side of the island, from where the mysterious ship had appeared, was rough. Endless breakers, sharp-toothed underwater reefs, and steep rock-faced cliffs made its coastline unapproachable, providing sanctuaries for the seals that elsewhere had been hunted to near extinction. But the island's east, where the *Perseverance* harboured, was peaceful, the Southern Hemisphere's waning summer offering a harmony of lulling earth tones, brown, rich dirt, green sea, and cloudless blue skies. High bluffs blanketed by wild red thistles shielded a sandy, safe haven used by sealers and whalers to socialize, pass mailbags to ships bound home, and replenish wood and water.

As he came closer, Delano could see the ship's name, the *Tryal*, painted in English in faded white letters along its bow. He could also see that its deck was full of black-skinned people, who looked to be slaves. And when he climbed on board, the alabaster-skinned New Englander discovered himself surrounded by scores of Africans and a handful of Spanish and mulatto sailors telling their 'stories' and sharing their 'grievances' in a babel of languages.

They spoke in Wolof, Mandinka, Fulani, and Spanish, a rush of words indecipherable in its details but soothing to Delano in its generalities. Earlier, as his men rowed toward the ship, he could see that its sails were tattered. What should have been an orderly web of rigging and tackle was a wooly mash. Its hull, calcified, moss covered, and pulling a long trail of sea grass, gave off a greenish tint. But he knew it was a common pirates' ploy to make ships appear distressed in order to lure victims on board. Napoleon had just crowned himself emperor of the French, Madrid and Paris were at war with London, and privateers were raiding merchant ships at will, even in the distant South Pacific. Now, though, hollow cheeks and frantic eyes confirmed that the misery was real, turning Delano's fears into 'feelings of pity.'

Amasa Delano was on board the *Tryal* for about nine hours, from around seven in the morning to a little after four in the afternoon. Having sent his away team back to the island to fill the *Tryal*'s casks with water, he spent most of the day alone among its voyagers, talking with its captain, helping to distribute the food and water he had brought with him, and securing the ship so it didn't drift. Delano, a distant cousin of Franklin Delano Roosevelt, from a respected shipbuilding and fishing family on the Massachusetts coast, was an experienced mariner in the middle of his third sail around the world. Yet he couldn't see that it was the *Tryal*'s slaves, and not the man who introduced himself as its master, who were in command.

Led by an older man named Babo and his son Mori, the West Africans had seized control of the *Tryal* nearly two months earlier and executed most of its crew and passengers, along with the slave trader who was taking them to Lima. They then ordered Benito Cerreño, the vessel's owner and captain, to sail them to Senegal. Cerreño stalled, afraid of rounding Cape Horn with only a handful of sailors and a ship full of mutinous slaves. He cruised first up and then down the Chilean coast, before running into Delano's *Perseverance*. The slaves could have fought or fled. Instead, Babo came up with a plan. The West Africans let Delano come on board and they acted as if they were still slaves. Mori stayed at Cerreño's side and feigned to be a humble and devoted servant. Cerreño pretended he was still in charge, making up a story about storms, doldrums, and fevers to account for the state of his ship and the absence of any officer besides himself.

Delano didn't know what to make of Cerreño. He remained uneasy around him, even after he had convinced himself that he wasn't a brigand. Delano mistook Cerreño's vacant stare—the effect of hunger and thirst and of having lived for almost two months under a death threat, after having witnessed most of his crew being executed—for disdain, as if the aristocratic-looking Spaniard, dressed in a velvet jacket and loosely fitting black pants, thought himself too good to converse with a pea-coated New Englander. The West Africans, especially the women, also made Delano uncomfortable, though he couldn't say why. There were nearly thirty females on board, among them older women, young girls, and about nine mothers with suckling infants. Once the food and water had been doled out, the women took their babies and gathered together in the stern, where they began to sing a slow dirge to a tune Delano didn't recognize. Nor did he understand the words, though the song had the opposite effect on him than did the soothing mix of languages that had welcomed his arrival.

Then there was Cerreño's servant, Mori, who never left his master's side. When the two captains went below deck, Mori followed. When Delano asked Cerreño to send the slave away so they could have a word alone, the Spaniard refused. The West African was his 'confidant' and 'companion,' he insisted, and Delano could speak freely in front of him. Mori was, Cerreño said, 'captain of the slaves.' At first, Delano was amused by the attentiveness Mori paid to his master's needs. He started, though, to resent him, vaguely blaming the black man for the unease he had felt toward Cerreño. Delano became fixated on the slave. Mori, he later wrote, 'excited my wonder.' Other West Africans, including

Mori's father, Babo, were also always around, 'always listening.' They seemed to anticipate Delano's thoughts, hovering around him like a school of pilot fish, moving him first this way, then that. 'They all looked up to me as a benefactor,' Delano wrote in his memoir, *A Narrative of Voyages and Travels in the Northern and Southern Hemispheres*, published in 1817, still, twelve years after the fact, confusing how he thought the rebels saw him that day with how they actually did see him.

It was only in the late afternoon, around four o'clock, after his men had returned with the additional food and supplies, that the ploy staged by the West Africans unravelled. Delano was sitting in the stern of his away boat, about to return to the *Perseverance*, when Benito Cerreño leapt overboard to escape Mori and came crashing down at his feet. It was at that point, after hearing Cerreño's explanation for every strange thing he saw on board the *Tryal*, that Delano realized the depth of the deception. He then readied his men to unleash a god-awful violence.[1]

Over the years, this remarkable affair—in effect a one-act, nine-hour, full-cast pantomime of the master-slave relation performed by a group of desperate, starving, and thirsty men and women, most of whom didn't speak the language of their would-be captors—inspired a number of writers, poets, and novelists, who saw in the masquerade lessons for their time. The Chilean poet Pablo Neruda, for example, thought the boldness of the slaves reflected the dissent of the 1960s. In the last years of his life, Neruda started first a long poem and then a screenplay that he called 'Babo, the Rebel.' More recently the Uruguayan Tomás de Mattos wrote a Chinese box of a novel, *La Fragata de las máscaras*, which used the deception as a metaphor for a world where reality wasn't what was hidden behind the mask but the mask itself.[2]

But by far the most famous story inspired by the events on the *Tryal*, and one of the most haunting pieces of writing in American literature, is Herman Melville's *Benito Cereno*. Whether he was impressed with the slaves' wile or intrigued by Amasa Delano's naïveté, Melville took chapter 18 of Amasa Delano's long memoir, 'Particulars of the Capture of the

Spanish Ship Tryal,' and turned it into what many consider his other masterpiece.

Melville uses the ghostly ship itself to set the scene, describing it as if it came not from the other side of the island but out of the depths, mantled in vapours, 'hearse-like' in its roll, trailing 'dark festoons of seagrass,' its rusted main chain resembling slave chains and its ribs showing through its hull like bones. Readers know there is evil on board, but they don't know who or what it is or where it might lurk.[3]

Apart from a wholly invented ending, *Benito Cereno*, published in installments in a magazine called *Putnam's Monthly* in late 1855, is mostly faithful to Delano's account: after the ruse is revealed, the ship is captured and its rebels turned over to Spanish authorities. But it is what happens on the ship, which takes up two-thirds of the story, that led reviewers at the time to comment on its 'weird-like narrative' and to describe reading it as a 'creeping horror.'[4]

Most of *Benito Cereno* takes place in the fictional Delano's mind. Page after page is devoted to his reveries, and readers experience the day on board the ship—which was filled with odd rituals, cryptic comments, peculiar symbols—as he experiences it. Melville keeps secret, just as it was kept secret from Delano, the fact that the slaves are running things. And like the real Delano, Melville's version is transfixed by the Spanish captain's relationship to his black body servant. In the story, Melville combines the historical Babo and Mori into a single character called Babo, described as a slight man with an open face. The idea that the West African might not only be equal to the Spanish captain but be his master was beyond Delano's comprehension. Amasa observes Babo gently tending to the unwell Cereno, dressing him, wiping spittle from his mouth, and nestling him in his black arms when he seems to faint. 'As master and man stood before him, the black upholding the white,' Melville writes, 'Captain Delano could not but bethink him of the beauty of that relationship which could present such a spectacle of fidelity on the one hand and confidence on the other.' At one point, Melville has Babo remind Cereno it is time for his shave and then has the slave psychologically torture the Spaniard with a straight razor, as Amasa, clueless, watches.

Melville wrote *Benito Cereno* midway between the critical and commercial failure of 1851's *Moby-Dick* and the beginning of the American
Civil War in 1861, at a moment when it seemed like the author and the
country were going mad. Crammed into one day and onto the deck of
a middling-sized schooner, the novella conveys a claustrophobia that
could be applied either to Melville (he had at this point shuttered himself away from the world, in the 'cold north' of his Berkshire farm) or to
a nation trapped (as Amasa Delano was trapped) inside its own prejudices, unable to see and thus avert the coming conflict. Soon after he
finished it, Melville collapsed and America went to war. It's a powerful
story.[5]

So powerful, in fact, that it is easy to forget that the original incident it
is based on didn't occur in the 1850s, on the eve of the Civil War, or in the
usual precincts where historians of the United States study slavery, such
as on a ship in the Atlantic or on a plantation. It happened in the South
Pacific, five thousand miles away from the heartland of US slavery,
decades before chattel bondage expanded in the South and pushed into
the West, and it didn't involve a racist or paternalist slave master but
instead a New England republican who opposed slavery. The events on
the *Tryal* illuminate not antebellum America as it headed to war but an
earlier moment, the Age of Revolution, or the Age of Liberty. The revolt
took place in late 1804, nearly exactly midway between the American
Revolution and the Spanish American wars for independence. 1804 was
also the year Haiti declared itself free, establishing the second republic in
the Americas and the first ever, anywhere, born out of a slave rebellion.

Writing in the 1970s, Yale's Edmund Morgan was one of the first modern historians to fully explore what he called the 'central paradox' of this
Age of Liberty: it also was the Age of Slavery. Morgan was writing specifically about colonial Virginia, but the paradox can be applied to all of
the Americas, North and South, the Atlantic to the Pacific, as the history
leading up to and including events on the *Tryal* reveals. What was true
for Richmond was no less so for Buenos Aires and Lima—that what

many meant by freedom was the freedom to buy and sell black people as property.[6]

To be sure, Spain had been bringing enslaved Africans to the Americas since the early 1500s, long before subversive republicanism, along with all the qualities that a free man was said to possess—rights, interests, free will, virtue, and personal conscience—began to spread throughout America. But starting around the 1770s, the slave trade underwent a stunning transformation. The Spanish Crown began to liberalize its colonial economy and the floodgates opened. Slavers started importing Africans into the continent any which way they could, working with privateers to unload them along empty beaches and in dark coves, sailing them up rivers to inland plains and foothills, and marching them over land. Merchants were quick to adopt the new language associated with laissez-faire economics to demand the right to import even more slaves. And they didn't mince words saying what they wanted: they wanted *más libertad, más comercio libre de negros*—more liberty, more free trade of blacks.

More slaves, including Babo, Mori, and the other *Tryal* rebels, came into Uruguay and Argentina in 1804 than any year previous. By the time Amasa was cruising the Pacific, a 'slavers' fever,' as one historian has put it, had taken hold throughout the continent. Each region of America has its own history of slavery, with its own rhythms and high points. But taking the Western Hemisphere as a whole, what was happening in South America in the early 1800s was part of a New World explosion of chattel bondage that had started earlier in the Caribbean, and was well under way in Portuguese Brazil. After 1812, it would hit the southern United States with special force, with the movement of cotton and sugar into Louisiana and across the Mississippi, into Texas.

In both the United States and Spanish America, slave labour produced the wealth that made independence possible. But slavery wasn't just an economic institution. It was a psychic and imaginative one as well. At a time when most men and nearly all women lived in some form of unfreedom, tied to one thing or another, to an indenture, an apprentice contract, land rent, a mill, a work house or prison, a husband or father, saying what freedom was could be difficult. Saying what it wasn't, though, was easy: 'a very Guinea slave.' The ideal of the free man, then, answerable to his own personal conscience, in control of his own inner passions, liberated to pursue his own interests—the rational man who stood at the centre of an enlightened world—was honed against its fantasized opposite: a slave, bonded as much to his appetites as he was to his master. In turn, repression of the slave was an often repeated metaphor for the way reason and will must repress desire and impulse if one were to be truly free and be able to claim equal standing within a civilization of similarly free men.[7]

It might seem an abstraction to say that the Age of Liberty was also the Age of Slavery. But consider these figures: of the known 10,148,288 Africans put on slave ships bound for the Americas between 1514 and 1866 (of a total historians estimate to be at least 12,500,000), more than half, 5,131,385, were embarked after July 4, 1776.[8]

The South Pacific *pas de trois* between the New Englander Amasa Delano, the Spaniard Benito Cerreño, and the West African Mori, choreographed by Babo, is dramatic enough to excite the wonder of any historian, capturing the clash of peoples, economies, ideas, and faiths that was New World America in the early 1800s. That Babo, Mori, and some of the rest of their companions were Muslim means that three of the world's great monotheistic religions—Cerreño's Catholicism, Delano's Protestantism, and the West Africans' Islam—confronted one another on the stage-ship.

Aside from its sheer audacity, what is most fascinating about the day-long deception is the way it exposes a larger falsehood, on which the whole ideological edifice of slavery rested: the idea not just that slaves were loyal and simpleminded but that they had no independent lives or thoughts or, if they did have an interior self, that it too was subject to their masters' jurisdiction, it too was property, that what you saw on the outside was what there was on the inside. The West Africans used talents their masters said they didn't have (cunning, reason, and discipline) to give the lie to the stereotypes of what they were said to be (dimwitted and faithful). That day on board the *Tryal*, the slave-rebels were the masters of their passions, able to defer their desires, for, say, revenge or immediate freedom, and to harness their thoughts and emotions to play their roles. Mori in particular, as a Spanish official reviewing the affair later wrote, 'was a man of skill who perfectly acted the part of a humble and submissive slave.'[9]

The man they fooled, Amasa Delano, was in the Pacific hunting seals, an industry as predatory, bloody, and, for a short time, profitable as whaling but even more unsustainable. It's tempting to think of him as the first in a long line of American innocents abroad, oblivious to the consequences of their actions, even as they drive themselves and those around them to ruin. Delano, though, is a more compelling figure. Born in the great upswell of Christian optimism that gave rise to the American Revolution, an optimism that held individuals to be in charge of their destinies, in the next life and this, he embodied all the possibilities and limits of that revolution. When he first set out as a sailor from New England, he carried with him the hopes of his youth. He believed slavery to be a relic of the past, certain to fade away. Yet his actions on the *Tryal*, the descent of his crew into barbarism, and his behaviour in the months that followed, spoke of a future to come.

Herman Melville spent nearly his whole writing career considering the problem of freedom and slavery. Yet he most often did so elliptically, intent, seemingly, on disentangling the experience from the particularities of skin colour, economics, or geography. He rarely wrote about human bondage as an historical institution with victims and victimizers but rather as an existential, or philosophical, condition common to all. *Benito Cereno* is an exception. Even here, though, Melville, by forcing the reader to adopt the perspective of Amasa Delano, is concerned less with exposing specific social horrors than with revealing slavery's foundational deception—not just the fantasy that some men were natural slaves but that others could be absolutely free. There is a sense reading *Benito Cereno* that Melville knew, or feared, that the fantasy wouldn't end, that after abolition, if abolition ever came, it would adapt itself to new circumstances, becoming even more elusive, even more entrenched in human affairs. It's this awareness, this dread, that makes *Benito Cereno* so enduring a story—and Melville such an astute appraiser of slavery's true power and lasting legacy.

I first learned that *Benito Cereno* was based on actual events when I assigned the novella for a seminar I taught on American Exceptional-isms. That class explored the ways an idea usually thought of exclusively in terms of the United States—that America had a providential mission, a manifest destiny, to lead humanity to a new dawn—was actually held by all the New World republics. I began to research the history behind *Benito Cereno*, thinking that a book that focused narrowly on the rebel-lion and ruse could nicely illustrate the role slavery played in such self-understandings. But the more I tried to figure out what happened on board the *Tryal*, and the more I tried to uncover the motives and values of those involved, of Benito Cerreño, Amasa Delano, and, above all, of Babo, Mori, and the other West African rebels, the more convinced I became that it would be impossible to tell the story—or, rather, impos-sible to convey the meaning of the story—without presenting its larger context. I kept getting pulled further afield, into realms of human activ-ity and belief not immediately associated with slavery, into, for instance, piracy, sealing, and Islam. That's the thing about American slavery: it never was just about slavery.

In his memoir, Delano uses a now obsolete sailor's term, 'horse mar-ket,' to describe the explosive pileup of converging tides, strong enough to scuttle vessels. It's a good metaphor. That's what the people on board the *Tryal* were caught in, a horse market of crashing historical currents, of free trade, US expansion, and slavery, and of colliding ideas of justice and faith. The different routes that led all those involved in the drama to the Pacific reveal the fullness of the paradox of freedom and slavery in America, so pervasive it could trap not just slaves and slavers but men who thought they were neither.

PART I

FAST FISH

First: What is a Fast-Fish? Alive or dead a fish is technically fast, when it is connected with an occupied ship or boat, by any medium at all controllable by the occupant or occupants,—a mast, an oar, a nine-inch cable, a telegraph wire, or a strand of cobweb, it is all the same.

—HERMAN MELVILLE, *MOBY-DICK*

1

HAWKS ABROAD

In early January 1804, a one-armed French pirate cruised into Montevideo's harbour. The Spaniards in his multinational crew had trouble saying his name, so they called him Captain Manco—*manco* being the Spanish word for cripple. François-de-Paule Hippolyte Mordeille didn't mind the nickname. It was the rank he didn't like.

Mordeille was a seafaring Jacobin. He presided over men who wrapped red sashes around their waists, sang the 'Marseillaise,' and worked the deck to the rhythms of revolutionary chants. *Long live the republic! Perish earthly kings! String up aristocrats from the yardarms!* Commanding ships called *Le Brave Sans-Culottes*, *Révolution*, and *Le Démocrat*, he patrolled the coast of Africa from Île de France (now Mauritius) in the Indian Ocean to Senegal in the Atlantic, harassing the French Revolution's enemies and guarding its friends. Mordeille, true to his republican spirit, preferred to be addressed as *citoyen*—citizen—or *Citoyen Manco* if need be. But not *captain*.

Coming south from Brazil, Mordeille tacked to starboard and hugged the coastline as he entered Río de la Plata, the great water highway to Montevideo and Buenos Aires and points beyond. The broad sea gulf seemed welcoming. But it was shallow, shoaled, and rock strewn. Its fast-flowing tributaries—it was the mouth of several rivers—ran through some of the driest regions in South America, pouring tonnes of silty sediment into the estuary, raising sandbars, and rerouting sea lanes. Strong dark-cloud winds coming off the pampas were especially treacherous when

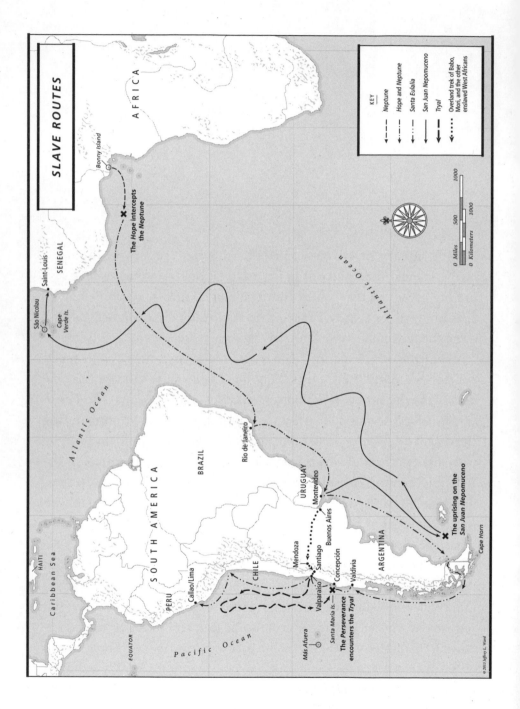

SLAVE ROUTES

KEY

Neptune
Hope and Neptune
Santa Eulalia
San Juan Nepomuceno
Tryal
Overland trek of Babo,
Mori, and the other
enslaved West Africans

AFRICA

Bonny Island

Saint-Louis

SENEGAL

São Nicolau

Cape Verde Is.

The Hope intercepts
the Neptune

Atlantic Ocean

Caribbean Sea

HAITI

EQUATOR

Pacific Ocean

Más Afuera

Santa María Is.

The Perseverance
encounters the Tryal

Valparaíso

Valdivia

Concepción

Santiago

Mendoza

Callao/Lima

PERU

SOUTH AMERICA

BRAZIL

Rio de Janeiro

URUGUAY

Montevideo

Buenos Aires

CHILE

ARGENTINA

The uprising on the
San Juan Nepomuceno

Cape Horn

Atlantic Ocean

0 Miles   500   1000

0 Kilometers   1000

© 2013 Jeffrey L. Ward

they hit the water at low tide. Just a few years earlier a windstorm had wrecked eighty-six ships in a single blow. Even the north shore, considered the safest route in and along which Mordeille sailed, was known as 'carpenter's coast,' since woodworkers made a living salvaging the timber of washed-up broken ships.[1]

Of Río de la Plata's two cities, Buenos Aires, located farther in on the south shore, was wealthier. But sailors preferred Montevideo on the north. It was littered with sunken hulls and still didn't have a wharf or a pier, but its harbour was deeper than the shallow riverbed off of Buenos Aires and thus preferable for loading and unloading cargo. Mordeille sailed in, driving his ship, the *Hope*, through the bay's muddy water to safe anchorage. Behind him came the *Neptune*, a prize Mordeille and his crew had taken near the Bight of Biafra.[2]

Copper-bottomed, teak-framed, three-masted, and three-decked, the 343-ton *Neptune* had a sharp-angled cutwater topped with an ornately carved prow: a lion without a crown, as the Spaniards would later describe the figurehead. It was big and looked warlike. Its purpose, though, was to carry cargo and not to fight. It was no match for smaller, better-armed vessels like the *Hope*, a fact that its captain, David Phillips, learned at great cost.

While the ship was anchored off Bonny Island, Phillips had heard reports that a French corvette was cruising the sea lanes, standing between him and open water. But with his hold full, he decided to risk a confrontation and make for Barbados. When he saw the *Hope* coming in fast on portside, Phillips gave the order to run. But his pursuer was faster, sweeping the trader's bow, forcing it to give up the wind. Mordeille then boxhauled around, bracing his ship's sails and returning on the *Neptune*. Phillips was trapped.

If the objective was to destroy the target, the fight would have been over quickly. But the rules of privateering meant that Mordeille got to keep what the *Neptune* was carrying, so his men aimed their guns not at its hull but at its rigging. The firing continued as boys ran back and forth watering the *Hope*'s deck to make sure blown powder didn't set it alight. A party of men readied themselves with boarding axes to take the *Neptune* by hand. The weapons weren't needed. A ball hit the rudder head, making it impossible to steer, and after about an hour more of firing, with eleven of his crew dead, another sixteen wounded, and his sails pocked and rigging frayed, Captain Phillips surrendered.

When Mordeille's men opened the *Neptune*'s hatch, they found close to four hundred Africans, mostly boys and men between the ages of twelve and twenty-five, but also a number of women and children.

They were in chains and dressed in blue cotton smocks.

Spanish documents indicate that some of the *Tryal* rebels were among them. But they don't say who or how many. The name Mori was common for captives embarked at Bonny. According to one database of African names, of all the recorded men called Mori to leave Africa as slaves, a plurality of them, just under 37 percent, did so from Bonny. Variations of Babo—Baboo, Babu, Baba, and so forth—were likewise found among slaves put on ships at nearby ports. Court records give the names of only thirteen other participants in the uprising, all men: Diamelo, Leobe, Natu, Quiamobo, Liché, Dick, Matunqui, Alasan, Yola, Yan, Malpenda, Yambaio, or Samba, and Atufal. The *Tryal*'s fifty-seven other West African men and women remain anonymous.

Most of the men and women Mordeille found on the *Neptune* would already have travelled weeks, in some cases months, moving along the trunks and tributaries of the enormous Niger, an ever-expanding grid reaching deep into the interior. Bonny was a popular station during these years, as big ships of considerable draft could anchor on the hard sand bed and take on large cargos, as many as seven hundred Africans in some cases. The river was 'spacious and deep,' reported one English sailor around the time the *Neptune* would have arrived, 'wider than the Thames.' At any given moment there'd be a queue of up to fifteen vessels, many of them Liverpudlians, forming along the island's shoreline, waiting for the black traders who came down from the inland once a fortnight. The traders would arrive in flotillas of twenty to thirty canoes, each holding as many as thirty captives, to be bartered for guns, gunpowder, iron, cloth, and brandy.[3]

The Europeans at Bonny and elsewhere in West Africa had no idea where the cargo came from. As late as 1803, the British Royal African Company instructed its agent in nearby Cape Coast Castle, on the Gold Coast west of Bonny, to survey the African merchants from whom they brought their slaves: did they come to the coast in 'small parties' or 'caravans'? What were the names of the 'towns or villages passed through'? Were the people in these towns 'Mohamedans or pagans'? If they came from the 'Great Desert,' 'what were the names of their tribes?' If they came 'from beyond the Niger,' what did 'they know concerning its course'? Did they have any information about the 'great chain of mountains that are reported to extend from Manding to Abysinia'? The British had been on the Gold Coast for well over a hundred years—they had controlled Cape Coast Castle since 1664—and yet their agent could give only the vaguest answers to these questions.[4]

The Africans embarked at Bonny, even if their enslavers didn't know their origins, had a reputation for being wilful and prone to fatalism. Those two qualities might seem opposing but they often resulted in the same action: suicide. One ship surgeon, Alexander Falconbridge, in his 1788 condemnation of the slave trade, tells of fifteen slaves put on a ship at Bonny who, before the ship left port, threw themselves into a school of sharks. Another voyager on a Bonny slave ship, a young boy kept awake by the 'howling of these negros,' described three captives who managed to break free and jump overboard: they were 'dancing about among the waves, yelling with all their might what seemed to me to be a song of triumph' until their 'voices came fainter and fainter upon the wind.'[5]

The *Neptune* was a Liverpool slave ship, which meant that, for Mordeille, its taking was more than potentially profitable. It was personal. The Frenchman had lost his arm escaping from a Spanish dungeon, but it was during a long lockup in Portsmouth, after having been captured by a Liverpool corsair, that he developed his 'tenacious hatred' of the British.[6]

Liverpool had joined the fight against republicanism with exceptional fervour. When news arrived in early 1793 that the French had executed their king, Louis XVI, city fathers lowered the Union Jack that flew over the city's Custom House to half mast. Mourning led to anger, and anger to action against the regicides, lest, warned one newspaper, the 'red cap of liberty be raised, the flag of death unfurled, the Marseillaise chanted, the age of reason proclaimed, and the goddess and her guillotine be made permanent' in Piccadilly. Liverpool's slavers, planters, and shippers financed a large mercenary fleet made up of about sixty-seven privateers, trim, fast ships mounted with twenty guns or better to take the fight against Jacobinism to the sea. For a time, French vessels were at their mercy.

But then Paris began to field its own privateers, including Mordeille, and Napoleon's rise led to an improvement in the republic's naval forces. By the time the *Hope* fell on the *Neptune*, France could not only better defend itself on the open sea but go on the offensive, harassing British cargo and slave ships as they travelled to and from Caribbean sugar plantations. Sailing under a Dutch flag with a French letter of marque, Mordeille was among the most tenacious of these avengers, hailed by the Napoleonic press as the scourge of Liverpool: 'Mordeille! Mordeille! Small and frail, but in the breach he has the strength of heroes.'[7]

The *Neptune* was owned by John Bolton, one of the largest backers of the city's mercenary fleet and an outfitter of a private anti-Jacobin squad of nearly six hundred men he named Bolton's Invincibles, armed to protect Liverpool from enemies within and without. Born the 'poor boy' son of a village apothecary, he started his career as an apprentice clerk in the West Indies, and legend has it that he parlayed a sack of potatoes and a brick of cheese into the start-up capital of what became a slaving empire. Leaving his 'coloured' wife and children behind penniless in the Caribbean, he returned to Liverpool, splitting his time between the bustle of his Henry Street counting house and Storrs Hall, a country mansion built in the middle of an ornamental grove on a wooded promontory overlooking Windermere Lake, where he entertained Tory politicians and Romantic poets, including his friend William Wordsworth.

Bolton might have come into life humble, but the wealth produced by at least 120 slave voyages let him leave it in a fine coffin shrouded in black velvet and studded with silver nails. His funeral cortege included:

eight gentleman abreast, three hundred boys from the Blue Suit School six
deep, two hundred and fifty Gentlemen on foot, six deep, sixty gentlemen
on horseback, thirty gentlemen's private carriages in a line. Several
gigs. . . . Four mutes on horseback. Three mourning coaches, each drawn
by four horses. Mr. Bolton's private carriage, drawn by four, beautiful
blood horses, bringing up the rear.

It was a Scouser send-off to remember, and observers thought the bells of
St. Luke tolled with exceptional beauty the day Bolton was laid to earth.[8]

As they made ready to sail across the Atlantic, the *Hope* and the *Neptune*
were floating contradictions of the Age of Revolution. On board one ship
were enslaved Africans understood to be property, which meant that
according to some interpretations of natural-law liberalism they could be
bought, sold, and traded as cargo. On board the other, a multihued crew
lived the French Revolution's promise of *liberté*, *égalité*, and *fraternité*.
Europeans, mostly French and Spanish, worked alongside dark-skinned
Portuguese mulattos and black Africans and Haitians who served as gun-
ners and musketeers. They assigned no title to skin colour and spoke an
egalitarian patois sounding sort of like French but with traces of Arabic,
Spanish, Portuguese, and old *langue d'oc*, along with words picked up from
around the Caribbean and the coasts of West and East Africa. Mordeille
himself, born on the Mediterranean, not far from Marseilles and a short
sail from North Africa, was once described as 'black as an Ethiopian.'[9]

The colour line did not, strictly speaking, divide the Atlantic between
masters and slaves. In the navies and merchant fleets of all the seafaring
empires and republics at the time, men of colour—among them, Africans, South Sea islanders, Arabs, Indians, Chinese, and freed American blacks—worked on ships, including slave ships, as cooks, cabin
boys, sailors, and even, in a few instances, captains. Nor did white skin
protect against the kind of arbitrary rule over body and will associated
with chattel slavery. Press gangs roamed the wharves and piers of port
cities throughout the British realm on the hunt for men to fill the ships

of the Royal Navy, looking nothing so much as like the slave gangs that stalked the coasts and rivers of Africa.[10]

In Liverpool, the vanguard of merchant reaction, savage fellows patrolled the streets, often led by a 'dissipated, but determined-looking officer, in a very seedy uniform and shabby hat.' Men would flee and children scream upon catching sight of them. Word quickly went out that there were 'hawks abroad.' Pity the poor sailor who didn't keep his door bolted and shades drawn: 'he was seized upon as if he were a common felon, deprived of his liberty, torn from his home, his friends, his parents, wife or children, hurried to the rendezvous-house, examined, passed, and sent on board the tender, like a negro to a slave-ship.'[11]

Once at sea sailors were subject to rule as feudal as the ancien régime and as brutal as the plantation. They could be flogged, tarred, feathered, keelhauled—dunked in the ocean and dragged under the hull, barnacles doing to backs in a minute what it took the whip fifteen lashes—or executed, made to walk the plank or hung by the yardarm. Even on ships like the *Hope*, which sailed with an insurgent élan and did away with rank, the authority of Mordeille, whether he be called citizen or captain, was absolute.[12]

The African slave trade, however, was a different kind of bondage. It not only survived the dawn of the Age of Liberty but was expanding and becoming even more lucrative. And so back on the *Neptune*, after it had been secured, its dead heaved overboard, its British prisoners shackled, and its African cargo counted, Mordeille did the maths and guessed that the ship's slaves were worth, wholesale, at least 80,000 silver pesos (it's nearly impossible to do a straight conversion into today's currency, but this princely sum was roughly equal to the annual salaries of the viceroys of Mexico and Peru, the highest Spanish officials in the Americas).

It doesn't seem that Mordeille gave much thought to the contradiction, the fact that he was a Jacobin believer in the rights of man and the liberties of the world who made his living seizing British slaves and selling them to Spanish American merchants. After all, he swore allegiance not to ideals but to the French nation, which had abolished slavery in its colonies in 1794 only to restore it eight years later. Napoleon's 1802 announcement of its restoration was terse: 'Slavery shall be maintained';

the slave trade 'shall take place.' In any case, the revolution's to-ing and fro-ing when it came to slavery and freedom mattered little to the privateer or, apparently, to his men.

When everything was ready on board the *Neptune*, the inventory complete, the rudder repaired, the damaged sails replaced, and the rigging redone, the two ships, the victor and its vanquished prize, set sail for Montevideo. The British, including the officers, had been placed in a hold, not the one that contained the Africans but a smaller one, below the *Neptune*'s quarterdeck.

Until about the 1770s, most Africans who made the Middle Passage to America didn't travel much farther once they crossed the Atlantic. The main slave harbours of the Americas—New Orleans, Havana, Port-au-Prince, Alexandria, Bahia, Rio de Janeiro, Cartagena, Baltimore, and Charleston—were portals to coastal, river, and island plantations, haciendas, and cities where most of the captives who survived the voyage would spend the rest of their lives.

But the West Africans brought into Montevideo by Mordeille on the *Neptune* were arriving as part of slavery's new extreme, the motor of a market revolution that was remaking Spanish America. They had already travelled more than five thousand miles from Bonny to Río de la Plata. They were about to be thrust into the wheels of mercantile corruption, though for them there would be no difference between what was called crime and what passed for commerce. And for those captives who would be driven on toward the Pacific, including those who would find themselves on the *Tryal*, their journey was not even half over.

2

MORE LIBERTY

Montevideo was a city of roof dwellers, much like how Nathaniel Philbrick describes Nantucket in the 1800s. Its houses were tightly packed on a small spit of land wedged between a handsome hill and a curved bay, leaving little room for gardens. Women arranged plants and flowers on rooftop promenades, where men in the evenings relaxed over coffee and cigars. From below came the ballads of strolling minstrels. 'Love is, in general, the subject of these songs,' one British traveler to the city reported.[1]

Another sound rising from the narrow streets was the long, drawn-out cries of itinerant peddlers. These hawkers were all slaves, many of them recently arrived from Africa, a fact they worked into their sing-song pitches for empanadas, sweets, milk, bread, and fish. They switched Spanish *r*'s for African *l*'s and rolled out the vowels in a great lamenting dirge, as if all the pain in the world were needed to announce that the barley cakes were made that morning:

> ¡Toooltas . . . toooltítas! ¡Toltitas son de cebáa!
> (Cakes . . . cakes . . . Cakes made of barley!)
> ¡Chaá que soy negla boba, pala que tanto glitá!
> (I'm a black straight from Africa, that's why I'm shouting!)
> Toooltas . . . toooltítas! ¡Ya no me queda ná!

This last sentence meant the item was sold out. But its literal translation is more plaintive, especially considering the circumstances of the vendor's arrival: *Now I'm left with nothing.* The free people of the city had to have liked this mix of melancholy and commerce, the bittersweet sound of slaves selling their wares, for later residents would remember these rhymes long after the vendors had disappeared from the city streets. Today in Uruguay, children recite them in school pageants.[2]

Montevideo was smaller than its sprawling sister city, Buenos Aires, which with its cowboys and muleteers still wasn't even sure it was a port town. The waterfront in Buenos Aires was a muddy slope to a shallow river, filled with taverns, drunken sailors, and garbage. The biggest ships couldn't get closer than eight miles to the coast. Cargo had to be put on small tenders, brought near to the shore, transferred again to amphibious carts with large wheels that jacked the wagon bottom over the surf, and then pulled by horses to the beach. Later, after the river had been dredged and adequate docks built, its residents would come to call themselves *porteños*—people who live in a port city. In the very early 1800s, though, most 'had their back to the river.' They looked inward toward the pampas.[3]

Montevideans looked to the sea. Many of the city's sky lounges were crowned with a watch tower and telescope, which, when viewed from the harbour, made Montevideo seem like a ramparted monastery. Merchants would climb their towers like monks up the bulwarks, scanning the sky for storms and the estuary for ships, with 'many an anxious feeling for the safety or expected arrival of some vessel.'[4]

Most goods out of and into Argentina, which was fast becoming butcher and breadbasket to the Atlantic world, passed through Montevideo's deepwater bay. Out went hides, lard, dried beef, wheat, brass, copper, wood, cacao, Peruvian bark, yerba maté, and vinegar. In came Havana rum, Boston and British textiles, English furniture and paper, French hats, candy and gilded bracelets from Cádiz, and sugar, tobacco, and hard cane liquor from Brazil.

And slaves. There was a 'hunger' for slaves, said an observer at the time, a 'thirst.' Montevideo was Río de la Plata's official slave harbour. All slave ships, even if they were bound for Buenos Aires, had by law to stop there and be inspected by the port's doctor and assessed by its tax collector. Slaves headed to upriver ports would be transferred to regularly scheduled cargo ships connecting the gulf to Paraguay. Most of the slavers that came in were accounted for, their cargo part of an importer's consignment.

Every day, though, merchants would mount their roof towers to see what else the tide brought in, hoping to make a little extra money with the arrival of an unanticipated ship. In late January, one expectant merchant noticed the *Neptune* shortly after it had dropped anchor, its deck filled with what he underestimated to be a 'hundred and something' slaves. 'I doubt they will permit their sale,' he wrote in a note to Martín de Alzaga, among Buenos Aires's wealthiest men, 'but I'm sure it will happen anyway.'[5]

When Mordeille arrived in Montevideo, its half-moon harbour was filled with moving men and ships sitting low in the water, their holds heavy with cargo and sails struck in repose. There was a busy wharf beach, lighted with fires burning pitch, and back behind that a crescent row of workshops where blacksmiths and colliers, carpenters, joiners, block makers, junk pickers, and caulkers readied vessels for their return to the sea. Stevedores, many of them black- and brown-skinned slaves themselves, hauled casks and crates and other slaves from the newly arrived ships. In the counting rooms of the city's warehouses, clerks and cash keepers in high-backed chairs recorded who owed what to whom in the business of moving humans halfway across the world. They managed the long trail of paperwork—promissory notes, exchange bills, current account books, insurance policies, consignment invoices, freight and tax receipts—that tied the ports of the Río de la Plata to interior cities, Chile, and Peru and, in the other direction, out into the Atlantic, to London, Liverpool, Boston, New York, and trading ports in Africa and Brazil.

This was what historians call Spanish America's market revolution, and slaves were the flywheel on which the whole thing turned.

For centuries, the Spanish Crown had tried to regulate slavery, along with all other economic activity in the Americas, under a system called mercantilism. Spain prohibited its colonies from trading with one another, banned foreign ships from entering American ports, prohibited individual

merchants from owning their own fleets of cargo ships, and limited manufacturing. Selected countries or companies were granted the monopoly
right to import slaves, and only into a handful of ports, principally Cartagena in Colombia, Veracruz in Mexico, and Havana in Cuba. The idea was
to prevent the development of a too-powerful merchant class in America,
making sure its colonies remained a source of gold and silver and an
exclusive for goods made in or shipped through Spain.

That was the theory, anyway. The practice was something else. Con-
trabanding flourished from the early days of the Conquest. The city of
Buenos Aires was conceived in corruption. During its early years in the
1500s, its Spanish founders did well skimming off the Andean silver that
passed through the city to Spain, and over the centuries smuggling
made up a large part of Río de la Plata's trade. When one early Spanish
governor tried to stop the smuggling of slaves by Portuguese traders
from Brazil, he was poisoned to death. By the late 1700s, illegal, untaxed
trade, much of it coming from the new United States or Great Britain,
made up nearly half the gulf's commerce. Merchandise flowed in and
out of the Atlantic, back and forth through the porous border with Brazil, and up and down the Paraná River, which connected both Buenos
Aires and Montevideo to Paraguay.[6]

Africans were often the contraband. They might be unloaded at night
on a dark beach down the coast from Buenos Aires and brought unnoticed into the city's market. Or their importer could march them into the
city during the day and simply say they were negros descaminados—'lost
blacks'—found someplace in the interior, which meant their sale was
exempt from import licenses or tax receipts. At times, though, Africans
were the cover for what was really being smuggled, with merchants using
permission to import a small consignment of slaves to mask a hold full of
Parisian toilet water or New York pickles. And on some British ships coming into Spanish American ports, black sailors temporarily pretended to
be slaves, just long enough to convince customs inspectors that they
were the ship's cargo and not whatever it was that was being smuggled.[7]

By the late 1770s, Spain was under increasing pressure to grant its
colonial subjects 'más libertad,' more economic liberty. The Atlantic
world was becoming more commercialized, with new opportunities for

colonials to engage in contraband and more openings for enemies like Great Britain to make inroads. The Crown therefore needed to find ways to regularize illegal trade, both to keep the loyalty of its colonial subjects and to check London. Madrid also hoped to stimulate the economy and thereby generate more revenue to fight the many fronts in its seemingly never-ending wars with one empire or another.

So starting with the American Revolution, Spain responded to each burst of insurrectionary ardor, each declaration of the rights of man, by issuing yet another decree allowing freer trade, including the 'free trade of blacks.'[8]

In November 1776, after the signing in July of the Declaration of Independence in Philadelphia, Spain opened Cuban ports to North American ships, including slave ships. Following the French Revolution of 1789, the Crown allowed individual Spaniards and foreigners to bring slaves into the ports of Caracas, Puerto Rico, Havana, and Santo Domingo. After the start of the Haitian Revolution in 1791, Madrid added Montevideo to the growing list of free-trade slaving ports, lowered taxes on the sale of slaves, and allowed merchants to set their prices according to the 'principle' of supply and demand, selling their Africans with the 'same liberty' that they could 'any other commercial good.' In 1793, the year the French executed their king, Spain again lowered export duties on goods traded for slaves, exempting slave ships from sales and registry taxes, and permitted colonies to trade among themselves, as well as with Portuguese Brazil, to acquire slaves.[9]

Then, in January 1804, Haiti became an independent nation, having defeated French troops trying to restore slavery on the island. 'We have dared to be free, let us be thus by ourselves and for ourselves,' its leaders declared, shocking those who would use the word *freedom* to mean freedom to buy and sell Africans as they would. A few months later, Spain extended the right of its American subjects, as well as that of any other resident in its dominion, to sail their own ships to Africa and 'to buy blacks wherever they were to be found.'*

---

* Neither Spanish American merchants, when they called for more 'liberty' and 'more free trade,' nor the Crown, when in response to those calls it deregulated the economy, tended

The gulf's merchants were notoriously grasping, and when they did get freer trade they used corruption as the thin edge of the wedge to get more. Each concession Spain made to its American subjects only provided new opportunities to skirt revenue collectors. For instance, Madrid eventually allowed merchants to buy foreign-built vessels and either trade directly with neutral countries or sail straight to Africa, buy Africans, and bring them back, practically tax free. But many Río de la Plata merchants found it cheaper to conspire with Boston and Providence shippers than to spend money to build up their own fleets. New England captains, upon approaching Montevideo or Buenos Aires in ships laden with Manchester broadcloth, New Haven pistols, or Gold Coast slaves would lower the stars and stripes, raise the royal Spanish standard, ready their counterfeit papers, and prepare to tell port authorities that the ship they were sailing was owned by a local Spaniard. A 'sham sale' was how New Englanders described the practice. And thus with the extension of free trade, slavery, an institution already founded on a lie, became, with this trick and those mentioned earlier, even more associated with illusion.

By the time Mordeille arrived on the *Hope*, with the *Neptune* following behind, slave trading in Río de la Plata had become a free-for-all. More African slaves arrived in 1804 than in any previous year. Buenos Aires was growing by a third every year, Montevideo was doubling, and by 1804 Africans and African Americans made up more than 30 percent of their populations.[10]

Slavery was the motor of Spanish America's market revolution, though not exactly in the same way it was in plantation zones of the Caribbean, coastal Brazil, or, later, the US South. As in those areas, Africans and

---

to invoke the idea of individual rights. Rather, they used the language of 'utility,' of achieving a greater 'good,' as needed to increase the prosperity of the empire. Spanish theologians did recognize that individuals possessed what they called a *fuero interno*, a realm of inner sovereignty, and they even had come to believe, as did English-speaking Protestant religious thinkers and philosophers, that the pursuit of personal gain could generate public virtue. But the Crown didn't accept the subversive natural-law idea that individual self-interest was itself a virtue.

African-descendant peoples might be used to produce commercial exports for Europe, mining gold, for instance, diving for pearls in the Caribbean and the Pacific, drying hides, or cutting cane.[11] But a large number, perhaps even most, of Africans arriving under the new 'free trade in blacks' system were put to work creating goods traded *among* the colonies.

Enslaved Africans and African Americans slaughtered cattle and sheared wool on the pampas of Argentina, spun cotton and wove clothing in textile workshops in Mexico City, and planted coffee in the mountains outside of Bogotá. They fermented grapes for wine at the foot of the Andes and boiled Peruvian sugar to make candy. In Guayaquil, Ecuador, enslaved shipwrights built cargo vessels that were used to carry Chilean wheat to Lima markets. Throughout the thriving cities of mainland Spanish America, slaves worked, often for wages, as labourers, bakers, brickmakers, liverymen, cobblers, carpenters, tanners, smiths, rag pickers, cooks, and servants. Others, like Montevideo's doleful itinerants, took to the streets, peddling goods they either made themselves or sold on commission.

It wasn't just their labour that spurred the commercialization of society. The driving of more and more slaves inland, across the continent, the opening up of new slave roads and the expansion of old ones, tied hinterland markets together and created local circuits of finance and trade. Enslaved peoples were at one and the same time investments (purchased and then rented out as labourers), credit (used to secure loans), property, commodities, and capital, making them an odd mix of abstract and concrete value. Collateral for loans and items for speculation, slaves were also objects of nostalgia, mementos of a fixed but fading aristocratic world even as they served as the coin of a new commercialized one. Slaves literally made money: working in Lima's mint, they trampled quicksilver into ore with their bare feet, pressing toxic mercury into their bloodstream in order to amalgamate the silver used for coins. And they were money, at least in a way. It wasn't so much that the value of individual slaves was standardized in relation to currency. Slaves were the standard: when appraisers calculated the value of any given hacienda, slaves usually accounted for over half its worth, much more valuable than inanimate capital goods like tools and millworks.

The world was changing fast, old lines of rank and status were blur-
ring, and slaves, along with livestock and land, often appeared to be the
last substantial things. Slaves didn't just create wealth: as items of conspicuous consumption for a rising merchant class, they displayed wealth.
And since some slaves in Spanish America, especially those in cities like
Montevideo and Buenos Aires, were paid wages, they were also consumers, spending their money on items that arrived in ships with other
slaves or maybe even, in a few instances, with themselves.[12]

French privateers like Hippolyte Mordeille made the promise of 'free
trade in blacks' a reality, both because the smuggling they excelled at
was an application of the principle and because Spain, as an ally of Paris
in the Napoleonic Wars, tended to allow them to sell their British-taken
prizes in Spanish American ports. The romance of pirates often imagines them as anarchists, sailing the 'ever free' sea bound to no law and
respectful of no property. In fact, they were vanguard merchant capital-
ists, or at least they were in the case of Buenos Aires and Montevideo.
Starting in 1800, the local commercial guild collected an informal tax
from its members to fund corsairs to protect their freight against enemy
ships. The guild then began issuing its own private letters of marque,
authorizing pirates to seize and sell enemy merchandise. Soon, individual merchants were entering into formal, contractual relations with privateer companies incorporated in France.[13]

Mordeille, who had been sailing to the Río de la Plata for nearly a
decade, worked closely with commercial houses in Cádiz, Spain, and
merchants in Montevideo and Buenos Aires. He is credited with pio-
neering Río de la Plata's comprehensive privateering contracts, which
stipulated the rights and obligations of all involved—merchants, captain,
and crew—and the percentage each would get from the seizure of 'good
prizes,' distributed according to the 'onboard hierarchy and the importance of tasks each performs.' Money was raised, loans were advanced,
weapons and munitions purchased, crews assembled, and ships outfitted
and dispatched to seize the cargo of merchant vessels flying the flags of
enemy nations. The Frenchman brought whatever cargo he might take

off British ships into Montevideo, including guns, tools, textiles, as well as luxury items like silk shawls, fine handkerchiefs, Brittany linen, Flemish lace skirts, ornate fans, pearls, silver mirrors, gold combs, and filigreed rosaries. But by a large margin, Mordeille's most valuable cargo was slaves.[14]

Even in this new world of freer trade, Mordeille still needed royal permission to convert his plunder into salable commodities. So shortly after arriving in Montevideo that January of 1804 with the *Neptune* in tow, he sat down and wrote a letter to the Spanish viceroy, Joaquín del Pino, whose residence was across the water in Buenos Aires.

3

A LION WITHOUT A CROWN

'The actions I have been compelled to take as a corsair have hardened my heart,' Mordeille wrote in his letter to the viceroy, in French-laced Spanish. The voyage across the Atlantic was rough, his men were hungry, and his ships were badly in need of repair. 'But what brings me the most sadness and melancholy,' he continued, 'is that my work has not benefited the blacks.'

The management of a slave ship took skill. Many alert men were needed to feed the captives, to distribute the victuals and stand watch, because every captain knew that revolts often took place at mealtime, to dole out water, rationing it so it lasted the journey, and to disinfect the slave hold. All this activity required patience and attentiveness.[1]

The *Hope*'s crew had those virtues when it came to sailing and fighting, Mordeille told del Pino, but not to slaving. 'Natural diligences'—defecation and urination—were problems, Mordeille said, particularly during the night. Slaves needing to relieve themselves were to inform the sailor on duty, who was supposed to accompany them to a makeshift latrine on deck. 'But it terrified my men to go into the hold,' the privateer admitted. Guards had to maneuver past cramped bodies, fumbling with heavy keys in the fetid dark, and then guide shackled men and women up the hatch ladder. It was easier to ignore the calls and let the enslaved defecate on themselves, adding to the layers of already dried vomit and excrement that encrusted the hold's floor. It was disgusting, Mordeille said.

During the Atlantic crossing, the *Neptune*'s surgeon, James Wallace, had supervised the handling of the slaves. But circumstances made the trip from Bonny to America worse than usual. The ship was adequately stocked for its scheduled run to Barbados but its provisions had to be stretched to cover Mordeille's seventy-two sailors, who were short on supplies. Water had run low. (Wallace had tried to make the slaves' water ration last by having the casks sealed, then cutting a small hole on top, through which was inserted a musket barrel, its breech broken off, to be used like a straw.) The mortality rate on this trip wasn't exceptionally high. On the *Neptune*'s previous voyage, in 1802, 395 Africans were boarded at Bonny; 355 disembarked in British Guiana. This time, 349 out of an original shipment of about 400 had survived.

But they were in a bad state, emaciated, their blue smocks having fallen off in tatters. 'They were completely naked,' Mordeille told del Pino. He didn't have the money to clothe or feed the captives and in fact was hoping to sell them so he could pay his crew, make repairs to his ships, and stock provisions. Nor could he count on Dr. Wallace, who had jumped ship and escaped. Mordeille told del Pino that he dreaded heading into the open sea without the surgeon.

'In the name of humanity,' Mordeille implored, in language the viceroy later said he thought exaggerated, 'I ask permission to sell the slaves.'

The viceroy stalled on the request. With his drooping eyes and aquiline nose, the only angular feature on flesh otherwise plump and bald, the seventy-five-year-old del Pino didn't look like a crusader. But he was committed to holding America for Spain. When he had taken office three years earlier, he had launched a campaign to stop contraband, which continued to flow in and out, untaxed. One of the reasons he was reluctant to let Mordeille's slaves come ashore was because he knew that the corsair worked with some of Río de la Plata's most powerful merchant-smugglers, exactly the people whom his antismuggling efforts were targeting. They had made the viceroy their enemy and he didn't want to do anything that might make them more money.

And everybody was complaining about how black the two cities had become, troubled that 'slaves of all ages and sexes were living together in close quarters' in dens of 'lasciviousness and vice.' True, everybody wanted slaves. Most well-off women wouldn't attend mass without a black slave in tow and most wouldn't give birth without a black or mulatta nursemaid. Even poor families owned slaves.

But there was no shortage of them. There were about ten big sailing ships moored in the bay around the time Mordeille made his request. Many, maybe most, held slaves. The frigate *Venus* had recently come in, sent by French colonists on the British-besieged Île de France in the Indian Ocean who hoped to trade the 198 Africans on board for desperately needed wheat. The French naval ship *L'Egypte* was about to appear with two more Liverpool prizes in tow, the *Active* and the *Mercury*, carrying 441 Africans. And just last December, Mordeille had brought in another prize, the *Ariadne*, a 130-ton snow-rigged British brig, with its hold full of Africans, gunpowder, and bullets. (All told, within a few months of either side of Mordeille's arrival, thousands of Africans were disembarked in Montevideo, likely including most of all the rest of the *Tryal* rebels.)[2]

Del Pino also had to consider the rising violence, including incidents of slaves murdering their masters. The crime was called parricide, or *parricidio*, in Spanish, since killing one's master was considered the moral and legal equivalent of killing one's father or killing the king. The offence was still rare. But not as rare as it once had been. In 1799, the gardener Joaquín José de Muxica was stabbed in the back by his slave, Pedro, who was subsequently hung for his crime. In early 1803, two slaves, Simón and Joaquín, were hung for executing an infantry captain, Manuel Correa, in his home outside of Montevideo, along with six others, including the officer's wife and son. In response to these and other crimes, Montevideo's city council erected a permanent gallows in its plaza, a warning against the 'pride and audacity,' the 'insubordinate spirit,' and the 'excessive hubris that blacks' were increasingly displaying.[3]

In the minds of many local Spaniards, these little parricides all stemmed from one source: the parricide of parricides, Louis XVI's execution in Paris. A few years earlier, a rumour had spread through Buenos Aires that slaves, Frenchmen, and seditious Spaniards were plotting an uprising. An investigation, led by a zealous slaver who presided over excruciatingly painful torture sessions, failed to find anything other than general discontent. The inquiry did reveal, however, snippets of conversations suggesting that slaves were paying close attention to events in revolutionary France: *The viceroy will be beheaded because he is a thieving dog. The French had good reason to execute their king.* And fueling the fear that the guillotining had a start date: *On Good Friday, we will all be French.*[4]

This was in 1795, when Spain was allied with monarchical Great Britain against revolutionary France, so discontent was easy to quash. But by 1804, Madrid had broken with London and sided with Paris. Now, the city's poor could casually mention the guillotine and still sound royalist.

Some Spanish officials blamed the cities' problems on French privateers, whose crews combined the worst of sailor boisterousness and revolutionary insolence. 'Their arrival isn't appreciated,' wrote one administrator; they 'come from a nation governed by principles opposed to ours in matters of religion and politics.' Not long after these remarks and just a few months prior to Mordeille's most recent arrival, scores of enslaved and free Montevidean blacks, apparently after having spoken with black Haitian sailors working on a French ship anchored in the harbour, fled to a river island north of the city, where they proclaimed an independent republic. They named it 'Liberty, Fraternity, and Equality' and decreed that it would be governed by the 'Law of the French.' The island republic was quickly suppressed. But slaves continued to run away.[5]

The subversion wasn't just political. For centuries, starting with the Conquest, the Spanish Crown and the Catholic Church restricted not just production and trade but consumption as well. Clothing, for instance, was understood to be a reflection of the grandeur of God's earthly estate, in all its Baroque hierarchal glory. As such, dress was regulated according to rank and race: gold, pearls, velvet, and silk for the better born of purer blood, cotton and simple wool for the king's coarser subjects. Spain policed the 'outrageous excess of the clothes worn by blacks, mulattos, Indians, and mestizos of both sexes,' as one Spanish administrator wrote, complaining about the 'frequent thefts committed in order to be able to afford such expensive attires.'* But as society became more commercialized, as Mordeille and other privateers brought in their handkerchiefs, lace skirts, fans, mirrors, perfume, combs, and rosaries, what one wore increasingly became a matter not of heavenly assigned status but of personal taste. Slaves, who were sold as commodities and put to work as labourers, were also customers. In Buenos Aires and Montevideo, as throughout the colonies, they, along with others in the poorer classes, began to sew velvet fringes onto their dresses, drape themselves in silk, and put on pearls and gold earrings and 'dress like the Spaniards and great men of the country.' The line between appearance and substance continued to blur.[6]

Del Pino took all these considerations in mind. The last thing he wanted was hundreds of starving slaves dumped onto Montevideo's beach, especially starving slaves who had just spent sixty or so days listening to pirates singing the 'Marseillaise.' What del Pino did want was

---

* There was a similar relationship between fashion and subversion in the United States. On November 17, 1793, a fire that started in the backyard stables of the Albany home of Leonard Gansevoort, Herman Melville's great-uncle, nearly burned Albany to the ground. It was part of a rash of arsons (including another one in the barn of Peter Gansevoort, Melville's Revolutionary War hero grandfather) blamed on slaves who, some of Albany's Dutch gentry feared, were inspired by the Haitian Revolution. The police arrested a slave named Pompey as the conspiracy's leader. They never found out his true motive, but they were sure he was guilty not just of arson but of another transgression: he liked nice clothing. During the hard years of the American Revolution, Albany dressed grey on grey, as wartime austerity reinforced the Dutch merchant gentry's staid reputation. Cut off from trade, families weaved their own drab linsey-woolseys. But when the fighting stopped, ships again came up the Hudson carrying 'rich silks, satins, and broad-cloths.' 'Colours of the rainbow took the place of the sombre brown and the heavy black previously worn by females, while blue, pea green and scarlet broad-cloths were selected by the males for dress coats.' Just as Spaniards accused 'blacks, mulattos, Indians and mestizos' of stealing to dress better than their birth, the Albany slave Pompey was accused of robbing money from his mistress to buy 'what he desired in the way of dress.' He was said to be 'foppish,' a 'gay fellow among the wenches' who hoped to 'imitate in dress those who mingled in a different society.' His name even changed with the times. Instead of the neoclassical Pompey (his first master, like other slavers of his day, apparently had taken to reading the 1770 English edition of *Plutarch's Lives*), he went by the frolicsome Pomp. At some point before the fire, Pomp, having fled to Manhattan, was caught 'parading' on Broadway 'wearing a bright red cloth coat, cut in the prevailing fashion, adorned with gilt buttons.' He was captured and returned to Albany. Later, Pomp, along with two other slaves convicted on the charge of arson—Bet, a sixteen-year-old girl and the property of Herman Melville's cousin Philip van Rensselaer, and Dinah, a fourteen-year-old girl and the slave of another Melville relative, Volkert Douw—were executed, hung from an elm tree not far from Melville's grandfather's Albany mansion.

Mordeille out of the harbour as soon as possible. And for that to happen, his ships needed to be restocked and repaired. That cost money, which Mordeille claimed he didn't have. So the viceroy told the Frenchman he could sell seventy slaves but he had to leave with the rest.

Mordeille had a fallback plan, which he had already worked out with local confederates, in case his request for permission to sell all the *Neptune*'s slaves wasn't approved. The scheme, as one of del Pino's subordinates would put it, was part of the standard 'repertoire of lies and tricks' the privateer and his allies 'used to pursue their sordid personal interests.'

The plot was simple. Mordeille would legally sell the seventy slaves to Andrés Nicolás Orgera, a Lima-based merchant who was at the moment in Montevideo. They would be boarded on the *Santa Eulalia*, a frigate then in transit from Cádiz, Spain, bound for Lima. Port taxes would be paid and customs forms filled out. Then the *Eulalia* and the *Neptune* would depart Montevideo within a day of each other, rendezvous at a beach on one of Río de la Plata's islands, and secretly transfer all the rest of the Africans save for forty young men.

The *Neptune* would get a makeover. Its privateer crew would be switched for Portuguese merchant sailors, its sails barque rigged in the Spanish style to make it look less British. Its hull and figurehead—its lion without a crown—would be painted black. Renamed the *Aguila*, the *Eagle*, it would sail to a small cove town forty miles east of Buenos Aires. There the Liverpool slaver would be sold, along with its remaining forty Africans, to a new owner, Don Benito Olazábal, one of Buenos Aires's leading merchants.

Mordeille would have to wait a month or so until the *Santa Eulalia* arrived from Cádiz before the plan could be put into motion. In the meantime, he occupied himself with supervising repairs on his vessels. The *Hope* had been about fifteen years in service, the last three the hard life of a privateer. The hull creaked badly and leaked constantly, and the ship's pumps needed to be worked without rest to keep it afloat. The *Neptune* too was showing signs of wear from its many trips from Liverpool to West Africa to the Caribbean and back again.

One of the advantages of Montevideo's sheltered bay, with its marked high and low tides, was that his two vessels could be careened there. That is, they could be towed close to the shore and left to fall gently into the bay's soft mud bottom as the water went out with the tide and then tilted to one side. Short of having access to a dry dock, this was the best way Modeille's men could scrape the barnacles off the *Hope* and *Neptune*, hull, recaulk their seams, and paint their hull boards with a mixture of tallow, tar, and sulfur to protect the wood against worms. The operation required some skill to carry out, but Mordeille could count on Montevideo's experienced corps of carpenters and shipwrights. They first would remove the sails, yards, and riggings from the masts of the two ships and brace the heels of their decks and inner hulls with props. Then they would ready supports to catch the masts as the ships were let down, using heavy rope threaded through portholes as pulleys.

Before any of this work could begin, the vessels had to be emptied. Anything that couldn't be lashed down had to be removed, including their cannons, cargo, and captives. The British prisoners were transported to a nearby French brig, where they were kept for a time before being released. The slaves were sent in lighters, about forty at a time, to shore.

4

BODY AND SOUL

The West Africans were taken to a place called *el caserío de los negros*—
'the Negro village'—where slaves waiting to be sold or transferred to
Buenos Aires were housed. It was on the western flank of the bay, just
behind the beach and upwind from well-kept Montevideo, with its roof
gardens. It was squalid, consisting of a large compound made of thick
adobe walls and not much else, though when city officials had dedicated
it a few decades earlier they did so to the 'pious mind of the sovereign,
who does nothing but shower his subjects with tender love.' An open pit
was used as a latrine and rat-infested garbage was piled high. Under the
old monopoly or licensing system, Spanish officials could occasionally
compel the companies who ran the slave trade to clean up their pens.*
But with slavery now liberalized, it was difficult to hold any one slaver
responsible for the filth, and it fell to the city to maintain the 'village,'
and about the only thing it did on a timely basis was to bury corpses, in
a patch of land just outside the walls.[1]

For Mordeille and the merchants he served, Montevideo was a central hub in an expanding Atlantic economy. For untold numbers of Afri-

---

* 'Free trade' is often thought of as a removal of the government from the economy. But
Spain's deregulation of slavery actually made the treatment of slaves within its colonies
more of a public policy problem; as the trade and the ownership of slaves became more
widespread, no one person, class, or company could be held accountable for its excesses. In
tandem with the liberalization of slavery came a series of laws and decrees regulating slave
hygiene, slave burial, slave punishment, and slave education.

can slaves, however, it was their terminus. Over the course of the next few weeks, while they waited in the *caserío* to see what the next step of their ordeal would be, fourteen more of the West Africans put on the *Neptune* at Bonny would die, adding to the fifty-one who didn't survive the Atlantic crossing. Death was everywhere around them.

Just a few days after the *Neptune* showed up, a Portuguese brig named *Belisario* dropped anchor. Of the 257 Africans boarded in Mozambique, ninety-one had died and most of those still alive were dying. Then came *La Luisa*, another Portuguese ship from Mozambique. Nearly a third of its original consignment of three hundred Africans had perished during the crossing. By this point, more and more slaves were arriving from the other side of Africa, from its eastern coast on the Indian Ocean. It took almost four months to make the trip, around the Cape of Good Hope and then running against the South Atlantic's westerlies, an agonizingly long and often lethal voyage.[2]

Along the way, Africans died from contagious diseases or from the miseries of crossing the ocean in a claustrophobically small space. Some went blind. Others lost their minds. Even when the circus followed the best practices of the early nineteenth century, the holds were never cleaned fast enough to counter the accumulating strata of excrement, vomit, blood, and pus. With poor ventilation, baking under the equatorial sun, cargo bays festered and putrefied. Slave ships could be smelled from miles away. 'The confined air, rendered noxious by the effluvia exhaled from their bodies, and by being repeatedly breathed, soon produces fevers and fluxes, which generally carries off great numbers of them,' observed a British slave ship surgeon in the 1780s. When bad weather forced the portholes and hatches to be closed for a long period of time, the floors of the holds would become so covered with 'blood and mucus' that they 'resembled a slaughter-house.' 'It is not,' said the surgeon, 'in the power of the human imagination to picture to itself a situation more dreadful or disgusting.'[3]

Montevideo's harbour doctors tried to identify the most serious illnesses: scurvy, consumption, dropsy, malaria, measles, yellow fever, typhoid, ophthalmia, flux (or unending dysentery, which easily spread in the packed-tight holds), something called *el mal de Luanda* (Angola sickness, a vitamin C deficiency that Spaniards distinguished from scurvy), ringworm, and gonorrhoea and syphilis, also known as *mal de Gálico*, Galician sickness. Smallpox was especially deadly. Before a working vaccine was fabricated in the early 1800s, Africans who arrived in Río de la Plata suffering from the disease were unloaded for less than half of their expected price had they been healthy. But those who had recovered from smallpox were sold at a premium, since it was assumed they had built up immunity.[4]

Slave ships were more than floating tombs. They were floating laboratories, offering doctors and scientists opportunities to examine the course of diseases in fairly controlled, quarantined environments. Often learning of cases from a ship's surgeon, medical professionals used high slave ship mortality to identify a bewildering number of symptoms and classify them into diseases, to hypothesize about causes and isolate variables, and to advance medical knowledge.*

---

* Africans were the primary victims of smallpox in the New World. But they also played a crucial role in its eradication. In 1803, after his daughter died from the disease, Spain's King Carlos IV ordered its vaccine (a practical version had been recently fabricated by the British) to be disseminated throughout his dominion. Francisco Xavier de Balmis, the doctor who headed the royal expedition appointed to carry out the task, decided it was best to transport the vaccine live. Twenty-two foundlings aged three to nine were boarded on a ship: doctors made a small incision on the arms of two of them and inserted a mixture of lymph and pus, which after a few days produced the pustules that would provide the material to vaccinate the next two boys. The procedure was repeated until the ship reached America. Once there, the foundlings were feted and praised, laid at the foot of church altars, and adopted by the king himself as 'special children of the country.' But Balmis's team didn't have the funds to cover all of Spanish America. It turned to the one institution that already reached across the far-flung realm: slavery. In Havana, Balmis bought four young slave girls, whom he used to send the vaccine to the Yucatan (once they performed their service, the two girls were sold). At first, slaves were sent on journeys specifically organized to transport the vaccine. But as time passed, it became easier just to use already established commercial routes, sending the vaccine 'arm to arm of the blacks' who were being shipped as cargo. Portugal had from the beginning relied on African slaves to get the vaccine across the Atlantic, sending it to Brazil in the arms of seven enslaved children. It was then taken to Río de la Plata in a shipment of thirty-eight vaccinated slaves who were to be sold in Montevideo. An African woman 'with pustules in perfect development' carried the vaccine to Buenos Aires. And from there, slaves took the 'miracle discovery'—which made slavery much more profitable for slavers—through the rest of Argentina, over the Andes, and into Chile. Interestingly, before the Spanish began to disseminate the vaccine through the arms of orphans and slaves, the naturalist Alexander von Humboldt reported

Among the sugar plantations of the British Caribbean, as well, a corps of doctors, some of them committed to relieving the sufferings of their charges, others looking to make the slave system more efficient, did important early work on epidemiology. They identified types of fevers, learned how to decrease mortality and increase fertility (more slaves were dying than being born), experimented with how much water they needed to give slaves in order for them to survive on a diet of salted fish and jerk, and identified the best ratio of caloric intake to labour hours. And when slaves couldn't be kept alive, their autopsied bodies provided useful information. Medical knowledge then filtered out of the slave industry to benefit the broader international community; slavers made no proprietary claims on the techniques or data that derived from treating slaves.[5]

For instance, an epidemic of blindness that broke out on the French slaver *Rôdeur*, which sailed from Bonny Island in 1819 with about seventy-two slaves, helped eye doctors identify important information concerning ophthalmia, or trachoma. The disease appeared not long out to sea, first in the hold among the slaves and then on deck, blinding all the voyagers save one member of the crew. According to a passenger's account, sightless sailors worked under the direction of the one seeing man 'like machines,' tied to the captain with a thick rope. 'We were blind—stone blind, drifting like a wreck upon the ocean.' Some sailors went mad and tried to drink themselves to death. Others cursed through the day and night. Still others retired to their hammocks, immobilized. Each 'lived in a little dark world of his own, peopled by shadows and phantasms. We did not see the ship, nor the heavens, nor the sea, nor the faces of our comrades.' But they could hear the cries of the slaves in the hold.[6]

This went on for ten days, through storms and calms, until the voyagers heard the sound of another ship. A Spanish slaver, the *San León*, had drifted alongside the *Rôdeur*. But the entire crew and all the slaves of that ship had been blinded by disease as well: when the sailors of each vessel

---

that young African slaves and Native American cow herders on the slopes of the Andes knew that exposure to the tubercles of cow udders protected them from the pox. Africans and Indians, Humboldt said, 'display great sagacity in observing the character, habits, and diseases of the animals with which they live.'

realized this 'horrible coincidence,' they fell into silence, 'like that of death.' Eventually the *León* drifted away and was never heard from again.

The *Rôdeur*'s one seeing mate managed to pilot the ship to Guadeloupe. By now, a few of the crew members, including the captain, had begun to regain some of their vision. But thirty-nine Africans hadn't, so before entering the harbour the captain decided to drown them, tying weights to their legs and throwing them overboard. The ship was insured and their loss would be covered. (The practice of insuring slaves and slave ships, which had become common by this point, extended a new kind of economic rationality into the trade, helping slavers decide that a dead slave might be worth more than living labour.) The case of the *Rôdeur* caught the attention of Sébastien Guillié, director and chief of medicine at Paris's Royal Institute for Blind Youth. He wrote up his findings and published them in *Bibliothèque ophtalmologique*, which was then cited in other medical journals.*

What killed the Africans on the *Joaquín*, which arrived in Montevideo a few months after the *Neptune*, was the subject of a long debate. Of the 301 East Africans who boarded the Portuguese frigate in Mozambique on November 19, 1803, only thirty survived the nearly half-year journey to Montevideo. The deaths started shortly after setting sail, one a day until the ship reached the Cape of Good Hope forty-six days later. The mortality rate steadily increased as the slaver rounded into the Atlantic and continued on to Santa Catalina Island, off the coast of Brazil. After a layover, the *Joaquín* made for Río de la Plata.[7]

Montevideo's surgeon, Juan Cayetano Molina, along with the harbourmaster, boarded the *Joaquín* the afternoon it arrived in port. When

---

* An 1846 ophthalmology textbook, *A Manual of the Diseases of the Eye,* called the case of the *Rôdeur* a 'melancholy instance of the ravages of this ophthalmia, under circumstances propitious to its extension.' For his part, the Quaker abolitionist John Greenleaf Whittier drew from Guillié's article to compose his 1834 antislavery poem, 'The Slave-Ships,' which describes the throwing of 'fettered and blind' slaves overboard: 'one after one, / Plunged down the vessel's side. / . . . God of the earth! what cries / Rang upward unto thee? / . . . / The last dull plunge was heard, / The last wave caught its stain.'

they opened its hatch, they were horrified by what they saw below: thirty bone-thin East Africans in a foul, bare room, otherwise empty save for hundreds of unused shackles. Told that the most recent death had occurred just that morning and that a few Africans had died the day before, Molina and the harbourmaster panicked and ordered the ship's captain to weigh anchor and leave immediately. The captain at first refused. The barometer was dropping and a storm was coming. He yielded, though, when the harbourmaster threatened to seize the ship and throw him in jail if he didn't comply. After food and water were brought on board, the *Joaquín* sailed back out into the gulf with its exhausted crew and emaciated slaves.

Almost as soon as the ship left Montevideo's snug harbour, a fierce wind came out of the pampas, creating a strong tidal bore that rolled through the estuary. A *pampero* is a sight to see: as the pressure falls, grasshoppers, moths, and other insects fly off the land, driven forward by gusts of air. Thick black-cotton clouds advance like a wall from the west, mixing water with blown dirt to rain mud. At times, the wind can be so strong as to push an enormous amount of gulf water into the Atlantic, exposing large patches of the riverbed. The storm turned the *Joaquín*, nearly capsizing it. First its furled sails blew out of their gaskets and then all three masts snapped, leaving the ship 'half-destroyed.' With what was left of its jib and foresail, the ship limped back into Montevideo, beaching on a sandbar close to shore.

There now began a lengthy, drawn-out legal battle of charges and countercharges. The merchant who imported the slaves, Martín de Alzaga, accused Molina of incompetence. Alzaga is a familiar type in Argentine history, a staunch antisubversive who defined subversion as any understanding of *libertad* beyond his right to buy and sell Africans (it was Alzaga who, during the investigation into Buenos Aires's rumoured French Revolution–inspired rebellion, had personally presided over the torture sessions of suspects, black and white, who exhibited 'dangerous egalitarian leanings'). The slaver wanted to disembark the survivors and sell them, to recoup some of his loss. City officials, going on Molina's diagnosis that they were carrying a transmittable disease, refused his request.[8]

Alzaga sued the doctor for malice. The Africans perished not from an infectious disease, the slaver insisted, but rather from lack of water and from the extreme variations of temperature they suffered on their long voyage, which, he said, had a debilitating effect on the 'miserable uprooted beings.' There was proof that Montevideo wasn't in danger: none of the Portuguese crew members had died on the crossing.

Royal officials convened a commission of inquiry, which became a curious exercise in the limits of inductive reasoning, the kind of reasoning that held that matters of law, science, and medicine were to be decided through observation. The commission took testimony from the *Joaquín*'s crew, since they witnessed the sickness spread over the course of the voyage. And it called on the expertise of five surgeons—two British doctors, a Spaniard, a Swiss Italian, and one from the United States. They all had firsthand experience ministering to ailing slaves, either because they had previously sailed on a slave ship or because they had spent time in Mozambique. Everybody, the doctors, the sailors, and the ship's officers, gave their opinion about what had killed the East Africans. No one, though, thought to ask the surviving East Africans themselves, who were being confined to the hold of the *Joaquín* for the duration of the investigation.

The doctors agreed that the slaves had died not from an infection but rather from dehydration and chronic diarrhoea, aggravated by the physical and psychological hardships of slavery. Those surgeons who had been to Mozambique confirmed that long before being boarded on the ship, the captives would have felt extreme anguish, forced to survive on roots and bugs and arriving at the coast emaciated and with their stomachs distended. Then, once on the ocean, crowded in a dark hold with no ventilation, they'd have had nothing to do other than listen to the cries of their companions and the clanking of their chains. Many would have gone mad trying to make sense of their situation, trying to ponder the 'imponderable.' They had developed a 'total indifference to life,' the Swiss Italian doctor, Carlos Joseph Guezzi, testified. No one illness was to blame for their condition. Rather, they had wasted away emotionally. An 'abandonment of the self,' in Guezzi's opinion, had led to their demise.

———

The commission decided that the East Africans had died from an intestinal illness aggravated by *nostalgia*, *melancolía*, and *cisma*—nostalgia, melancholia, and brooding, or mourning. Montevideo had nothing to fear. Alzaga could disembark the survivors and sell them.

It was a strange ruling, holding in favour of an individual trader while condemning, implicitly at least, the trade itself. In doing so, the decision revealed the way that medical professionals were beginning to use in a more clinical fashion terms that in the past had been associated with religion, morality, and emotions. *Cisma* literally meant schism. In Spanish theological texts, the word referred not just to the political division of Christianity between Catholicism and Protestantism but to the spiritual split of fallen man: Adam's rebellion against God resulted in a *cisma* 'between body and soul, between flesh and spirit.' As to *melancolía*, two decades prior to the arrival of the *Joaquín* in Montevideo, the Royal Spanish Academy was still associating the term with nighttime demon possession, with dreams that 'compress and squeeze the heart.' In Great Britain, melancholics could be geniuses, sublime souls capable of producing beautiful poetry; more often, though, moral and religious philosophers of the time tended to think of extreme sadness as a vice, as a dissipating self-indulgence manifesting itself in a fondness for 'love-tales,' 'melodramatic escapades,' and other 'popular nonsense' that leads to a softening of the brain.[9]

The doctors investigating the *Joaquín*, however, used these concepts in a decidedly secular, matter-of-fact manner and, more importantly, in ways that unmistakably affirmed the humanity of the slaves. To diagnose enslaved Africans as suffering from nostalgia and melancholia was to acknowledge that they had selves that could be lost, inner lives that could suffer schism, or alienation, and pasts that could be mourned over. The Spanish doctor, Josef Capdevila, was the most empathetic, emphasizing the 'sadness' that overcame captives when they realized they were being forced to leave behind their 'family, their homeland, their freedom—all the familiar objects that soothe the senses and make people happy.'

After reading the opinion of the five surgeons, who collectively represented the state of medical knowledge in the United States, Protestant

Great Britain, and Catholic Spain, one comes away with the sense that slavery must have played an important but largely unacknowledged role in disenchanting medicine, in taking concepts like melancholy out of the hands of priests, poets, and philosophers and giving them to doctors. The intellectual historian Thomas Laqueur notes that, starting in the 1700s, a new kind of forensic writing, at once clinical and humane, began to reveal 'in extraordinarily detailed fashion' the 'pains and deaths of ordinary people in such a way as to make apparent the causal chains that might connect the actions of its readers with the suffering of its subjects.' There was an unprecedented outpouring of 'fact, of minute observations, about people who had before been beneath notice.' Laqueur includes the 'realistic novel, the autopsy, the clinical report, and the social inquiry,' to which could be added the observations of slave ship doctors.[10]

Two decades after the incident involving the *Joaquín*, the Spanish medical profession no longer considered *melancolía* to be caused by an incubus or a sign of moral weakness. It rather was understood as a type of delirium, related to dementia and mania. Spanish doctors also began to use the word to refer to seasickness, describing, though they didn't directly mention slavery, the condition in terms very similar to the way critics of the Middle Passage did, as caused by rancid food, too close contact, extreme weather, and above all the 'isolation' and the 'uniform and monotonous life' one experiences at sea, which can induce violent nervous disorders and intestinal disease. It was as if with each time a doctor threw back a slave hatch to reveal the human-made horrors below, it became just a bit more difficult to blame mental illness on demons and personal failings.[11]

The doctors, however, didn't extend the logic of their own reasoning to condemn the slave trade. They instead focused on the hardships of the Middle Passage as a technical concern. 'It is in the interests of commerce and humanity,' said the Connecticut-born, Edinburgh-educated member of the inquiry, John Redhead, 'to get slaves off their ships as soon as possible.'[12]

———

The West Africans brought to the 'village of blacks' must have thought they had landed in some combination of hell and heaven. All around, there were clusters of sick, fevered, and suppurating Africans, either recovering or dying from their Middle Passage. Yet after three months in the ship's hold, they were at least on land, in an open-air compound located on the bank of a freshwater stream where they could bathe.

In the United States, as well as in the Spanish, French, British, and Dutch Caribbean and some areas of Portuguese Brazil, the torments of the ocean voyage continued on land, as Africans left behind one totalitarian system, the slave ship, and entered another, the plantation. In the Río de la Plata region, however, there was a dizzying disjuncture between the terror regime of the Atlantic, as revealed in the inquiry into the *Joaquín*'s crossing, and life on shore.

Africans shipped out of Montevideo or Buenos Aires to work in mines or plantations would be in for more suffering. But those who stayed in the two cities found themselves in a plebeian world of considerable liberty. Many worked as assistants to tradesmen and artisans who were not their owners; the main obligation to the person who claimed them as property was a weekly or monthly percentage of their cash wages. As their trade skills increased, so did their degree of freedom. Many negotiated their own terms of employment and housing arrangements and some slaves became independent artisans themselves. There were no large concentrations of plantation slaves in the Río de la Plata region. Bakers, brickmakers, ranchers, wheat growers, and beef salters were the biggest slave owners. The majority of enslaved peoples belonged to households with only one slave or two. Thousands of the city's slaves went about their lives with little or no oversight, dancing, drumming, drinking, gambling, and generally ignoring regulations trying to get them to do otherwise.*

---

* The Río de la Plata was the southernmost outpost of what the musician and historian Ned Sublette calls the Atlantic Ocean's 'saints and festivals belt,' a fusion of Catholic and African rituals and rhythms: similar to New Orleans's Mardi Gras Indians and its second-line clubs, in Montevideo and Buenos Aires, enslaved Africans and, after slavery had ended, free people of colour, organized mutual-aid societies. Often based on their places of origin, these organizations comprised a startlingly diverse array of 'nations,' including *nación congo, nación benguela, nación moro, nación bornó, nación lubono, nación angola*, and *nación mozambique*, electing 'kings' and 'queens' and staging collective dances and public processions. By

The *Neptune*'s Africans caught a glimpse of this world at the compound. It really was, in a way, a village, a permanent refugee camp for people from all over the African continent, from Senegal, Guinea, the Congo, Angola, and Mozambique. Families, mostly making a living in low-skilled trades, had settled in, raising ragtag lean-to homes around cooking fires. During the day, the the newly arrived slaves would have seen black laundresses leaving the compound's gates early in the morning and coming back late at night, working hard but being left alone to live on the margins of freedom, singing: '*Acuchú chachá acuchú chachá . . . al cubo del sur, vamo a lavá . . . vamo todo a lavá.*'[13]

In all the many hundreds of pages of official documents having to do with the case of the *Neptune*, there is not one description of the West Africans, not a scrap of information about them other than that they were embarked on Bonny Island, that when they were taken by Mordeille's crew they were dressed in coarse blue cotton smocks, and that the adult men wore beads around their necks and waists and had a thin, shaved line running through their scalps, from forehead to nape.

One thing is known for sure: they would have done anything not to get back on the *Neptune*, or any other slave ship. It appears they were afflicted with the same disease the slaves on the *Joaquín* were said to have been suffering from—from *nostalgia*, defined by one Spanish dictionary as 'a violent desire compelling those taken out of their country to return home.'[14]

---

the late 1700s, Spanish officials were regularly complaining about neighbourhoods where 'black men and women are found in various houses using the *tambo* and *tango*,' words that could mean either the instruments (drums) or the dance.

5

A CONSPIRACY OF LIFTING AND THROWING

By the end of February, with the careening of his ships completed and the *Santa Eulalia* in from Cádiz, Mordeille, anxious to get back out to sea, made arrangements to reboard the *Neptune*'s slaves. Fourteen had died at the compound and nine were too sick to be moved, which left about 320 to be loaded. They were divided into two groups. The seventy del Pino gave Mordeille permission to sell were put on the *Eulalia* and the rest, over 250, returned to the *Neptune*.

The *Neptune* was the first to revolt. Coming on board in the morning, naked except for makeshift loincloths and the beads the men still wore around their waists and necks, the West Africans grew increasingly frantic as the day went on. At dusk, on the deck of the anchored ship, one of them seized a sailor and threw him overboard, crying out, 'I would rather kill all the whites than return to sea.' With that, what Mordeille would later describe as 'the conspiracy of lifting and throwing' had begun.

The ship erupted. At first, Mordeille's crew tried to hold its ground, fighting the captives hand to hand. After the slaves pushed a few more into the water, the mariners retreated to the ship's boats and rowed away. A nearby Spanish man-of-war, the *Medea*, sent a detachment of marines to retake the ship from the unarmed Africans. Firing musket shots over the heads of the rebels, the troops boarded the vessel. When it became clear that their revolt had failed, a number of the rebels began to throw themselves over the gunwales into the bay.

As already mentioned, of all the Africans taken during the four-century-long slave trade, those from West Africa, especially those boarded at ports in the Gulf of Guinea and the Niger Delta region, and especially Bonny, where the *Neptune* sailed from, were known for their high rates of suicide. Descendants of slaves who worked the rice plantations of Georgia's coastal islands handed down a legend that captive Igbos would fling themselves into the Atlantic rather than submit to slavery, not committing suicide but 'flying' or 'walking' on the water—or dancing on the waves—home. 'Negros did not' kill themselves, remembered Esteban Montejo, a former Cuban slave.* 'They escaped by flying. They flew through the sky and returned to their own lands.'[1]

None of the *Neptune*'s West Africans managed to get away. They were all pulled out of the water alive. Skirmishes like this were so common on slave ships that they were hardly ever reported, much less were inquiries made into the motives of the rebels. Mordeille did send a note to Viceroy del Pino reporting the event, writing that the Africans had risen up after spending time on shore among 'their kind.' Seeing how the others 'dressed and ate,' he said, they were 'determined not to return to sea.' It took 'indescribable effort' for his men to force them into the hold.

Once order was restored and provisions were stocked, including five barrels of black paint, the *Neptune* set sail on March 21. The ship's papers said it was going to Guiana but it dropped anchor a day later at one of the estuary's island beaches, where, as planned, it rendezvoused

---

* In this instance, Montejo identifies Congolese Africans as those most likely to fly away: they 'flew the most; they disappeared by means of witchcraft . . . without making a sound. There are those who say the Negros threw themselves into rivers. This is untrue. The truth is they fastened a chain to their waists which was full of magic. That was where their power came from. I know this all intimately and it is true beyond a doubt.' The equation of suicide and flight runs through Toni Morrison's *Song of Solomon*. After hearing children singing lines from an old blues song ('Solomon done fly, Solomon done gone, Solomon cut across the sky, Solomon gone home'), Milkman, the novel's twentieth-century protagonist, realizes his connection to a long-ago 'flying African.' Working in the cotton field one day, Milkman's ancestor 'flew off. . . . He flew. You know, like a bird. . . . Went right back to wherever it was he came from.'

with the *Santa Eulalia*. That night, with the help of paid-off royal coast guards, their crews transferred all except forty of the *Neptune*'s Africans to the *Eulalia*. While Mordeille's carpenters and painters began work to make the *Neptune* look like something other than a Liverpool slaver, the *Santa Eulalia* hauled anchor and started out, bound for Lima.[2]

The *Eulalia* made it as far as the mouth of the Río de la Plata, with the open sea ahead, when a number of slaves got 'loose.' They didn't take the whole ship, just the part in front of the *barricado*, the midsection containment wall built for these kinds of occasions, about eight feet high and projecting two feet out from either side of the vessel, punched through with holes for blunderbusses. The stern and quarterdeck remained in Spanish hands. The rebels ordered the *Eulalia*'s captain, Tomás Lopatequi, to sail to Africa, but Lopatequi, still in control of much of the mechanics of the ship, including the wheel, capstan, and mizzenmast, instead made for Punta del Este, the northern head of the gulf, where the water is deep to the coastline. Nearing land by the end of the day, Lopatequi ordered a launch dropped and sent a messenger to get help from a nearby garrison.

Anchored from the stern and swinging with the tide, the *Eulalia* bobbed quietly, as the Africans in the fore and Spaniards in the aft sized each other up through the night and over the barricade. Saber-carrying, black-hatted cavalry soldiers, led by Second Lieutenant Josef Casal, arrived the next morning. Unsure how to proceed, Casal put half of his forty men on the *Eulalia*'s stern and kept the rest in his boat.

Nothing much happened for another half day. At some point, the women, who had been locked in a separate hold, had broken free. Now the forward deck, about a twenty-by-forty-foot space, was packed with 290 or so insurgents, most of them naked. The rebels seemed to realize that there was no such thing as a standoff in this kind of situation. The advantage of time and waiting went to their captors. Having taken over half the ship, freed the women, and issued a demand to be returned to Africa, there was nothing else they could do that would have an effective result. They therefore threatened to destroy the ship's cargo.

The *Eulalia* carried a rich hold, filled with pipes of wine, candles, iron, nails, paper, maté, leather shoes, and mercury, used to extract silver from ore, and Captain Lopatequi demanded that Lieutenant Casal do something to not lose it. Mounted on the quarterdeck were two twenty-four-pound carronades. A magazine of case shot—tin cylinders filled with six- to eight-ounce iron balls—was stored in the stern as well. When case shot is fired, the force of the discharge rips the flimsy tin apart, propelling the balls forward independently in a cone-shaped cluster, inflicting maximum pain on humans, especially on targets gathered closely together, as the insurgents were in the fore of the ship, while limiting damage to infrastructure.

Only the 'rigour of fire,' Casal wrote his superiors later, would force *la negrada*—the 'black mass'—to submit. Two blasts ended the revolt. Casal had his men pull a hundred of the 'most robust and terrible' African men off the ship, twenty of whom were identified as leaders and marched in chains to the garrison. The rest were returned to the ship. After a halfhearted, inconclusive investigation as to why the ship had so many Africans on board, local officials allowed the *Santa Eulalia* to proceed to Lima.

It was a long, frightful sail south and through the Strait of Magellan. The *Eulalia* was not a big ship. Over 250 humans were kept in storage rooms designed to carry no more than a hundred slaves. The West Africans, laid in on their sides, the front of one body pushed against the back of another, listened in the dark as the ship's beams groaned with each lurch through the rough straits. With rancid food, poor ventilation, little water, and no medical attention, they began to die. Fifteen were gone by the time the ship reached the Pacific, another ten before calling on Arica in northern Chile, six before Pisco in Peru, and twenty-three more by the time the ship dropped anchor at Lima.

The *Eulalia* ended its journey in June 1804, its surviving cargo having spent most of nine months in the hold of a ship on the high seas.

Meanwhile, Mordeille's scheme proceeded as planned: he handed over the disguised *Neptune*, now called the *Aguila*, to a group of Portuguese mariners under the command of Simão de Rocha, a cabin boy he had promoted to the rank of captain. Rocha sailed the counterfeit vessel to Ensenada de Barragán, a small port village on the Buenos Aires side of the Río de la Plata, and delivered it, along with its forty remaining captive Africans, to its new owner, a Buenos Aires merchant.

But port officials figured out the swindle. Acting on orders from Viceroy del Pino, who had been alerted to the uprising on the overloaded *Santa Eulalia*, they seized the ship, imprisoned Rocha, and embargoed the slaves. They had recognized the *Neptune* by its blackened figurehead: its lion without a crown.

Mordeille—Citizen Manco—had already cruised out of the Río de la Plata on the *Hope*. He would return again and again over the next three years, delivering at least eight more prize ships and nearly a thousand more enslaved Africans to Montevidean and Buenos Aires merchants.[3]

When the British Royal Navy tried to capture Buenos Aires and Montevideo, Mordeille and his men helped defend the two cities. He put his knowledge of the estuary, earned over the years avoiding Spanish officials, to good use, hitting British ships and then running, drawing them into shallow water to ground on sandbars and shoals.

British troops took but couldn't hold Buenos Aires and Montevideo. But Mordeille died driving them out, on February 3, 1807, killed by a bayonet on the Montevideo beach where, over the years, he had unloaded thousands upon thousands of Africans, including the ones who came in on the *Neptune*.[4]

Those sixty of the *Neptune*'s slaves who didn't continue on to Lima on the *Santa Eulalia*—the forty embargoed from the disguised *Neptune* and the twenty 'robust and terrible' rebels taken off the *Eulalia*—were sent on to Buenos Aires, where they would be auctioned in the city's slave market. They had arrived as booty, twice-stolen goods. Now, thanks to the alchemy of 'free trade in blacks,' they were about to complete their transition from pirate's prize and contraband to salable merchandise.

I Never Could Look at Death without a Shudder

Herman Melville believed in abolition. 'Sin it is, no less,' he wrote of slavery, 'it puts out the sun at noon.' Yet he tended to treat bondage as a metaphysical problem and freedom as an idea best suited to some inner realm of personal sovereignty. It was a common position for his time. Individuals, wrote Henry David Thoreau in *Walden*, published a year before *Benito Cereno*, needed to achieve 'self-emancipation even in the West Indian provinces of the fancy and imagination.' All human beings, Melville believed, oscillate somewhere between the two extreme poles of liberty and slavery that defined much of the political rhetoric of antebellum America. His stories contained characters who were slaves yet made to seem free, and freemen, like Ishmael and Ahab, who were slaves, mostly to their own tangled thoughts and uncontrollable passions. All the tomes of 'human jurisprudence,' Melville wrote in *Moby-Dick*, could be reduced in essence to the whaler's rule distinguishing 'Fast-Fish' (harpooned or hooked on a line, and thus in the possession of a given party) from 'Loose-Fish' (unclaimed and therefore fair game). 'What plays the mischief with this masterly code,' Melville said, 'is the admirable brevity of it, which necessitates a vast volume of commentaries to expound it.'[1]

And once expounded, it turns out that there is no such thing as a completely Fast or a completely Loose Fish. 'What are the Rights of Man and liberties of the world but Loose-fish? . . . And what are you, reader, but a Loose-Fish and a Fast-Fish, too?' 'All men live enveloped in whale-lines,' he said elsewhere in *Moby-Dick*, 'All are born with halters round their necks.' 'Who aint a slave?' Ishmael asks. 'Tell me that.' There's joy in the question, as well as in the implied answer—*no one*—an acceptance of the fact that humans, by sheer stint of being human, are bound to one another.[2]

There was one moment in Melville's writing career, though, when he admitted that the chattel slavery of dark-skinned people from Africa, or descendants of Africans, was different. It's in a scene from one of his earlier novels, *Redburn*, partly based on his visit to Liverpool in 1839, when he came upon a statue of Rear Admiral Horatio Nelson. Nelson had led the British to their greatest naval victory, over the combined French and Spanish fleet at Trafalgar in October 1805, but he died in the battle, cut down by a French bullet. Most of the memorials that went up afterward throughout Great Britain to honor Nelson's sacrifice were simple tributes, like the column in London, which supports the regally posed admiral in full dress uniform.

But Liverpool's monument, located in Exchange Flags Square, in the shadow of city hall, was darkly symbolic, more befitting, thought one observer, a 'barbarous' nation ruled by savages or Catholics rather than by true Christians: a naked Nelson falls back in uneasy repose in Victory's arms, his left foot trampling down a dead man, as Death, in the form of a cowled skeleton, its ribs separated by dark recesses, grasps at his heart. Around the pedestal sit four pitiful figures chained to the stone.[3]

They were supposed to be French and Spanish prisoners of war. But they made Herman Melville think of slaves:

> At uniform intervals round the base of the pedestal, four naked figures in chains, somewhat larger than life, are seated in various attitudes of humiliation and despair. One has his leg recklessly thrown over his knee, and his head bowed over, as if he had given up all hope of ever feeling better. Another has his head buried in despondency, and no doubt looks mournfully out of his eyes, but as his face was averted at the time, I could not catch the expression. These woe-begone figures of captives are emblematic of Nelson's principal victories; but I never could look at their swarthy limbs and manacles, without being involuntarily reminded of four African slaves in the market-place.

And my thoughts would revert to Virginia and Carolina; and also to the historical fact, that the African slave-trade once constituted the principal commerce of Liverpool; and that the prosperity of the town was once supposed to have been indissolubly linked to its prosecution. And I remembered that my father had often spoken to gentlemen visiting our house in New York, of the unhappiness that the discussion of the abolition of this trade had occasioned in Liverpool; that the struggle between sordid interest and humanity had made sad havoc at the fire-sides of the merchants; estranged sons from sires; and even separated husband from wife.

Melville was especially impressed with the way the monument's 'hideous skeleton' insinuated 'his bony hand under the hero's robe,' groping for Nelson's heart. 'A very striking design, and true to the imagination; I never could look at Death without a shudder.'[4]

Considering that Melville resisted imagining chattel slavery as a singular problem, distinct from other forms of domination, the proposition set forth in the second paragraph is interesting: Liverpool's wealth, as well as Carolina's and Virginia's, was built on the backs of enslaved Africans. But what is especially compelling is the cascading flow of the prose, the way an initial, fleeting impression kicks off an 'involuntary' stream of associations revealing slavery's outsized role in Western history, the way the trade made seemingly random coincidences fit into a meaningful pattern.

One such coincidence involves the Nelson statue itself. Melville probably didn't know it, but the monument was raised by a civic committee made up mostly of slavers, shippers, and sugar planters who were grateful that the Royal Navy, thanks to Nelson, had established its dominance over the Atlantic, so that they could sail their vessels to and from the slave plantations in the Caribbean in relative safety. Among them was John Bolton. This meant that the slaver responsible for the arrival in America of some of the West Africans who would later inspire Melville to write *Benito Cereno* was also responsible for the 'fleeting images' that prompted Melville, years earlier, to write about slavery in the first place.

Melville's vision would soon pass and he would return to discussing slavery as a proxy for the human condition in general. Yet while in Liverpool, he circled the ghastly memorial 'repeatedly.' 'How this group of statuary affected me,' Melville wrote in *Redburn*, based on that visit, 'may be inferred from the fact, that I never went through Chapel-street without going through the little arch to look at it again. And there, night or day, I was sure to find Lord Nelson still falling back, Victory's wreath still hovering over his sword point, and Death grim and grasping as ever, while the four bronze captives still lamented their captivity.'

Melville returned one more time to look at the monument, in 1856, a year after he wrote *Benito Cereno*. 'After dinner went to Exchange,' he recorded in his diary, 'Looked at Nelson statue, with peculiar emotion, mindful of 20 years ago.'[5]

PART II

A LOOSE FISH

What is the great globe itself but a Loose-Fish?

—HERMAN MELVILLE, *MOBY-DICK*

6

A SUITABLE GUIDE TO BLISS

Amasa Delano was born into one of those sprawling pilgrim families that, if not for their pedigree then because of their numbers, seemed to have had a hand in everything America was becoming. His great-great-great grandfather Philippe de Lannoy arrived in Plymouth in 1621, one ship behind the *Mayflower*. Within less than a decade, he had joined with other colonists to sail his family across the bay, settling what became the town of Duxbury on a spit of forest and meadowland nestled between the ocean and salt marshes and fed with freshwater springs.

Philippe married twice, had five sons, four daughters, and thirty-eight grandchildren—who each in turn had a prodigious number of offspring, eagerly so: one of Philippe's sons, Amasa's great-great grandfather, was fined ten pounds for having committed 'carnall copulation' with a woman he subsequently married. 'They are so plentiful they roost in trees like turkeys,' a Duxbury neighbour once said. The Delanos, as the name came to be written, were soon found across New England, from Maine to New York, and beyond, and included branches that produced some of America's most successful businessmen, artists, and statesmen, among them three presidents: Ulysses S. Grant, Calvin Coolidge, and Franklin Delano Roosevelt. Amasa's mother's ancestors also arrived early in Plymouth, descended from a Devonshire man said to have been knighted by Queen Elizabeth.[1]

At the time of Amasa's birth in 1763, Duxbury was a poor fishing town made up of horse trails and cottages stocked with rough-edged, homemade furnishings. Only one home had anything that could be called a carpet and nobody had a four-wheel cart and just a few families owned African slaves. Marshfield, one town over, was wealthier. Its sons went to Harvard or enlisted in the British Royal Navy. Duxbury stayed stocked with farmers, fisherman, wood cutters, colliers (charcoal makers), and shipwrights, 'iron-nerved' men who could 'hew down forests and live on crumbs.' All were poor, but some were poorer, mostly the elderly who had outlived their kin and couldn't survive on their own. Families took turns 'keeping' a distant cousin of Amasa's, for instance, 'old Jane Delanoe,' and then paid for her coffin when she died.[2]

Amasa's parents, Samuel and Abigail, called the rest of their boys Alexander, William, and Samuel Jr. But they named their firstborn after his uncle Amasa, which in Hebrew means burden or to carry a heavy load. There is only one Amasa in the Old Testament. He is King David's nephew, murdered by his cousin Joab, who with his right hand pulls Amasa's beard in friendship as if to kiss him as he uses his left to thrust a dagger into his side. Amasa's intestines spill out on the ground and he dies in his own blood. 'The more plot there is in sin, the worse it is,' was how an eighteenth-century commentary on the Bible interpreted this passage. And if the biblical reference weren't forbidding enough, the circumstances of his namesake uncle's death were even darker.[3]

On October 4, 1759, Amasa's uncle Amasa Delanoe, a sergeant in Rogers Rangers, a celebrated British militia, took part in an attack on Saint Francis, a French-allied Abenaki settlement near the Saint Lawrence River. The village's men had gone out patrolling, leaving behind mostly children, women, the sick, and the old. Dressed as Indians, the Rangers set the village on fire. In 'less then a quarter of an hour the whole town was in a blaze, the carnage terrible,' Robert Kirk, a Scottish member of the Rangers, recorded in his diary. 'Those who the flames did not devour were either shot or tomohawk'ed.' Kirk called it 'the bloodiest scene in all America.'

The killing was over in a few hours, but the retreat down the Connecticut River valley, with the British pursued by the French and Abenaki, lasted weeks. Short on food and water and badly exposed to the elements, the Rangers, now broken up into small bands, got lost in the woods. Exhausted and starving, they survived through cannibalism. Kirk's unit killed a captive they had taken from Saint Francis, Marie Jeanne Gill, the daughter of the Abenaki chief. 'We then broiled and eat most of her,' Kirk wrote, 'and receive great strength thereby.' Delanoe's group, reduced to three soldiers, did the same to its prisoner, who might have been the Abenaki leader's other child, his son Xavier. The next day, the Abenaki caught Delanoe and his men near Lake Champlain, and when they learned the British 'had killed and eat a Little Boy,' the Indians 'killed and scalped' them 'in revenge.'[4]

The younger Amasa took first to freshwater, then to salt, and by the age of five could plunge into the cold ocean and stay under for unusual lengths. Even as a boy he had a compact physique, as if he were composed of condensed energy. Along with his younger brothers, Samuel and William (Alexander died an infant), Amasa learned to build ships from their shipwright father and to navigate on fishing trips to the Grand Banks, bringing back cod, mackerel, and herring to sell in Boston. He quit school after a few years, rebelling against the 'severity of schoolmasters,' though he continued to be a voracious reader.

Duxbury was a small town and a large part of Amasa's moral education took place in his family's pew in its clapboard First Parish Church. Reverend Charles Turner was the village pastor through the whole of Amasa's first thirteen years. He was a severe-looking man who wore an unusually large white wig as he made his rounds calling on families and scaring children. 'I was exceedingly afraid of him,' recalled one of Amasa's contemporaries.[5]

Turner projected authority but his theology was subversive. He was a man of 'practiced eloquence,' part of a generation of preachers who were planting the seeds of what would later become known as Unitarianism. They were leaving behind the cold Calvinism of Delano's parents and grandparents, which held that there was little an individual could do to change the course of his afterlife (and which thought it nothing to name

a baby boy Amasa). The people of Duxbury were embracing a more liberal faith, which included the notion that man possessed free will.
Turner had an opportunity to rehearse this new outlook in Boston in
1773, before an audience of royal magistrates. He had been selected to
give that year's annual Election Sermon, a prestigious honour in recognition of a long and distinguished career in the ministry.[6]

Preached before the British governor of Massachusetts, Thomas
Hutchinson, at a time when Boston newspapers were openly debating
the question of independence, Turner's sermon was practically insurrectionary. 'The scriptures,' he said, 'cannot rightly be expounded without
explaining them in a manner friendly to the cause of freedom.' Turner
said that he had lived for nearly two decades among the good men and
women of Duxbury. London opinion thought of them, along with the
rest of America's 'common people,' as 'little superior to Indian Barbarians,' but they, better than the king and his deputies, were the true
source and guardians of virtue.

Turner also included in his sermon a formulation that would become
increasingly common in public debate, the idea that the 'avarice' of individuals could contribute to 'publick advantage.' By increasing available
wealth and resources, the pursuit of personal gain, he said, could benefit
the community as a whole. In this new equation, qualities that Christians in the past had considered vices, such as ambition, were placed in
the category of 'interests.' They weren't to be *repressed* but *balanced* by
virtue—or, as Turner put it, 'enriched' by 'higher principles' that would
protect the 'publick good' from the 'vile affections of a few.' Man's passions, appetites, and interests needed to be, he said, regulated with what
'if we please we may call a constitution.'[7]

Turner's remarks are a clear example of one of the things that the historian Gordon Wood says made the American Revolution radical: the
equation of the governance of the self and the governance of society, a
reliance on a moral constitution to check and balance passions in individuals and a written one to check and balance them in politics. Governor Hutchinson 'winced and changed colour during the sermon' and
'pointedly did not invite Turner to the festive meal that followed the
preaching.' Samuel Adams, though, was so impressed with Turner's ser-

mon that he distributed its text far and wide, throughout the colonies and to London, where it reached the desk of Benjamin Franklin.[8]

Back in Duxbury, Turner would take his flock to the shores of the revolution and leave them there. He retired from the ministry in early 1776 due to ill health. On July 3, 1776—the day after the Continental Congress voted to break with Great Britain and the day before it adopted the Declaration of Independence—the town's new minister, Zedekiah Sanger, was ordained, and Reverend Elijah Brown, pastor of nearby Sherborn's First Parish Church, gave the sermon.[9]

Brown's optimism concerning human nature was even greater than Turner's. 'There is nothing in divine revelation inconsistent with, or contrary to the prime dictates and requirements, of pure, unabused reason,' he said in his lecture introducing Sanger. 'Reason, that shining ray of the Deity—that bright effulgence of eternal light, when first implanted in the human soul,' he continued, choosing a set of luminous words that radiated pure love, 'was a suitable guide to bliss and glory.'[10]

But Reverend Brown had a problem. Like many of its neighbouring towns, Duxbury had sided with Boston's Sons of Liberty against London. Three years earlier, Amasa's father and uncles helped raise the village's first company of minutemen, promising to 'stand or fall' with the Congress. Duxbury paid a price. Even before the Battle of Lexington, royal troops were harassing its residents, encircling its church during services and political meetings, and impeding its fishermen from going to sea. The Royal Navy burned one schooner just off shore, transferring its crew, which included a number of Amasa's cousins, to a prison ship in New York Harbour, where some perished. Elsewhere, too, the war against the British had exacted a heavy toll. And the losses suffered at the hands of the British were nothing compared with the smallpox epidemic that swept North America, from New England to Mexico, beginning in 1775, laying siege to cities and villages and claiming more than 100,000 victims by the time it abated.[11]

And so, at the end of his sermon celebrating the brightness and bliss of God-given reason, Brown turned gloomy. He told the Duxbury congregation that he supported independence from Great Britain and he urged the town to continue 'struggling for our natural rights.' But the situation is 'calamitous,' he said; 'heaven is angry with us.' The wasting plagues, the groans of our wounded, the blood of our brethren, the horrors of war—how else could such a procession of woe be understood other than as punishment? Have we not, he asked, 'wickedly forsaken the lord?'

Brown had given up the doctrine of predestination for individual souls, yet he held on to the idea that God spoke through history, that history was more than the accumulated tally of individual acts derived from free will. It was an expression of divine favour or disfavour. If the good people of Duxbury had used their free will to act virtuously—to fight for their natural rights—then how to account for their suffering?

Amasa was thirteen years old in 1776. By all accounts he was a thoughtful boy. Yet sitting in the Delano family pew, he probably missed the depth of Brown's paradox, that individual lives might not be foreordained but the course of history was still guided by God. It wouldn't be until the end of his life that he questioned the idea that if reason and discipline were put to controlling appetites and impulses, success would follow. In any case, the reverend's dark turn was brief, coming at the very end of a long, long sermon.

When Brown finished, he yielded the pulpit to Duxbury's new minister, who started with the subject on everyone's mind. Reverend Sanger began by quoting Leviticus: 'Proclaim liberty throughout all the land unto all the inhabitants thereof.'

The revolution changed Duxbury. Samuel Delano, Amasa's father, did well as the owner of a small shipyard, moving from being 'poor and without any literary attainments' to, in 1783, able to buy a decent-sized plot of land. Yet though he is often listed among the men whose skill and hard work made Duxbury rich, his name doesn't appear on the rolls of those who became rich themselves, like his neighbour Ezra Weston. Weston also started as a poor freeholder and shipwright, but he came to dominate the town's economy by the end of the 1700s, owning a large shipyard, a blacksmith shop, timberlands, a ropewalk, a sawmill to cut spars, and a fleet of fishing ships. He acquired so much wealth and influence that he would earn about as damning a nickname as could be imagined in republican New England: King Caesar.[12]

Duxbury's postrevolutionary prosperity led to an increase in harlotry, hard drinking, cursing, gambling, and other iniquities concentrated near its shipyards. 'Keep away,' one old timer warned a bunch of back-country farm boys looking for work with the town's fishing fleet. 'It's Sodom, and it's going to be sunk, it is.' Individuals like King Caesar, who reigned over Duxbury's little Sodom, accumulated riches that would have been undreamed of just decades earlier. Weston's son, Ezra Weston Jr.—who was about the same age as Amasa—inherited not just his father's business and property but his title as well. He was King Caesar II, presiding over the further expansion of his family's shipping empire.[13]

With wealth came poverty. The kind of occasional family and church charity that paid for old Jane's coffin was no longer enough to deal with spreading destitution. In 1767, the town had voted to 'drive the poor' into a workhouse, and soon thereafter a standing committee was established to administer the institution. In exchange for food and clothing, the insolvent picked oakum (like Charles Dickens's Oliver Twist), pulling strands of hemp or jute out of old rope, which would then be mixed with tar and used to caulk the hulls of ships.[14]

The changes in Duxbury were slices of larger ones taking place throughout the new republic. Gordon Wood describes this period in American history, in the decades following the triumph of the revolution, as a great unravelling. 'Everything seemed to be coming apart,' he writes, 'and murder, suicide, theft and mobbing became increasingly common responses to the burdens that liberty and the expectation of gain were placing on people.' Far from creating a nation founded on 'benevolence and selflessness, enlightened republicanism was breeding social competitiveness and individualism.' Reverend Turner's idea that 'higher principles' could temper private ambitions was put on its head. For many, private ambition *was* the higher principle. Everywhere rude men were accumulating great fortunes, speculating, lending money at high interest, price gouging, or seeking political office to advance not the ideals of the republic but the interests of

their particular class, or worse, just themselves, by 'exploiting the revolutionary rhetoric of liberty and equality.' 'The Revolution,' Wood writes,
'was the source of its own contradictions.'[15]

In Duxbury, one response to these changes was to go abroad. Even
before the revolution, Reverend Turner had defined knowledge of the
world as a positive good, a way of cultivating civic virtue. 'If a few general terms can give no tolerable idea of the blessings of freedom,' he
preached, then 'let them be learnt from the story of the world.' By the
turn of the century, leaving Duxbury was thought to be a way to both
learn about the world and rise in it. An unwritten law governed the
town, a 'natural decree,' as one resident put it, 'that every boy should
take his place on board a ship as soon as he was able to go aloft.' The
experience would allow the sons of Duxbury to 'expand their sympathies' and better their circumstances—that is, to improve themselves
morally and materially.[16]

Beginning his life when the idea of an independent America was dim in
the minds of a few radicals and ending it in 1823, when all of the Western
Hemisphere (excepting Cuba, Puerto Rico, and Canada) had declared
itself free, Amasa Delano was truly a new man of the American Revolution. He held deeply and certainly the most radical of all the revolutionary ideas then coursing through the new nation: human beings were
born equal. What they made of this equality, however, was their own
doing. Tutored by ministers like Turner and Sanger, Delano thought the
idea of 'self-government' to be a personal virtue as much as it was a
political program, perhaps even more so, and he strived for self-mastery.
He admitted to being ambitious, to having wanted very much to be successful, respected among his peers for his talent and honest nature and
financially secure enough to support a family.[17]

Like many other republicans of his day, Delano made a distinction
between ambition and envy. Envy was a vice, ambition a virtue, a force for
self-improvement, a way to better one's self and one's community. Had
Delano been envious, he might have responded to an increasingly divided
Duxbury by turning inward and demanding a levelling of wealth. Instead,

he struck outward, believing that he could fulfil his ambition by enlarging his world. Delano hoped to escape Duxbury's parochialism and see the world as it really was, liberated from the 'exaggerated accounts' found in books and the tall tales told by sailors who returned from long voyages peddling 'false statements of things a great way from home.'

He wanted to do what his pastor had urged him to do: learn the story of the world.*

War gave him the chance. Shortly after hearing Reverend Sanger proclaim liberty, Amasa, against his father's wishes because he was underage, signed up with Duxbury's rebel militia and marched to Boston to fight the British. From that moment on, to the day three decades later when he picked up a pen to write his memoirs, Amasa seemingly didn't have a moment's rest.

Like some republican Zelig, Delano witnessed, or came close to witnessing, many of the most storied episodes that mark the start of modern times. He guarded British prisoners taken at the Battle of Saratoga and observed the destruction of Yorktown, reflecting afterward on the 'melancholy sensations' that overcame him upon 'viewing scenes of devastation and blood.' He sailed many times to Haiti in the years before that country's revolution, on merchant ships built by King Caesar carrying New England salt cod to sell to plantation owners to feed their slaves. Amasa was in the port cities of Canton and Macao just as China was opening to Western trade. He dropped anchor in Hawaii shortly after the death of Captain Cook. When he left he took with him two young men. One, the son of the legendary King Kamehameha, later disappeared in China. The other made it to Boston, where he would earn

---

* Going to sea did for plebeian citizens like Delano what landed property did for republican gentry, whose large estates were not so much commodities, to be traded like so many hogsheads of tobacco. Rather, landed wealth buffered them from the jostle of the marketplace and sheltered them from all its petty, parochial, divisive interests. It allowed men like Thomas Jefferson and George Washington to cultivate their cosmopolitanism, to rise above the fray and advance an uplifting vision of the republican good. As Washington said, to be a republican was to be 'a citizen of the great republic of humanity at large.' While it didn't afford the same kind of financial security, going to sea, living a close-quartered life with people of many races, did allow a person like Amasa Delano or Herman Melville to imagine himself, as Melville wrote, an 'untrammeled citizen and sailor of the universe.'

good reviews for his performance in the *Tragedy of Captain Cook*. Amasa witnessed battles fought between the British and French navies and among the inhabitants of the Palau islands, leading him to reflect on the moral superiority of the latter. When he asked the king of Palau why his followers destroyed the property of their defeated rivals in a spirit of revenge, he was told: 'The English do so.'

A dreamscape of abundance passed before his eyes in Africa, South America, and the South Sea Islands: clusters of antelopes and herds of deer that seemed never to end, enormous stands of flamingos and companies of parrots, banks of swans that covered the whole of the coast of Chile, marching colonies of penguins blanketing the Malvina, or Falkland, Islands. Decades before Darwin observed the Galapagos's giant turtles, Delano compared them to Indian elephants; 'their mouths, heads, and necks,' he said, 'appeared to quiver with passion.'

While in Lima, Delano visited the offices of the Spanish Inquisition and toured the Spanish mint and gave a remarkable account of African slaves casting gold into bars and coins. Delano was the first to tell in detail the story of the mutiny on the *Bounty* against Captain Bligh. He had his cargo seized by French revolutionaries in Île de France and was present at the beginning of British rule in India and European colonialism in the Pacific's island archipelagos. Delano described the Dutch roots of apartheid in South Africa, thoughtfully considering the implications of what we today would call the racial division of the world. He smoked opium with Moors in Malaysia, conversed on matters of ethics and war with Polynesian chiefs, and considered the resemblance between the Christian Holy Trinity and a three-headed statuette he came across in Bombay representing Vishnu, Shiva, and Brahma.

All told, Amasa Delano spent the better part of three decades at sea.

Delano thought that traveling the world would enlarge his mind and add to his wisdom, helping him to 'subdue his prejudices,' rise above petty provocations, and master the 'divine art of extracting good from evil.' But since, as he put it, he owed his tolerance and open-mindedness to his ability to 'generalise his observations, principles, and feelings,' he was, in a way, expecting to confirm what he already believed, ideas concerning reason, free will, and man's capacity for self-mastery that he had been taught by ministers like Turner and Brown. But what he found in the world was quite different, something that didn't confirm his certainty but crushed it.[18]

7

THE LEVELLING SYSTEM

One of Delano's first commissions as an officer was on a British East India Company ship engaged in smuggling opium and mapping Pacific islands. After two years on board, Delano cashed out. He took part of his wages in the drug, which he smuggled into China and sold, doubling his earnings. It was early 1793 and, wanting very much to leave Canton and return home, he took command of a ship bound for Europe called the *Eliza*, freighted with sugar by a Dutchman named Van Braam.[1]

The *Eliza* was not a good ship. It was 'dull in sailing' and 'very leaky.' Water seeped into the hold and mingled with the sugar, which dissolved into a syrup that the ship's pumps then ejected back into the ocean. This sweet mixture began to attract fish, first a small escort, then a detachment, more and more until the *Eliza* was enveloped in a vast, shimmering silver troop of maritime life.

Across the Indian Ocean, from the Straits of Sunda to Île de France, the *Eliza* was followed by 'an immense multitude of fish,' of 'all varieties, from the largest whale down to the smallest sprat.' It was a movable feast, a never-ending banquet: a few hooks and a bit of grain were enough to catch a ship's worth. But one of the species, Delano didn't know which though suspected the bonito, proved noxious. 'The greater part of the crew was poisoned.'[2]

Delano arrived in Île de France, east of Madagascar in the Indian Ocean, in July 1793. A harbour pilot rode out to the *Eliza* and told

Amasa the news: King Louis XVI had been guillotined; France was now a republic and aristocratic Europe had joined together to crush it; the island was under siege from without and governed by radicals within; mobs roamed the street, sacking the stores of rich merchants and forcing them to sell their wares in exchange for the revolution's practically worthless paper currency; privateers filled the port, some of them pierced for forty or more guns, armed to seize ships and cargo. No vessels were safe, not even if they flew under a flag friendly to the republic.

'The information struck us dumb,' Delano said.

With its sweet wake in trail, the *Eliza* had cruised into a tropical hot-house of revolutionary passion. Ideas then convulsing Europe were embraced with even more fervour on that small sugar and slave island. Delano was horrified by what he saw. He knew the people of Île de France to be honest and honourable, he said, recalling an earlier visit. In the decades prior to the regicide, the colony had prospered from increasing trade between Europe and Asia, and many of its merchants, sugar planters, and slavers had become rich. The price of sugar was high and the island's Port Louis serviced ships sailing between Europe and Asia. But the colony was also home to a growing number of poor whites and free people of colour, natural-born sansculottes. And when news arrived of Louis's beheading, everything fell apart.

Amasa Delano had lived through revolutionary fervour before. The people of Duxbury had united in near-unanimous support of the Sons of Liberty and the Continental Congress. He was a young boy when the town raised a liberty pole. 'We had a very high one,' recalled one Duxbury resident. Yet his hometown had been spared much of the internal strife that gripped other communities. Throughout New England, patriots gave suspected Tories a choice: kiss the liberty pole and proclaim support for independence, or be tarred and feathered. Duxbury, though, had very few 'liberty-pole recantations,' remembered one veteran of the revolution, because there 'was none to recant.' There was one incident where patriots caught a Halifax trader named Jessie Dunbar selling butchered meat to the British. They beat him in the face with cow tripe.

Yet for the most part, war against the British bred neither 'bigots nor enthusiasts' among Delano's neighbours, who, once the fighting was over, returned to their shipbuilding and seafaring businesses—despite the fact that a few in town were getting richer, and many other were becoming poorer.[3]

In Île de France, however, Delano watched a world unhinged by revolution. A Jacobin club was formed that effectively seized power from the colony's merchant- and slaver-dominated assembly. Women dyed their hair red, white, and blue, planters renamed their slaves after Greek gods, and Jacobins held one 'festival' after another: one celebrated 'Virtue,' another 'the Harvest,' yet another extolled 'Innocence.' The girl who played Innocence was dressed in a white tunic and garlanded with flowers, but she was left exposed too long to the cold and died the next day. The Festival of the Grape Harvest featured two female 'citizens' who 'enacted scenes of debauchery.'[4]

'They soon learned to cry, "liberty and equality,"' Delano wrote. There were other slogans as well: 'The tyrant is dead.' 'Oppression is destroyed.' 'The rights of man are triumphant.' A guillotine was raised in the plaza, hung with a sign that read, 'A cure for aristocracy.'

The island's slaves didn't rise up, and the colony's planters managed to ignore Paris's 1794 decree abolishing slavery. But paranoia increased and conspiracies multiplied. The planter class lived in constant fear. Rumours flew that artisans were plotting with slaves and that sailors were arming them both. English spies and counterrevolutionaries were thought to be everywhere. Food supplies dwindled.

One of the things the French Revolution did that Delano found especially distressing was to democratize piracy. In the past, as with Mordeille's merchant partners in Montevideo and Buenos Aires and the slavers' mercenary fleet in Liverpool, it was the wealthy and well connected who financed privateers, men who could afford to outfit a corsair ship and send it off to see what it could catch. Now, though, in Île de France, privateers were selling cheap shares in their operation, as many as 500 per ship, to anyone who would buy them. 'All ranks of men,' Delano noted, could now profit from piracy (similar to the way 'free trade' was at this time democratizing the slave trade in Spanish America). Later, after Napoleon came to power in Paris, these privateers would be nationalized, their actions coordinated with the French republican navy to disrupt British commerce. But in the years immediately following the execution of Louis XVI, piracy was open to all: every man a privateer.

Though Delano as a young man had for a short time served in the crew of an Atlantic corsair, he now condemned the practice. He had known many a fellow captain laid low by privateers and had himself escaped them on more than one occasion. Privateering was little more than a 'system of licensed robbery,' a 'wicked' commerce that he compared to slavery. Just as humans could be seized from their homes, losing everything they held dear, an 'honest sailor' who had his life's work invested in his hold could be robbed of 'every cent'—and the thievery 'done according to law.'

Delano was immediately affected by the island's lawlessness. His cargo of sugar, that part which hadn't melted into the ocean, was arbitrarily embargoed by the colony's authorities. Prohibited from leaving port, Delano was furious. The island's administrators didn't 'treat us with respect or justice,' he complained. It was 'mortifying' to see 'very low men, without talents or integrity, in possession of power, and using it for the worst purposes, under the name of liberty.'

A child of the American Revolution, Delano found himself trapped in a place that was a perversion of the world of morality and reason promised by that revolution. 'I soon discovered,' he later wrote, that what French revolutionaries meant by the word *liberty* 'was to do as they pleased, while others should be bound to conform, or die.' 'Those who declaim the most vehemently in favour of the levelling system, are, as far as my experience has extended,' Delano thought, 'among the greatest tyrants when they get the power. . . . The attempt to establish perfect liberty, or what the unthinking sometimes call perfect liberty, must of course fail.'

Delano's ship was registered in the United States, but its cargo was owned by a citizen of Holland. And France was at war with the Dutch. Delano therefore had to hide his bills of lading to make it seem the sugar was his. Weeks passed and nothing was resolved. His crew was 'eating out' his supplies and worms were 'eating up' his ship. Delano secretly managed to sell his sugar. But it was too late. The *Eliza* was rotted through and through and had to be scuttled.

With proceeds from the sugar, along with the money he had made from selling his opium, Delano joined with another American captain and purchased from a privateer a large 1,400-ton prize, the *Hector*. The island's port was filled with such ships, taken by corsairs, for sale. Delano's need to get off the island overcame whatever misgivings he might have had about buying a seized vessel. 'Ships at this time,' he wrote his brother in Duxbury, are 'as cheap as you could wish them.'[5]

The idea was to sail to Bombay and take on a cargo of cotton, which Delano would then sell in Canton. 'We thought that we might be able to do something handsome for ourselves,' as well as pay Van Braam back for his lost sugar, he said. He soon realized that the 'undertaking was too much for us.' Daily expenses to cover provisions, wages, and repairs exhausted whatever money the two Americans had. And the port's Jacobin authorities 'laid one embargo after another' on them, saying that because the *Hector* mounted sixty guns it wouldn't be allowed to sail to an 'English port in India,' where it might be taken by the British and used to blockade the island. Delano and his associate were forced to borrow money at an 'exorbitant interest to be paid at Bombay,' in order to cover their operating costs.

Although Delano and his partner finally got away, their fortunes didn't improve. A few days out from Île de France the *Hector* hit an eight-hour hurricane and nearly broke apart. 'We lost three topsails,' Delano reported, and the foreyard split in its sling. They repaired the ship and made it to India. But since the French were seizing American vessels, they found no merchant willing to ship their cargo with them. They were stuck in Bombay for months, missing the best sailing season to China. The debt contracted in Île de France mounted. It now stood at $20,000. Taking out a second loan to pay the first, the two men moved on to Calcutta. They still couldn't find a merchant willing to risk the run. The captains were forced to sell the *Hector* when the holder of their new loan demanded payment, with the proceeds barely covering the debt.

Delano was broke, down and out in Calcutta. His 'accumulated losses' weighed on him 'constantly.' He was dismayed that he had lost Van Braam's property. He knew that his motives were 'pure and honest' when he used the profits from the Dutchman's sugar to buy a prize ship. He had felt that he had been held hostage in Île de France, that Jacobin island, and he wrote Van Braam telling him every detail of his misfortune, saying that he had planned to pay him from the profits made on the *Hector*. He just couldn't make it work. 'On reflection, the attempt to manage so large an enterprise with so small a capital was unwise, and now caused me much self reproach.' 'We went beyond our depth,' he said. His soundings were off.

Delano caught a schooner back to Philadelphia, arriving with 'but one gold moore,' his 'high hopes' disappointed, his 'mind wounded and mortified.'[6]

8

SOUTH SEA DREAMS

After five years at sea, Amasa Delano came home to Duxbury with his hands 'empty,' his 'dress thread bare,' and 'nothing but his wants abundant.' 'I never saw my native country with so little pleasure,' he wrote of what he called the 'disastrous termination of my enterprises and my hopes.' Successful captains return from prosperous voyages with their holds full of exotic gifts and are warmly welcomed by friends and family. He, in contrast, had nothing to give. As Delano walked the streets, he was 'alive to every symptom' of 'affected pity' and 'scanty sympathy.' When he ran into acquaintances, he feigned good cheer. But his 'downcast eye and wounded mind' were turned away from the indifferent world. 'The heart must feel its losses.'[1]

Amasa went back to work at his father's shipyard, determined to recover from his defeat. He began building his own vessel, finding a few investors in Boston so he could buy the best material. He worked methodically, being careful to choose the right wood for each part of the ship. Delano used hard white oak and hackmatack, or larch, which was brought into Duxbury's shipyards on oxcarts and cut into thick wide and long boards. Once they were seasoned, he estimated they would stay strong and staunch for thirty years. Pine was used for the masts and thrice-tarred spruce for the spars. Delano planed yellow pine for deck planks and beams and sheathed the ship in the best copper he could find.

'There should never be a doubt as to the fitness of a ship' for a long voyage. Rather than rely on 'luck,' since luck 'partakes of the miraculous,' one should take care to prepare for any 'hazard, without an *if* or a *but* remaining.' The vessel had two good chain pumps on the lower deck, front and aft of the mainmast, made of hard pine and iron.[2]

When the sleek ship was finished it was eighty-four feet long, twenty-four wide, and twelve deep. It had two decks, two raked masts inclined slightly aft, and a proud bowsprit. Amasa named it the *Perseverance*.[3]

As Delano was building his ship and thinking about ways he could redeem himself, both economically and emotionally, from his disastrous last voyage, his options were limited. There was one industry he probably could have done well in, a trade so vital and dynamic that in a way it made all other trades possible: slavery.

Slavery, as the historian Lorenzo Greene wrote half a century ago and many scholars, such as Harvard's Sven Beckert and Brown's Seth Rockman, are today confirming, 'formed the very basis of the economic life of New England: about it revolved, and on it depended, most of her other industries.' The expansion of slave labour in the South and into the West was still years away, but slavery as it then existed in the southern states was already an important source of northern profit, as was the already exploding slave trade in the Caribbean and South America. Banks capitalized the slave trade and insurance companies underwrote it. Covering slave voyages helped start Rhode Island's insurance industry, while in Connecticut some of the first policies written by Aetna were on slaves' lives. In turn, profits made from loans and insurance policies were ploughed into other northern businesses. Fathers who 'made their fortunes outfitting ships for distant voyages' left their money to sons who 'built factories, chartered banks, incorporated canal and railroad enterprises, invested in government securities, and speculated in new financial instruments' and donated to build libraries, lecture halls, universities, and botanical gardens.[4]

The use of slave labour in the North was ending by the time Amasa was building his *Perseverance*, but throughout New England there were merchant families and port towns—Salem, Newport, Providence, Portsmouth, and New London among them—that thrived on the trade. Many of the millions of gallons of rum distilled annually in Massachusetts and Rhode Island were used to obtain slaves, who were then brought to the West Indies and traded for sugar and molasses, which were boiled to make more rum to be used to acquire more slaves. Other New Englanders benefited indirectly, building the slave ships, weaving the 'negro cloth' and cobbling the shoes to dress slaves, or catching and salting the fish used to feed them in the southern states and Caribbean islands. Haiti's plantations purchased 63 percent of their dried fish and 80 percent of their pickled fish from New England. In Massachusetts alone, David Brion Davis writes, the 'West Indian trade employed some ten thousand seamen, to say nothing of the workers who built, outfitted, and supplied the ships.'[5]

If slavery was economically indispensable, it was also, for many, morally reprehensible and indefensible. There were fewer and fewer actual slaves in New England by the end of the 1700s, but many of its sons, as they went out to learn the 'story of the world,' encountered the horrors of the trade abroad. In 1787, for instance, a childhood friend of Amasa Delano's, Gamaliel Bradford, had an opportunity, while serving as an officer on a ship purchasing salt from the Cape Verde Islands, to board a French slave ship just north of the Gambia River. He recorded in his diary the impression the visit left on him and his companion:

> We were now to behold a scene new to both of us. The ship had on board three hundred of those miserable wretches, who form the chief branch of trade carried on at this coast. It has ever been painful to me to behold a fellow mortal in chains, even when they had been riveted by the hands of justice, for crimes committed, or were thrown on by the fortune of war for a season. But here the sight was doubly shocking. Those we now saw before us were poor innocent creatures, who had been snatched from their peaceful habitations by the rapacious hands of their fellow men, brought to market and sold like beasts to the highest bidder, now loaded with chains they are thrown into this floating prison in which, terrified with the thoughts of they know not what, they are to be transported from their country, parents, and friends to a distant region, where hunger, grief, inhuman usage with the incessant toil, must hang upon their latter days, and

close their scene of ills. The women and children were disposed of upon the quarter deck, where you might see the smiling infant playing upon the breast of its anxious mother, who with looks the most expressive of grief, dropped the tear of tenderness upon her baby. Pitiable wretch thus thou shalt soon, perhaps, be deprived of this thy fond care. My heart bleeds for thee now, how then could I behold thee arrived at the place of thy destination thy child plucked struggling from thy bosom and sold to a severe master, who perhaps lives remote from him who has just made a purchase of thee. Thy tears then are all in vain—In vain shalt thou wish to be slave to the same tyrant—thy master wants thee, but wants not thy child—thus deprived of this only solace in all thy afflictions, thou are delivered over to thy merciless keeper, chilled with horror & stupefied with grief, thou art motionless untill the lash of thy barbarous driver arrouses thee again to the sense of thy misfortunes—but to compensate for this variety of ills, mayst thou hereafter be happy, and mayst thou see thy babe happy also.[6]

As the historian Bernard Bailyn writes, 'slavery' was a 'central concept' for men of Bradford's and Delano's generation. 'As the absolute political evil, it appears in every statement of political principle, in every discussion of constitutionalism or legal rights, in every exhortation to resistance.' British colonists and then American republicans didn't actually think that they were in danger of being seized from their homes, taken to a foreign country in chains, and sold as property to labour in plantations and mines. They understood the concept as signifying many different conditions, including a lack of personal or political self-control, economic dependence, or absence of fair representation in a larger political collective. Delano himself compared the plunder of privateers to the depredations of slavers. And as a young boy, he heard Duxbury's pastor, Charles Turner, make frequent references to slavery from the pulpit. 'How distressing the thought of being slaves,' said Turner in the 1773 sermon he preached before the British governor in Boston, 'how charming that of being free.'[7]

After independence, though, the use of the word *slavery* as a political concept, and the problem it signalled, shifted. It was still an allegory for all sorts of enthralment, yet when New England sailors like Bradford returned to towns like Duxbury describing such 'new scenes,' they had an increasingly clear sense of who was a slave and who wasn't.

It wasn't too long after Bradford's return that slavery became a contentious issue in Duxbury itself. 'Ought it not to diminish our relish,' asked the town's minister, John Allyn, in an 1805 sermon, for items that 'are the produce of slavery'? King David, he said, would not drink water brought to him by slaves.* Duxbury was one of those towns that derived secondhand profits from slavery, so Allyn's remarks were pointed. The Bostonian Mungo Mackay, who grew wealthy on the Middle Passage, purchased at least one ship from King Caesar Weston. On the River Walk in Savannah, Georgia, there's a plaque that today reads, 'The schooner *Gustavus* of Duxbury, Mass., disembarked 26 Africans at the Port of Savannah on October 6, 1821. The men, women and children ranged from two months to thirty-six years.' The *Gustavus* was owned by Nathaniel Winsor Jr., another prosperous Duxbury shipbuilder and merchant. And Weston's large fleet, which provided jobs for Duxbury sailors, also ran fish to plantations in Haiti, Cuba, and Virginia and brought sugar and cotton, picked and cut by slaves, to northern and European ports.[8]

Reverend Allyn, though, wouldn't follow his premise to its radical end. 'We, Christians, advocates for liberty and the rights of men,' he said, 'stimulate our appetites and feast our palates, daily, and without remorse, upon luxuries produced—' Suddenly, there, in midsentence, he interrupted himself. Before changing the topic, he admitted that to continue would prove too provocative: 'I stop, lest something unwelcome should obtrude itself in regard to the social condition of some of our sister states.' 'The sea of popular liberty' is 'tempestuous,' he warned, 'the rich and the poor, the north and the south, form into parties to injure

---

* Decades after Allyn's 1805 sermon, Ralph Waldo Emerson, in 1841, made the same point, criticizing the conceit that one could remain clean from the stink of commerce simply by choosing a noble career. The 'trail of the serpent,' Emerson said, 'reaches into all the lucrative professions and practices of man.' 'We are all implicated'; all one had to do was ask a 'few questions' about the goods that enter one's home to realize that 'we eat and drink and wear perjury and fraud in a hundred commodities.' 'How many articles of daily consumption are furnished us from the West Indies' or the 'Spanish islands,' he asked, where one man 'dies in ten every year . . . to yield us sugar'?

and destroy each other; and under the specious cover of preserving liberty, liberty is at length annihilated.'

Allyn was beginning to get a sense of the dilemma the next generation of northern Americans, including in Duxbury itself, would confront head-on: make war to end slavery, which might end America's experiment in liberty, or leave southern states alone and admit that liberty for some meant slavery for others. Most good opinion in Duxbury, a community well-versed in natural law, a town that was unanimous in its support for revolution, opposed slavery. But in the years to come, the argument would be over how to end it, or even if ending it was worth the cost of endangering the union. Duxbury's Christian congregations would split and then split again over slavery.*

These schisms were still well in the future as Delano thought about what to do with his *Perseverance*. It wasn't built to be a slaver but he could have used it to trade with Caribbean slave islands. That is how as a young man he served his seafaring apprentice, on ships carrying salted cod to Haiti. Then as a young officer and captain, he travelled enough times to other slave islands in the Caribbean, including Trinidad, Tobago, Puerto Rico, as well as Guiana on the mainland, that a good part of the experience that made him a master mariner was owed to slave hunger (Haitian slaves, writes Amy Wilentz, 'often could not consume enough calories to allow for normal rates of reproduction; what children they did have might easily starve'). But like his friend Gamaliel Bradford, he found slavery abhorrent.[9]

---

* Allyn's way out of the impasse was to support the deportation of Africans and African Americans to Africa. Others, though, demanded more forceful leadership from their religious leaders. Divisions in Duxbury over slavery eventually led to the founding of the Wesleyan Church because the Methodist Episcopal Church wouldn't vote on a motion saying slavery 'is sin' and that 'liberty and slavery cannot exist together.' Duxbury resident Seth Sprague, just three years older than Amasa Delano, led these splits. Of the Methodists, Sprague said: 'by degrees the sin of slavery crept into the church; and when an attempt was made by a few of its members to expel that enormous sin, all the influence of the Church was arrayed against them.' The Church, Sprague said, was but 'one great prop in support of slavery.' 'So long as I remain a member of that Church, I am virtually giving my influence in support of slavery.'

Delano might have tried his hand as a whaler. Whaling was still on the upswing, and though Atlantic whales by this time were mostly gone, Delano could have outfitted his ship as a whaler and tried to tap the Pacific's 'living sea of oil.' Duxbury was just a daylong dog's leg sail around Cape Cod to Nantucket and a bit farther to New Bedford, the twin capitals of American whaling. But few Duxbury men got into the business, either as common sailors or as captains.[10]

Once, when he was in the harbour at Valparaiso, in Chile, Amasa had tried to harpoon a whale. A large one had fallen asleep not far from the harbour's clutch of anchored ships. Delano had his men row him softly out to within twenty feet of the animal. He threw his lance and hit his mark but 'on feeling the hurt' the whale raised its enormous tail and brought it down with frightening force, throwing up enough water to half fill Delano's boat. 'Had it hit the boat it would have been staved to atoms, and probably some of us been killed.' The whale swam away bellowing and spouting blood till out of sight. 'Thus ended our first and last enterprise in killing whales,' wrote Delano. The outing convinced him that 'it was a difficult and dangerous business, and ought never to be attempted by any, except those who have been bred up to and perfectly skilled in the art.'

Even had he been able to master the kill, the business of whale hunting was a complex, hierarchical affair, with many interests and skills at play. By the late 1700s, most whaling expeditions were organized by heavily capitalized firms or groups of investors, underwritten by established insurance companies, and supplied by makers of specialized equipment, including barbed harpoons, cutting knives, and hooks. Windlasses had to be fortified and blocks and tackle calibrated to counterpoise the buoyancy of the ship with the deadweight of the whale as it was hauled out of the water and its blubber peeled off. Ships also needed to be outfitted with a large number of casks and pots and their decks reinforced to hold the heavy brick stoves that rendered the blubber into oil and that turned whalers into floating furnace-factories.

Herman Melville provided a famous description of these tryworks, set in motion by the 'unconscious skill' of men from many nations who gracefully kept their footing so that the raging furnace didn't set their windswept, wave-tossed, night-enveloped ship ablaze: with 'huge pronged poles' the men 'pitched hissing masses of blubber into the scalding pots, or stirred up the fires beneath, till the snaky flames darted, curling, out of the doors to catch them by the feet. The smoke rolled away in sullen heaps. To every pitch of the ship there was a pitch of the boiling oil, which seemed all eagerness to leap into their faces.' The men laughed and talked and spat 'as the wind howled on, and the sea leaped, and the ship groaned and dived.'[11]

It wasn't just that Amasa Delano didn't have the capital and contacts to organize such a collective, synchronized enterprise. He also didn't have the sentiment.

In a section of *Moby-Dick* describing the labour involved in squeezing the jellylike spermaceti oil taken from a whale's head into liquid, Melville conveys a sense of intense human interconnectivity, the way self-abandonment can produce ecstatic solidarity:

Squeeze! squeeze! squeeze! all the morning long; I squeezed that sperm till I myself almost melted into it; I squeezed that sperm till a strange sort of insanity came over me; and I found myself unwittingly squeezing my co-labourers' hands in it, mistaking their hands for the gentle globules. Such an abounding, affectionate, friendly, loving feeling did this avocation beget; that at last I was continually squeezing their hands, and looking up into their eyes sentimentally; as much as to say,—Oh! my dear fellow beings, why should we longer cherish any social acerbities, or know the slightest ill-humour or envy! Come; let us squeeze hands all round; nay, let us all squeeze ourselves into each other; let us squeeze ourselves universally into the very milk and sperm of kindness. Would that I could keep squeezing that sperm for ever![12]

After reading Delano's lengthy memoir, one gets the feeling that the Duxbury captain would have recoiled in horror from such a scene. Not because of Puritan sexual repression. He doesn't present himself

as particularly chaste.* Rather, as someone obsessed with self-creation
and self-mastery, Delano would have been repelled by the sense of self-
abandonment that the passage conveys. It is hard to imagine him plung-
ing into a mass of blood, sinew, smoke, or, for that matter, organizing it
into a profitable venture.

Amasa was too self-aware, too preoccupied with his efforts at
improvement and with why those efforts never amounted to much. He
was steeped in natural law, yet there was something artificial, or estranged,
about his relationship to the world. He thought too much while at the
same time not enough.

An episode that took place during Delano's earlier commission with the
British East India Company reveals the depths of his isolation. Delano
liked his fellow officers on the opium-trading *Panther*. They were 'all
North and South Britons by birth,' educated in 'good schools in England
and Scotland' and possessed, he thought, of a 'liberality of mind.' And
he liked to think that they liked him. They called him 'Brother Jonathan,'
a nickname the British had for Americans suggesting intrepidity and
curiosity but also gullibility and worldly innocence.[13]

So he had no reason to doubt his shipmates when, on the small Pacific
island of Pio Quinto to load wood and water, they reported finding gold
a few miles inland, along the narrow river that spilled into the harbour.
As he listened to his companions talk, 'every time this word, *gold*, was
pronounced,' Delano said, 'my imagination became more heated.' The
British officers said that they weren't going back themselves since they
didn't know much about minerals and wouldn't be able to extract the
valuable gold from the useless rock.

'*Odds mon*,' said one of the Scots, slapping Delano on the shoulder
and telling him to make a go of it, offering the American his canvas bag

---

* He didn't refuse the chief of Palau's gift of a female concubine, which he characteristically
describes as satisfying the virtue of inquisitiveness rather than sating the vice of lust: 'I was
curious to know whether any of the women would be unwilling to go with those by whom
they were chosen; but I discovered in their countenances only cheerfulness and pleasure.'

and 'Malabar boy'—a slave from the Indian region of Kerala—for a guide. 'He knows the place where we found these curious ores, and you can return with a back load of gold.'[14]

Delano spent that night dreaming 'South Sea dreams.' The next morning, he lit out early with the young slave boy. The riverbank they followed was a delight at first, level and easy. But as the ground gradually rose, broken ravines and strewn rocks began to block their way. They walked hours more and still didn't come upon the gold. Growing tired, Delano kept asking the boy how much farther. The boy didn't speak English but he kept gesturing ahead. 'The gold inspired me,' Delano said, 'and banished all sense of hardship.' They kept moving.

After about five hours, the boy, reacting to Delano's now frantic questioning, cried out and collapsed. Delano realized he was the brunt of a joke by his fellow officers. The slave was only half in on the trick; he had been instructed by his Scottish master to simply point upriver whenever Delano asked him a question. 'From the very moment that the idea of a hoax entered my mind, all the evidence on this subject struck me in a new light. I saw how to put the circumstances together, and how to account for every thing,' wrote Delano more than two decades later. The prank had left an impression. 'The intrigue unfolded itself with perfect clearness and I saw myself in a wilderness, a fatigued, disappointed, and ridiculous dupe.'

It was a 'hard struggle' back. Delano tried to make the best of the situation, filling his bag with insects, flora, rocks, soil, and birds he shot with his musket. He was acting the part of a naturalist, hoping to return with 'something to check the force of the laugh against me.' But he soon gave up the pretense. Fear of scorpions, centipedes, and tarantulas, along with a thick underbrush of thorns and nettles, kept him on the river's banks. And as the day wore on, the insects he thought to observe bit his ankles and drove him to seek refuge on rocks in the middle of the river. Every retraced step back to the *Panther* 'renewed . . . the consciousness' of his 'foolish credulity.'

They made it back to the beach just before night fell, 'completely worn down with fatigue.' Delano sat on a boulder in the middle of the river's mouth as feelings of humiliation washed over him:

When I was seated in perfect silence, on a rock in the river near its sources, and could hear the echo of the waters through the awful stillness of the desert, mingled with the occasional but unintelligible expressions of anxiety by the poor Malabar boy; and when I remembered that I was at an almost immeasurable distance from my native country, in the service of a foreign power, the victim of an imposition which appeared to me under various aspects, and now in a savage spot where the natives might be every moment upon me, I confess I was not very far from that fixed mood of melancholy, mortification, and terror, which required but little more to overcome me.

It must have been some image: a seated, silent towheaded Amasa Delano, head in hands, and a dark Kerala slave boy prostrate at his feet, convulsed and crying with fright, two isolated figures on a barren rock island in a river mouth in the middle of the Pacific, the waste of an empty white beach all around them and the green of a tropical forest behind. Delano was so lost in the 'perfect silence' and 'awful stillness' of his own misery that he was barely aware of the indecipherable wails of the young Indian.

Later, once the episode was behind him, Amasa said that the intense distress he felt sitting on his beach promontory helped him be more empathetic to the pain of others. As a 'child of misfortune,' he was extremely sensitive to the 'sufferings and wants of men, whose spirits fail, when they are at a distance from home, and appear to themselves to be cast out from the sympathies of the human family.' Though he was talking about the hard life of sailors, Delano's description of vulnerability and loss could be describing the condition of slavery: 'Many are the instances, in which generous and feeling minds have been ruined, and only relieved by death, when they were subject to the command of others, and during a period of depression were inhumanly treated without the means of redress.' He said in retrospect that the episode helped him understand the loneliness that is a part of 'human nature' and made him a better leader of men.

Yet here on a South Sea beach, he ignored his Malabar slave boy, who undoubtedly was feeling the same 'melancholy, mortification, and terror' he was. Even if he had wanted to pay attention, the boy 'could not speak English.' 'And I,' Amasa said, 'could not speak anything else.'

Not too long after this event, the German philosopher G. W. F. Hegel published *The Phenomenology of Spirit*, which contains what the historian David Brion Davis describes as the 'most profound analysis of slavery ever written.' Davis is referring to a short chapter that starts with the master believing he is a sovereign consciousness, independent of and superior to his slavish bondsman, even as he grows materially and psychically dependent on his slave. Soon, the solipsism of the master gives way to an intense awareness of the slave's being, so much so that he can't imagine the world without him. He comes to realize his utter dependence on the slave, not just on his labour but on the slave's recognition of his very existence. In turn, the slave becomes aware of this dependence and realizes his equality. One philosopher has called Hegel's description an 'existential impasse.' But it isn't really an impasse, since there is an exit: the whole point of Hegel's parable is to identify how human consciousness evolves, how it moves toward a higher level of freedom. It is out of the struggle between the master and the slave that a new world consciousness emerges. As Hegel wrote elsewhere, it wasn't 'so much *from* slavery as *through* slavery that humanity was emancipated.'[15]

It is Amasa on his rock who is at an impasse, so trapped within himself that he can't even enter into the dialectic of dependence and interdependence, he can't even begin the process of seeing himself in another. In this particular case, he is insensate to the cries of his own, at least for a day, slave lying at his feet. But throughout his memoir he seems blind to the larger social world around him. Being from New England, he thinks he is 'free,' not only in a political sense, as compared with the legal enslavements of Africans and others, but in every other sense. Free from the past, from the passions that soaked human history in so much blood. Free from vices; reason is his master. And of course free from slavery itself, from relations of bondage and exploitation. After every one of his many other moments of crisis or of disappointment, including this one, he affirms his faith in the idea of self-mastery and self-creation. And his faith is repeatedly proven to be misplaced.

Amasa's feelings began to regain their elasticity after his British

mates arrived in the ship's boat. 'Brother Jonathans' were known for
their cheerfulness, and so the players of the joke pressed him to 'join in
the common laugh.' Delano obliged. But when he jumped into the boat
to go back to his ship, he felt a sharp sting. A 'large centipede eight or
nine inches long' had crawled out of a pile of firewood and given Delano
'a most venomous bite' on his throat. The infected area 'swelled very
much, and caused an extremely painful night.'

'Thus ended my dreams and my excursion in search of the golden ore.'

Morals wouldn't let Amasa run a slave ship or trade with slave islands.
Insufficient access to capital, along with other deficits, ruled out whaling.
There was, though, one maritime profession that well suited Delano's
resources, talents, and temper: sealing.

Black Will Always Have Something Melancholy in It

Largely ignored throughout the nineteenth century, *Benito Cereno* was hailed as a masterpiece at the beginning of the twentieth. It was, wrote one critic, a 'flaming instance of the author's pure genius.' But what did it mean? *Moby-Dick*'s symbolism was so fluid and open-ended it could be debated endlessly. *Benito Cereno*, in contrast, seemed unrelentingly to be about one thing, the most divisive subject in American history: slavery.[1]

Except that for a long time scholars said it wasn't about slavery. *Benito Cereno* 'equals the best of Conrad,' wrote Carl Van Doren in 1928. And like those who read Joseph Conrad's *Heart of Darkness* for its 'Freudian overtones, mythic echoes, and inward vision' but ignored its true story of homicidal Belgian imperialism in the Congo, scholars didn't think *Benito Cereno* was about the slave trade and the racism it bred. Some said it was an allegory of the clash between European decadence (Cereno) and American innocence (Delano). But more often, critics read it as a parable of the cosmic struggle between absolute virtue and absolute evil.[2]

Article after academic article fixated on Babo's blackness (recall that in Melville's novella, it is Babo, not Mori, who plays the role of deceptive servant). 'Blackness and darkness are Melville's predominant symbols of evil, and Babo is blackness, not simply a Negro.' He is 'pure deviltry . . . a creature of undiluted evil.' The West African who in the story presides over the murder of his enslaver and much of the ship's crew is a 'manifestation of pure evil.' He is the 'origin of evil,' a 'monster,' and 'the metaphorical extension' of 'the basic evil in human nature.' Babo isn't a symbol of evil or a human being who does evil: 'Babo is evil.'

Most early-twentieth-century scholars couldn't see any rational reason for his violence. Babo's is a 'motiveless malignity.' He hates for the 'happiness of hatred' and is evil 'for the sake of evil.' He is 'everything untamed and demoniac—the principle of unknown terror.' He is 'the shark beneath the waters.' Some, such as Harvard's F. O. Matthiessen, cautiously suggested that the slaves' actions were justified by their captivity, since 'evil' had 'originally been done to them.' But most white scholars continued to insist that the 'morality of slavery is not an issue in this story.' 'Babo, after all, as perhaps his name suggests,' wrote Yale University's Stanley Williams in 1947, 'is just an animal, a mutinous baboon.'[3]

African American critics saw things differently. As early as 1937, Sterling Brown, a professor of literature at Howard, himself the son of a slave who trained a generation of writers, poets, activists, and actors, including Toni Morrison, Stokely Carmichael, Kwame Nkrumah, Ossie Davis, and Amiri Baraka, wrote that he wasn't troubled by the portrayal of the West Africans as 'bloodthirsty and cruel.' They weren't villains, Brown wrote, much less incantatory exclamations of cosmic evil. They were human men and they 'revolt as mankind has always revolted.' In the wake of the civil rights movement of the 1950s and the black power protests of the 1960s, African American writers and activists started to celebrate Babo as an 'underground hero' and to read Benito Cereno as subversive, seeming to take the side of the whites while skewering their idiocy.[4]

Then there's Amasa Delano's whiteness. The image of the Duxbury captain that accompanies his memoir is striking. His cropped hair is colourless and his face is white, as intensely so as the starched, ruffled white cravat that grabs his round neck a bit too tightly. The retreating flanks of Delano's scalp are curved and his arched eyebrows seem to continue their circumnavigation around fleshy cheeks. There's a hint of a sailor's squint, yet his eyes lack depth. They are fishlike. In fact, the combined effect of the whiteness and the roundness calls to mind a sea creature, a whale or maybe an otter. D. H. Lawrence described Herman Melville as 'half a water animal': 'There is something slithery about him. Something always half-seas-over.' Delano, too, according to an acquaintance, was 'almost amphibious.'[5]

Delano sat for the portrait when he was about fifty years old. It is a full-frontal bust image done in stipple engraving, where the contours of his face are created by thousands of black dots pressed on a white page. All its shading and texture come from contrasting black to white. The denser the dots, the brighter Delano's cetacean whiteness. Melville was fascinated by this kind of black and white interplay, the way that blackness defines whiteness. He used the imagery of a dark backgrounded portrait or a lighted sphere 'shrouded in blackness' as a symbol of sublime terror—the feeling a person gets when contemplating his or her smallness in relation to the 'ghostly mystery of infinitude.'[6]

He didn't, though, assign a simple colour code to morality, where black meant bad and white meant good. That he didn't is clear in one of *Moby-Dick*'s most famous chapters, 'The Whiteness of the Whale,' which has the book's narrator, Ishmael, offering an extended meditation on what it is about the colour white, despite its association with things 'sweet, and honourable, and sublime,' that strikes 'panic to the soul.'[7]

To write the chapter, Melville read, among other things, Edmund Burke's *A Philosophical Inquiry into the Origin of Our Ideas of the Sublime and Beautiful* (1757), which argues that there is something inherent in blackness that causes a shared repulsion in 'all mankind.' Darkness doesn't just conceal potential dangers, Burke writes, but causes a 'very perceivable pain': as light dims, pupils dilate, irises recede, and nerves strain, convulse, and spasm. To prove his point that darkness is 'terrible in its own nature,' Burke gives the example of a young, presumably white, boy born blind who, after having his vision restored at the age of thirteen or fourteen, 'accidentally' sees 'a negro woman' and is 'struck with great horror.' People can become accustomed to 'black objects,' and once they do, the 'terror abates.' But 'black will always have something melancholy in it.'[8]

Melville says the same about the colour white. The thought of Virginia's Blue Ridge Mountains calls forth 'soft, dewy, distant dreaminess.'

Yet just a 'bare mention' of New Hampshire's White Mountains causes a 'gigantic ghostliness' to pass 'over the soul.' The Yellow Sea merely 'lulls us,' while the White Sea casts 'spectralness over the fancy.' Melville doesn't say that he believes the origin of this fear is to be found in slavery, yet he does have Ishmael mention in passing that the association of whiteness with goodness allows the 'white man' to gain 'mastership over every dusky tribe.'

He never really explains where the power of whiteness comes from. Maybe it is a matter of contrast. The polar bear's whiteness, for instance, drapes its 'irresponsible ferociousness' with a 'fleece of celestial innocence and love,' uniting 'opposite emotions in our minds.' 'Were it not for the whiteness,' Melville writes, 'you would not have that intensified terror.' Or it could be that since white isn't 'so much a colour as the visible absence of colour,' it reminds man that other, more pleasing hues are 'subtile deceits' covering up the 'charnel-house within.'

PART III

THE NEW EXTREME

There is boundless theft . . .
The sun's a thief, and with his great attraction
Robs the vast sea; the moon's an arrant thief,
And her pale fire she snatches from the sun;
The sea's a thief, whose liquid surge resolves
The moon into salt tears; the earth's a thief,
That feeds and breeds by a composture stolen
From general excrement; each thing's a thief;
The laws, your curb and whip, in their rough power
Have unchecked theft.

—A PASSAGE MARKED BY HERMAN MELVILLE IN
WILLIAM SHAKESPEARE, *TIMON OF ATHENS*

9

THE SKIN TRADE

On April 19, 1804, in Buenos Aires, Juan Nonell, a twenty-year-old Cata-lan recently arrived in the Americas, sold sixty-four Africans to Alejandro de Aranda, a merchant from the inland Argentine province of Mendoza. Among the slaves were a man named Babo and his son Mori.

The sale could have taken place in any of the many fetid human pens that dotted the city. Earlier, most slave transactions occurred in a few centralized locations, including in El Retiro, a large open-air compound built by the British when they had the slave trade monopoly with Spain, or in an auction house along the waterfront. But with the advent of free trade, the auction house was converted into the city's customs building, while Retiro gave way to smaller corrals that had sprouted throughout the city centre and near the wharves. Officials constantly complained of merchants who made no effort to keep up these enclosures or provide care for people 'full of lice, skin diseases, and scurvy, and exuding from their body a foul and pestilential odour.' Those Africans who didn't attract a buyer were simply 'liberated,' turned out into the streets with no clothes, no Spanish, and no way of surviving. Nearly all died quickly following such midnight emancipations. Slavers wouldn't even bury the bodies; instead, they'd have the corpses 'dragged through the street' and 'thrown in city ravines.'[1]

Aranda paid Nonell 13,000 pesos for the sixty-four Africans, a third in silver and a promissory note for the balance, which he committed to pay within a year after he had returned from Lima. Nonell had acquired the slaves in the lot from various sources. Some were the captives pulled off the *Neptune* and *Santa Eulalia* by royal officials, purchased by Nonell at public auction. The Catalan did most of his business with US slave ships that worked the western bulge of Africa, between the Senegal and Gambia Rivers. In the months prior to the sale, Nonell had imported 188 Africans into Buenos Aires, including seventy-one that came in on the *Louisiana* and another ninety on the *Susan*, both US brigs that embarked their cargo at the Gambia River. Of the fifteen *Tryal* rebel names that we do have, Samba is typical among the Fulani, as is Leobe, though it is also found among the Wolof. Atufal might have been the slavers' compression of a first and last name—Fall is a common surname in Senegal. Alasan was a popular West African Muslim name. They all referred to West African peoples who could have been seized anywhere in Senegambia.[2]

The slaves purchased by Aranda probably hadn't been branded. In 1784, Spain had dropped the requirement that a royal mark be seared into slaves' skin as a receipt to prove that they had been imported legally and that the branding tax, *el derecho de marco*, had been paid (though some US, French, and British ships continued using the brand as a way of distinguishing their lots). They weren't named in the promissory note he received from Aranda. When Spaniards referred to slaves as merchandise or cargo they generally used the word *piezas* (pieces or units). When Africans were huddled together in pens they were usually referred to simply as *la negrada* (the black mass) or *la esclavitud*—which roughly translates as a combination of servitude and slavery but was often applied collectively to the people subject to that condition, reducing them to that condition, as 'in the *esclavitud* was fed' or 'the *esclavitud* was disembarked.' In Nonell's case, the import documentation just referred to the humans he was buying and selling as *negros* and *negros bozales*—that is, 'raw' blacks, straight from Africa.[3]

It's not that Spain didn't encourage record keeping and paperwork. On the contrary, the Spanish empire floated on ink. To a far greater degree than any of their imperial rivals, Spaniards were obsessed with legalisms. Spain sent not just warriors, priests, and would-be aristocrats across the Atlantic but a legion of scriveners and notaries to create one of the most comprehensive bureaucratic edifices in world history. Content mattered.

Spanish theologians debated for centuries the moral and religious justifi-cations of conquest and slavery. They revived Roman law. They reread Aristotle and Saint Thomas Aquinas. And they reinterpreted Scripture.

Forms, elaborate forms, mattered as well. Royal decrees, commercial transactions, tax and tariff records, legal inquiries and testimonies were copied again and again and deposited in archives throughout Spain's dominion. The copying might be rushed, done in illegible handwriting. Or it could be ornate, adorned with elaborate flourishes left over from when Arabs ruled the Iberian Peninsula, and filled with phrases so oft repeated they had become meaningless. Sales receipts frequently said a given slave was 'subject to servitude' or 'taken in a just war and not in peace.' It was legalese from an earlier time, when Catholic theologians were consciously arguing that the enslavement of Africans was legitimate since they were prisoners of a war deemed to be just. By the late eighteenth century the expression was used by rote, applied not only to slaves cap-tured in the field but to those who had been in America for generations.[4]

Another term, employed throughout the four centuries of Spanish American slavery, said a given slave was to be sold *como huesos en costal y alma en boca*, 'like bones in a sack and with its soul in its mouth.' It was a vivid way of saying 'as is'—what you see is what there is—providing a blanket exoneration to the seller should the goods expire after the transaction.

By the early 1800s, the descriptive power of this paperwork was over-whelmed by the giddiness created, and the fast money to be made, from trading slaves. The Crown tried to stem the vertigo. With deregulation came new rules for how to document the commerce. It was now required that each slave ship have an individual register listing the number of imported Africans and their breakdown by sex. Importers, though, were not obligated to give the names of the Africans or where they were from. Ship captains were supposed to describe their itinerary, but writing down 'sailing to the coast of Africa to buy slaves' was good enough.

Despite his young age, Juan Nonell had already established himself as a rancher and hide trader who was taking good advantage of Spain's liberalization of commerce to diversify his operations. In other places in the Americas, especially the Caribbean and the US South, the growth of slavery mostly created single-crop-plantation societies, founded nearly exclusively on the forced, uncompensated labour of large numbers of slaves concentrated in individual enterprises. In Río de la Plata, however, 'free trade of blacks' helped make a more varied commercial society. Nonell, for instance, now could use the increasing number of available slaves to pick the small scale insects that live on prickly pear cacti and then have them boil, dry, and mash the bugs into a red dye called cochineal, popular in those revolutionary years in Buenos Aires' local textile industry. Mostly, though, he bought and sold Africans wholesale to support his ranching and shipping operations. He expanded slowly, investing the profits in his business. Soon Nonell was sending twenty thousand hides to Liverpool at a time, selling them for eight to ten cents apiece.[5]

He had become a successful player in Buenos Aires's skin trade. Spaniards in Buenos Aires had been exchanging the skins of cows, oxen, and bulls for slaves for nearly two centuries. Holds that had just been filled with humans were packed with dried hides laid flat one on top of the other until they reached close to the beam of the top deck. The pile would be covered with brine and then laid over with canvas to prevent damage from leaks. Since the weight of hides was relatively light, they didn't provide sufficient ballast, so casks of boiled-down fat—tallow—were also packed to deliver draft and steady the vessel. Through the eighteenth century, one healthy, male slave fetched 100 hides, worth 200 pesos, and if a given ship wasn't big enough to carry an equal exchange, the difference would be paid in contraband gold and silver.[6]

Pampas leather was valued in Europe; softened and scented, it sold well in Paris and London. Using a method learned from Arab artisans, craftsmen soaked the hides in limewater, scraped off the epidermis and hair, then pickled and tanned them with oak and sumac bark into tawny book covers, altar mantels, mural hangings, church vestments, casket linings, and cloaks, boots, and gloves perfumed with orange and jasmine.

It was a slow, steady trade. But starting in the late 1700s, with Spain's deregulation of commerce, the industry exploded—not just for hides but for everything related to flesh and skin. For over a century, gauchos, or cowboys, and ranchers had left most of the carcasses of the animals they skinned to rot. There wasn't a large enough local market for the meat, only a small part of which was preserved by salting, smoking, or sun drying. But once Spain granted permission to merchants and ranchers to sail directly to Brazil and the Caribbean and sell salted beef and horsemeat as food for plantation slaves, teamsters set off for the salt flats in the foothills of the Andes and brigs sailed down the coast to Patagonia, bringing back load after load of salt. Flesh was cured by the ton and then exported to points north. At the same time, the increase in the number of slaves arriving in Río de la Plata provided ranches and slaughterhouses the labour to keep this growth going.

The drying of skins had once been crude and cheap, performed in the open pampas or on ranches where the cattle were slaughtered. The expansion of slavery concentrated and intensified the manufacturing process. Most of this at first took place on the Montevideo side of the Río de la Plata. But starting in the early 1800s, travellers coming into and out of Buenos Aires would have noticed gradual changes along the roadside. There would be one more slaughterhouse on the outskirts of the city, one more *saladero*, or salting plant, on the banks of the river. This was the birth of Argentina's modern meatpacking industry, which would drive the country to the heights of the world economy in the early twentieth century. And it was all made possible by slave labour and the slave trade.[7]

The London weekly magazine *Household Words*, edited by Charles Dickens, described the scene by first asking its British readers:

> Whence come the thirty-five thousand tons of ox-hides annually imported into this country? Whence a large proportion of the seventy thousand tons of tallow? Whence the twenty thousand tons of dry bones (for sugar-refining, ornamental turnery, and fancy articles)? Whence the millions of horns? Whence do the great slave populations of Brazil, Bahia, Pernambuco, and Cuba obtain the dry and salted beef which is their staple food?

The answer was a Río de la Plata *saladero*, explained the magazine, in an essay that was anonymously written yet Dickensian in style. The workday starts, it said, with the cowboys

pushing, and goading, and hallooing with might and main, till the beasts
are wedged together as tightly as people at the pit-door of a theatre on the
night of a popular play; but, unlike the pit entrance, the door of the vreté
or smaller inclosure is of the portcullis kind; and when the performances
inside are to commence, it is lifted up. The bovine victims rush in; but the
moment they enter, they encounter sights and smells portentous of their
coming fate, which impel them to make a sudden retreat. Alas! The instant
the last tail has passed under the opening, down falls the door to oppose
all egress; and the unhappy oxen find themselves as completely imprisoned as rats in a trap.[8]

Slavery wasn't fully abolished in Argentina until 1853, a few years
after this description was written. Until then, the kind of operation the
article was describing relied heavily on enslaved labour. The personnel
of the first modern salting plant, for instance, set up on the Montevideo
side of the Río de la Plata in the late 1780s, consisted entirely of slaves
who worked every part of the line.[9]

Saladeros were early factories, combining new and old. They oper-
ated with near-assembly-line coordination, synchronizing the movements
of workers toward a common goal (as opposed to the old craft method of
one artisan working on one thing start to finish): men herded cattle
into a corral, where they would be lassoed by a horseman, slaughtered
by a knifeman, hauled off by trolleymen, trimmed by butchers, boiled
by cooks, and so on.

Saladeros didn't eliminate artisan expertise, as would modern factories, but rather harnessed it—especially the use of lassos and the *facón*,
or long butcher knife—to mass production. Once the animals were
herded into a smaller corral, a very 'ingenious process' would take place. A
man stood on a raised platform holding a rope, tied on one end to a lasso.
The other end of the rope was wound around a wheel and latched to a
horse. With 'unerring aim' he'd throw his noose and, after hitting his target, yell *¡Déle!—Go!*—to the horse, which would move forward until the
cow's head was braced against the wheel. In one motion, the man would
draw his *facón* and plunge it into the exposed neck, between skull and
spine. 'Death is instantaneous.' Thus the industrialization of Argentine

gaucho skill: 'so dexterously and rapidly is this sort of battue kept up, that during the twelve hours from four to five hundred animals are daily disposed of, . . . killed, skinned, dissected, salted, and distributed to every commercial quarter of the globe.'[10]

Where in the past the bodies of oxen, cows, and horses were left to decay in the sun, under the new system—created by the demand for salted meat to feed slaves and the use of hides and tallow to buy slaves—even the 'meanest bit' of the carcass was used. Butchers cut the flesh into two-inch pieces, pickled them in brine, layered them in salt, and then laid them on the ground, over a dried hide used like a tarp. As the pile reached higher, pressure from its weight forced liquid out of the meat. When the strips were sufficiently dry, they would be placed on racks in the sun until they turned into hard, imperishable dark jerk.[11]

Trimmers scraped off all the remaining skin and fat from the hides, which then were either stretched out on the ground with stakes to dry in the sun or salted in layers of brine. Scrap meat, along with bones, fat, and viscera, was taken to the boiling room and thrown into large vats, where the mix would be steamed into tallow. Wood was at a premium, coal even rarer, so thistle harvested from the pampas was used to boil the water to make the tallow. Waste from this reduction would be thrown in the fire, along with the carcasses of old horses and sheep, to help it burn a little longer and save thistle. Like the tryworks made famous by Melville, where pieces from the whale were used to keep the flames going, the livestock provided the fuel for its own rendering, like a 'plethoric burning martyr, or a self-consuming misanthrope.'

Defective hides were used for glue stock, and at the end of the day bone ash was collected for road pavement. The tripe was fed to pigs, jawbones were sent to Europe to make combs, and hoofs were used to make gelatin, oil, and glue.

About the only thing not used was runoff blood. Each salting plant gushed red into the Río de la Plata. The noise was hideous. Charles Darwin, who visited a *saladero* before his trek over the Andes, described a 'death' bellows that came out of the plants, 'a noise more expressive of fierce agony than any I know.' And the smell was unbearable.

Darwin thought the 'whole sight' was 'horrible and revolting.' The 'ground is almost made of bones and the horses and riders are drenched with gore,' he said. 'A thousand horrible butcher's shops pervading everything,' wrote another visitor, each sending columns of soot and smoke rising above the city's skyline.[12]

The primary products—dried hides, salted meat, horns, and tallow—would be loaded on vessels. Some of these ships set out for Cuba or Europe to trade the hides, meat, and grease for goods like rum, guns, and textiles, which they would then bring to the coast of Africa to exchange for captives bound for Río de la Plata. Other merchantmen made straight runs to Brazil, the Caribbean, or Africa to buy slaves.[13]

Juan Nonell did well with the liberalization of slavery. Others found breaking into the trade more difficult. A Montevidean named José Ramón Milá de la Roca jumped in after Spain announced that colonials could skip the middleman and sail straight to Africa to buy slaves. But he lost one shipment after another to piracy, war, and at least one slave revolt. He came close to 'near total ruin,' he said, looking back on his venture. Certainly compared with the tight regulations and restrictions on the trade in the past, there was now more room for midlevel merchants and ranchers like Nonell to make money—and for men like Milá de la Roca to think that they could make money. But it was Río de la Plata's already established large merchants who were best positioned to take advantage of deregulation, to pay the freight on large shipments, to shield themselves against frequent loss, shipwrecks, or revolts, to pay taxes and duties, which, even though they had been greatly reduced, still added up. By the early 1800s, about two-thirds of the exploding trade was controlled by a handful of extremely powerful men based in Buenos Aires and Montevideo.*

---

* First among them was Tomás Antonio Romero, who exercised near 'vertical domination' over large parts of Río de la Plata's economy. He controlled land, ships, slaves, and *saladeros*. He worked closely with merchants in Cádiz, bankers in London, and shippers in Boston and Providence. Described as an 'arch-corruptor' of Spanish administrators, Romero played all sides against the others with unrivaled skill. At different moments, he held exclusive monopoly contracts to provide Spain's royal navy with salted meat from his *saladero*,

It was especially hard for provincials like Alejandro de Aranda, from Mendoza, to succeed in the commerce. The residents of Mendoza practically lived under the long shadow cast by Potosí, the storied silver mountain in what is today Bolivia, the main source of the famed Spanish dollar, or piece of eight, then among the world's most circulated currencies. Yet actual cash was hard to come by. Most of the minted coins were sucked up by Spain to cover its ballooning military budget to fight its endless wars. Trade was conducted almost exclusively through loans or promissory notes. Well-established Buenos Aires businessmen could negotiate credit from financiers in Cádiz and London, but even they complained about the terms. Traders in hinterland cities like Mendoza were several links down the chain, with each deal pushing them further into debt.[14]

Even before purchasing the West Africans from Nonell, Aranda was already fairly deeply in arrears from past transactions. He had bought Africans in Buenos Aires before, but only one or two at a time, bringing them over the pampas and reselling them in Mendoza or Santiago. But now he was beginning a new stage of life. He had just gotten married and was starting a family and he hoped his large deal with Nonell might get him out of debt and improve his position—or at least steady it.[15]

---

to import Brazilian twist chewing tobacco, which was sweetened with molasses and popular with Buenos Aires's sailors, market women, and teamsters, and to freight quicksilver, or mercury, used to amalgamate silver, to Potosí, and then ship the silver out of Potosí to Spain. Yet he was eloquent in defence of 'free trade,' fighting 'cape and sword' for the right to diversify his trading options, even as he used his political connections to cut out his rivals. All told, between 1799 and 1806, Romero organized at least thirty-two slave expeditions, exporting about a quarter of a million pesos in hides and importing almost twice that value in Africans. And that is only what he officially reported. It was Romero who was the target of Viceroy del Pino's anticorruption campaign.

10

FALLING MAN

Among the stories that Jorge Luis Borges's grandmother used to tell him, one that Borges himself enjoyed sharing in the many interviews he gave in his later life, had to do with where she bought her slaves. 'The slave market, my grandmother used to tell me, was in Plaza El Retiro,' Borges once said. 'That's where they sold slaves.' By Borges's time, in the mid-twentieth century, El Retiro, laid out in Parisian style, was one of Buenos Aires's most elegant parks. The wealthy set up their town residences here in stately four- and five-story apartment buildings overlooking ornamental ponds and hundreds of shade trees.

Borges didn't keep bringing up the fact that Plaza El Retiro was once the city's principal slave market out of sympathy or solidarity; he was known to hold exceptionally negative opinions of Argentines of African descent. He was, rather, carrying on a family grudge.

The Argentine writer could trace his family's lineage back centuries to the first days of the Conquest. His ancestors included royalists—the men who founded and built the Spanish empire in the Americas—and republicans who fought to break from Spain and create the new Argentine nation. But Borges's family, especially his mother's side, had largely let the market revolution pass them by. They weren't able to convert their reputation into financial success and they repeatedly found themselves on the losing side of political conflicts. Dispossessed by merchants and cattle ranchers and persecuted by politicians, the family had become fallen gentry.

Having lost her wealth, Borges's grandmother passed down to young Jorge tales of her family's golden age like jewels. One of her favourite stories had to do with her parents' slaves: where they got them, how many they had, and how often the slaves came to visit after they were freed. Borges, in turn, liked repeating the anecdotes, a wry way of reminding the city's nouveau riche—nouveau, anyway, during his grand-mother's lifetime—that much of their money could be traced back to slav-ery and that the parks they liked to stroll through on Sundays were built over the bones of enslaved Africans. 'Members of our gentry,' he said in one interview, 'administered El Retiro's slave market.' As to the park's luxury apartment buildings, 'the first tall building ever put up there,' he said, was 'a bunk house for slaves.'

Some of Borges's distant cousins grew prosperous off slavery. 'Among those who enriched themselves by selling slaves were relatives of mine,' he said.* 'Wealthy households' were able to hold 'thirty or forty' slaves. Others, like the Borges family, were able to keep only a few as their lustre faded. 'In the house of my great-grandparents, there were just five slave servants,' Borges said, which didn't represent any 'great fortune.' And once slavery was finally abolished, downwardly moving families would hold on to their memory of slavery: Borges often talked about how the descendants of the slaves of his grandmother kept her surname and how, when he was a child, they used to call on his family home to pay respects.

Many in Buenos Aires's elite liked to claim contrived coats of arms and flaunt aristocratic-sounding Spanish family names. So Borges would repeat the story of how he once picked up a newspaper that was published by Afro-Argentines and was surprised to see 'all of Buenos Aires's great surnames' on its masthead. 'Except they belonged to blacks.' He singled out one in

---

* Borges is here talking about Jaime Llavallol del Riu, an emigrant from Barcelona who founded one of Buenos Aires's most successful commercial houses. He is credited with mod-ernizing the city's port facilities, which, according to Borges, also included the slave market at El Retiro. Later, in the 1840s, as Argentina moved toward abolishing slavery, Llavallol and Sons began to import thousands of indentured servants from Gallegos and the Canary Islands, 'treating them like slaves' (Isidoro Ruiz Moreno, *Relaciones hispano-argentinas: De la guerra a los tratados*, Buenos Aires, 1981, p. 16).

particular, Alzaga, the name of descendants of slaves who had been owned by Martín de Alzaga (the importer of perhaps the most lethal slave ship to have ever harboured in Río de la Plata, the *Joaquín*). 'Around here not too long ago,' Borges recalled, speaking of his own neighbourhood, 'there lived a number of very snobbish blacks'—*muy snobs*, he said, using the English noun as an adjective. 'They were named Alzaga, and had been for many generations the slaves of the Alzaga family.' Like their Spanish namesakes, these black Alzagas were also very conceited, he remembered, 'looking down' on those with more plebeian names, such as Gómez or López.[1]

Alejandro de Aranda was born in Mendoza, on the far side of the Argentine pampas, though he called himself Spanish. His real surname was Fernández, but he came from a line of men who preferred to use, generation after generation, de Aranda, reportedly inherited from a distant aristocratic ancestor from Andalusia. He was a year old in 1769 when his father, who came to Argentina from Spain hoping to reverse what had been a precipitous decline in his family's fortune, died. He was eight when his widowed mother, Rosa Ventura, remarried into one of Mendoza's wealthiest and most politically connected families.[2]

Born into fading prestige, wedded into money, Alejandro lived on the margins of advantage. Having acquired a vineyard outside of Mendoza, his father had left the family land rich but worse than cash poor, passing on his debts to his widow, who couldn't pay them off until she married Alejandro's stepfather, José Clemente Benegas. After Alejandro and his older brother, Nicólas, moved into Benegas's well-accommodated home, a compound really, they were attended to in all the genteel comfort that their times allowed.

Then Rosa Ventura and José Clemente began to have boys of their own. Alejandro and Nicólas were by no means pushed out. When they grew up and went into business together as merchants, the Aranda brothers were able to count on their stepfather, along with his extensive network of relatives, for financial and political support. But their standing in the family was more like wards, or visiting cousins, than true sons of the father.

Mendoza is just east of the Andes, encircled by haciendas and wineries, its arid soil turned fertile by melting mountain snow. Beyond this agricultural belt was a great desert plain, the western fringe of the Argentine pampas. Mendoza's merchants had done well as middlemen for goods shipped from Buenos Aires, more than a month's wagon ride away, over the mountains to Santiago, Chile. They also exported their own products east and west, including wheat, barley, alfalfa, and wine.

A well-kept town of midday naps and simple adobe homes, Mendoza struck a precarious balance between isolation and prosperity and worked to maintain an equally difficult equipoise between commerce and custom. The town's women were courteous and elegantly composed, wrote one Frenchman traveling through in the early nineteenth century. Its men wore ponchos as a matter of pride, even as formal wear, covering short pants cinched by gold or silver buckles. The style was 'bizarre' and 'extravagant,' whereby the city's elite mixed and matched the ostentation of medieval Spain with clothing associated with the pampas gaucho. Residents of Mendoza, the Frenchmen said, were 'hostage to their traditions.'[3]

As young men in their twenties, the Aranda brothers led separate private lives. Nicolás stayed in town, while Alejandro moved back and forth between Buenos Aires and Santiago, selling wine fermented on the vineyard they had inherited from their father and buying wholesale goods to bring back to Mendoza. Military rosters from the time record that Nicolás, a five-foot, five-inch cavalry lieutenant, was always present, and Alejandro, an inch shorter and a sergeant, was always 'travelling.'[4]

By 1804, Alejandro, the half-orphaned son of a migrant who had come to America hoping to get rich but died without succeeding, had burrowed deep into the incestuous heart of aristocratic power in Mendoza. In January, he married his first cousin María del Carmen Sainz de la Maza.[5] She was the daughter of his mother's sister, who, like his mother, had married into a wealthy family. Alejandro, therefore, wasn't so much rising in as sidestepping through Mendoza society. A month later, his mistress, Francisca de Paula Puebla, gave birth to his daughter, whom they named María Carmen, after Alejandro's new bride. Francisca was the daughter of one of Mendoza's largest vintners, Juan Martín

Puebla, but his wealth was self-made and over time his vineyards had run down. By the turn of the century, his two hundred wine barrels were considered 'old but serviceable.'[6] And later that year, Alejandro, at the advanced yet unaccomplished age of thirty-six, learned he would be starting a proper family. His wife was pregnant.[7]

Alejandro was comfortable with black slaves; they were part of his world. His stepfather's house had more slave servants than family members. He and his brother were raised by enslaved women and played with enslaved children. Since women from well-off families generally had servants do their breast feeding, Alejandro might even have been a *hijo de leche*—a 'milk child' whose nursing by a black slave often established a lasting relationship of affection. The houses of the Aranda brothers' next-door cousins had even more slaves than theirs, the majority of them children their own age. When Alejandro was nine, the home of his cousin María Carmen, his future wife, had over sixteen blacks and mulattos living in it, ten of them under the age of twelve.[8]

Every year during his childhood, a few hundred captive Africans regularly travelled through Mendoza on their way over the Andes to Chile. When the Crown began to liberalize the slave trade in the late 1770s, the numbers steadily increased. By the mid-1780s, nearly one mule train in three leaving Mendoza for Santiago carried slaves. Most of these shipments were small; through the 1790s, only a handful of very wealthy importers could afford to freight large numbers of slaves overland.[9]

Things changed with the new century, as more ships arrived in the Río de la Plata with more slaves. It began to seem that every shipment of shoes from Spain or candy from France making its way to Santiago was accompanied by a considerable number of Africans. Supply still couldn't keep up with demand and the value of slaves kept rising. By 1804, Africans were considered a much better investment than land.[10]

When historians talk about the 'slavers' fever' that overcame Spanish America, most virulently in the early 1800s, they are generally referring to expectations of profit to be made from the commerce. The delirium,

though, was about more than economics. Slavery shaped the most intimate realms of life: men like Aranda drank human bondage in at the
breast (black women were held in higher esteem than mulattas as wet
nurses); familial networks of fathers, sons, cousins, and friends carried
out the maritime and continental trade, and slavery worked its way into
prized bloodlines through concubinage and rape, weaving together relatives in a shadow tapestry of unrecognized heraldries, the most famous
examples being those of America's founding republican fathers: Thomas
Jefferson's slave children and Simón Bolívar's reputed slave ancestor. In a
world where fashion vied with religion and law in maintaining rank,
slaves served as signifying adornments. Well-dressed slaves tended to
the women of well-off families everywhere they went in public, to the
market, to church, or after mass on their Sunday stroll, and these women
treated their enslaved servants as if they were jewellrey. The best families
kept troupes of African musicians, including violinists and harpists,
who entertained the lavish dinner parties that filled society's calendars,
and the choruses of the finest churches and convents were comprised of
slaves. One Buenos Aires priest, in Montserrat, a neighbourhood
where many of Buenos Aires' black servants lived, said that slaves sang
Mozart's *Laudate Dominum* 'to perfection.'[11]

For the Aranda brothers, whose business venture so far yielded more
debt than profit, further undermining their supposedly noble standing,
free trade, of slaves and other goods, was a threat and an opportunity. It
was a threat because it enriched even the city's mule drivers, decreasing
the distance between commoners and lords and pushing the mannerly
world of their childhood farther into the past. But the profits that could
be made on slavery also offered a chance to stem the erosion of their
own position, to secure the noble name their ancestors had long claimed.
As the solidity of Spanish mercantalism gave way to a fast-churning
economy, slaves, along with livestock and land, often seemed to be the
last substantial things. Men like the Aranda brothers latched themselves
onto black bodies and held tight.

11

THE CROSSING

There were two ways to get slaves to Lima from Buenos Aires. One was how the *Santa Eulalia* went, down the coast of Argentina, through the Strait of Magellan, then up the Pacific to Lima. That route was dangerous and expensive, costing between sixty and one hundred pesos per slave for food and freight, nearly a quarter of the slaves' retail value. Alejandro de Aranda could save money and take the slaves he purchased from Nonell overland for a third that amount.

They set out in early July, two hours before the sun rose, part of a long teamster train carrying not just Aranda's cargo but the goods of many merchants hoping to make it across the pampas before the start of the rainy season, which could come as early as September. The caravan had the feel of a travelling village, moving forward not just merchandise but also the bustle and hierarchy of Argentine society. There were hundreds of mules and scores of ox teams and wagons carrying the freight, followed by a few coaches for well-off passengers, including merchants like Aranda who were accompanying their merchandise. Not quite mansions on wheels, these carriages still were nicely accommodated. Behind these came the rickety, overflowing wagon homes of the muleteers, many traveling with wife, children, and other relatives in tow. Then the cooks and the carpenters, blacksmiths, and other specialists needed to repair the damage caused by the rough road on the carts.

Conveying privilege, wealth, and labour, the procession also had law and order—the hired armed men who rode front and rear. The caravan was traveling west, parallel to a line not too far south that was the frontier of Spanish authority, beyond which lived what some called the 'pirates of the pampas,' yet-to-be-subdued Native Americans and lawless gauchos.[1]

The trip was easiest in the dry winter, between May and August, when the bridgeless rivers were at their lowest. But this was the season when wind blew from the west, wiping away trails as if they were surface currents on the ocean. Called *buques*, or boats, the wagons that made up the train had their beds high off the ground, on big wheels set wide apart, designed to glide over shifting sands and muddy grasslands. They were practically rolling carcasses, covered with hides, 'hair outward,' stretched over ribs made of sugarcane, to protect from the blown dust. Cow skins were also used to strengthen the cart's woodwork. Cut into narrow strips, the hides would be soaked in water and then wrapped around the wagon's shafts, wooden springs, and wheels. As they dried, they'd contract, adding a layer of tensile strength to protect the vehicle as it moved over furrowed roads.

The stretch leaving Buenos Aires was covered in clover and dark-purple thistle. It was boggy, even during the dry season, yet made passable by the bones of cows and other animals thrown into the marshy ground as landfill. After a week, the caravan would have entered the pampas proper, a wide-open 'misty expanse' that often reminded travellers of the desolate ocean. Charles Samuel Stewart, a navy chaplain who crossed in the middle of the nineteenth century, described 'a vast sea of grass and thistles, without roads or enclosures, and without a habitation, except at long intervals. Nothing breaks the unvarying outline, unless it be now and then an ombu [an immense, solitary shade tree] rising on the distant horizon, like a ship at sea.' It took a bit over a month for a large caravan to travel from Buenos Aires to Mendoza, about the length of the Atlantic crossing.[2]

The Argentine writer Victoria Ocampo said that the pampas destroy perspective. They offer 'no middle ground': everything is either urgently close or impossibly far away. Only someone in love with emptiness could be comfortable in them, Ocampo observed, invoking T. E. Lawrence's fascination with the Arabian Desert. Lawrence himself quoted Shelley, who, referring to the ocean, wrote, 'I love all waste. And solitary places: where we taste the pleasure of believing all we see is boundless, as we wish our souls to be.'[3]

For Babo, Mori, and the other slaves, the boundlessness must have been unnerving. Not because the landscape was alien but rather because it was almost similar to what they had left behind. Along the way, their carts crossed reedy marshes like the swales and swamps of Senegambia, Guinea, and the Niger delta. Though now mostly gone, Argentina's famed never-ending blanket of grass that so enthralled travelers was then still unbroken, resembling, in a way, West Africa's inland steppe. Its absolute flatness made it seem even more enormous than the African expanse. Observers looking out at the pampas often commented that they could see the curve of the earth, the horizon bending as it yielded to the sky.

The pampas were full of strange animals, wrote one traveller, herds of deer, solitary ostriches, small owls, and four-inch-long locusts that flew up from the feet of the horses and oxen like small birds. The West Africans passed cows, some of them of the same stock found in their homeland, and goats grazing in open grassland, licking saline soil, and drinking from muddy lagoons. The cattle were tended to by dark-skinned mestizos and Amerindians, calling to mind the wandering Fulbe pastoralists who roamed the African savanna. Gauchos were skilled horsemen, like the Mandinkas (though if any of Aranda's captives were from the forested areas of West Africa, where the tsetse fly was prevalent, they might never have seen a horse, since the sleeping sickness spread by the fly was fatal to most domesticated animals). Babo, Mori, and the others travelled during the blue-sky season, when the pampero constantly blew dust and caused occasional whirlwinds ('like a thick column of smoke issuing from a large chimney') similar to the dry Harmattan that comes down from the Sahara.[4]

The hide-covered, cane-ribbed, constantly rocking wagons were less fetid and crowded than the hold of a slave ship. The West Africans had more opportunities to relieve themselves by the side of the road. They could bathe in the rivers, in fresh cold water. Even during the dry season, these rivers were hard to cross, and the effort to do so broke the tedium of the journey. Horsemen plumbed them to make sure they were passable, their steeds braying if they weren't, advancing reluctantly if they could, followed by the mules and oxen, water rushing to their chests.

Most often, time passed with nothing to do but sit and suffer the jolts from the rough road, rutted by the burrows of vizcachas, fat, rabbitlike rodents, and listen to the almost deafening squeak of the wagon's ungreased wheels. The vast plain went on and on, covered in grass, green clover, alfalfa, and occasional patches of giant sunflowers, with 'scarcely an undulation to break the dead and boundless monotony.' It was an 'ocean of grass,' a 'sea of verdure.'[5]

In his inquiry into the beautiful and the sublime, Edmund Burke wrote that a large tract of land, like an open level plain, provokes nothing like the fear 'as the ocean itself.' The voyage across the Atlantic was undoubtedly more terrifying to the West Africans than the trip across South America. Burke, though, also recognized boredom as its own terror. 'Melancholy, dejection, despair, and often self-murder,' he wrote, 'is the consequence of the gloomy view we take of things in this relaxed state of body.' The coerced kind of boredom that Babo, Mori, and the others suffered must have been especially so. It stole, along with their freedom, another thing that made them human: the experience of time as the ordering of purposeful activity. Hour after hour they looked out from their carts and watched something that seemed like their world pass by, with slightly different smells and subtly different colours.[6]

Two-thirds through their journey, after the caravan crossed a major river, the Quinto, they came upon an even more desolate stretch of land called *la travesía*, the crossing, a phrase also used by Spanish slave traders to refer to the Middle Passage. The stony road gave way to sand, and they went long periods seeing not a tree or a drop of water, not a variation in the topography, only the occasional ox or mule skeleton lying on the side of the road. One English-speaking traveller said this part of the journey looked like nothing so much as 'similar tracts in Africa.' The day would have been searing, hotter than their homes during the dry season. The austral nights were cold.

Then, even before ending *la travesía*, about the time they reached yet another river—'as broad as the Thames at Windsor,' thought an English traveler—they'd have caught their first glimpse of the Andes.

The Andes are the longest mountain chain in the world. What makes them stunning, however, is that they are the thinnest. The Himalayas are wide and sprawling, with long, slow ascents of hundreds of miles that gradually raise the traveller up and dilute the view, so much so that some of their highest peaks give the impressions of hillocks. In contrast, only a short distance separates Andean crown from foot, making them appear like a great wall running the length of South America. The effect is especially striking if the Andes are approached from the pampas. The haze that occasionally hangs over the far horizon blocks the view but also heightens the impact, drawing one's eye to snow-covered summits that seem to float in the sky like 'stationary white pillars of clouds.' As Babo, Mori, and their companions moved closer, the full 'view of this stupendous barrier' would become clearer. They were still days away, yet they would have had to lift their 'necks back to look up' at the mountains.

Just beyond *la travesía* was Mendoza, Aranda's hometown, with its poplar-lined roads, fenced farms, vineyards, and orchids. Having crossed the pampas before the summer rains came, the West Africans now had to wait until the winter's mountain snows melted before moving on. By early December they were on the move again, on a straight road west heading toward the Andes.

12

DIAMONDS ON THE SOLES OF THEIR FEET

Enslaved peoples had been travelling along, and dying on, this road for centuries, ever since the Spaniards arrived in the area in the 1540s. When Pedro de Valdivia led an expedition down from Peru to claim the territory today known as Chile, he named the city he founded Santiago de la Nueva Extremadura. Santiago was the patron saint of Spain, also known as Santiago Matamoros, or the Moor Killer, for having intervened in an early battle to drive Islam off the Iberian Peninsula. And Extremadura was the name of the Spanish province where Valdivia was born. Sometimes, though, the Spaniards simply called this far edge of empire, wedged between the Andes and the Pacific, La Nueva Extrema, the New Extreme.

Africans died on one of the first Spanish attempts to find a way over the Andes, in 1551, during Francisco de Villagrán's disastrous trek. Villagrán only made it across with the help of Native Americans, wrote a Spanish chronicler, and along the way he lost 'two slaves and two horses' to the ice and cold. In 1561, Mendoza was established as an outpost of Santiago, and soon Spaniards were passing back and forth regularly over the mountains. The going was still treacherous. Even during the summer months, when the passes were open, travellers moved slowly along narrow paths, tethered together by guide ropes for support. Native Americans would fly by them. They 'travelled liberally, without these ropes,' wrote one Spaniard, 'as if they had diamonds on the soles of their feet.'[1]

The valleys that spread out from both sides of the mountains enjoyed a mild climate, leading settlers to think they could re-create the great feudal estates of Europe in the Americas. Workers, though, were needed to plant wheat, grow grapes, and raise cattle. And before Africans started arriving in great numbers, the colonists tried to turn Indians into slaves. The Mapuche, or *araucanos*, on the Pacific side of the Andes were difficult to subdue, so the Spaniards turned to the Huarpes, who lived in small villages in the region north of Mendoza. Most of the demand for labour came from Santiago, which sent raiding parties over the mountains. It was the Huarpes who had saved the Spaniards from certain death when they first tried to cross the mountains, teaching them the best trails.

Now they found themselves dragged in irons over those very trails. Many froze to death. 'When I crossed the cordillera,' Santiago's archbishop wrote to King Philip II in 1601, 'I saw with my own eyes the frozen bodies of Indians.' Twenty years later, his successor wrote that he had witnessed 'things that made my heart cry tears.' Indians were brought over the Andes in chains and collars, and when one collapsed or died, it was easier to cut off his hands or his head rather than break the iron. The weakest were left alive to freeze to death, some of them crawling into caves to find shelter. Many tried to commit suicide by using their iron collars to choke themselves. Enslaved Indians arrived in Chile 'thirsty and hungry, treated worse than the barbarians and gentiles treated the Christians of the primitive church.' The Huarpes soon disappeared as a distinct people.[2]

In 1601, the same year Santiago's archbishop wrote Spain about the treatment of Native Americans, the first large consignment of Africans made the crossing. Ninety-one 'Guinea Angolans' were shipped from Brazil via Buenos Aires to Santiago, with Mendoza as a transit point. They were on their way to be sold in Lima. From this point forward, the overland slave trade steadily increased, though the Crown tried at first to route all slaves into Peru through Panama. As part of the general system of mercantile restrictions, only a small number of merchants were allowed to ship slaves overland from Río de la Plata.[3]

But slave smuggling, especially of small groups of two or three Africans, was rampant. By the early 1600s, royal officials were complaining that there was nothing they could do to stop it. 'Every year,' one wrote the king in 1639, 'many unregistered blacks cross the Andes into Chile from the port of Buenos Aires.' If they were caught, merchants simply said that the slaves they were bringing over the mountains to sell in Santiago were their personal servants. In 1762, a slaver named José Matus, in order to gain the cooperation of his two slaves during the trek, told them that a land of freedom existed on the other side of the Andes and that once over they would be emancipated. When they arrived in Santiago, Matus sold them.[4]

No record exists of the details of the West Africans' trip across the Andes, what Aranda's slaves thought or felt as they began the ascent. If it weren't for what came next, after they arrived at Valparaiso and boarded the *Tryal*, their journey would have slipped into history unnoticed.

The first leg of the trip, the road out of Mendoza, is dead flat and wide open, like most of the rest of the pampas. It enters the foothills through a deep valley, turning into a path that winds between two high ridges. At that point, the mules, teamsters, travelers, and about 170 Africans (Aranda had combined his shipment with those of other slavers) would have moved in a single line. After just a few turns on the switchback trail, the open pampas would have disappeared behind them. Officials had built some rudimentary bridges, and, after postmen caught in a storm were forced to burn the mail to stay alive, a few limestone-and-brick shelters to protect travelers. Otherwise, the road had changed little from when those first two Africans died on it in 1551.[5]

The voyagers went on foot, linked together with neck chokers made of either iron or tightly woven hemp. It was steep going, with no vegetation to bind the loose and slippery soil. The path zigzagged north by northwest along deep ravines and through gaps as narrow as eighteen inches. For much of the way up, a river of rushing snow melt followed the trail on one side, and overhanging rocks on the other. Small wooden crosses marked the places where someone had lost his footing and tumbled into the ravine. At this point, slavers took the time to remove the neck collars, afraid that if one slave decided to commit suicide they would lose the whole procession to the abyss.

Born and raised somewhere along the warm flatlands of West Africa, Aranda's slaves had spent most of their lives in terrain where mangrove swamps and savannas gently rise into foothills. Some of them might have been from one of West Africa's highland regions, such as Fouta Djallon, made up of sandstone plateaus out of which flow the headwaters of the Gambia and Senegal Rivers, as well as some of the tributaries that feed into the Niger. On average, Fouta Djallon stands at about 3,000 feet above sea level, with its tallest point not much more than that. Now, though, the voyagers were climbing up a steep path that passed under the two tallest mountains in America. Mount Aconcagua, at 23,000 feet, is 'startling in its magnitude,' wrote one nineteenth-century traveler, 'overwhelming in its solitude and isolation.' Behind that, the slightly smaller yet more imposing Mount Tupungato, its vertical face scoured 'crude and naked' by a never-ending 'fury of wind,' looked like a rock avalanche suspended in motion that at any moment might resume its fall. The whole scene, another traveller observed of the approach to the two peaks, offered an 'immense, inanimate but magnificent view of desolation.'[6]

Everywhere the climbers looked, they would have seen giant overhanging precipices and signs of violent earthquakes, landslides, and avalanches. Turn one way, and there was 'nothing but broken, sterile mountains covered with ice.' Turn another, and there was an even 'more horrible view' of 'even blacker mountains, covered with even more ice.' After three days of climbing, the procession came to the Puente de Inca, a narrow, icy natural rock bridge that spanned a deep gorge. It was here that, nearly three centuries earlier, an observer had commented that Native Americans must have 'diamonds on the soles of their feet,' as he watched them glide across. It sounds like an attribution of grace but perhaps merely meant that their feet were rough and hard and had traction. In any case, the bridge terrified the Spaniards. 'Only the man who has made his confessions' should venture across it, said yet another traveller.[7]

The higher the group went and the colder it became, the more intense the disorientation. After about three days, it would have reached the trail's high point, around the spot where Charles Darwin, travelling along this road decades later, would notice what he called the 'perfect transparency of the air' and 'increased brilliancy of the moon and stars.' Like Ocampo commenting that the pampas offered 'no middle ground,' Darwin said it was hard to gauge perspective and to judge 'heights and distance.' Not, as in the case of the flatlands, because of the boundlessness of the view but because the air contained no moisture that might refract light. Darwin described the effect as bringing 'all objects . . . nearly into one plane, as in a drawing or panorama.' The air was so dry that the naturalist's wooden instruments shrank noticeably and his bread petrified. Static electricity flashed from nearly everything. When Darwin rubbed his flannel waistcoat in the dark, it 'appeared as if it had been washed with phosphorus.' The hair on a dog's back 'crackled' and his linen sheets 'emitted sparks.'[8]

All this strangeness must have increased the disorientation Babo, Mori, and the others felt, of moving through a physical world that seemed not of this world. Altitude sickness would have added to their exhaustion. Africans forced along this road suffered horribly from the penetrating cold, and, like the Huape slaves before them, were often found 'frozen in place.' Those who hadn't completely succumbed were whipped to get them moving again. The sweat they built up (despite the cold) on their daylong marches froze on their skin and made the night that much more horrible. Extreme fatigue weakened resistance. The year before, in 1803, smallpox had struck a group of about a hundred Africans as they were making the crossing, killing two. The rest arrived in Valparaiso 'full of scabs.' At least four Africans who left Mendoza around the time Babo and the others started out didn't make it across. There are stories today that still circulate among the region's surviving Native Americans, handed down by their ancestors, of coming upon the frozen bodies of Africans, their heads or arms cut off so that their handlers didn't have to waste time breaking their chains or cutting and then retying the hemp. A Frenchman who witnessed Africans being brought along this route a few years after Aranda's slaves made the climb said he wished that his 'prideful' countrymen could be forced to 'travel through such a forsaken, steep, and ice-covered place, so that they would understand suffering.'[9]

The experience, he said, would strip them of their 'pride and soften their hearts.'

One of the things that must have seemed familiar yet different to Babo, Mori, and their fellow captives would have been the progression of the Southern Hemisphere moon. Lunar phases are the same on both sides of the equator, yet they move in opposite directions. In the Northern Hemisphere, where all the Africans brought by Aranda were from, the bright part of the moon grows bigger from right to left. Then, halfway through the cycle following the full moon, the dark part grows larger from the same direction. But Buenos Aires, Mendoza, and Valparaiso are located well below the equator, where the moon waxes and wanes from the left.

It had to have seemed strange, this inverted moon, made brilliant by the high, dry Andean air. It was yet another sign of not just their world but heaven turned upside down. But since the new moon and the full moon are the same on either side of the equator, the West Africans had been able to mark the passing of lunar months on their more than year-long journey from the coast of Africa, across the Atlantic, then over the American continent to the foothills of the Andes.

And from what happened next, it appears they knew that December 3, 1804, about a week before they started up the mountains, was the first full day of Ramadan. And that December 27, a week after they boarded the *Tryal* bound for Lima, was the eve of the holiest day of that holy month: Laylat al-Qadr, or the Night of Power.

Heaven's Sense

In *Moby-Dick*, out of all the *Pequod*'s many hands, Herman Melville chose to give Pip, a young African American cabin boy, the ability to truly see, a gift that comes to him after he nearly drowns in the Pacific.

Pip has already jumped out of the whaleboat on that 'beautiful, bounteous, blue day,' frightened by a rap a harpooned whale gives to the boat's bottom with its tail. The whale has to be lost so that Pip can be saved, a trade that earns him a rebuke from Stubb, the *Pequod*'s second mate. 'Stick to the boat,' Stubb says. 'We can't afford to lose whales by the likes of you; a whale would sell for thirty times what you would, Pip, in Alabama.'

But Pip is soon in the water again. True to his word, Stubb leaves him to drift while he chases another whale. The young boy is absolutely alone. 'Bobbing up and down in that sea, Pip's ebon head showed like a head of cloves,' the 'ringed horizon' expanding 'around him miserably.' 'The intense concentration of self in the middle of such a heartless immensity, my God! who can tell it?'

Pip is finally rescued, but before he is pulled from the sea he has a vision. He sees the totality of the world, its origins and inner workings, in a single moment:

> The sea had jeeringly kept his finite body up, but drowned the infinite of his soul. Not drowned entirely, though. Rather carried down alive to wondrous depths, where strange shapes of the unwarped primal world glided

to and fro before his passive eyes; and the miser-merman, Wisdom, revealed his hoarded heaps; and among the joyous, heartless, ever-juvenile eternities, Pip saw the multitudinous, God-omnipresent, coral insects, that out of the firmament of waters heaved the colossal orbs. He saw God's foot upon the treadle of the loom, and spoke it; and therefore his ship-mates called him mad. So man's insanity is heaven's sense; and wandering from all mortal reason, man comes at last to that celestial thought, which, to reason, is absurd and frantic; and weal or woe, feels then uncompro-mised, indifferent as his God.[1]

Pip is not the only one on the *Pequod* given a glimpse into the abso-lute. Ishmael, standing among a pile of whale bones, is also 'borne back to that wondrous period, ere time itself can be said to have begun; for time began with man.' But the vision doesn't disturb Ishmael the way it does Pip. The two characters are about as distant from each other in social status as possible. Ishmael makes it clear that his decision to sign on the *Pequod* is entirely his own. He does say his purse is light. But the main reason he joins the voyage is because he is bored by and alienated from the artificiality of modern city living. Ishmael hopes going to sea will be a bracing experience, or at least provide entertainment to distract him from his ennui. And he makes clear that he could have joined as an officer rather than as a common sailor, but preferred not to. 'Who aint a slave? Tell me that,' he says to explain his decision.

It is a curious question coming from Ishmael, who is about as free a man as one can imagine. White, educated, mobile, and a man, he has, as far as we know, no family and no debt. Yet he thinks his own condition can be generalized—and in antebellum America, no less—to all human-ity. And so, standing amid the whale bones, Ishmael sees infinity but isn't troubled. He still thinks that he is the subject of history, that 'time began with man.'

Pip, though, comes out of the sea seemingly made mad by God's indifference, and his madness is Melville's. Melville had read the geolo-gists, naturalists, and other scientists of his day, including Charles Lyell and Charles Darwin, and immediately grasped the frightening potential of their arguments: that existence had no meaning, that the earth was so old, that time itself was so incomprehensible, that it rendered belief and faith in man's centrality in the order of the universe impossible.

Over the last decades, literary scholars have scoured Melville's writings for political meaning. Some have found the influence of a racist, expansionist culture. Others see a generous humanism, reading works like *Moby-Dick* and *Benito Cereno* as sophisticated indictments of 'American values and institutions,' of slavery, empire, alienating individualism, and white supremacy. There are, though, many Melvilleans who resist turning the author into a scolding social critic. Melville could, they admit, write in sly and cutting ways about his country's shortcomings, but he was too much of a metaphysician, and too much of an agnostic concerning his metaphysics, to turn his criticism into a political program. Melville would later pay close attention to the Civil War. There is no evidence, though, that in the 1850s he was especially concerned about the plight of actual existing slaves in the South. After the disappointment of *Moby-Dick*, he became preoccupied with philosophy, with larger questions of ethics, withdrawn into himself to the point that he broke down. His disquiets were at once psychic and cosmic but not, apparently, primarily political.[2]

Yet it is exactly Melville's existential digressions that speak directly to the problem of slavery in Western society, that go straight to the heart of what the massive and systemic subordination of millions and millions of human beings over the course of hundreds and hundreds of years meant to the societies that prospered from slavery and to the slaves who suffered creating that prosperity. Melville wrestled with whether life had meaning, and if it had, whether its meaning was rooted in radical individualism, in human interconnectivity, or in larger moral structures; he grappled with the despair of losing one's self in a godless cosmos, with the conflict between notions of free will and predestination and thus between belief and disbelief, with the idea that the physical world was a mirage, that one needed to punch through the pasteboard mask of surface things and grasp the underlying reality. Slavery, in a way, was the concrete manifestation of such metaphysical terrors, for it represented the same threat to real individuals as the possibility of a meaningless universe posed to the idea of the individual: obliteration.

And so it is Pip, 'the most insignificant of the Pequod's crew,' told just before his near death that his labour is worth less than the energy produced by an animal's oil, whose free will consists entirely of choosing between life on board a whale ship and life on an Alabama slave plantation (if he even had that choice; the terms of Pip's service are not revealed), whom Melville has fully realize the implication of infinity: that man's existence itself is insignificant. And it is Pip to whom Melville gives the power to see. What the rest of the crew thinks is babble is really an expression of his ability to take in everything all at once from every perspective; Melville has him going about the deck chanting a visionary conjugation: 'I look, you look, he looks; we look, ye look, they look.'

Melville read Darwin's account of the voyage of HMS *Beagle*, most likely during his own sea travels in the early 1840s, when he visited many of the same shores and islands Darwin had less than a decade earlier. And Pip's vision might have been inspired by one of its most dramatic passages.

There is a section where Darwin, during his trek over the Andes at an altitude of about 7,000 feet, comes across a grove of calcified trees standing white and straight 'like Lot's wife.' He looks back behind him toward the pampas and realizes he is standing in what had once been a sea, a vast tectonic elevator that had been lifted up, brought down, and then raised up again. Darwin unfolds a quarter-billion-year history in a single burst:

I saw the spot where a cluster of fine trees once waved their branches on the shores of the Atlantic, when that ocean (now driven back 700 miles) came to the foot of the Andes. I saw that they had sprung from a volcanic soil which had been raised above the level of the sea, and that subsequently this dry land, with its upright trees, had been let down into the depths of the ocean. In these depths the formerly dry land was covered by sedimentary beds, and these again by enormous streams of submarine lava—one such mass attaining the thickness of a thousand feet; and these deluges of molten stone and aqueous deposits five times alternately had been spread out. The ocean which received such thick masses must have been profoundly deep; but again the subterranean forces exerted themselves, and I now beheld the bed of that ocean forming a chain of mountains more than seven thousand feet in height.

Having dived, like Pip, down to the ocean's bottom, Darwin soars up over the Andes. Gazing east at what millennia ago was a 'green and budding' valley but is now the desert pampas, he pronounces that 'all is utterly irreclaimable.'[3]

Darwin didn't know it, but the mountain pass where he had this vision was the old slave road connecting Argentina to Chile. The naturalist was moving along exactly the same route that, three decades earlier, Babo, his son Mori, and their other captured West African companions had travelled, past the exact same grove of white stone trees.

PART IV

FURTHER

Sealer, Slaver & Pirate are all of a trade.

—CHARLES DARWIN, *BEAGLE* DIARY, MARCH 24, 1833

13

KILLING SEALS

The *Perseverance* left Boston on November 10, 1799, captained by Amasa Delano, with his brother Samuel as first officer. The currents were contrary and the weather unhelpful. Constant rains and hot, sultry air were followed, after the ship passed the 12th parallel north, by a maddening calm that mildewed the ship's sails and covered everything on board with a 'blue mould.' Then, rounding Cape Horn, the brothers hit a 'violent head sea' that rolled into them like a 'mountain,' tossing their ship into the 'foul' shallows, where it wandered in the night fog.

But by early 1800 they had made it into the calm blue Pacific, to the many islands that dotted Chile's southern coast, ready to enter on the upside of one of the most dramatic boom and busts in economic history.

With increasing frequency starting in the early 1790s, and then in a mad rush beginning in 1798, ships left New Haven, Norwich, Stonington, New London, or Boston, calling first on the Cape Verde Islands off the coast of Senegal to pick up a load of salt and then cutting southeast to the great half-moon sealing archipelago of remote islands running from Argentina in the Atlantic to Chile in the Pacific. They'd be on the hunt for a certain species of Pacific fur seal, the kind that wears a layer of velvety down like an undergarment just below an outer coat of stiff greyblack hair. Some of the skins would be brought to Europe, where furriers had recently perfected a technique for peeling the fur intact off the hair, turning the skins into capes, coats, muffs, and mittens for ladies and

belts, sashes, wallets, and waistcoats for gentlemen. Most would go to
Canton and be traded for silk, tea, and ceramics.[1]

Along with whalers, sealers like Amasa and Samuel were part of a
first generation of republicans who, with the Alleghenies not yet completely breached, saw America's frontier as lying not to the west but to
the south, past Brazil and Argentina, around Cape Horn, bringing New
Englanders deep into the Pacific, to the Hawaiian Islands and beyond,
to Japan and China. Whaling, though, took place in the bountiful,
unclaimable sea. Whalers might fight over whether any given fish was
fast or loose, but they hunted in a watery commons open to all. Sealing,
in contrast, happened on land, and it was through the spectacularly
rapid growth of the industry that New Englanders took their first informal possession of island colonies—one sailor indeed described his ship
as a 'floating metropolis,' moving from one island to another, leaving
behind 'little colonies' of skinners to stake their ground.[2]

Bostoneses—as the Chileans called New England mariners—brought
with them the ideas and institutions of the American Revolution, of rule
and revolt. There among the coves, gulches, and beaches of islands hundreds of miles off the coast of Chile and many thousands of miles from
the United States, a strange order took shape. Seal ship captains planted
the stars and stripes and on the Fourth of July celebrated the independence of the thirteen colonies by setting ablaze thirteen coils of oil-
soaked rope. They presided over makeshift courts of law that settled
disputes related to property and debt. They even had their own secular
sacred texts: if no Bible was available, witnesses swore on the collected
plays of William Shakespeare, found in the libraries of most ships.[3]

For a brief few years on his first sealing expedition, from November
1799 to November 1802, Amasa Delano was able to reverse the humiliation of his last long voyage. He was making money, and taking hundreds
of thousands of sealskins to Canton. Delano was being treated as an
equal by men he respected and he enjoyed the authority he felt his character and talents deserved, helping to bring law and order to these distant islands—a far cry from the piratical levelling he witnessed in Île de
France. By this point, the British had mostly left sealing in the eastern
part of the South Pacific to the Americans, so there were no Scots to play

practical jokes on him. But the prestige couldn't last, as the promise of fast and unprecedented profit set off a rage to slaughter that would fast sweep away this archipelago republic of seal killers.

As the Delano brothers were making preparations to sail, they kept hearing reports of one place above all so full of seals that 'if many of them were killed in a night, they would not be missed in the morning.' And that's where they headed.[4]

Sitting five hundred miles dead west of Santiago, Chile, the island of Más Afuera, round, mountainous, and shrouded in mist, looks like a movie-set ideal of a misty deserted island. Rock walls rise quickly to a height of 6,000 feet, forming a plateau cut by cascades and deep chasms that seal hunters called 'gulches' and circled by a craggy, cave- and cove-dotted shoreline. A 'gold mine,' sealers said. And as if to make the island's striving promise of wealth that much more perfect, its name, Más Afuera, means 'even further' in English.

Más Afuera's lack of a safe harbour or easy landing beach completed its allure as an object of desire. Enormous rookeries of fur seals remained out of easy reach. Seal ships anchored far from shore had to dispatch their launches through dangerous waves and boulders to land men and supplies. 'Whale boat upset on the bar and 3 men drowned & 4 saved with great difficulty,' reported one ship's log from the time.[5]

'In every bay there are such Multitudes of great Sea-Lions, and Seals of several Sorts,' Captain Edward Cooke said in 1712 of the archipelago of which Más Afuera is a part, 'all with excellent Furs, that we could scarce walk along the shore as they lay about in Flocks, like Sheep, the young ones bleating like lambs.' They were so 'thick on the shore' that Cooke's men were 'forced to drive them away' before they could land. Especially in November, when they 'come ashore to whelp and ingender . . . the Shore is so full of them for a stone's throw, that 'tis impossible to pass thro them. . . . When we came in, they kept a continual noise day and night, some bleating like Lambs, some howling like Dogs or Wolves, others making hideous noises of various sorts; so that we heard 'em about, tho a mile from Shore.'[6]

When the Delano brothers arrived at Más Afuera in March 1800 there were fourteen ships anchored at different points around the island's circumference.

Away teams left ashore on Más Afuera and elsewhere to acquire seal-skins also hunted sea elephants, found on the same islands where seals birthed and nursed their young. These mammals were enormous, some-times twenty feet tall and twelve feet around, the largest in the world that live both in the sea and on land. They were big, like whales, and like whales they were taken for their oil. A single bull yielded as much as two hundred gallons. Unlike whales, they were easy to kill.

The difficulty and danger involved in the high-sea hunt of a whale created respect among the men for the leviathan. The slaughter of sea elephants, in contrast, was easy sport, a game that bred cruelty and con-tempt. As the sea elephants opened their mouths to bellow, their hunters would take turns tossing in rocks. 'There was no difficulty in killing them, since they were incapable of either resisting or escaping.'

At times, rousing them from their slumber took more effort than dispatching them. When bulls did lift themselves up to protect their cows, their blubber-rich skin undulated in great waves up and down their bodies, a trance-inducing index of their market value, and a signal to begin the kill. The animals 'being soft and fat' and the lances 'being sharp and long,' the men would perforate their prey in 'a dozen places.' The sea elephant's heart pushes an enormous amount of warm blood through its circulatory system, as much as twenty gallons. When the animal is underwater, its circulation slows down. But on land, blood courses through its body in a high-pressure flow. Pierced in multiple places like Saint Sebastian, the creature begins to gush 'fountains of blood, spouting to a considerable distance.' At other times, the hunters would give just one quick thrust to the heart, 'the blood flowing in tor-rents, and covering the men.'[7]

Sea elephants rarely fought back. There is one account, though, of a sailor 'foolish and cruel enough' to slay a young one in the 'presence of his mother.' She came up on her child's executioner from behind and took his 'head in her mouth,' scoring 'his skull in notches with her teeth.' The sailor soon died.[8]

When the killing was finished, the men skinned the carcasses and cut the hides into two-by-two-foot squares, each as thick as eight inches with blubber. About fifteen to twenty of these 'horse pieces' were then strung on poles and carried to the tryworks, which were usually set up by a stream or a river where the sand and blood could be washed off the blubber. The pieces were then ripped into two-inch strips, scored, and tossed into the pots, which were fired during the first round with wood. But as in the rendering of beef tallow and whale blubber, the animals assisted in their own consumption: once the initial batch was boiled into oil and ladled into casks, the crisp, nearly fried pieces of sea elephants, still unctuous enough to combust, kept the heat going. On the South Georgia Islands and elsewhere, penguin carcasses were also heaped on the flames, their feathers used as a 'wick for the fat.'[9]

It hardly took more skill to kill seals. Here's Delano's description:

> The method practiced to take them was, to get between them and the water, and make a lane of men, two abreast, forming three or four couples, and then drive the seal through this lane; each man furnished with a club, between five and six feet long; and as they passed, he knocked down such of them as he chose, which are commonly the half-grown, or what are called young seals. This is easily done, as a very small blow on the nose effects it. When stunned, knives are taken to cut and rip them down on the breast, from the under jaw to the tail, giving a stab in the breast that will kill them.[10]

Most of the farmers who made up these gangs were used to slaughtering and butchering livestock. But not on this scale.

The attack on a rookery was like a military operation. The men set out early in the morning, before daybreak, and, divided into two groups, flanked the target at either end of the beach, lying low behind outcroppings of rocks, 'so as to be hid from the seals.' When a signal was given, both groups would start their rush to the seals, beginning the 'dire work of slaying as fast as possible.'

The men might hide in place for hours waiting. Normally, it was the 'old whigs'—that is, the mature males—that were first to appear, so named because of a tuft of curly hair on their heads. Then came the mature females, called clapmatches (either because there was a spark in their quick movements, like that of a match, or because their hooded-looking heads resembled a cap with earflaps, which in Dutch is called a *klapmut*). They'd be followed by their pups. Green hands would be anxious to start, while veterans urged patience until the rookery was filled, sometimes, in the early years of the trade, with as many as twenty thousand seals.

Usually the signal was given at around eleven in the morning. The sealer George Little described an assault he participated in: 'We rushed with impetuosity down the rocks on the beach, between the seals and the water, and with our unsparing hand began the work of death. A slight blow with the club on the head was sufficient for the "young" pups, but it was not so easy a task with the old "whigs" and "clap-matches."' Whigs might try to protect their harems, yet soon there would be a dash to the sea. Most seals in any given attack would escape, but sealers would force a large number upland, where they would be trapped and killed. If a man happened to fall in the scramble, wrote Little, 'he would be torn to pieces by these huge animals, for their mouths are as large as that of a lion.'

Fur seals growl and snort, occasionally letting loose rhythmic barks. One alone can sound like a cross between a dog and a cow. When they are crowded together in the hundreds or thousands on the beach, their noise, punctuated by snapping teeth, is thunderous, competing with the howl of the Pacific wind. 'This battle caused me considerable terror,' Little confessed. 'What with the roaring of the old seals, maddened to desperation, and the yelping of the young pups, together with the shouts of the crew, formed, to my mind, a kind of pandemonium scene, from which I should have been exceedingly glad to have escaped.' For coats and capes, furriers preferred the larger pelts of mature seals, so they could avoid cross seams. But the dense fur that kept the 'very small pups' warm was the plushest. 'Too tiny' for most garments, it made fine wallets and mittens.[11]

The slaughter went on until dark. Since only skins were valuable, carcasses were left on the ground, 'strewing in such numbers,' according to one account, 'as to render it difficult to avoid treading on them in walking around.' The 'smell infected the atmosphere.' By the end of the day, the men would be drenched in saltwater, blood, 'squalor and filth.'[12]

Sea elephants were monstrous, their blubber and lumber almost perverse. Seals, though, were the size of humans, and their hunters talked about them as if they were: 'They are gregarious, very intelligent, sociable, and affectionate'; they are 'curious'; 'when churchbells ring, they swim to the shore'; they 'kiss each other, and die with grief at the loss of their young.' 'I have myself,' said one traveller, 'seen a young female shed tears abundantly, whilst one of our wicked and cruel sailors amused himself at the sight, knocking out her teeth with an oar, whenever she opened her mouth. The poor animal might have softened a heart of stone; its mouth streaming with blood, its eyes with tears.' Occasionally, if a fiddle, fife, or flute was available, sealers would play music to lure the animals to shore.[13]

Some glimpsed beauty amidst the frenzy. 'They have the finest eyes imaginable, and there is no fierceness in their countenance,' said a visitor to the Malvinas, or Falklands, in 1797 who watched one being clubbed. Just before expiring, the seal's 'eyes changed colour, and their crystalline lens became of an admirable green.'[14]

What came next, after the 'work of death,' as Little put it, was over, did require talent. Skinning had to be done fast, before rigor mortis set in. If a shore gang had enough men, the work would be broken up into tasks. One group to club, another to stab, and yet another to 'rip and flip,' that is, to cut an incision along the neck, bellies, and flippers. Then a final gang of men would follow to separate the skin from the blubber. Dividing the work like this ensured that their skinning knives, made of the highest quality steel, remained razor sharp. Had the knives been used for other tasks, such as cutting through sandy hair and fur, they would have quickly lost their edge. An experienced man would work with grace and speed, taking about a minute per seal to remove a skin intact.

The skins were then soaked in water, so that the flesh and fat (which could be used to keep cooking fires or tryworks burning) could be scraped off more easily. Then they would be either salted or stretched and pegged on the ground to dry. Drawn-out skins would cover vast expanses of beach, their hair shimmering black-blue in the sea wind. There was one stretch of land nearly two miles long on the coast of Patagonia used by Connecticut captains to dry skins. They called it the 'New Haven Green.'[15]

Amasa Delano compared the drying and stacking of sealskins to that of salt cod, yet more care had to be taken to ensure that the fine underfur of the pelts wasn't ruined. On land, waiting for months for a ship to return, stacked skins had to be protected from rats and rain. Once on a ship, sealskins, like Buenos Aires hides, could be piled from the floor of a hold to its rafters. They needed to be absolutely dry before being stacked and the hold made waterproof. If they got wet on the voyage, the fur would come out in clumps and the skin would fester, selling, with luck, only for fertilizer.

Whaling knowledge grew slowly over centuries, expanding alongside the gradual extension of the hunting radius, from the waters around Nantucket to all of the Atlantic and then the Pacific. In contrast, the sealing industry boomed in a remarkably short period of time, starting in the early 1790s. And the drive to kill, dry, and ship skins to Canton fast outpaced technique. There was confusion among the officers, and even more among the men, about what constituted best practices.

In 1792, Edmund Fanning's expedition caught sight of its first rookery, on the Malvina Islands. Fanning had been told that the best way to kill seals was to get between them and the water, yell loud, and drive them inland. But that method worked best with fur seals. What Fanning had come upon were hair seals, a larger species with different instincts.

One of Fanning's hands had a doubt: 'Do you think these overgrown monsters are seals?'

'Surely they are,' Fanning answered.

When the men advanced on the beach from the water, letting out a collective yell and raising their clubs, the hair seals 'sent forth a roar that appeared to shake the very rocks on which we stood, and in turn, advancing upon us in double quick time, without any regard to our persons, knocked every man of us down with as much ease as if we had been pipe stems, and passing over our fallen bodies, marched with the utmost contempt to the water.'[16]

Years later, some away teams still didn't know that the piled-up heaps of skinned corpses left on the beach from previous kills repelled living seals, discouraging them from coming on shore. On one island, men hid behind boulders for days waiting for a rookery to fill up. The seals would 'just land in the surf, stick their heads up and look about for a moment . . . and go to sea again.' It took the keenest among the waiting men to realize that the seals 'were afraid to come on shore, on account of the carcasses . . . strewn all over the beach.'[17]

Another captain, George Howe, master of the *Onico* and supposedly an experienced sealer, didn't know how long skins should be soaked. When told by his away team that the skins they had gathered were 'damaged by lying too long in the water,' Howe asked why they were not taken 'out sooner.' When his men reminded him that it was he who ordered that they stay in water for 'five days,' the captain said that 'they were not soaked enough.' Howe asked if the skins 'stank.' Yes, his men told him. Good, he said, 'they ought to stink.' The pelts were soon worthless.[18]

At first, missteps like these didn't much matter. There were so many seals.

Amasa Delano estimated that when New Englanders first arrived at Más Afuera and 'began to make a business of killing seals, there is no doubt but there were two or three millions of them on the island.' The *Eliza*, out of New York, had dropped anchor in 1792 and taken 38,000 skins off the island. From then on, more and more vessels arrived carrying away bigger and bigger hauls. Between 1797 and 1799, the shore crew of a New Haven ship called the *Neptune* killed and skinned 18,000 seals. The numbers in the margin of the diary kept by one of its crew members, David Forbes, records the steady pace of the killing, which took place every day but Sunday: 'Killed 370 whigs.' '500 whigs.' '700 whigs.' 400. 370. 230. 400. 160. 260. 440. 270. 280. 350. 300. In 1800, the *Betsey* took 110,000 sealskins off the island.[19]

It did indeed seem as if you could kill them all one day and start fresh again the next. Yet within a stunningly short time, the intense slaughter that took place on Más Afuera and elsewhere flooded the Chinese market. During just one week in December 1801 alone, thirty-two ships were in Canton selling hundreds of thousands of skins. With so many pouring in, their price was rapidly dropping. 'You see how fluctuating these markets are,' Delano's agent in China said.[20]

The market wasn't fluctuating. It was plummeting. To compensate for the falling prices, ship captains pressured their away teams to step up the killing, which in turn led to the rapid disappearance of rookeries. Oversupply and extinction went hand in hand.

Falling prices and vanishing herds rapidly changed the nature of the industry. In the early 1790s, it would take only a few weeks, or at most a season, for small gangs of six to ten men on an island like Más Afuera to fill a ship's hold with skins. Less than a decade later, the size of away teams had tripled, and they were staying on islands two or three years at a stretch.

As the seal population diminished, desperation grew. Cooperation among different seal ships and away teams, which was common early in the boom, gave way to a scramble for territory. In 1803, a Nantucket gang that had laid claim to Más Afuera's valuable 'northwest plain' was sending 'all hand round the cove to put a stop to Capt. Britnall sealing.' A few days later, they 'stopped Mr. Butler from destroying the clapmatches at the cove.' To prevent such conflicts from escalating, seal ship captains signed 'treaties' dividing up the island's hunting grounds. But the fighting continued.[21]

Efforts to self-regulate the hunt were too little and too late. There were 'sudden and large fortunes to be made,' wrote one sealer of his experiences, yet little accumulated wealth was built up 'in consequence of the animal's being almost annihilated.' Within a few years, seal rookeries would be gone for good on many of the Argentine and Chilean islands, with some subspecies of seals becoming extinct.[22]

'On island after island, coast after coast,' the historian Briton Cooper Busch says in *The War against the Seals*, 'the seals had been destroyed to the last available pup, on the supposition that if sealer Tom did not kill every seal in sight, sealer Dick or sealer Harry would not be so squeamish.'

14

ISOLATOS

Work on a whale ship required intense coordination and camaraderie. Out of the gruesomeness of the hunt, the peeling of the whale's skin from its carcass, and the hellish boil of the fat, something, as Melville wrote in *Moby-Dick*, sublime emerged. The enormous profit derived from whaling integrated not just capital and technology but human sentiment. And like the whale oil that lighted the lamps of the world, divinity itself glowed from the labour, a value shared by working people throughout America: 'Thou shalt see it shining in the arm that wields a pick or drives a spike; that democratic dignity which, on all hands, radiates without end from God; Himself! The great God absolute! The centre and circumference of all democracy! His omnipresence, our divine equality!'[1]

Sealing was something else entirely, pitting desperate captains and officers, racing to make a voyage pay off, against equally desperate foremast hands, who, left alone on remote islands, had plenty of time to gripe and plot. It called to mind not industrial democracy but the isolation and violence of conquest, settler colonialism, and warfare, men brutally exploiting one another and nature, not for something elemental and needed by all like light and fire but for the raw material of conspicuous consumption. Sealers seized territory, fought one another to keep it, and pulled out what wealth they could as fast as they could, before abandoning their claims empty and wasted.

Some sealing islands were stocked with black cattle, wild hogs, and goats left by previous visitors. Others were nothing but barren clay mixed with stones and sand. Sealers, often schooners and brigs like the *Perseverance*, dropped off away gangs for ever-longer stretches. The men left behind by captains like Delano were given little instruction and few provisions, aside from start-up casks of hard bread, lard, and liquor, axes to build a shelter, salt to dry the skins (unless they were to be sun dried), a few muskets, balls, and powder. They were expected to live off the land. The island called Desolation at the southern tip of the Americas especially lived up to its name, even during the summer months, when the seals came ashore to give birth.

Away teams survived by wading into freezing water to harvest mussels, shooting birds, and boiling maidenweed for tea. Carrion crows could be mistaken for turkeys until they were shot; then their stink announced that they were vultures. Other islands had only seals to eat. Men cut steaks out of the meat, boiled the organs, salted the tongue, ate the brains as sweetbreads, and made black pudding with the blood. With luck they could occasionally trade with passing ships, exchanging sealskins for 'oranges and English nuts.' They lived Jonah-like, so to speak, inside the animals, as if they were the viscera themselves: they used the skeletons of whale bones as beams for their huts, sheathing them with the skins of seals and sea elephants. Sometimes, away teams would find traces of those who preceded them. After their first kill on a small, rocky, waterless Pacific island, a group of sealers came across a 'sight which petrified them with horror': the skeletons of seven men and the remains of a hut, all that was left of a team that had been put ashore 'for the purpose of getting elephant oil and seal.'

It was a harsh, brutal life, and one, for both officers and foremast hands, considerably lower in standing than whaling. Many involved were unskilled, part of a revolutionary generation of land men who learned the job on the spot, hoping to make enough money to return home and buy a farm. The only experience they had that prepared them for the work was slaughtering and butchering farm animals. As William Moulton, from inland New York, put it, the 'object of my voyage was to acquire property.'

Left alone for months or years at a time, the men suffered the 'severity of winter in this rigorous climate,' wrote Moulton. The snow was constant on the islands of the southern latitudes. Where there wasn't snow, there were ticks, flies, and other insects. 'Tormented by Buggs,' ran one entry in a sealer diary. The diet was monotonous and tough. The seal blood that went into black pudding was fibrous, causing bouts of intense vomiting. Scurvy was common. Some men were reported to have died shortly after eating a seal liver steak. They didn't know it at the time, but the livers of seals contain a staggering amount of vitamin A, which could produce 'purgings, dysenteries, and other complaints.'[2]

When the men weren't killing and skinning, they cooked, drank, and played checkers or cards. Occasionally, another ship would drop anchor and relieve the boredom. 'Held a ball on Captain Bunker's craft,' read the journal of a sealer who had spent twenty months on Más Afuera. 'Music was a flute, drum and violin.' But months of isolation bred vague resentments, cutting into the ability of sealers to enjoy the company of others: 'A great disliking of this ship and crew among us.'[3]

Days and nights were lonely and dreary, as diary entries testify: 'Rain all day.' 'Stormey rainy weather.' 'Cloudy misty weather.' 'Misty dirty weather.' 'Cold, snow.' 'Making a pair of trousers.' Then: 'Rainy day again. Finished trousers.' 'Little to eat and nothing soon but seal.' The men tried to keep the holidays: 'The two hands returned with 4 goats . . . to keep the birthday of our saviour. Not much to do except look for the ship, for which I employ the greater part of my time.' On islands where the water was warm enough, some lonely hands took breaks from the slaughter to play with the seals, gamboling alongside them in a bay, as if they were seals themselves.

Dreams washed over the men. 'Cartwright dreamed of home last night.' Another 'dreamed of the young virgins.' After months of solitude and slaughter, even pleasant ones were interpreted as ominous: 'Last night drempt of a wedding at home which I've heard say is a sign of a funeral.' 'Last Night drempt of home again which makes me fearful of what has happened there.'[4]

Quick relief was not to be expected: 'One year yesterday since I landed on this uninhabited Craggy Dismal place and in less then one more hope to depart from it with gods will.' Nor could one assume it would even arrive: 'Many a look do I cast on the distant ocean to descry our ship & many a sigh for fear she will not come.'[5]

Whaling bound men tightly together in a small space for a long time, their solidarity made possible by the reliably high price of whale oil. Sealing was a more frayed affair. A seal ship might pick up hands in different ports as needed to fill out away teams, which meant that the ties linking crew to officers and captain were weak and unravelled quickly under pressure. When the margin of profit on skins collapsed due to oversupply, the only way to make up the difference was to reduce the daily operating budget of the ship. Officers cut meals to two a day and reduced portions. They diluted the rum and rationed medicine. And they drove men to kill more seals and to find more space on the ship to pack the extra pelts. First mates put seamen's chests on shore to make more storage room and captains converted forecastles into cargo holds, forcing their men to sleep in whatever nook they could find, often on deck and exposed to the elements. The skins, not the men, needed to stay dry. And once the skinning was done and a ship's hold packed from its bilge flats to its deck beams, officers might see away men as redundant, abandoning them 'to perish on some maroon island' and keeping their rightful proceeds of the voyage.[6]

Whale men were cheated as well. In his history of maritime New England, Samuel Eliot Morison describes the kickbacks and double dealings that filched sailors out of their cut, usually calculated at around a hundredth part of a voyage's earnings. There were any number of things that hands had to pay for, from fees for 'fitting out' and insurance to items taken from the ship's 'slop chest,' like tobacco and clothing. The charges would be added to what was called a portage bill, an account of debits and credits, and deducted from their share. Some arrived in a final port at the end of a voyage to learn they had been running a deficit and had to pay, or take out another loan, just to disembark. Yet in an established industry with the backing of complex institutions including corporations and underwriters, there was some accountability and oversight.[7]

Seal ship captains, however, even more than whalers, earned a reputation for exceptional deceit—not because this particular trade attracted a more vile sort of man but because its economy and ecology were unsustainable, forcing captains and officers to find new ways of limiting labour costs. 'The oppression of these tyrants,' wrote William Moulton, talking about his own experience as second mate on the *Onico*, 'was insufferable.'

Moulton was older than most of his shipmates. From a farming family in upstate New York, he was a veteran of America's Revolutionary War. So he had an idea what tyranny looked like, describing seal ship captains as if they were British aristocrats or Hudson Valley landlords. 'These gentry,' Moulton wrote, 'can never fleece, drive, nor starve enough out of their men, nor devise too many pleas to cull and consume everything on themselves, to gratify their lusts of avarice and appetite.'

Sealers on Más Afuera, as well as on other islands, who began to think that the abuse wasn't worth the share or who realized that the chances were dim that they would ever see their share, increasingly decided to strike: they quit, either collectively or individually.*

In 1803, the entire crew of the *Mentor* jumped ship at Más Afuera,

---

* The phrase *to strike* to refer to a labour stoppage comes from maritime history and is an example of how revolutionary times can redefine a word to mean its exact opposite. Through the seventeenth and much of the eighteenth century, *to strike* was used as a metaphor for submission, referring to the practice of captured ships dropping, or *striking*, their sails or flags to their conquerors and of subordinate ships doing the same to salute their superiors. 'Now Margaret / Must strike her sail,' wrote William Shakespeare in *Henry VI*, describing an invitation extended by the 'Mighty King' of France to Margaret, the weaker queen of England, to join him at the dinner table 'and learn a while to serve / Where kings command.' Or as this 1712 account of a British privateer taking a Spanish man-o-war off the coast of Peru in 1709 put it: 'fir'd two shot over her, and then she struck' and bowed 'down to us' (Rogers, *A Cruising Voyage*, p. 160). In 1768, London sailors turned the term inside out. Joining city artisans and tradesmen—weavers, hatters, sawyers, glass grinders, and coal heavers—in the fight for better wages, they struck their sails and paralyzed the city's commerce. They 'unmanned or otherwise prevented from sailing every ship in the Thames.' From this point forward, *strike* meant the refusal of submission.

with only 350 skins and thirty barrels of sea elephant oil in its hold. Its captain had to sell the ship in Chile for a pittance to cover passage home for him and his remaining officers. Around the same time, the away team from the *Jenny*, under the command of a Boston captain named Crocker, refused to return to the ship. Amasa Delano heard the news from his agent in Canton, who warned him to keep an eye on his own men: 'The People left on Massafuero by Crocker have most all deserted.'[8]

Most of these islands were uninhabited, so there was no local source of labour. If their men deserted them, captains would have to travel some distance to recruit new hands, one way or another. At some point after his men abandoned him, Crocker, now in command of the *Nancy*, visited Easter Island, located about eighteen hundred miles west of Más Afuera. After a 'bloody' battle with the island's inhabitants, the Rapa Nui, Crocker captured twelve men and ten women and locked them in his hold. According to the captain of a Russian sealer, he was going to maroon them on Más Afuera to establish a slave 'colony' of sealers. Three days out of Easter Island, however, the men jumped overboard and drowned. 'They preferred perishing in the waves, to leading a miserable life in captivity.' The women tried to follow and were 'prevented only by force.'[9]

Officers needing to fill their ships' holds used all their power to stop desertions and forcibly 'carry' men back. And men did all they could to avoid being brought back. Here are the March 1799 entries from the captain's log from the *Concord*, a sealer off an island south of Más Afuera:

17th. In the course of the night Glover and Drown, two of our seamen stole the yawl and run on shore with all their clothes. We found the boat, but can't find the men.

18th. Saw those two fellows that run ashore, but there is so much wood and swamp that it is impossible to catch them.

22d. Sent the boat on shore to fill three barrels of water which were empty. Moser, one of our hands, gave us the slip. We supposed at first that he went to take a walk and did not come back in time to come off in the boat. . . . We saw him on the beach, sent the boat after him, but he ran into the woods. The people are all dissatisfied [and] have been mutinous of late.

23rd. Sent two boat crews on shore to try to catch those Infernal Rascals. Caught Drown but Moser kept his distance. Night calm, some hands ashore to catch the Villain. No Moser to be found. The fellow must be a plagy fool, for he's got no clothes but what he has on.

Then later, on Más Afuera:

April 12th. Drown, one of the fellows that run away, swears by all that's good that he will not work. I suppose we must tie him in the shrouds and give him a plagy flogging which is very disagreeable, but there is no help for it.[10]

Sealing was as nearly an all-or-nothing system of labour relations as possible: until a ship had its complement of skins, workers had leverage in their dealings with officers. They might desert one vessel and bargain with another for better terms. Yet once their ship's hold was full, their bargaining position completely and absolutely vanished, leaving them at the mercy of the officers. Before that point, though, masters were desperate to maintain their authority. Whipping was common, as the Concord's refractory Drown, threatened with a plagy flogging, learned. And seal ship captains could use their far-reaching contacts to financially punish runaways. Later, when a number of men abandoned the Perseverance on its second sealing voyage, Delano sent their names to China, instructing his man there to embargo the 'proceeds of their share' should they show up as hands on another vessel.[11]

By 1801, there were on Más Afuera more than a hundred 'alone men,' a phrase used to describe sealers who lived and worked independently, unaffiliated with any ship. They were of 'all descriptions and characters.' Some, 'badly used' by officers, were refugees from coercion and abuse who had escaped the 'clutches of their tyrants.' Others were at loose ends, left stranded far from home after their ships had been seized by Spanish authorities for smuggling. Still others were left-behinds, abandoned after having worked for months or a year to fill a hold of a ship. Ship captains described these castaways as 'felons, pirates & murderers.' Amasa Delano's agent in China warned him to guard his skins: 'There are so many fellows or rascals on the Island that what one gets cant be call'd his own they steal so.' The island became an oxymoron, a society of hermits. 'Not acknowledging the common continent of men,' to use Melville's description of the 'isolatos' on the *Pequod*, each lived on a 'separate continent of his own.' On Más Afuera, they were islands living together on an island, federated along its gulches and mountain ledges.[12]

One of these isolatos was an 'English lad, by the name of Bill' who took the idea of freedom further than most did during his day. Having fled his ship, he lived in one of Más Afuera's many caves, deciding he wanted nothing to do with either shipboard discipline or the modern world's new master, money. 'He keeps at work sealing,' said a sailor who spoke with him, 'and says if he can get bread and rum he shall be contented.' Bill sold the sailor sixty skins, asking only to have his 'keg filled' in exchange.

The sixty skins were worth twenty dollars, the sailor said, which would buy much more than two gallons of rum. Bill didn't care. 'He says he was never so happy before; there is no larboard watch, no reefing topsails, no body to quarrel with, and he sleeps when he pleases and works when he pleases.'[13]

'Want nothing else?' the sailor asked. 'No,' answered Bill.

15

A TERRIFIC SOVEREIGNTY

Second mate William Moulton also tried to flee from his captain, George Howe, master of the sealing schooner *Onico*. Howe had become abusive shortly after the *Onico* left New London in late 1799. At first Moulton and the rest of the crew thought he was afflicted by drink. Howe 'clipped his words' and suffered long 'spells of hiccupping.' He slept most of the day on the quarterdeck, 'so profoundly' that he didn't wake when the sea broke 'over him with an impetuosity that almost threatened to wash him off.'[1]

Moulton began to see a deeper malice behind the captain's cruelty, which couldn't be explained by alcohol or by the pressure caused by the falling price of sealskins. Howe, decided Moulton, was intoxicated by unchecked power. Maimed and blind in the right eye, he was impressive. One can't read Moulton's 1804 account of his eventful voyage without thinking of Melville's Captain Ahab. Moulton describes Howe as tall and lean, with a sharp nose, thin lips, and a 'sneerful smile.' He was a 'genius,' a 'monocular master,' who compensated for what he lacked in mathematical and astronomical talent by cursing God and nature: 'no Son of Neptune can excel him in execrating the elements and their author, the winds, and him that sent them.'

Where Ahab tapped into wells of dark emotion to bind his men to him, making them think they were joining his mania out of their own free will, Howe ruled only by fear and division. He invented useless chores, like heaving seawater up in a bucket and passing it awkwardly along up a line of men in the rigging, until the bucket was empty and the men soaked. 'Discord among his crew was the basis of his strength.' He often ordered one group of hands to give their biscuits to another. Without cause, he lashed men to the deck cannons to be 'cobbed,' forcing all hands to participate in the paddling lest they themselves incur 'like punishment.' Howe commanded other 'victims' of his 'vengeance' to 'hold their faces fair' to his 'strokes.' If they turned away, he would direct his blows to 'the more sensitive and vital parts' of their body.

Disfigured, damning God and nature to hell, and exercising a 'terrific sovereignty' over his crew, Howe took pleasure, Moulton said, 'proportionate to the misery of others.' When the *Onico* dropped anchor to hunt seals at Staten Land, a craggy, mountainous island off the tip of Tierra del Fuego, where the sea surged 'against all sides of it with great violence,' the abuse continued. Howe forbade his men from building their own shelters until they had raised his own commodious fifty-rafter hut and covered it with the thickest sealskins. He withheld medicine and food, kept them 'on seals' till they were sick, and refused to let them wear warm clothing. Howe watered down the ship's rum and taxed the crew's own liquor supply, whipping all who dared protest until they were bloody. Howe became obsessed with Moulton, who, having fought in the American Revolution, represented a living symbol of rights and a challenge to arbitrary authority.

Moulton tried to escape. Setting out on a twelve-day trek to the other side of the island, he slept in caves, climbed precipices, and slipped down into deep valleys, barely avoiding landslides. With Howe following on his heels carrying 'fire arms well loaded with powder and ball' and swearing 'revenge,' Moulton crawled 'up a gulch to gain the top of a mountain' and called to God to rescue him from 'covetous one-eyed self interest.' 'Oh! Pride and ambition, what havoc have you made,' he cried, 'let me be delivered from malice, deceit, and envy. . . . Lord, save or I perish.' Howe caught him on the far side of the island and dragged him back to the *Onico*.

———

The extent of George Howe's hatred of Moulton was extreme, but his power over his crew was typical. Both maritime law and custom granted captains of whalers, slavers, merchantmen, sealers, and naval vessels absolute authority over their men. 'A Captain is like a King at Sea, and his Authority is over all that are in his Possession,' thought one eighteenth-century mariner. Captains could whip at will; the quarterdeck where floggings took place was often referred to as the 'slaughter-house.' Sailors were punished for the most minor offences: losing a whaleboat's oar, breaking a dish, or letting an African slave drink out of the wrong water cask. Captain Francis Rogers of the *Crown* told his crew that he would 'skin them alive,' while another shipmaster told a sailor that he would 'split his Soul or Stab him and eat a piece of his Liver.' Captains doled out their punishment with a 'brutal severity,' said one account, describing what happened when an old hand on a slave ship anchored off Bonny Island complained about his water allowance: a deck officer beat him until his teeth fell out and then jammed 'iron pump-bolts' in his mouth, forcing him to swallow his blood.[2]

Legally, ships remained redoubts of the old regime well through and beyond the Age of Revolution. It wasn't until 1835 that the US Congress passed an act that tried to place merchant ships under the rule of law and due process, making it a crime punishable by $1,000 or five years in prison for 'any master or other officer, of any American ship or vessel on the high seas' to, with 'malice, hatred, or revenge, and without justifiable cause, beat, wound, or imprison, any one or more of the crew . . . or withhold from them suitable food and nourishment, or shall inflict upon them any cruel and unusual punishment.' And it wasn't until 1850 that the navy outlawed flogging on its vessels. But these practices continued well past their legal abolitions. 'No southern monarch of the slave,' said a sailor in an account of his voyages in 1854, could best the 'brutality' and 'want of moral principle' of sea captains.[3]

Still, the new language of rights spreading around the Atlantic and Pacific following the American, French, and Haitian Revolutions provided sailors with new ways to think about shipboard sovereignty, along with ways to contest it when they felt it was unfairly exercised.

By the time Moulton returned to the *Onico*'s sealing camp, he found most of the rest of his shipmates ready to join him against Howe. They were younger than Moulton, but most of their fathers had fought in the revolution, so they did what their parents' generation did: they elected an assembly, drafted a declaration, and voted to rebel against a man named George.

Like the Declaration of Independence, on which it was clearly modeled, the document the sealers of the *Onico* composed in September 1800 was both a litany of specific grievances and a treatise on natural law and just rule. There, on a remote island at the bottom of the world, its drafters identified themselves as 'citizens of the United States of America' and announced they were opposing Howe's 'authority without reason.'

They listed many of the captain's specific abuses and quickly moved on to their main point: 'It would be an endless, endless talk, should we attempt to enumerate all the instances of your tyranny, though of sufficient magnitude to deserve particular notice. What power is there that you could have assumed, which you have not assumed?' 'If you exercise this mighty power by right,' they asked, where 'did you derive this right?'

Most of the *Onico*'s sealers deliberated on every stage in planning their mutiny, taking direct votes before proceeding on any action. As in the American Revolution itself, there were limits. The crew's one unnamed 'negro' was, Moulton wrote in his journal without further comment, 'excluded from the knowledge of these proceedings.'

The rebellion was called off before it started. Faced with the threat of having his ship seized and being placed in chains, Howe not only capitulated but 'embraced substantially' the spirit of the crew's petition. With goodwill restored, the near-mutinous men boarded the *Onico*, hauled anchor, and made for Más Afuera.

They arrived on the island—which at this point was serving as the capital of what might be called the Oceanic Republic of Sealers—on October 30, finding it crowded with the gangs from at least ten ships along with the hundred or so unattached 'alone men.' Amasa Delano was there with the *Perseverance*, as were the Nantucket Swain brothers, captains of the *Mars* and the *Miantonomoh*. Out of New Haven was the *Oneida*, which had on board an 'apostate Methodist priest.' Though he declared himself an atheist and spent his nights 'drinking and carousing,' the minister continued to preach during the day.

Open-minded Amasa Delano believed the doubting priest to be a 'man of fine sense and liberal principles' and invited him to give a sermon on board the *Perseverance*. Moulton, having befriended the cleric, suggested he take 2 Corinthians 4 as his text:

> We faint not. But have renounced the hidden things of dishonesty, not walking in craftiness, nor handling the word of God deceitfully; but by manifestation of the truth commending ourselves to every man's conscience in the sight of God. For God, who commanded the light to shine out of darkness, hath shined in our hearts, to give the light of the knowledge of the glory of God in the face of Jesus Christ. . . . We are troubled on every side, yet not distressed; we are perplexed, but not in despair; persecuted, but not forsaken; cast down, but not destroyed.

Good republicans like Moulton interpreted the verse as supporting natural, inherent rights: the fact that every man had his own God-given conscience shining in his heart—the 'light of nature,' as Delano put it elsewhere—meant that sovereignty, reason, morality, and justice were vested in individuals and didn't spring from 'fountain head' despots like George Howe.

Once at Más Afuera, Howe didn't return to his old generalized arbitrariness but rather concentrated his bile on Moulton, threatening to leave him stranded on the mainland, where the Spaniards would take him prisoner and put him to work 'in the mines.' Moulton responded by composing another declaration, this time directed not to Howe but to all the 'American Masters' at Más Afuera, including Amasa Delano, who were acting like the informal island colony's ad hoc governing council. Once again,

Moulton recounted Howe's many insults, concluding his defence by asking to be released from all his obligations to Howe and the *Onico*'s owners.

The council of captains convened a hearing on March 15, 1801, hosted by Valentine Swain, master of the schooner *Miantonomoh*. Around a head table in the captain's quarters sat Delano, the Swain brothers, and four other seal shipmasters, who conducted the inquiry with decorum and solemnity. They called witnesses and considered evidence but the case came down to the balance of Moulton's portage bill, the record kept by ships listing a sailor's credits and debits. Moulton didn't contest that his share of the voyage was worth less than what he owed on cash advances and for the tobacco and other provisions he had taken from the *Onico*'s slop chest. But he said his debt should be deducted from Howe's earnings, since it was Howe's erratic rule that made the voyage unprofitable.

The captain-judges decided in Moulton's favour, ruling that he was no longer obligated to Howe. Moulton was elated, until he realized that the Swain brothers, who were employed by the same Norwich merchant company that owned the *Onico*, were using the dispute to best Howe. They wanted his ship, crew, and what few skins he had. They weren't so much absolving Moulton's debt as transferring it to Valentine Swain and the *Miantonomoh*. That's why Valentine Swain had had Moulton's chest brought on board his ship before the hearing, to make it difficult for Moulton to flee.

Captain Swain demanded to know Moulton's intentions, but Moulton hedged. He was fighting here for a principle, the doctrine of 'free labour,' the idea that since every man possessed his own conscience in the eyes of God, he also possessed his own labour. For Moulton, this meant 'sealing for myself or whomever I pleased.' Yet now he was being passed from one master to another like, as he put it, a 'tool.'

Standing before these lords of the island in the oak-lined cabin of one of their 'most consequential,' Moulton was acutely aware that there were forms of power that might not exactly be called slavery yet were coercive nonetheless. The captains' recommendation that he join the crew of the *Miantonomoh* was presented to him merely as 'advice.' Moulton, however, had no doubt that it was the 'advice of those who commanded nearly all the ships and property of merchants belonging to the United

States in this ocean, and who dictated, divided, and parceled out the sealing ground on this island.'

'You will at once see how near that advice approached to a command,' was how Moulton described his predicament in his memoir.

Moulton thanked the captains for releasing him from Howe's authority. He then muttered 'some ambiguous expressions' to evade Swain's question and conceal his intentions. The *Miantonomoh*, set to sail the next day for Valparaiso, was leaving a sealing gang behind, which Moulton said he would join. That night, he removed his chest and bedding from the ship and fled to the interior of the island.

Swearing never to sign his name to 'another portage bill, under any ship-master whatever,' Moulton set out to live 'independently in every respect, . . . to seal by and for myself.'

Swain's crew didn't make it easy. Moulton built a hut and started to hunt seals, joining the ranks of Más Afuera's hundred or so masterless alone men. He was treated as a deserter, constantly harassed by the men of the *Mars* and the *Miantonomoh*, who stole his skins and chased him from the island's rookeries.

Moulton had made his bid for freedom in mid-1801, just as the skinning season was about to start. After six or seven years of intensive slaughter, there were fewer seals on the island. By the end of the year, 'very few clapmatches' or 'young seal pups' were to be found. The only seals coming on shore were 'old whigs.' Despite the shortage, the market in Canton was still saturated and prices were still falling. The result was more clashes among the seal gangs attached to specific ships on Más Afuera, more stealing, and more fighting over territory.

In response to what today would be called an ecological crisis, some of the alone men formed an association. Having recently helped draft a 'declaration of independence,' Moulton now joined with others to compose a constitution. The alone men's 'rules for their government' stipulated that any motion that was made, seconded, put to a vote, and carried by a majority would be 'binding on all.' The association was an almost perfect example of the principle of government by consent, of men coming together in a state of (despoiled) nature and agreeing on a set of laws to protect their interests and freedoms.

The charter mandated that all the alone men would collectively decide when the skinning season was to start. It allowed that whigs that wandered inland could be hunted freely but permitted 'not a seal to be taken' on the beach until 'we all go a sealing.' The idea was to give rookeries a chance to form and grow before they were assaulted. The members of the association would club, rip, and flipper the seals collectively as a group but they would flay the carcasses individually, with 'every man' taking 'what he skins' as the product of his labour. No sealing would be done on Sundays and any man caught violating the rules or stealing the skins of another member would be fined appropriately. Members, if possible, would sell their skins to ships as a group, to get a better price.

It would have been remarkable if all the association did was to try to regulate hunting in response to vanishing seals and the predations of captains and shore gangs. Yet one of its rules went beyond that, expanding the idea of freedom to mean not just individual liberty but mutual interdependence and social security: 'If any of us get disabled by sickness, or being bitten or wounded,' the members agreed, 'there shall be an equitable proportion of sealing ground set off for the disabled person or persons; or that his deficiency of skins occasioned thereby, shall be made up to him by the rest of us, in an equal ration proportionate to the number of skins taken by each individual.' Each would do what he could, but each would have what he needed.

For the brief few years in the late 1700s and early 1800s when the council of American sea captains, among them Amasa Delano, governed Más Afuera, they ruled less like republican emissaries than like rival emperors divvying up a continent: they signed treaties defining boundaries, commanded expeditions that fought one another over resources and wealth, came together to enforce common rules governing property and debt, and even issued their own currency.* At the same time, an odd

---

* Ships purchased skins from alone men with promissory notes to be paid in the United States, often postdated thirty months. See 'Extract from the Journal of Joel Root,' *Papers of the New Haven Colony Historical Society* 5 (1894): 149–72.

lot of 'felons, pirates & murderers' survived in the nooks and crannies of this 'terrific sovereignty,' men who might either renounce Jesus and money and live in caves or decide that being free 'in every respect' meant organizing a half-anarchic, half-social-democratic seal-hunting guild.

As to Captain George Howe, he fell apart after Más Afuera's captain's council ruled against him. The *Onico* became infested with rats, which he couldn't smoke out. Depressed and anxious, he was, as Moulton guessed he would be, relieved of his command by the Swain brothers, who took his skins and crew.

Howe wound up in Valparaiso, confined to the back room of a home of a respected Spanish family, gravely sick with fever. Amasa Delano considered Howe an honest and noble-minded friend, despite joining the Swain brothers to rule against him, and was surprised to learn of his whereabouts. Delano himself had dined a number of times in the house, yet his hosts never once told him that Howe was a few feet away, dying. When he paid a visit, he found the captain untended, in a room 'no better than a hovel, in a most deplorable situation.' Alone in a 'miserable bed,' Howe looked 'wasted,' like a skeleton.

Just before Howe died, the owner of the house brought out his ledgers and had the captain 'acknowledge the different charges' he had incurred during his stay. The Spaniard already held the captain's cash for safekeeping. Now he presented him with a bill for his room and board. 'So far gone,' Amasa wrote, Howe could only say 'yes—without probably knowing what he said.' Thus Captain Howe left this world in debt, having signed his last portage bill. His own.[4]

In mid-October 1801, after tending to George Howe's affairs, Delano returned to the *Perseverance*, gathered the men he had scattered on Más Afuera and other islands, and sailed to China to deliver his haul. For once, his timing was good. He had heard from his agent that the market was volatile but he made it to Canton and sold his skins just before prices truly collapsed.

In the Chilean Pacific, seal rookeries continued to disappear. 'Seals were scarce' said the log of the *Minerva* in 1802. In 1803, after three weeks on Más Afuera in what should have been the height of the skinning season, one away team could barely kill enough seals to 'cover a hut, during which time we had no other shelter than an old boat, turned bottom upwards.' Prospects were 'dreary' and 'gloomy,' made worse by the fact that 'most of the time it was rainy.' In 1804, there were more men than seals on Más Afuera. Two years later, there were no seals at all.[5]

'No seals,' reported the *Topaz* sailing off of Chile, 'no seals.'

16

SLAVERY HAS GRADES

Unable to seal, since there were no seals, sealers turned to smuggling to make a profit. That's how Benito Cerreño, a young Andalusian shipmaster new to the Americas, wound up owning the *Tryal*—a vessel that, even before serving as the stage for a South Pacific slave uprising, had already been involved in another fight concerning labour, back in New England.

Flat-decked, three-masted, square-rigged, and built in New Bedford in 1794, the *Tryal* was purchased by the Nantucket Quakers Paul Gardner Jr., Thomas Starbuck, Moses Mitchell, and Thomas Coffin Jr. in early 1801. The four men might have intended to use the vessel for sealing, as they told its crew, yet by the time the ship left Woods Hole on the first day of March 1801, with Coffin at the helm, it had been refitted with secret holds and false-bottom crates.

Coffin arrived at Más Afuera in December, planning to use the island as cover to make quick runs of contraband cargo, including cigars, guns, and textiles, into Valparaiso. It was a dangerous business. Spanish officials might be tolerant in general, but their tolerance could quickly disappear with shifting wartime alliances, as Madrid broke with London to join Paris or argued with Washington over tariffs. In one swoop, a Spanish man-of-war could descend on an island, confiscate skins, embargo and auction ships, along with the personal belongings of the crew, and imprison sailors and officers.

That's what happened to Valentine Swain's brother, Uriah, who was also a Quaker.* Caught with $2,000 worth of banned luxury goods in his schooner *Mars*, his men were sent to Lima, where they were 'robbed, plundered, and put into prison.' And that's what happened to Thomas Coffin when, in June 1802, the *Tryal* was seized by the Spaniards in Valparaiso and its voyage ended.[1]

Crossing the Andes, travelling through Brazil, and then catching a ship north, Thomas Coffin took three years to make it back to Nantucket. He arrived home just in time to learn that he along with the other three owners of the *Tryal* were being sued for 'deceit.'

The plaintiffs claimed to be the masters of James Mye, a young cabin boy who had shipped out on the *Tryal* in 1801. Half African American and half Wampanoag, Mye was born in Mashpee, a 'praying village'—as the Puritans called their Indian reservations—that had been settled at the base of Cape Cod.[2]

Before the arrival of Europeans in the early 1600s, the Wampanoag, an Algonquin-speaking people, numbered many thousands and lived throughout southern New England, including on Martha's Vineyard, Nantucket, and eastern Long Island. Even before the establishment of Plymouth Bay Colony, epidemics, brought by Europeans, had devastated the population. Settlers took Wampanoags as slaves, using them as servants and labourers or trading them to the Spanish and French in the West Indies for goods or African slaves. By the early 1800s, the Wampanoag had almost disappeared. Only about sixty families were left in Mashpee, which survived largely due to the arrival of a number of free or escaped 'foreign-Negros and Molatoes' from points south. 'Too many Negroes,' reported an 1800 census of the town, 'have mixt with these people.'[3]

---

* Quakers prohibited 'fraudulent' commerce, but the sanction was hard to maintain since they tended to abhor 'any restrictions on their ability to trade' and were 'ambivalent about any authority except their own.' Trade was a moral imperative that transcended politics, and Europe's revolutionary wars only made their 'inner light,' like the *fuero interno* of Río de la Plata merchants, that much stronger.

The Wampanoag in Mashpee had tried to get by picking wild fruit, catching clams, and making brooms to sell on Martha's Vineyard and Nantucket. This commerce wasn't enough to live on in a world where cash and credit ruled. More and more Wampanoag took advances from local merchants. Ever deeper in debt, men signed on to whaling ships to pay off their mounting loans. 'An Indian having gotten into debt obliges himself,' wrote one minister in the mid-1700s, 'to go a whaling till he pays.'*

Many, though, found their debt actually increased on long voyages, built up by their 'buying' tobacco and other goods from the ship's slop chest during the voyage. The obligations would pass on to their children, who then too would be 'bound to serve.' 'Children were sold or bound as security for the payment of their fathers' debts as soon as they were seven or eight years old. . . . These Indians and their children were transferred from one to another master like slaves,' said one observer in 1758. 'Every Indian had his master.'[4]

During the colonial period, just prior to the American Revolution, London granted Wampanoag villages like Mashpee some autonomy. Yet granting nominal freedom to a subjugated people trapped in debt bondage just led to more subjugation: the only thing the Wampanoag were truly free to do was take on more debt, to bind themselves or their children to merchants, artisans, and whalers. Then, after the revolution, the Commonwealth of Massachusetts imposed a 'guardian system' on Mashpee, supposedly to protect its residents from falling 'very easy prey' to creditors who plied 'them with spirituous liquor.' But this reform also worked to institutionalize bondage, giving a board of white 'guardians' nearly unlimited power to administer village affairs, including authorizing all debt, indenture, apprentice, and other labour contracts.

Under this new system, when a Nantucket ship owner wanted a Mashpee Wampanoag for a whaling or sealing crew, he made his request to the Mashpee guardians. When indebted families signed over their

---

* In *Moby-Dick*, Tashtego, a Wampanoag from Nantucket, is a skilled harpooner. Some Wampanoag, like Amos Haskins, who became master of the whaler *Massasoit*, might sail as skilled hands or officers, but most Native Americans were low-share deckhands. The 'captaincies and mateships were the "exclusive preserve" of white Nantucketers.'

young children to white masters, they needed the approval of the guardians. When masters willed their apprentices to their children or when they sold their indentures to another master, the guardians had to give their permission. And when masters bound out their apprentices on whaling or sealing ships, with the expectation they would turn over half of their shares when the voyage was complete, they required the authorization of the guardians.

That's how James Mye wound up on the *Tryal*. Two Mashpee guardians, Joseph Nye and David Parker, both direct descendants of *Mayflower* Pilgrims, 'did bind out' the boy to one Joshua Hall. On Hall's death, Mye's indenture passed to Hall's two sons, Stephen and Joshua, who in turn 'bound out' Mye to Thomas Coffin, for a period of five years.

Stephen and Joshua Hall wanted their share of what they thought Mye was owed for his time on the *Tryal*, had the ship done what its owners said it would do: go sealing. In exchange for his labour, Mye was to receive 'a one-hundredth part of the produce of all the skins'—a 'proportion' of which was to be paid to the Hall brothers. Instead, Coffin and his associates used their ship to 'deceive, disappoint, wrong and defraud,' said plaintiffs, and as a result their enterprise was 'defeated, broken up, and lost, altogether.'[5]

Barnstable County's Court of Common Pleas decided in favour of the Hall brothers, ordering the *Tryal*'s owners to pay the plaintiffs $100. But the Massachusetts Supreme Judicial Court overturned the decision on appeal.

The three-member higher court ruled that sons couldn't inherit indentures as if they were personal property. When the plaintiffs' counsel argued that the Mashpee guardians had verbally sanctioned the transfer, the justices unanimously held that an oral agreement wasn't enough 'to send a man round the globe and bring an action for his service.' The decision, in a sense, was based on a narrow reading of the law: it didn't challenge the legitimacy of Wampanoag guardianship or the practice of indenture, implying that had the guardians approved the transfer in writing the Halls would have been in their rights to send Mye wherever they wanted.

One of the judges did offer a more far-reaching opinion. Justice Simeon Strong argued that even if Mye had been bound to the Halls by a formal contract, the brothers still wouldn't have had the 'right to send him to the south-pole, to the end of the globe, in their service.' Strong also said that Mye himself couldn't, even if he wanted to, agree to such an arrangement, since he was a young boy with 'no will of his own.' Strong here was clearly defining labour as something that required wilful, rational consent.

Hall et al. v. Gardner et al. was an early precedent in a growing body of case law that helped move America away from apprenticeships and indentures, which tied workers in various ways to their place and person of employ, toward modern notions of free labour. In the decades before the Civil War, lawyers cited the case to reform child indenture, to limit the 'boundless license' of masters to send their apprentices and indentured workers wherever they wanted, and to rein in third-party 'brokers' who in some states acted much like slavers, carrying out a 'lively trade in apprentices well into the nineteenth century.'[6]

The case was even cited at least twice by Hawaiian lawyers after the Civil War to restrict the near-absolute power of plantations over indentured migrant workers. In 1870, for example, attorney W. C. Jones used it in his successful bid to free Gip Ah Chan from prison. Chan had left China five years earlier on the ship *Matador*, part of a fleet that since 1849 had been carrying tens of thousands of 'coolie' labourers to Peru. This time the *Matador* sailed to Hilo, Hawaii. During the voyage, representatives of a plantation owned by Theodore Metcalf 'thrust' a half-Spanish, half-English contract at Chan, who, though he couldn't understand its contents, had no choice but to sign it.

In Hilo, Chan was put to work on Metcalf's sugar plantation. When Metcalf died shortly thereafter, Chan quit the plantation. In response, Metcalf's partners had local authorities arrest him for violating Hawaii's statute covering master-servant relations. They claimed that Chan's labour contract was still in force and that it had passed to them upon Metcalf's death. Chan's lawyer, Jones, cited, along with other precedents, *Hall et al. v. Gardner et al.* to argue the contrary, that contracts couldn't be bequeathed from one partner to another. The judge agreed with the defendant and freed Chan. At some point during the proceedings, Metcalf's associates had objected to accusations leveled by Jones that they had treated his client like a slave. There was, they said in their defence, 'nothing similar to chattel slavery in the prisoner's condition.' Chan was a free man who could stop working whenever he paid off his obligations. 'A slave,' in contrast, 'had no right to wife, child, or to anything on earth.'

'Slavery has grades,' Mr. Jones answered.[7]

As he was defending himself in court against the Hall brothers, Thomas Coffin continued efforts he had started in Chile to get his ship back, petitioning the US government to intervene on his behalf against Spain. He was too late. Spanish authorities had long since auctioned the *Tryal* off.[8]

The ship was purchased by José Ignacio Palacio, a wealthy Lima merchant who then sold it, on credit, to Benito Cerreño. Cerreño kept the vessel's English name and, even before Coffin arrived back in Nantucket, had started using it to run freight up and down the Spanish Main's Pacific coast, from Concepción in the south to Lima in the north and Valparaiso in between.[9]

A Merry Repast

During his Pacific voyages in the 1840s, Herman Melville visited many of the same places Amasa Delano had passed through four decades earlier, such as Lima and Más Afuera. At the Galapagos, both men were struck by the size and slowness of the islands' famous giant tortoises. The insistence of these animals on moving in a straight line no matter what immovable obstacle stood in their way seemed to awaken in the two men thoughts of destiny and free will.

After bringing a few of these enormous creatures on board his ship and observing their movements, Delano came to believe that they could 'easily be taught to go to any place on the deck.' The trick, he wrote, was to be found in 'whipping them with a small line when they are out of place, and to take them up and carry them to the place assigned for them; which being repeated a few times will bring them into the practice of going themselves, by being whipped when they are out of their place.'

Years later, in a series of sketches about the islands called *The Encantadas*, Melville's narrator also spends time considering their movements. 'There is something strangely self-condemned in the appearance of these creatures,' he says. 'Lasting sorrow and penal hopelessness are in no animal form so suppliantly expressed as in theirs.' It is as if some 'malignant, or perhaps a downright diabolical enchanter' had bestowed on them a 'crowning curse': a 'drudging impulse to straightforwardness in a belittered world.'

Melville then relates a common sailor superstition regarding the animals. 'All wicked sea-officers,' especially captains and commodores, 'are at death transformed into tortoises' and sentenced to long, lonely lives walking across barren, solitary islands—much like the castaways, left-behinds, and runaways tormented by shipmasters like George Howe.

Then, as if to underscore Melville's own tortoiselike faith in cosmic reason—his hope that, despite living in a world littered with evidence proving otherwise, things that go round will come round—he has his narrator sit down with his shipmates and make 'a merry repast from tortoise steaks and tortoise stews.' The reincarnated becomes the digested.[1]

PART V

IF GOD WILLS

Therein come down the Angels.

—THE QUR'AN, 97:4

17

NIGHT OF POWER

It was a coincidence, and a bad one for Alejandro de Aranda. In 1804, Ramadan, the holiest month of the Islamic lunar calendar, fell just before he began to move his slaves over the high Andes. Islam is a prophetic religion, like Christianity and Judaism. It promises deliverance from earthly pain. Even more so does Sufism—the kind of Islam found in the part of West Africa where Babo, Mori, and the others were captured—which charges the faith's already powerful universalism with a potent mysticism.

Mystics often describe their efforts to become one with the absolute as a journey 'upward and outward.' 'The road on which we enter is a royal road which leads to Heaven,' wrote Saint Teresa. 'We ascend,' said Saint Augustine. Islam, too, uses the metaphor of journeying to imagine an individual's approach to God, enacted in the obligation of Muslims to visit Mecca once in their lives. Sufism especially associates religious faith with a quest. The 'Sufi who sets out to seek God calls himself a "traveller" (*salik*), he advances by slow "stages" (*maqamat*) along a path (*tariqat*) to the goal of union with reality.' Islamic mysticism is popularly associated with dervishes whirling in an effort to achieve self-annihilation. But in West Africa, Sufism also has a strong quietist tradition that encourages a contemplative submission of one's interior self to divine will. The British anthropologist Edward Evans-Pritchard, based on fieldwork he conducted in the 1920s among the Azande people in southern Sudan, writes that the aim of Sufism is to transcend the senses to the point where there is 'no longer a duality of "God" and "I," but there is only "God."' West African Muslims did this through asceticism, contemplation, and prayers until a 'state of ecstasy' took over the soul, freeing the believer from his or her 'bodily prison.'[1]

Whichever of these traditions Babo and the other Muslims among Aranda's captives were part of, their climb up the Andean slave road—where years later Darwin would notice how the extreme clarity of the air distorted perspective—collapsed their physical and spiritual worlds into each other. Christians who willingly made the journey described the climb in mystical terms. 'A very extraordinary effect is often produced on the mind,' wrote one early nineteenth-century traveller of his experience approaching the summit, making him feel a 'strong vibration,' as if his whole being was 'harmonizing' with the universe. 'It seems as if crowds of ideas were dancing in the mind, with associations so rapid and figures so intricate, that I could not make any of the performances out: something like a cadenced shake alone was sensible.' Such a feeling of disorientation must have been even stronger for those force-marched up the mountain pass.

In the evening, after their daily ascent, or in the morning before starting out, or maybe during short breaks along the path, the West Africans might have been ignored by their handlers long enough that they could face east and pray. But the extreme conditions of the climb would have made it hard to wash themselves and probably impossible for them to fast, adding to the intensity of their journey. As did the fact that they were moving west, not east, away from Mecca. The cold was extreme, sparks might have flown from their clothes, and the radiance of the moon, the movement of which told them it was Ramadan, was unlike anything they had seen before. What was routine fearfulness for those used to the heights would have been an all-consuming anguish for a people coming from a land of grassy flats, having just survived a two-month ocean voyage only to be forced on a nearly equally long trek over the pampas. Probably not all of Aranda's captives were Muslim. But their extreme experience might have allowed those among them, like Babo and Mori, who could make prophetic sense of their journey, who could use the moon and the stars not just to explain their movements but to promise deliverance from their sufferings, to rise as leaders. Among West African Muslims there is a belief that the hardship of travelling by foot on pilgrimages to Mecca helped fortify spiritual powers that could be used to defeat evil spirits, or jinns, that might be encountered along the way.[2]

It was worse luck for Aranda that once in the port town of Valparaiso he didn't have to wait to embark his cargo. The schooner *Tryal* was already there in the harbour, loaded with cargo from southern Chile, including wheat, cypress and pine timber, butter, cheese, casks of lard and wine, and biscuits, bound for Lima, where Aranda had planned to sell his slaves. They were able to board quickly, just before the ship hauled anchor, which meant they would be on the high seas for Laylat al-Qadr, translated as the Night of Power or the Night of Destiny. Every year Muslims celebrate this day, which falls at the end of Ramadan, when the angel Gabriel appeared to Mohammed, a reminder of Allah's promise to deliver the faithful from history's suffering. The promise is told in the Qur'an: 'The Night of Power is better than a thousand months. Therein come down the Angels. . . . Peace! . . . This until the rise of morn!'[3]

Early on the eve of Laylat al-Qadr, three hours before sunrise and five days after setting sail from Valparaiso on December 22, the West Africans rose up and took control of the *Tryal*. The ship's cargo hold was full; as a result, the slaves had been sleeping on deck amidships since leaving port, guarded by a night watch but unshackled. Aranda, mistaking exhaustion and emaciation for docility, told Cerreño that they were 'tractable.' At this point, there were seventy-two slaves in the shipment, eight more than Aranda had purchased from Nonell eight months earlier. The additions might have been the infants that were occasionally mentioned in Spanish documents, born along the way. Or perhaps Aranda purchased them from other sources. The records don't say.*

---

* Spanish documents related to the event report seventy-two slaves were on board the *Tryal* but give inconsistent information regarding their breakdown by age, gender, and origin. The following is an approximation: thirty-two men from Africa (twelve of whom were specifically identified as coming from Senegal), three other men (perhaps men not in Aranda's shipment who joined the rebels), twenty-eight African women, and eleven 'suckling babies' of both sexes. Twenty of the men were twelve to sixteen years old; twelve were between twenty-five and fifty.

Most of the ship's thirty or so hands also slept on deck, in a make-shift canvas tent pitched off of the foremast. What was the *Tryal*'s bunk room in the bow of the ship, the forecastle, had been converted into quarters for Aranda and his travelling entourage, six people, including three clerks, a cousin from Spain, and his brother-in-law. At least three other slaves were on board the vessel, and they had, a few days before the revolt, begun to conspire with the West Africans.

Two of them, José and Francisco, were Aranda's servants. Islam was a strong bond, yet slavery forged other kinds of alliances. The nineteen-year-old José was from Africa. He had been purchased by Aranda six years earlier and might have spoken the West Africans' language. Prior to the revolt, the ship's pilot caught him several times 'having secret conversations' with Mori and chased him away. The mulatto Francisco, born in Buenos Aires and with Aranda for most of his life, probably spoke only Spanish.

The third slave who joined the West Africans was Joaquín, the ship's thirty-five-year-old caulker, one of the many 'people of colour' (the term is associated with late-twentieth-century racial politics yet it was commonly used in colonial Spanish America in the early 1800s) who worked as tars, carpenters, blacksmiths, and shipwrights, a corps of free and enslaved labourers who kept the Spanish Pacific maritime fleet running. Joaquín was described as a Christian who had 'lived many years among the Spaniards.' Later, in his testimony, Benito Cerreño said he was *de los más malos*—'among the worst' of the rebels when it came to murdering Spaniards.[4]

At around three o'clock on the morning of the revolt, about thirty West Africans moved quietly toward the bow, led by Babo and Mori and armed with knives and axes secreted for them by José and Joaquín. For some of the men—the ones who had come to America on the *Neptune* and been transferred to the *Santa Eulalia*—this would be their third bid to free themselves. They first attacked the ship's carpenter and boatswain, who were on watch but had fallen asleep, wounding them badly. The insurgents then fell on the other sailors. Left behind around the mainmast, the West African women, even before the men overcame the guards, had begun to sing softly, their sound muffled by the waves. When the first scream broke the night, their voices grew louder, letting out a 'melancholic' dirge, a murderous sadness that was meant to give the men courage to kill.

What were they singing? They might have been reciting lines from the Qur'an. It was more common for men to memorize verses from the holy book through rhythmic chanting, but throughout West Africa, select women also participated in qur'anic studies. Or it might have been a praise song or call to war, one of many such songs and poems that made up West Africa's extensive musical repertoire. Whatever it was, one thing is certain: it added to the terror that the *Tryal*'s sailors felt as they succumbed to the slaves' assault. Spaniards generally thought African music was, as one observer wrote in the 1770s, 'the most barbaric and grotesque thing imaginable.' Slaves fashioned percussion instruments out of anything they could, including jawbones of asses, which when beaten made a rasping sound that Spaniards found particularly unnerving: their 'song is like a howl' and their 'dances call to mind rituals that witches perform for the Devil on their Sabbaths.'[5]

The rebels executed eighteen sailors, stabbing and hacking some to death and throwing others overboard. Three or four crew members managed to break away and hide. Seven begged for their lives and were spared.

The West Africans then took control of the ship's cockpit and three hatchways, tying the hands of their captives behind their backs and forcing them down the ladder of the middle hatch to the cargo hold. A few of the ship's hands had been belowdecks when the fighting started. When they tried to come up the forward hatch, the rebels drove them back into the forecastle with the ship's passengers, including Aranda.

The aft hatch led to the captain's quarters. Benito Cerreño was twenty-nine years old, thin and tall for his time. He was born in Calañas, Spain, a small orchard and goat town outside of Seville, into a gentry family that had begun to come apart as agricultural prices in Spain steadily declined throughout the late 1700s. Cerreño arrived in Lima in the first years of the 1800s, probably on a ship owned by his future father-in-law, Raymundo Murre, whose fleet included a number of cargo vessels that ran up and down the Pacific coast. It was through Murre's contacts that Cerreño financed his purchase of the *Tryal*.[6]

Like Aranda, Cerreño was using the expansion of Spanish American commerce to try to escape his family's downward fall—not with slavery but with shipping, an industry that grew in tandem with slavery. When Spain began liberalizing commerce, it allowed its American colonies to trade among themselves. Chilean merchants, for instance, wanted to sell their wheat and wine to Peru and other northern ports, and when they were permitted to do so, a vibrant merchant marine, run out of Lima, began to take shape. And though Cerreño wasn't a slaver and the *Tryal* wasn't a 'slave ship,' his trade's success depended on carrying slave-produced goods as well as, occasionally, slaves.

Cerreño was asleep when the revolt began but awoke to the noise and quickly realized the seriousness of the situation. Armed with two pistols and a musket he kept in his quarters, he moved into the passageway between his cabin and the main cargo hold, where the hatch ladder descended. He stayed there through the night, keeping the West Africans from either climbing down or coming through the hold's bulkhead door. The standoff ended at dawn, when Babo ordered three prisoners be brought to him. Without giving the Spanish captain an ultimatum, he had them thrown overboard, bound but not gagged, so their screams could be heard. Cerreño surrendered.

When he'd gone below to sleep the night before, the slaves, if Cerreño noticed them, had been heaped around the mainsail. Now he came out into the morning light of a different world.

The *Tryal* was seventy-five feet long and a bit less than a third that wide. Its stern was square and, with neither figurehead nor billethead, its prow was blunt and unadorned. Save for the masts, riggings, wheelhouse, and hatchway coamings, the *Tryal*'s top deck was flush and unbroken from stern to stem, almost like a barge, or a stage, allowing an open view to a new scene: everywhere Cerreño looked, there were West Africans, armed and in charge.

Mori spoke Spanish and he interpreted for his father, Babo. One of the first things the West African asked Cerreño was if there were any 'lands of black people in these seas where they could be taken.'

No, Cerreño said.

———

African captives being rowed to a slave ship anchored at Bonny.

A rendering of the hold of a Brazilian slave ship, by the Bavarian painter Johann Moritz Rugendas, c. 1827. One enslaved African stretches to raise a water bowl through the hatch while a group of sailors remove a corpse. Rugendas noted in the text accompanying this painting that lack of water was the main cause of both death and revolt among captive Africans.

Slaves in South America were involved in every aspect of economic life, as producers and consumers. The bottom image is of a group of shackled slaves, some of them wearing turbans, forming a queue to buy tobacco in Rio de Janeiro.

Amasa Delano in 1816.

The two-masted *Perseverance* displaying its banner, pennant, and flag.

Pampas wagons were called *buques,* or boats. Photograph by Samuel Boote, c. 1885.

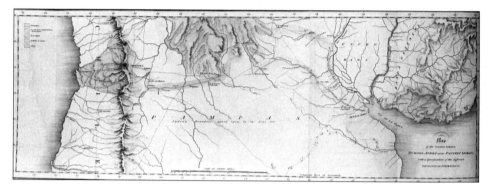

Map of the country between Buenos Aires and the Pacific Ocean, c. 1885.

Crossing the Andes from Mendoza. This drawing illustrates Charles Darwin, *Journal of Researches.*

A successful rancher and slaver, Juan Nonell sat for this portrait in the 1830s, more than twenty-five years after selling Babo, Mori, and the rest of the West Africans to Alejandro de Aranda.

Babo, Mori, and the other West Africans travelled along this road to Valparaiso before being boarded on the *Tryal*.

'It was too much like hitting a man when he is down': the technique of killing seals had not changed much between Amasa Delano's time and the late nineteenth century, when this illustration was done.

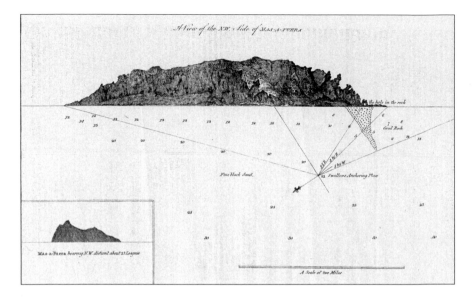

Herman Melville said Más Afuera looked like a 'vast iceberg drifting in tremendous poise. Its sides are split with dark cavernous recesses, as an old cathedral with its gloomy lateral chapels.'

This painting is of the square-sterned, flush-decked *Ann Alexander*, a ship that resembled the *Tryal*.

A West African Mandinka marabout.

Map of Santa María Island, 1804. The *Perseverance* met the *Tryal* in the island's leeward bay, to the left of the sandbar.

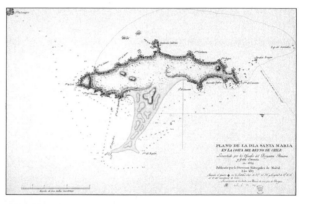

A wood engraving by Garrick Palmer from an illustrated edition of Melville's *Benito Cereno*: Amasa's boat approaching the Spanish ship.

Seal blubber is tendinous, so superb steel was used in the blades of skinning knives, like the kind used to disembowel and flay the *Tryal* rebels. Delano said that his were 'always kept exceedingly sharp and as bright as a gentleman's sword.' This knife, found in the New Bedford Whaling Museum, is five inches wide and forty-eight inches long. Note the knot work, which was needed to keep hands from sliding down the oily handle onto the double-edged blade.

Talcahuano viewed from the sea in 1793.

Concepción's finest families would have turned out to view the hanging of the leaders of the *Tryal*'s rebellion wearing their best dress.

He was lying. It was inconceivable that a man of Cerreño's class, skin colour, origin, and occupation didn't know that early the year before, in 1804, Haiti had declared its independence, establishing the second republic in the Americas.

The revolt had started in 1791 and the wars that followed had lasted more than a decade. The fight to end slavery on one of the world's most profitable slave islands had repercussions that were felt across the Atlantic world, from Montevideo, where a group of runaway slaves set up a short-lived Republic of Liberty, Fraternity, and Equality, to the Hudson Valley, where in 1793 slaves said to be inspired by Haiti started a series of fires (first in the barn of Herman Melville's great-uncle Leonard Gansevoort, then another in the stables of his grandfather Peter Gansevoort) that nearly destroyed Albany. Reports of the Revolution, rumours, including eyewitness testimony, songs, poetry, and slogans, ran through the Americas, carried by sailors from port to port.[7]

Consider this Victor Hugo–like image: In 1797, six years after the start of the Revolution, in the middle of the night on a bridge in La Guaira, a harbour town on Venezuela's Caribbean coast a short sail from Haiti, a young mulatto slave boy named Josef strolls out of the misty darkness singing in French. Alarmed authorities take him into custody and, in an effort to learn the lyrics, demand that he continue singing. Josef does, and, according to the historian Cristina Soriano, who found the transcript of the interrogation in the Venezuelan archives, every song has the same chorus: 'Long live the republic, long live liberty, long live equality.'[8]

It is also unlikely that some of the West Africans on the *Tryal* didn't know of Haiti, either from the time they spent in the harbours and holding corrals of Buenos Aires and Montevideo or on Citizen Mordeille's corsair ship, where French sailors had to have been talking about Napoleon Bonaparte's failure to restore slavery on the island. In 1801, Bonaparte sent fourteen generals and twenty thousand troops to the island. Less than three years later, they were gone, vanquished by rebels and disease, and the free republic of Haiti was proclaimed. Haiti had become a refuge for 'foreigners of colour' seeking freedom; black Haitian privateers stopped at least one slave ship bound for Cuba, 'declaring their intention to take the captives to Saint-Domingue so that they "might enjoy their freedom in the land of liberty."' Ada Ferrer, who has studied the influence of the Haitian Revolution in the broad Atlantic world, writes that after declaring independence the new nation's 'leaders made it increasingly clear that the "land of liberty" referred to Haiti and not to France.'[9]

Cerreño told the West Africans that no such place existed. After a long conference among themselves, the slaves demanded to be taken either to Senegal or to São Nicolau (San Nicolás, in Spanish), an island in the Cape Verde archipelago off the coast of Senegal.

Cerreño said it was too far a sail and his ship wouldn't make it in its condition. The rebels said they would do anything he required in terms of rationing food and water but they would kill him if he didn't return them to Africa.

Cerreño relented, but since the West Africans didn't know whether the passage back to the Atlantic was to the north or to the south, he continued sailing north to Lima. Mori told him he would die if they spotted any town or settlement, so the Spaniard stayed far off shore, away from coastal towns, even as he scanned the horizon hoping for a Spanish or foreign ship.

The West Africans held what Cerreño later described as 'daily conferences' early every morning to decide their course of action, a ritual that might have included prayers. After the uprising, many of the rebels had discarded their filthy, threadbare clothes, replacing them with tunics cut out of canvas the ship had in stock, and tied with rope belts strapped around their waists. With each passing day, they were, Cerreño said, becoming more 'restless' and 'mutinous,' anxious to feel that they were making progress home.

As they approached Callao, Lima's port town, Cerreño grew nervous that the West Africans would see the city's lights, so he turned the ship around and headed south. He didn't have a plan but settled on the idea of sailing past Valparaiso to the uninhabited island of Santa María, which was often used as a safe harbour by sealers and whalers. With luck, he might be able to quietly come upon another vessel. At least his ship would be able to replenish its water casks out of sight of a town.

On January 16, a few days after changing directions and about three weeks after the West Africans had taken over the ship, they decided in their morning meeting that they had to kill Alejandro de Aranda. There are other cases of slave ship rebels singling out their owners for execution. In 1786, on the Danish slaver *Christiansborg* sailing from Africa's Gold Coast, insurgents dragged Paul Erdmann Isert, who was travelling as a passenger to the Caribbean, to the bow, and slashed his face with a razor, barely missing his temple artery. Isert later learned that the rebels tried to kill him because they thought that, as one of the last white people to board the ship, he was their 'owner' and 'that it would be best to send me into the other world first, after which the Europeans, like mercenaries, would surrender all the sooner.' In that case, the West African slaves seemed to have imagined slavery as a unified, hierarchical institution, headed by one man. Kill the leader and his slaves would be set free.[10]

On the *Tryal*, the decision to execute Aranda was also calculated. Mori told Cerreño that he and the others had to kill Aranda—not for revenge or to administer justice but to secure their freedom. But it is hard to say what exactly the calculation was. Generally, in West African Islamic law, killing one's owner was not a legitimate means for gaining freedom from slavery (we don't know if the West Africans on board the *Christiansborg* were Muslim or not). Moreover, Babo, Mori, and their companions couldn't have thought that simply killing Aranda would result in their freedom. Over the course of more than a year, they had been passed from one master to another, one driver to another, and they would have seen that American slavery was extremely decentralized, entailing many different venues—ships, wagons, holding pens—run by a varied cast of captains, sailors, teamsters, and jailers. The fact that they repeatedly warned Cerreño to avoid other ships indicates that they knew that if they were discovered and subdued they would be returned to captivity, whether Aranda was alive or not. Maybe they thought they had to kill Aranda to make sure he wouldn't reclaim them as property in the event they did make it to Senegal or Cape Verde. Yet that wouldn't explain the sudden sense of urgency.[11]

Cerreño said later that he tried to stop the execution. Mori told him they would kill all the Spaniards and *Tryal* sailors if he interfered. '*La cosa no tenía remedio*,' Mori said—literally, *the thing had no remedy*, or, more loosely, *there was no option*, or *there was no other way*.

The words come to us from Cerreño's testimony and might only be conveying the fatalism often associated with Catholicism, heightened, in this case, by a harrowing ordeal. But Islam, too, has its fatalistic dimension. Like Christianity, it wrestles with the idea of free will, trying to understand the role that human action plays in a universe where a sovereign God determines all things.

Three weeks had passed since the revolt, restoring to the West Africans what their forced voyage across the Atlantic and America had nearly taken from them: their sense of time as the ordering of meaningful activity. For over a year, from one Ramadan to another, they had fought off their powerlessness by counting the months of the Islamic calendar, fulfilling, by sheer force of intellect and resolve, the Qur'an's promise of deliverance, when God would intervene in history: 'Therein come down the Angels.' They had risen up and seized the ship. But now the new moon of Eid had passed, and though life was hardly normal, another cycle had started.

Having taken control of their destiny, the rebels now found themselves lost in a strange sea on a meandering ship with dwindling supplies, perhaps trying to reconcile their belief that history was guided by some unknowable combination of free will and divine providence with the fear that they were drifting aimlessly, that the power to control the circumstances of their lives was again slipping out of their hands.

January nights in the South Pacific near the coast of Peru and Chile are extremely clear. The new masters of the *Tryal* would have been sailing under a firmament of stars and a low summer moon, settling on the idea that Aranda had to die immediately for them to keep the power they had so audaciously seized. As Mori told Cerreño, there was 'no other way.'

Just after dawn, Mori ordered Matunqui and Liché to bring Aranda on deck. They entered the forecastle, where Aranda had been confined since the uprising, with their knives drawn. Aranda was asleep in his bunk. His executioners raised their weapons and brought them down into the slaver's chest. Aranda's clerk Lorenzo Bargas was in the adjoining berth. Opening his eyes to see black arms and slashing daggers and feeling Aranda's warm blood spray his face, he threw himself out a porthole into the sea to drown.

Aranda was dragged on deck half dead and the women again began to sing a dirge urging the men to finish the deed. Matunqui and Liché tied Aranda's hands behind his back and, lifting his body by his head and legs, threw him into the sea. The rebels then did the same to Aranda's brother-in-law, Francisco Maza, and his other two clerks and, perhaps looking to save water and food, a number of sailors who were wounded during the uprising. The *Tryal*'s boatswain, Juan Robles, was a strong swimmer and he kept himself the longest above the waves, saying acts of contrition that could be heard on the deck of the ship as he drifted away, his last faint words begging Benito Cerreño to sponsor a mass in the name of Our Lady of Succour to save his soul.

When the killing ended, Mori turned to Cerreño and said, 'All is done.' He then threatened to kill the rest of the prisoners if the captain continued to stall in delivering the West Africans to Senegal.

Mori repeated the threat for the next two days. On the third day, he, Babo, and Atufal approached Cerreño and proposed signing 'a paper.' The West Africans had drawn up what in essence was a contract, perhaps in Arabic, whereby Cerreño would take them home and they, in exchange, would return the ship and its cargo once they reached their destination. 'Even though they were raw and from Africa,' Cerreño later said, 'they knew how to write in their language.' The three men signed the document, and with that, Cerreño testified, the West Africans were 'satisfied and appeased.'

18

THE STORY OF THE *SAN JUAN*

The odds were long that Babo, Mori, and the others would have been able to take the *Tryal* through the straits or round the treacherous Cape Horn into the Southern Ocean and across the Atlantic to Senegal. But it was not impossible. Just four years earlier, a group of Muslim slaves on a Spanish ship called the *San Juan Nepomuceno* had managed to complete a voyage nearly as audacious, carrying out perhaps the greatest escape in the history of New World slavery.

Built in Guayaquil, Ecuador, by free and enslaved people of colour, the *San Juan*, which also sailed under the name *God's Blessing*, was a fine display of Spanish American ship craft, displacing over a thousand tons of water and mounting thirty cannons. When it set out for Lima from Montevideo at the end of 1800, it carried ninety sailors, including its Basque captain, Anselmo Ollague, and between sixty-five and seventy slaves, mostly 'Negros and Moors from Senegal' who had been brought into Montevideo on another ship. The vessel was loaded with more than a quarter of a million pesos' worth of merchandise, including beeswax, oil, ivory combs, ribbons, glass windows, silver watches, silk handkerchiefs, cashmere wool, English sheets, floral cotton prints, bolts of muslin, 'finely worked cowbells,' vials of mercury, leather shoes, silk, hats, gold chains, and silver crosses. Nearly the whole lot, including the Africans, belonged to one man, the ship's owner, Ignacio Santiago de Rotalde, proprietor of the biggest commercial house in Lima and a member of one of the twenty richest families in Spain.[1]

The uprising took place about a week out of port, as the ship was nearing the Cape. The captain and officers were asleep in their bunks for their midday rest and the remainder of the crew members were in the fore of the ship with their guard down. The revolt was led not by one of the West Africans but by a thirty-year-old slave named Antonio, described as a determined and desperate fellow who had once worked as a ship carpenter but had run away from his master. Apparently he had been captured and was included among the other slaves to be sold.

Having come into possession of the ship's weapons, the slaves divided into two groups, one moving on the officer's quarters, the other advancing to the bow. Four officers were killed and the captain was fatally wounded, cut with a saber across the neck and stabbed with a knife in his side. The next day, Antonio, now in charge of the ship, transferred the dying Captain Ollague and twenty-four sailors to a small Spanish ship that the *San Juan* had come upon. Antonio then ordered the first officer, José de Riti, and the remaining crew to sail to Senegal.

Riti did what other Europeans in similar situations, including Benito Cerreño four years later, often did: he went one way but told the Africans he was going another. In this case, rather than sailing east, to Africa, Riti tried to make it northeast, to Brazil. The currents, though, in the part of the South Atlantic where the *San Juan* sailed are difficult to navigate, flowing mostly south and east—that is, away from Brazil. Riti had to both tack against the stream and conceal his true direction from Antonio and the others, probably sailing one way during the day and another at night. Unable to keep his bearings, he drifted deeper and deeper into the middle Atlantic.

Weeks turned into months. The ship had plenty of food—its holds were stocked with fifteen hundred eggs, five casks of lard, twenty-five barrels of bacon, ham, bread, wheat, beans, lentils, butter, cheese, vegetables, twenty-two quadrupeds (goats? pigs? cows?), and three hundred chickens, as well as delicacies such as figs, chocolate, dried peaches, capers, cloves, cacao, grapes, pears, and wine. But its water supply dwindled. And what was left had become contaminated. Twenty-four of the rebels died of scurvy and dysentery. That no sailors succumbed suggests that the West Africans' immune systems had been weakened during the Middle Passage that brought them to Montevideo. Along the way, the *San Juan* crossed paths with two other ships, which the rebels scared off by firing their vessel's cannons.

The situation deteriorated, and the ship's caulker, an older African said to be from Senegal named Daure, began to challenge Antonio's command. As the voyagers grew desperate, Daure became more suspicious and erratic. Fearing for his life, Riti gave up zigzagging and sailed northeast. The *San Juan* eventually came on São Nicolau, one of the windward islands of the Cape Verde archipelago, then a Portuguese colony. Riti tricked Antonio into accompanying him and a contingent of Spanish sailors to shore to find water. The ruse led to the rebel leader's capture and the *San Juan*'s flight from the island under fire from pounding battery cannons. With Daure now in command, the ship arrived at French-run Saint-Louis, a port city near the mouth of the Senegal River, ten days later. The *San Juan* entered the harbour flying the Spanish flag and giving a customary eleven-gun salute, which was returned in welcome by a harbour cannon. Led by Daure, the rebels went ashore, delivered the ship to the island's French governor, and claimed their liberty.[2]

The fact alone that the rebels managed to reverse the Middle Passage is extraordinary. According to one study, 493 slave ship revolts took place between 1509 and 1869. The actual number is at least twice that, since many obscure uprisings, like those attempted on the *Neptune* and *Santa Eulalia*, aren't included in the tally. The vast majority were unsuccessful. As many as six thousand Africans might have died in these 493 cases, either killed in the revolts or executed following their suppression. Others committed suicide after their bid failed, as some of the slaves on the *Neptune* tried to do. Revolts that did lead to freedom tended to take place close to the shores of either Africa or America, where rebels could run the ship aground and escape.[3]

Mostly what constituted success was to capture and hold a ship for some time, establishing fleeting floating communities of free men and women until catastrophe struck, until they were recaptured or, adrift in the ocean, they ran out of food and water and slowly died. Some decided not to wait: in 1785, Africans who had taken a Dutch slaver chose death, according to one report, when it became clear they were about to be recaptured. They ignited the ship's powder magazine, blowing it to timbers and killing between two and five hundred insurgent slaves. The *San Juan* rebels, though, had crossed the entire Atlantic, surviving a five-month journey that included at least three armed skirmishes.[4]

They arrived at the perfect moment. For a very short time, January 1801 to July 1802, Saint-Louis was being run by a former French Catholic priest turned revolutionary, Aymar-Joseph-François Charbonnier, who seemed to be more committed to abolition than either his predecessor or successor. Citizen Charbonnier, apparently acting without consulting his superiors, and perhaps even against their wishes since the *San Juan* was a Spanish ship and France was allied with Spain, auctioned the ship and its merchandise, used the money to send its crew and passengers back to America, and let the rebel slaves go free. As to the ship, soon after its auction, a British corsair sailing off the island of Gorée burned it to the sea.[5]

Back in Spanish America, the viceroy of Peru, upon learning of the loss of the *San Juan Nepomuceno*, used the case to make a suggestion that colonial officials had been making for nearly three centuries: he urged the Crown to prohibit the importation of West African Muslims to the Americas. Slaves who followed the teaching of Mohammed 'spread very perverse ideas among their own kind,' he said, meaning Africans in general.

'And there are so many of them in this realm.'[6]

19

MOHAMMED'S CURSED SECT

The viceroy didn't say what he thought those 'perverse ideas' were. Rarely did Spanish bureaucrats and Catholic theologians go into details when they discussed the problem of Muslims in America. They didn't have to. Islam was too familiar, too deeply pressed into the very identity of the Spanish people, to need explaining. Everybody knew what they were talking about when they were talking about Islam. The long, long fight against the religion in Europe gave rise to many of the beliefs that Spaniards took with them when they crossed the ocean to found their empire in America, and it played a fundamental role in shaping the institution, slavery, that made that empire possible.

Spaniards called their war against Muslims on the Iberian Peninsula, starting in 722 and ending in 1492, the *reconquista*, or reconquest. The word is deceptive for it implies a return to the old and a restoration of what was. The fact is, prior to the arrival of Islam, Iberia was a fractious place of Visigoth wretchedness on the margins of Christendom. Al-Andalus, as Arab and Berber Muslims called the land, was the true restoration, returning a magnificence that had been absent since the time of the Romans. The peninsula, especially under the caliphate of Córdoba, became a centre of law, science, architecture, engineering, and literature—even Christians called its gardened, fountained, lit, and learned capital, the city of Córdoba, the world's 'brilliant ornament.' The *reconquista* created something new entirely: the Catholic kingdoms of Spain and Portugal.

It is easy to think of the *reconquista* as a bloody clash of civilizations, the western front of a wider struggle between a besieged Christian Europe and an expansionist Islam. A large part of the God-sanctioned absolutism we associate with medieval Catholicism and Islam was forged during this conflict. Yet 770 years is a long time, throughout which there were sustained periods of peace. Even during the war's most violent phases, Catholics and Muslims lived among each other, trading goods and establishing refuges of hospitality. Iberia during these eight centuries was a crucible where each of the world's three major one-God religions—Catholicism, Islam, and Judaism—shaped the others in ways subtle and obvious.

Anyone who travels today through modern Spain can see evidence of the obvious. It's there in the cool, clean mosquelike interiors of Catholic churches and of synagogues. It's present in the food, of course, and in the Spanish language. The farther back in time one goes reading Spanish the more cursive the calligraphy, until by the sixteenth century it is absolutely arabesque, its flourishes and curlicues binding the two bookish cultures together. The syntax and structure of Spanish derives from Latin. But hundreds of common words come from al-Andalus, many used to describe the most primal experiences of what it means to be human and live together in a society: of pleasure and food, law and authority, trade and taxes, and will, fate, and acceptance. As such, they have something to do with this story. That is, they have something to do with slavery.

Azúcar means sugar in Spanish and comes from the Arabic *sukkar*. Muslims introduced the sweetener to Europe and had begun to plant it in Spain in the late thirteenth century. The Portuguese and Spaniards took the crop first to the Atlantic islands, including the Azores and Madeira, and then to the plantations of the New World, which needed large numbers of slaves for cutting the cane and grinding the stalks into juice. If the West Africans on the *Neptune* had made it to the Caribbean, that's most likely what they would have been put to work doing. The Arabic-derived *aduana* means customs, while *alcabala* and *almojarifazgo* refer to taxes, words that Spaniards used in America to regulate the importation and sale of Africans, among other items. *Azotar*, to whip, also comes from Arabic and describes a common punishment Catholic and Islamic masters inflicted on slaves. *Ahorrar*—to accumulate wealth—and *ahorrarse*—to save one's self, including by saving enough money to purchase one's freedom—come from the Arabic words *hurr*, which signifies free, and *harra*, which means to liberate or emancipate oneself from servitude, to be free.[1]

Military conquests and pirate raids were the chief sources of slaves for Christians and Muslims alike. Yet before being considered true slaves, prisoners were often considered hostages, or *rehenes*—from the Arabic *raha'in*, meaning captives used as pledges or security. It was common for Catholics to ransom Arabs or Berbers, either to obtain gold or black slaves or to free Christian ones. Muslims did the same to free Arabs and Berbers taken by Catholics. *Mulato*, a Spanish word referring to a person of mixed European and African race, is related to the Arabic *mulo*, or mule, as well as *muxālatah*, which means a 'mixture of things or people of diverse kinds,' often of an illicit or forbidden nature. The obsolete *mujalata* meant business dealings between Muslims and non-Muslims, including slave trading.[2]

Beyond wealth, power, and social standing, Arabic loan words conjure up a fatalism associated with slave societies, feelings of destiny, doom, and luck—resignation, or not, to one's place in society. *Mezquino* means 'wretched,' a word often used to refer to enslaved peoples. The origin of *afán*, which in Spanish means 'zeal' or 'desire,' is more difficult to trace. According to one lexicographer, it might derive from Arabic words signifying grief or worry. It could also mean mystical extinction, a spiritual experience like what Mori, Babo, and their other Muslim companions might have felt as they began their Andean ascent at the beginning of Ramadan. *Ojalá* and *oxalá* are popular Spanish and Portuguese expressions. They originate from the Arabic *inshallah* and mean 'if God wills.'[3]

———

If centuries of fighting and living together created a shared culture—including a shared culture of slavery—it also hardened divisions, deepened fault lines, and bred fundamentalism. There's no one instance that can be singled out as a turning point, a moment when tolerance, at least in practice, gave way to absolutism. The Catholic *reconquista* of Iberia had long been considered a religious war, since it was fought between people of two different faiths. And after years of bloodshed, religious theorists of both the crusade and the jihad elaborated ever more complex theories of 'just war' and slavery, sanctioning the captivity of nonbelievers while forbidding the enslavement of the faithful.

But, importantly, Catholic theologians didn't argue that the goal of their *guerra buena*—good war—was the conversion of Muslims. Rather, they legitimated the *reconquista* as a just retaking of territory rightfully Christian (since the Visigoths had accepted Christ before the Arabs arrived).

The turn to empire was different. In 1492, the reconquest ended and the conquest began. In January, Catholic soldiers drove Muslims out of Granada, Europe's last Islamic stronghold. In April, Christopher Columbus sailed to America, shortly followed by ships full of warriors who imagined themselves extending a fight that had begun in Europe. 'With the completion of the conquest of the Moors, which lasted more than eight hundred years,' wrote one chronicler in 1552, 'the conquest of the Indians began.'*

Catholic theologians, however, couldn't justify waging war on Native Americans the same way they justified doing so on Muslims in Iberia, because Spain—or Portugal, in the case of Brazil—couldn't invoke a

---

* Hernán Cortes, Mexico's conqueror, called the sedentary Aztecs *moors*, while at least one priest thought the nomadic peoples who roamed the deserts of northern Mexico reminded him of *alárabes*, or Arabians. Spaniards used the word *mosque* to describe Aztec and Incan temples and believed Andean ritual baths and animal slaughtering practices to be suspiciously similar to Islamic rites. When royal officials arrived to survey Castile's new possessions, local bureaucrats welcomed them by staging reenactments in town plazas not of the conquest of the Americas but of the reconquest of Spain. And the saint the Spaniards picked to be the patron of America was Santiago Matamoros: Saint James the Moor Slayer. Columbus himself described his voyage as the next step in the struggle against the 'sect of Mohamet and of all idolatries and heresies,' even though one of the reasons he sailed west was to avoid Islam, to find a way to bypass Muslim control of trade routes to Asia.

historical claim to the land. And the fact that Native Americans, unlike Muslims, had never 'known' Christ and therefore had never had the opportunity to reject him took away another pretext to subjugate them. For Spain, these facts posed, as one historian writes, a 'legal and moral problem of enormous proportions,' for other European empires were challenging Iberia's exclusive dominion over the Americas ('I wish someone would show me the clause in Adam's will that disinherits me,' the Catholic king of France reportedly said when he heard that the pope had given the New World to the Spaniards and Portuguese).[4]

Spain began to advance a series of religious arguments to make its case, the fine points of which were dense but the thrust of which was clear: its monopoly right to America was defended as a spiritual mission to save Native American souls. In order for the justification to work, America had to be kept pure. The Inquisition worked to purge native heresies (including those practices that reminded Spaniards of Muslim rites) while royal officials banned Jews, Jewish converts to Christianity, Muslims, and Muslim converts (who numbered as many as 400,000 people in 1609, almost 5 percent of Spain's total population) from settling in the Americas.[5]

One of the first royal prohibitions of this kind was issued as early as 1501, less than a decade after Columbus set foot on Hispaniola. The Crown instructed its new governor of the Americas to carry out the 'conversion of the Indians to our holy Catholic faith' with 'great care':

> If you find persons suspect in matters of the faith present during the said conversion, it could create an impediment. Do not give consent or allow Muslims or Jews, heretics, anyone reconciled by the Inquisition, or persons newly converted to our Faith to pass, unless they are black slaves.[6]

Unless they are black slaves. There lay the problem, for slavery was the back door through which Islam came to America. Of the more than 123,000 slaves brought to the Americas between 1501 and 1575, over 100,000 were from the area surrounding the Senegal and Gambia Rivers. A majority were Wolof, Fulani, Walo, Mandinkas, or other groups found in West Africa. Which meant they included Muslims.

Brought by Arab and Berber merchants and clerics, Islam had spread among the people below the Sahara hundreds of years before the first slave ship sailed to America. It created a strange kind of continuity, for even as Iberian Catholics were purifying Europe of Islam, they began sailing to West Africa and finding 'Mohammed's cursed sect' spread far and wide among its black-skinned peoples. 'Jalofofs, Fulos, and Mandingas,' in particular, wrote a Spanish priest in the late 1500s, were 'infected with the wicked fungus of Mohammed' and 'professed the false doctrine of the Antichrist.'

Belief in the 'reality of Allah' and his 'inaccessible mystery,' as the Qur'an writes, took diverse forms in West Africa. On one end of the spectrum was a tolerant strand that existed peacefully with animists, even combining pre-Islamic practices with Islamic rites like divination and sorcery, that in theory should have been forbidden by qur'anic law. In this sense, Islam in West Africa, especially in rural areas, looked much like the fusion of Catholic saints and Native American gods that took root in much of Spanish America. The historian Lansiné Kapa writes that West African ancestor worship could exist side by side with Islamic monotheism, with 'lesser spirits' believed to derive their power from Allah. On the other end was a jihadist orthodoxy that waged war on both nonbelievers and apostates.[7]

In both cases, West African Islam was a creed with a strong egalitarian ethos and sense of justice. Its menace was that it challenged Catholicism on its own terms, with a universal monotheism and belief in a mysterious, unseeable, and eternal god.* Catholics had recognized the threat in Iberia, where its theologians often depicted Islam as a profane plagiarizer, perverting the true Church's rituals, vestments, and beliefs (like celebrating its weekly holy day on Friday—*viernes*, in Spanish—

---

* According to one Christian traveler among the Fulbe in the early 1800s, West African Muslims recognized the resemblance as well: there was 'a belief that Islam *is*, in fact, true and primitive Christianity as really taught by Christ and his Apostles,—reformed by Mohammed, with equal authority, from the corruptions which had by his time been introduced.'

rather than Sunday, even though, as one Catholic priest wrote, 'we know that Venus was a shameless whore').[8]

And they recognized the threat in West Africa. Speaking of black Muslims along the Gambia River system, a sixteenth-century Portuguese trader reported that their clerics 'count months as we do.' Like Catholicism, West African Islam was a literate religion. They 'write in bound books,' he continued, in which 'they tell many lies.' Like Catholics, they had a clergy, but their 'heathen priests go about looking thin and worn out by their abstinences, their fasts and their dieting, since they will not eat flesh of a creature killed by a person who is not one of them.' Their clerics wore robes, like Catholic priests, 'with large black and white hats.' And they practiced rites similar to the Holy Mass: 'They make their ritual prayers with the faces turned towards the East, and before doing this, first wash their nether parts and then their face. They recite their prayers all together, in a high voice noisily, like a group of clerics in choir, and at the end they finish with "Ala, Arabi."' And 'black ears . . . believe the lies.'[9]

Yet unlike the Latin Catholic Mass, the Word in West Africa wasn't just received. It was discussed in language the faithful could understand. Literacy and faith were intertwined. One eyewitness account written in 1608 by a Jesuit describes Mandinka Muslims establishing mosques and schools through West Africa where 'they teach reading and writing in the Arabic script.' Books were written out and bound in cities like Gao and Timbuktu or arrived from northern Africa and Arabia, brought by 'trading moors,' and included not just Qur'ans and qur'anic commentaries but scientific treatises and Arabic language versions of the Psalm of David, the Book of Isaiah, and the Pentateuch of Moses. By the late seventeenth century, Timbo, in the northern highlands of Guinea with a population of 10,000, was a respected centre of learning. 'Considerable attention,' wrote one American observer, 'is devoted to the acquirements of knowledge,' which included law, arithmetic, astronomy, and languages. It was mostly men who had the privilege of literacy, but not always. A slaver traveling through the region said that he often had seen elderly women 'at sunset reading the Koran.' Other travellers reported seeing girls learning to read.[10]

Teaching could be rote. Most young men 'had read the Qur'an several times and copied it at least once.' The learned son of the Islamic ruler of Fouta Djallon, Abd al-Rahman Ibrahima, captured and made a slave in 1788, was literate in both Arabic and Pular and educated in schools in Timbo, Djenné, and Timbuktu. He said that he wrote out his lessons 'forty-eight hours a day.'[11]

Yet even with all the rigidity that memorization through endless repetition entails, this combination of pedagogy and religious instruction could still be empowering, creating a common community of believers among diverse peoples. Unlike the Latin Catholic Mass, which awed the faithful from a distance, Islam in West Africa fused together received truth, participatory education, and historical experience, giving it a force that the Jesuit Alonso de Sandoval, writing in the early 1600s, described like this:

This language sounds like the speech of demons in hell. . . . In Guinea, the main priests of this cursed sect are Mandingas, who live along the Gambia River and inland more than five hundred leagues. They not only drink the poison of Mohammed's sect themselves but also take it to other nations. They bring it with their trade goods to many kingdoms. . . . These priests have mosques and a clerical hierarchy similar to our rankings of archbishops and bishops. They have schools where they teach the Arabic letters they use to write their scrolls. When the high-ranking clergy travel, they are received in different places as if they came from heaven. When they arrive in a new town, they announce the day when they will begin their sermons so that many people from all over the region will know to gather there at that time. They decorate a plaza and hang a few scrolls that seem to give their lies some authority. Then the priests stand and raise their hands and eyes to heaven. After a while, they prostrate themselves before the infernal writings and bow to them. After getting up, they give thanks to Allah and to his great prophet Mohammed, sent to pardon their sins. Then they praise the doctrine written on the scrolls and ask everyone to pay attention. No one speaks, sleeps, or lets their eyes wander for two hours as they read and discuss the writings. Orators praise their kings and lords, puffing up their vanity, as the priests speak of their victories and those of their ancestors. They mix many lies into their stories, degrading our holy faith and praising Mohammed's cursed sect, eloquently persuading the kings and everyone else to reject Christianity.*

Centuries later, in the early 1800s, a Protestant traveler among the Fulbe similarly observed the importance of education in Islam conversion. Poor and rural families, he said, would embrace Allah in order to secure an education for their children. 'The spread of Islam has been by

---

* This paragraph is from Sandoval's 1627 treatise on slavery, originally titled *De instauranda Aethiopum salute*. Sandoval based his book on years of firsthand fieldwork on Cartagena's waterfront, one of the first slave ports set up by Spain on the American mainland, into which came tens of thousands of West Africans. By the early 1600s, when Sandoval was active, the city counted over seven thousand Africans or African-descended inhabitants, more than twice the number of Europeans. To communicate in the over seventy African languages or dialects that existed in the city, Sandoval worked through interpreters or used the Afro-Spanish pidgin that had evolved with the slave trade. Among the information he gathered were slave impressions of the forced collective baptisms performed on them before they left Africa, where sailors would push the heads of the captured Africans into pots of water as priests chanted Latin prayers. Compared with how Muslim clerics spread their faith in the regions south of the Sahara, these mass baptisms would do little, in Sandoval's view, to endear Christianity to African slaves. Some thought they were being marked, that the oil would be squeezed from their bodies and they would be eaten. Others believed it was a hex, meant to prevent them from rebelling on the ship. Sometimes slaves were baptized and branded during the same ceremony, their flesh seared with an R topped by a crown, a royal seal. They might not have understood the meaning of the water, but the pain made its point. Sandoval was especially pessimistic about the conversion of Muslim Wolofs, Fulanis, and Mandinkas. Sandoval's history didn't question the legitimacy of slavery. 'Only God knows if these blacks are enslaved justly,' he wrote. But he did depict Africans as suffering humans with souls equal to those of whites. He was one of the first Europeans to describe in graphic, horrible detail the torment we today associate with the slave trade, a description even more exceptional since it was based on the testimony of the slaves themselves. Sandoval was especially critical of 'Christians' who 'punish their slaves more in a week than' Muslim slave masters 'do in a year.' The priest was also among the first Europeans to understand slavery as a quintessential modern institution in the sense that it forced a psychic alienation, or schism, between appearance and reality, between one's interior thoughts and one's outer performance. Sandoval's Jesuit colleagues argued that as long as slaves didn't openly rebel against the Catholic Church, then their passivity could be taken as implicit consent that they had accepted Christ. But Sandoval recognized that slaves had inner lives and private thoughts concealed from their masters, that the brutality inherent to slavery forced slaves to use cunning to survive. The examples he gave of this deception were the rituals of branding and baptism: 'Think about how they do not fight off the burning brand used to mark them and permanently imprison them in their masters' power to be abused and threatened,' he wrote; 'branding hurts them, and they do not want it, but they passively receive it and suffer through it, meanwhile detesting it on the inside.' As to baptism, those Africans who understood it as a rite of religious conversion, often remarked afterward that, '"their heart said nothing to them" (using their own words).'

these means so rapid,' he wrote, that it would soon 'supersede Paganism throughout Western Africa.' He grudgingly admitted the attraction: its 'influence is to a certain extent humanizing,' offering something 'on which the tired spirit may rest.'[12]

No one knows how many Muslims were among the 12,500,000 Africans brought in chains to America. Some estimate as many as 10 percent. They were present in the earliest slave ships that began to arrive in 1501. Over three and a half centuries later, they were among some of the last. Muslims disembarked in America's northernmost slave ports, in New England, and its southernmost, in Buenos Aires and Montevideo.

For some enslaved Muslims brought to America, Islam was the religion of rule, the faith of expanding courtly states like the Mali and Songhai empires. These societies were highly literate in both Arabic and local languages and organized around urbane mosques, libraries, and schools. In other areas, Islam was a religion of resistance, of pastoral or farming qur'anic communities fighting to win or keep their autonomy from unjust or unholy overlords. In 1804, for instance, Fulani and Hausa nomads launched a jihad against the Islamic rulers of the city-state of Gobir, who were enslaving freeborn Muslims. The insurgency was led by a rural Sufi preacher named Uthman dan Fodio, who freed slaves who joined his cause and advocated for the manumission of those who converted to Islam. The war lasted for over a decade and transformed much of West Africa, an event the historian Manuel Barcia has argued was as important to the history of the Atlantic world as were the French and Haitian revolutions. As fighting convulsed the upper Niger valley, Muslims and non-Muslims alike were captured in raids, sold to Europeans, and shipped to America, their religious differences giving way to the shared horrors of the Middle Passage. It was around this time that Babo, Mori, and the other *Tryal* rebels were first enslaved.[13]

Islam, then, provided American slaves with the law (a set of rules and expectations governing what constituted righteous slavery), the spirit (the experience of jihad or insurgency against illegitimate enslavers) needed to contest their bondage, and the literacy and theology to process their experience. One English traveller noted that in Brazil, some Muslim slaves 'write Arabic fluently, and are vastly superior to most of their masters.'[14]

Muslims were part of the first major slave revolt in America, which took place on Christmas Day, 1521, on a plantation run by Christopher Columbus's son. Scores of Wolof men taken from Senegal revolted, killing Spaniards, burning plantations, and winning a week of freedom until they were captured and hung. After this rebellion, Spanish authorities issued the first edict, of many to follow, prohibiting the enslavement of Africans believed to be Muslims. Among those banned were blacks from the Levant or raised among Moors, people from Guinea, and 'Gelofes,' or Wolofs, inhabitants of the region around the Senegal and Gambia Rivers. The Spaniards thought Wolofs to be especially 'arrogant, disobedient, rebellious, and incorrigible.' They had, wrote one Spanish poet, 'vain presumptions to be knights.'[15]

Muslims kept being captured and shipped to America. And they kept revolting. They were among those Africans and descendants of Africans who fought for their freedom in the Haitian Revolution. They were found on George Washington's Mount Vernon farm and probably at Thomas Jefferson's Monticello. They were part of Simón Bolívar's army of freed slaves and mulattos that ended Spanish colonialism in South America. The largest concentration of Africans who professed Islam was in Bahia, Brazil, where well into the nineteenth century they read the Qur'an, worshiped in mosques, dressed in white linen, and kept Islamic holy days, fasting during Ramadan and celebrating under Eid's full moon. In 1835, they staged the largest urban slave rebellion in the Americas. The day they chose to start their uprising was the same day Babo and Mori started theirs three decades earlier—Laylat al-Qadr, the Night of Power.[16]

Abominable, Contemptible Hayti

When Herman Melville was trying to decide what to call the slave ship in *Benito Cereno*, one option was to keep the vessel's actual name, the *Tryal*. It was resonant enough. Abraham Lincoln hadn't yet, when Melville started writing the story in early 1855, used the biblical phrase *fiery trial* to refer to the slavery crisis. But it was a common metaphor in the oration Melville grew up on, often used to refer to the American Revolution. Instead, Melville settled on calling the ship the *San Dominick*, identifying it with Haiti's old French colonial name, Santo Domingo.[1]

Though the former slave colony had declared independence in 1804, it would take more than half a century before the United States would recognize the country. Washington would receive no 'black ambassadors,' said one Missouri senator, since to do so would be to honour the murderers of 'masters and mistresses.' Even many of the most passionate abolitionists didn't want to make much of Haiti, fearing defenders of slavery would use the savagery that had been unleashed during its revolution to discredit their cause. 'That abominable, contemptible Hayti' was how Harriet Beecher Stowe had a sympathetic character describe the country in *Uncle Tom's Cabin*. But others, despairing that slavery was growing ever stronger, started to celebrate the revolution and praise its founding father, Toussaint Louverture, declaiming poems, giving speeches, and staging plays honouring his memory.[2]

Throughout the 1850s, for instance, Frederick Douglass's newspaper reported on this Toussaint revival, including a review of the opening performance of a play titled *Toussaint L'Ouverture* in Paris, at the Porte St.-Martin theatre: 'A crowd collected round the doors as early as twelve o'clock; at the opening the throng was immense. In the first scene the population of St. Domingo was exhibited collected on the banks of the sea, upon whose blue surface was reflected the brilliant light of the sun; the black *Marseillaise* was sung with enthusiasm.' 'The slave owners are sleeping on slumbering volcanoes,' Douglass said in 1849. Six years later, Melville asked whether *Benito Cereno*'s *San Dominick* was 'like a slumbering volcano' waiting to 'let loose energies now hid.'[3]

Maybe Melville, in naming his ship the *San Dominick*, was extending a small literary recognition to the long-denied island republic. Or perhaps he was simply struck by the way the historical Benito Cerreño denied Haiti's existence to Babo, Mori, and the others and so decided to make him master of, and then held captive on, a ship named after the country.

Melville made other changes to Delano's true account, details that added to the atmosphere of the 'strange craft,' with its 'strange history,' and 'strange folks on board.' At the beginning of the story, he has Delano notice that the ship's prow is wrapped in canvas, underneath which is scrawled the phrase 'follow your leader.' Later, as Delano's men are retaking the ship, the tarp is pulled away to reveal a gruesome sight: Alejandro Aranda's skeleton. The rebels had substituted what had been the *San Dominick*'s Christopher Columbus figurehead with Aranda's bones, the implication being that they cannibalized him. It's also revealed that Babo forced each surviving crew member and passenger to come forward, asking them, as he pointed to the skeleton in the prow, 'whether, from its whiteness, he should not think it a white's.' 'Keep faith with the blacks from here to Senegal,' the West African warns, 'or you shall in spirit, as now in body, "follow your leader."'

Was Melville, in writing this scene, trying to symbolically reverse the 'entire story of New World history told from the European American point of view,' revealing the 'rudiments of its own carnage,' as one scholar has suggested? Did he intend to turn the slave master into 'the sacrificial emblem of his own vicious system of power'? Did he think that only by rendering flesh down to bleached bones could the sin of slavery be expunged from America?[4]

It is impossible to know—Melville left no letters or journal entries, or at least none yet found, indicating what motivated him to write *Benito Cereno*. But in February 1855, just two months before Melville submitted *Benito Cereno* to *Putnam's Monthly*, Charles Wyllys Elliott gave a lecture on the Haitian Revolution at the Mercantile Library on Astor Place in Manhattan. He started his remarks with the New World's first major slave revolt—the one led by West African Wolofs in 1521 on Christopher Columbus's son's Santo Domingo plantation. 'The slaves had risen, slain their overseers,' Elliott said, 'and been hung by scores.' Elliott, a writer and urban planner who travelled in the same circles as did Melville and whose lecture would be published by the same press that put out *Benito Cereno*, reminded his audience that Haiti used to be called Santo Domingo, where Christopher Columbus first landed. Soon after which, a 'million of the simple natives' would be 'sacrificed' for gold. Once this first New World genocide was complete, the Spaniards turned to Africa 'to steal, to seduce, and to buy negroes . . . blessed by the Pope, encouraged by the State.'[5]

'This was but the beginning,' Elliott said. Follow your leader indeed.

PART VI

WHO AINT A SLAVE?

Freedom is the name for a thing that is not freedom.

—HERMAN MELVILLE, *MARDI*

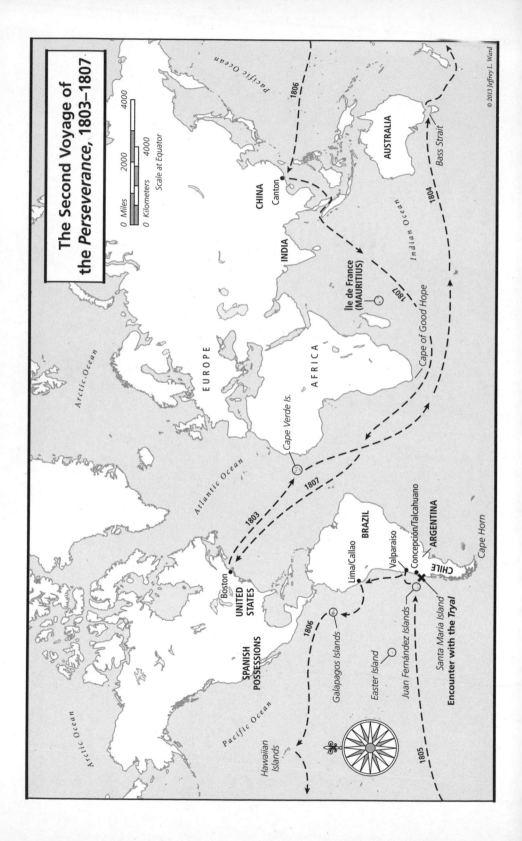

The Second Voyage of
the *Perseverance*, 1803–1807

Scale at Equator

0 Miles   2000   4000

0 Kilometers   4000

© 2013 Jeffrey L. Ward

Arctic Ocean

Pacific Ocean

Atlantic Ocean

EUROPE

AFRICA

Cape Verde Is.

Cape of Good Hope

Ile de France
(MAURITIUS)

Indian Ocean

CHINA

Canton

INDIA

AUSTRALIA

Bass Strait

1806

1804

1807

1803

1807

UNITED
STATES

Boston

SPANISH
POSSESSIONS

BRAZIL

Lima/Callao

Valparaiso

Concepción/Talcahuano

ARGENTINA

CHILE

Cape Horn

Santa María Island

Encounter with the *Tryal*

Juan Fernández Islands

Easter Island

Galapagos Islands

Hawaiian
Islands

Pacific Ocean

1806

1805

20

DESPERATION

In February 1805, as Amasa Delano cruised south along the coast of Chile heading to Santa María Island on the *Perseverance*'s second sealing voyage, the white-capped Andes took his mind off his troubles. From north to south, as far as Delano could see, mountains rose beyond mountains 'with awful sublimity.' The self-taught sailor meant that word as it was then used by men who had read Edmund Burke or some other eighteenth-century philosopher or poet. To describe a thing as sublime was to say that it evoked both terror and pleasure—terror from facing nature's infinity and pleasure from doing so at a distance. There's privilege implied, for only fortunate souls got to experience dread from a safe place, like Amasa Delano on his 'ship's deck, eight or ten miles off shore.'

The sky was clear, and starboard's near-setting sun cast its light on the range's western foothills, creating a lattice of light and shadow. The *Perseverance* was moving at a steady pace on a calm sea. Amasa's eye followed the rolling water as it flowed into the coast's undulating plains, tracing the contour of the land until it shot up with a startling steepness. The mountains were 'magnificent beyond description,' he thought. 'In some places beautifully shaded, where one mountain stands a little in front of another, making the most interesting and splendid appearance that can be conceived of.'[1]

The *Perseverance*, along with the *Pilgrim*, built in expectation that this second skinning expedition would do as well as the first, had set sail from Boston seventeen months earlier, practically almshouses for the Delano family. The *Pilgrim* was captained by Amasa's brother Samuel and carried his other brother, the 'badly-clubfooted William.' Amasa was on the *Perseverance*, along with his nephew and ward Charles, who was seven years old yet 'wanted as much attendance' as a child of three. The boy had lost the use of his arms and Amasa was obligated to care for him, a responsibility that had, he said, a 'more powerful effect' on him 'than all the other causes put together.'[2]

Though his last voyage had made a profit, family obligations and debts had built up while Amasa was away. In June, he married the widow Hannah Appleton, who ran a respectable Boston boardinghouse. But money remained a problem. On shore, Delano felt the burden of responsibility. Samuel was a shipbuilder and he had property in Duxbury, so he could take care of himself. The twenty-year-old William, who years later would die at sea, was a more hapless figure. And his three sisters, particularly Irene, just a year younger than him, were not well off.

The weight grew heavier as Amasa made ready to leave. 'Almost the whole of our connections, whom we left behind, had need of our assistance,' he wrote, and 'our absence would not be less than three years.'

He noted feeling 'more anxiety than I had ever experienced at the beginning of any enterprise.' He was taking from his 'parents all the sons they had, and one grandson, and from my sisters all their brothers.' And he was feeling his forty years: 'I found myself less active in body and mind than I was at the age of twenty-five.' He had no choice, though, but to face 'storms, dangers, and breakers' to take what he could 'from barren rocks in distant regions.'[3]

The *Perseverance* and *Pilgrim* first picked up a load of salt at the Cape Verde islands, where they signed up some Portuguese sailors and a few wayward 'Sandwich Islanders.' Then they sailed down the western coast of Africa, around the Cape of Good Hope, and across the Indian Ocean toward the Pacific, gaining additional men along the way.

The brothers had heard that seals were scarce in the waters off Chile

but the captain of a French ship had told them that the rookeries were full
at King Island, in the eastern mouth of Bass Strait, the wide, windy passage that separates Tasmania from mainland Australia. The island had
been home to the plentiful dark-plumed black emu. By the time the Delanos arrived in early 1804, the seals were gone and so were the emus. Over
the millennia, the ostrichlike birds had evolved to be able to kick most
predators to death, but within just about five years sealers hunted them to
extinction, using dogs specially trained to grab the birds by the neck.[4]

'Greatly disappointed at not finding any Seal on the Island of any
Consequence,' the brothers headed to the western side of the strait, to
Cape Barren Island. Along the way, they found the stranded *Integrity*, a
British cutter helping to found a new prison colony up the Derwent
River (which would eventually grow into the city of Hobart, Great Britain's first and largest settlement in Tasmania). The *Perseverance* stayed
with the ship and helped fix its broken rudder, while the *Pilgrim* took its
cargo and passengers up the Derwent. Afterwards, Amasa sent Samuel
to Sydney to present the British governor with an invoice for 400 pounds
for 'services performed.' The governor complained that the bill was
excessively high but he had to pay it since the *Integrity*'s captain had
signed off on the invoice. Delano, he thought, was a 'piratical fellow' for
taking 'extortionate advantage.'[5]

The *Perseverance* arrived in Kent's Bay on Cape Barren Island on
March 3 and set up camp. The surrounding waters were filled with
'rocks, shoals, and dangers,' and the land was made up of broken granite
and deep, wavy loams covered with grass trees, heath, and brushwood.
Sealing had just started here and elsewhere in the strait a few years earlier. Already, though, British officials were concerned about the promis-
cuous slaughter of adult seals, which was leaving pups to starve to death
on the beach by the thousands. If the market price had been high enough,
it would have been worth it to kill young seals, since their small patches
of fur could be used to make wallets and gloves. But with the China market saturated and the price of fur dropping, profit margins weren't enough
to pay for the time and effort it took to skin small seals (it was easier to
just cut larger pelts into smaller pieces).[6]

Delano's most immediate problem at Cape Barren was not too few seals but too many sealers. Some of them were fugitives from mainland Australia, working for Port Jackson and Sydney merchants. Others were escapees from the convict colony on the Derwent River, where the British had started sending its 'worst class' of criminals. 'Ill-behaved, useless, and lazy,' many of these 'abandoned hardened wretches' fled as soon as they arrived, stealing boats, muskets, gunpowder, and food and escaping into the dark of Bass Strait. They hoped to make it to New Zealand or Timor though most got only as far as Cape Barren, swelling the 'number of lawless runaways who for so long a time infested' the island. These 'sea-rats' joined already established merchant-contracted seal gangs or worked as alone men, living in wretched hovels and kidnapping indigenous women from Tasmania to keep as slave wives. They lit false guide fires to lure ships into shoals and then pillaged them when they wrecked.[7]

Amasa said later that he had tried to avoid 'open rupture' with the other sealers. It was hard, though, to withstand so many 'insults from such villains.' His boats were stolen and his ships cut adrift. Many of his men couldn't take the harassment. They deserted, either joining rival seal gangs or enlisting in the military service of 'His Britannick Majesty.' With his crew dwindling in numbers, Delano was forced to replenish its ranks with escaped convicts.[8]

Around mid-October, occasional hit-and-run skirmishes erupted into a full-on battle between Amasa's away team and a sealing gang led by James Murrell, who worked for the Sydney merchant house of Kable and Underwood. After Murrell and his crew broke up a camp set up by Delano, Delano's sailors retaliated. They pulled Murrell and a few of his men out of their cabins by their hair, dragging them over rocks and nettles to the beach, stripped them naked, tied them to trees, and flogged them till they bled. Murrell got loose and ran into the sea. He was chased down by a 'Sandwich Island savage'—one of the Hawaiians in Delano's crew—and given 'several violent blows with large stones.' Murrell raised his arm in defence and was struck lengthwise between his wrist and elbow 'so heavy as to cause the flesh to burst open.' He was finally dragged out of the surf half dead, abandoned on the beach in the 'most excruciating pains.'

The *Perseverance* and *Pilgrim* fled New South Wales the next day. The ships carried hardly any skins but left with at least seventeen English, Welsh, and Irish deserters or escaped convicts, along with canvas, tackle, and rigging pilfered from Murrell's sealing camp.[9]

The Delano brothers headed east to the more familiar hunting grounds off Chile, calling on one island after another yet still finding no seals. Realizing the voyage was a bust, their men began to jump ship, a few at each anchorage. The two brothers, deciding that if they split up they could cover more territory and perhaps find a full hunting ground, made a plan to rendezvous at an island called Santa María and went their separate ways. Samuel headed to the islands of San Ambrosio and San Félix and Amasa went north, to Juan Fernández, located between Más Afuera and the mainland.

The *Perseverance* dropped anchor about six miles off the island's northwest shore. Most of the men Delano could rely on had been left elsewhere to try to find seals, leaving him feeling isolated. Captain of his ship, he felt like its prisoner. His brothers were far away and he had no one on board he had confidence in to leave in command. Nor did he trust any of his ship's hands, especially the Tasmanian convicts, to take out the whaleboat on their own. He feared that if they made it to the island they wouldn't come back or, if they met up with other away men, they might ally with them against him. Delano, despite his misgivings about leaving the ship, had no choice but to lead the away team himself.

High breakers blocked his landing and his boat drifted east with the wind. The weather was overcast, and before long Delano noticed that his ship was receding away from the island, apparently having hauled anchor. It was disappearing into the west and soon looked as if it were only 'as big as a man's thumb.' Delano's men pulled hard on the oars but couldn't make headway. They came on a calmer bay with a small pier. The island's governor, who was there on the dock as if waiting for them, refused to let them come ashore. Delano begged to be allowed to stay the night. The governor, under orders from Lima not to let foreigners on the island, wouldn't relent. Delano had no choice but to head back out past the surf, where the wind and sea had grown even rougher.[10]

Waves began to break over the boat. The men rowed and bailed until ten at night and still couldn't find the *Perseverance*. Delano fired his musket, hoping his ship would see the flare, but the thick air muted the light. 'There was such a cross sea' that with each pull of the oars water filled 'half way up to the boat's thwarts.' Yet they couldn't wait out the storm by riding the waves without some kind of ballast. Every lift up by a crest of a wave was followed by a wet dive down into the trough of its swell. Delano had his men lash their oars together to make two spans, one on either side of the boat, each weighted down with stones to improvise a catamaran that helped steady the wave-tossed vessel.

The away team stayed like that through the night, 'suffering hardships in the extreme.' Amasa had almost drowned once already at Cape Barren. He, his brother William, and four other sailors were bringing barrels of fish to the shore in a small boat to smoke. But as they pulled toward land, they got caught in a horse market. Two colliding tides forced the waves to rise in a heap: their boat went up and then down and then filled with water and sank, leaving Amasa and the others 'floating on the surface.' Amasa took hold of a piece of wood to keep afloat. When he looked up, he saw one of his men, a Swede named John Fostram, swimming toward him. Panicked that Fostram would pull him under, Delano began to kick furiously to get away. He looked back to see Fostram drown. 'I remember but few incidents in the course of my life,' Delano later wrote, 'that were more gratifying to me than that of Fostram's sinking.' Then he saw that another sailor was also trying to reach him. He too went under. 'I never until then had experienced any satisfaction at seeing a man die, but so great is the regard we have for ourselves when in danger, that we would sooner see the whole human race perish than die ourselves.' Eventually the sea calmed and Amasa, along with William and two other men, was rescued.[11]

This time, though, Amasa couldn't count on his brothers. Samuel was far to the south looking for seals and William was on a nearby

island. He began to fear that the *Perseverance* had intentionally abandoned him. Cliques had formed on the ship, and on the sail from New
South Wales to South America their leaders were constantly testing his
authority. Absent the rousing power of an outside enemy to fight, like
Murrell, and no seals to kill, and therefore no money to be made, some
of his men had turned against him. Sailors who had been with the
brothers since leaving Boston a year earlier had begun to complain that
their 'share' of the voyage was so far pitifully small. Those who joined
along the way, especially the escaped convicts, felt little loyalty to the
Delanos. Fights broke out among the crew. Acts of petty insubordination
grew in frequency. His men ignored his orders. Worse, they started to
mock him. 'My crew were refractory, the convicts were ever unfaithful.'

He began to rely on his chief officer, Rufus Low, to administer more
frequent and heavier punishments. These retaliations worsened the situation, quickening the cycle between transgression and reprimand. Soon, a
desperate Delano was meting out floggings and withholding food for only
'minor offences.'* In turn, deckhands began to see Delano's command as
increasingly capricious. 'Nothing pleases him,' one sailor later testified.[12]

Floating in the rough sea on his rigged catamaran, Delano thought
that he had lost his ship and that his crew had cast him away to die.
He was thinly dressed, only in Nanking pantaloons, which were 'very
tight,' and a waistcoat and sleeved jacket of thin white cotton cloth. They
were tight, too. Amasa laid down in the bottom of the boat and passed
the night soaking wet, 'with the water washing over me all the time.' The
sea continued rough through the morning. By ten the storm had finally
broken, allowing the boat's men to dismantle the drag and begin again
to row. Finally, after another five hours, they came upon the *Perseverance*. A rope and pulley had to be used to haul Delano onto his ship,

---

* Rufus Low, from the town of Gloucester, on Massachusetts's Cape Ann, was, next to Delano, the *Perseverance*'s most experienced sailor. Low had been the captain of a merchant
ship that made several voyages to India. In 1794, he was master of the schooner *Industry*,
which was captured by first the British and then the French navy, before it was plundered
by French colonial officials in Haiti. In 1800, he also served on the USS *Essex*, one of the
modern US Navy's earliest ships, as sailing master, on a voyage where an exceptionally high
number of floggings took place.

since he was temporarily paralyzed from spending the cold night bound in waterlogged cotton. He asked the sailor he left in charge why he hadn't kept track of the boat and was given only a vague answer. The storm prevented the men from doing so, he told Delano, and the strong wind made them drop their masts.

Delano then gave an order to pick up the nearby away teams and proceed to Santa María. He needed to find his brother.

21

DECEPTION

The *Tryal* came down along the rough, windy side of Santa María Island hard around its southern head, rocking and pitching. Only by luck did Cerreño give a wide berth to a low ledge that ran about a mile out from the point, to land full stop in a quiet bay about half a league from the *Perseverance*, bow to stern.

Falling in with the Duxbury brig jolted the ship's voyagers out of their trancelike state. For fifty-three days since the uprising, Cerreño had sailed undetected, avoiding the busy sea lanes between Valparaiso and Lima crowded with merchant vessels and naval ships. Two West African women, along with their two babies, had died of hunger and thirst, leaving a total of eighty-seven people on board: sixty-eight West Africans, their three allies—Joaquín, Francisco, and José—ten surviving sailors, four cabin boys, one passenger left from Alejandro de Aranda's entourage, and Captain Cerreño. It had been a month since the rebels threw Aranda into the sea, and his murder had eased tensions. As did the pledge Cerreño signed to take the rebels to Senegal.

But the situation was dire. Food was short and water gone. There would have been dew in the evening, almost as dense as rain, though not enough to keep the travellers hydrated. After the deaths of the two women and their children, desperation had turned to stupor.[1]

The *Tryal* was broad-beamed, built like many of New Bedford's oak whaling and trading ships for seaworthiness. The voyagers, though, had eaten their way through much of the food merchandise that had served as ballast, the casks of lard, bushels of wheat, boxes of biscuits, chickens, pigs, and cows that weighted the ship and helped keep it steady. And they had run into a bad storm shortly after Aranda's murder. Waves tossed the ship like a log and water poured over the coamings into the hatches, more than the West Africans, pumping furiously, could kick back out. Cerreño had no choice but to jettison much of the rest of the ship's heavy cargo, including a load of timber from southern Chile, overboard.

Because the ship was lighter and riding higher on the waves, less water breached the *Tryal*'s gunwales. But its pitch increased. The ship was already worn and leaky when Cerreño had taken possession of it in early 1803, and it had grown worse with over a year of hard use and poor care. Now it was nearly ruined, its sails threadbare and its rigging a tangle. Long braids of kelp draped the vessel's bow and barnacles encrusted its hull. 'A ship grows foul very fast in these seas,' a sailor wrote of the waters in which the *Tryal* travelled.[2]

The morning the *Tryal* rounded Santa María's southern head, Amasa Delano was lying in his bunk thinking about the line that separated sport from insubordination. The *Perseverance* had dropped anchor four days earlier to wait for Samuel, who still hadn't appeared, and soon thereafter Delano cast eight men he had discovered plotting against him off his ship, putting them on the island. He allowed another eight to go to shore to have some fun, 'shooting, fishing, getting birds' eggs, and playing ball.' Though after the troubles in New South Wales, the tense voyage to Chile, and the suspicious actions of his crew off of Juan Fernández (Amasa never found out what really happened that night), he wasn't sure how many from this group would come back. Santa María wasn't a big island. It was just about five miles long and half that wide, but there were plenty of places to hide among its pines or in its marshes and coves. Delano would have to wait for his brother Samuel before he could hunt down deserters, since so many of the men left on the *Perseverance* were close to desertion themselves.

Dressed and on deck after being told about the appearance of the *Tryal*, Delano considered what to do. He feared privateers and knew firsthand their trick of feigning distress, then striking. But he also knew that maritime commerce, and the prosperity that came with it, couldn't exist without courtesy and trust. 'One ship may be in want of something that another can spare,' wrote Delano later. Besides, the ship could be an ally and might even help him with his own troubles.

Delano ordered the ship's boat to be loaded with fish, water, bread, and pumpkins and hoisted out quickly, since it looked as if the wind was pushing the *Tryal* toward the ledge. He had recently learned from a Captain Barney, master of the Nantucket whaler *Mars*, of yet another plot by some of his 'convict men' to steal his boat and make for the island. This time, though, unlike at Juan Fernández, he had men he could trust with him, including his first midshipman, Nathaniel Luther, and his brother William. He left William in charge of the ship and climbed into the boat with Luther.

Santa María sits fifty miles off a wide coastal gulf into which flows the Bio Bio River down from the Andes, the natural border separating Chile's tamed north from its wild south. Over the centuries Spain had tried to turn Santa María into a defensive garrison, an outpost against pirates, contrabandists, freebooters, unauthorized whalers and sealers, and rival empires.[3] But the island was still mostly uninhabited in 1805. In the opening scenes of *Benito Cereno* Melville paints the place grey on grey: 'Everything was mute and calm; everything grey.... The sky seemed a grey surtout. Flights of troubled grey fowl, kith and kin with flights of troubled grey vapours.... Shadows present, foreshadowing deeper shadows to come.' But as Delano made his way toward the *Tryal* the sun was breaking through the early mist, revealing a blue sky that would last the day long.[4]

The West Africans could have tried to stay ahead of their dwindling food and water by reducing the number of people on board their ship. Yet they needed the remaining crew alive if they were going to make it to Senegal. And as far as surviving documents suggest, they didn't turn on one another. Rather, in the weeks prior to the encounter with the *Perseverance*, the rebels sank into stillness. During calm days, the late summer sun waxed warm as the vessel rocked listlessly in the water and its yardarms creaked in their slings. Power slid into impotence. After the frenzied uprising and the rush of executions, followed by the heavy work needed to empty the cargo hold during the storm, there was nothing to do. Until the sight of the *Perseverance* rousted the rebels out of their resignation.

Witnesses say it was Babo and Mori who came up with the plan. Had they tried to flee, the *Perseverance* probably wouldn't have pursued. The West Africans, though, didn't know that. They could have immediately fought. Benito Cerreño later testified that, upon coming on Delano's ship, the rebels picked up their knives and broad axes and made ready. Instead, Babo and Mori thought of the idea of deceiving the boarding party, of acting as if they were still slaves. Mori warned Cerreño that he would be listening to his every word and watching his every move. If Cerreño gave 'any indication about what had happened on the ship,' as the Spanish report on the incident later said, 'they would kill him on the spot, along with all the rest of the crew and passengers.'

Babo, Mori, and possibly others on board the *Tryal* were lettered men, probably educated in qur'anic schools. They knew how to read the sky, at least enough to keep the calendar, and how to write in their own language. Legal contracts like the kind they had made Cerreño sign in exchange for his life were well established in Islam by 1805, as they were in Christianity. Mori knew enough Spanish to communicate with Cerreño. And Babo was held in high respect by the other West Africans, suggesting that he could have been a marabout (a cleric) or a *faqīh* (a scholar) in his former life.[5]

Slavery existed throughout West Africa. Babo, Mori, and some of the others might have been slave owners themselves. Or they might have been slaves, since neither status nor education would have necessarily protected them against being captured and sold to Europeans in one of the many conflicts that roiled parts of West Africa at the time. Beyond whatever firsthand familiarity Babo might have had with slavery, if he was a religious man or an elder scholar, he would also have been well versed in the theology of slavery. Many of the great Sufi manuscripts today found in Timbuktu and elsewhere throughout Mali, for instance, grapple with slavery as a moral, legal, and intellectual problem.* As did Christians, Muslim philosophers and clerics worked to reconcile their humanism— the idea that all could be saved, that, as a fourteenth-century Muslim jurist said, 'the basic principle for all children of Adam is freedom'—with the practice of slavery.

As it did in Christianity, this contradiction raised a number of questions that Islamic scholars struggled to answer: Who could legitimately be enslaved? Who has the right to enslave? What limitations should be placed on the power of masters? What obligations did slaves have to their owners? Muslim theologians, like Christian ones, elaborated strong ethical codes regulating servitude, urging slaves to obey their masters and masters to be righteous and merciful, to treat slaves as family.**

Also much like Christians, Islamic philosophers understood freedom and slavery broadly, as psychological and spiritual conditions. Desire, or worldly envy and pride, was slavery; the freeing of oneself of desire, giving up ambition, was freedom. Sufis in particular used slavery as an analogy for nurturing an intimate relation with Allah, of submitting one's will and being to God. Who aint a slave? The person who serves God like a slave. 'Let it be known,' wrote the tenth-century Sufi theologian, Abd al-Karim ibn Hawazin al-Qushayri, 'that the real meaning of freedom lies in the perfection of slavery.'[6]

In a way, giving themselves over is what Babo, Mori, and the others did. As they watched Delano cutting across the bay, they started to abandon the outward manifestations of the freedom they had won with their rebellion, a freedom that in any case was already slipping away with each day they spent in the Pacific. Drawing on their own experience with the master-slave relation, with its mannerisms that signalled

---

* These are the manuscripts that were recently threatened during Mali's northern insurgency, many of which were saved, as they have been repeatedly over the centuries, by the heroic work of librarians and scholars. See Lydia Polgreen, 'As Extremists Invaded, Timbuktu Hid Artifacts of a Golden Age,' *New York Times*, February 3, 2013.
** Among the most famous of West African philosophers was Ahmad Baba, born in Timbuktu in 1564 and enslaved himself by North Africans. He wrote an estimated forty books, including one of Islam's most influential treatises on just and unjust slavery. The historian Paul Lovejoy argues that West African Muslims brought to America as slaves were aware of Baba's writings, including his arguments against illegitimate enslavement.

duty, submission, and affection, they readied themselves to play their part, to inhabit their characters. They would try to 'perfect slavery.'

It took Delano and his men about twenty minutes to reach the *Tryal*, which was slowly drifting out of the bay, away from the ledge and away from the *Perseverance*. After he had boarded, and after he had quickly surveyed the state of the ship and finished distributing the food and water he had brought with him, Delano spent most of the rest of the day in the company of Cerreño and Mori. He had sent his midshipman, Luther, along with the rest of his away team, to obtain more supplies, so he was alone. Delano knew it would take a long time for them to return. They first had to go to a fresh spring inland on the island to fill the *Tryal*'s water casks and then back to the *Perseverance* for canvas and more food. Delano also told them to wait for the return of the *Perseverance*'s larger and better-built yawl, which was out on a fishing run, and to use that to bring the full casks and food back to the *Tryal*.

Cerreño had greeted him warmly when he first came on board, and the two captains began conversing in a mix of broken Spanish and basic English. Cerreño rallied himself to his part, telling Delano that his ship was out of Buenos Aires bound for Lima, Peru, but had run into a bad storm rounding Cape Horn, where he had lost a number of men overboard. He had made it into the Pacific only to fall becalmed. In the windless, tideless sea, the fevers had hit, he said, killing all his officers and most of the rest of his crew.

Cerreño seems to have tried to drop hints that things on board were not as they appeared, introducing Mori to Delano, for instance, as 'captain of the slaves.' A more suspicious mind perhaps would have picked up the irony, that it was Cerreño who was enslaved and Mori his master. But Delano didn't. Exhausted and wasted, Cerreño had trouble keeping the performance going. He grew distant. Delano kept asking him questions, which Cerreño tried to answer. But his responses became shorter and shorter. His change in demeanour had a noticeable effect on Delano, who began to think that his initial worries were justified, that Cerreño planned to kill him and, in alliance with the slaves, take his ship.

Those fears, though, began to fade, leaving Delano to feel a different kind of vulnerability. He started to think that he was being insulted, that Cerreño's 'neglect' was intentional. As he grew more agitated, Delano began to pay more attention to the black man at Cerreño's side. But he couldn't stay focused. His mind turned from one thing to the next, from Cerreño, to Mori, to the nursing, dirge-singing women, to the rest of the slaves, and then back to Cerreño.

The *Tryal* rebels didn't quite 'perfect slavery.' They were impatient. They seemed to have wanted to see what they could get away with and still have a white man think them slaves. At one point, a young African, with Delano standing nearby, pulled out a knife and slashed the head of a Spanish cabin boy, cutting him to the bone. Blood poured out and the startled Delano looked to Cerreño, who brushed off the attack as 'merely sport.' 'Rather serious sport,' said Delano. Delano noticed other, similar incidents that made him think that the slaves enjoyed what he called 'extraordinary liberty.'

Shortly after Luther returned with the supplies, around three o'clock in the afternoon, Delano felt a change in wind and looked up to notice that the *Tryal* had drifted nearly out of the bay and now was about three leagues away from the *Perseverance*. Delano asked Cerreño why he hadn't dropped anchor. Receiving no satisfactory answer, he took charge, ordering the ship be brought as close to his vessel as possible. When that was done, he had the anchor put out and made ready to leave. He had had enough.

Throughout the day, Delano had tried to talk to Cerreño about compensation. He was glad to offer his assistance but, as was the case with the *Integrity* at Bass Strait, he expected to be paid for his effort. Yet each time he asked if they could meet alone, away from Mori, he was rebuffed, told by Cerreño that whatever he wanted to say he could say in front of the slave. The idea of talking about money in front of Mori must have unsettled him, for Delano kept putting the conversation off. Just before he was ready to leave, he asked one last time if he and Cerreño could go below to talk. He was again refused. Delano then invited the Spaniard to take tea or coffee on his vessel. Cerreño said no. 'His answer was short,' remembered Delano. He decided to retaliate. 'In return, I became less sociable, and said little to him.'

But just as Delano was going over the side of the *Tryal*, about to climb down into his boat, Cerreño came toward him. Delano's hand had been holding on to the top rail and Cerreño placed his over it, pressing down and squeezing tight. A surge of relief flowed through Delano. He immediately returned the warmth. That Cerreño seemed reluctant to let go of his hand, that it even had to be pulled it free. The release from his worry that the Spaniard held him in low regard was so powerful that, over a decade later in his memoir, he recounted his experience on board the *Tryal* as if it were his relationship to Cerreño that was driving the action, as if he didn't know, though of course he did by then, that the West Africans were the ones who were choreographing that relationship.

'I had committed a mistake,' Delano wrote of his attributing Cerreño's 'coldness to neglect; and as soon as the discovery was made, I was happy to rectify it, by prompt renewal of friendly intercourse. He continued to hold my hand fast till I stepped off the gunwale down the side, when he let it go, and stood making me compliments.'[7]

For his part, Mori's acting had been almost flawless, as Spanish officials would later say. But Mori, too, succumbed to pride. As Amasa Delano was climbing down the ladder, the West African slipped out of character, stepped up to Cerreño, and quietly asked him how many men the American had on the *Perseverance*. Thirty, the Spaniard answered, but many of them were on the island. 'Good,' Mori nodded, then whispering: 'We will only need three blacks to take it, and before night falls you will have two ships to sail.'

The boast shocked Cerreño out of his torpor. He looked at his black captain, stepped on the gunwale, and threw himself overboard.

22

RETRIBUTION

Delano's men, with Delano sitting in the rear of his boat, had just pushed off far enough from the *Tryal*'s hull to lower their oars, when Benito Cerreño fell into the boat. As soon as he landed, he yelled up to his men: 'Into the water all who can swim, the rest up the rigging.' He was speaking fast and frantically, and Delano, with his simple Spanish, couldn't understand him. For a moment, Delano thought he himself was being attacked, that his earlier fears were correct after all. But after a Portuguese hand helped translate, Delano finally realized what was happening.

Events then moved fast. After pulling three of the *Tryal*'s four sailors out of the water, Delano's crew began to row toward the *Perseverance*. When they reached earshot, Delano, still in the stern of his boat with one arm pressed on the tiller and the other wrapped around a collapsed Cerreño, ordered his men on deck to run the cannons out their portholes. But the West Africans had cut the *Tryal*'s anchor cable, letting the tide swing the bow and point the ship out of the bay. The *Perseverance* was left in a bad position, with only its aft gun facing the fleeing vessel. It fired six shots, missing each time save for one cut of the foremast rigging.

The *Tryal* was moving, but the *Perseverance*, with two dropped anchors, couldn't immediately follow. Cutting his cables would have allowed

Delano to set sail quickly. But that would have resulted in a financial loss either to the *Perseverance*'s investors or to its insurers. In *Moby-Dick*, when the *Pequod*'s first mate, Starbuck, tells Ahab his obsession isn't economically rational and will hurt the profits of the ship's owners, Ahab responds by cursing rationality: 'Let the owners stand on Nantucket beach and outyell the Typhoons. What cares Ahab? Owners? Owners, Owners? Thou art always prating to me, Starbuck, about those miserly owners, as if the owners were my conscience.'[1]

Delano, in contrast, not only almost lets the *Tryal* get away in order to save the two anchors but years later, telling the story in his memoir, interrupts the chase to provide readers with a long lecture on the responsibilities and duties of sea captains as defined by insurance law. To cut his ship's cables, he says, 'would be to break our policy of insurance by a deviation, against which I would here caution the masters of all vessels.' Whenever possible, it was best not to do anything to harm the interest of the underwriters, shareholders in the ship, and financers of the voyage. 'All bad consequences,' he continues, 'may be avoided by one who has a knowledge of his duty, and is disposed faithfully to obey its dictates.' Delano would take risks when it came to storms, seals, and other perils of sailing. But regarding the institutions that had evolved to govern commerce—like insurance and law—he remained faithful and duty bound. He preferred to risk letting the *Tryal* slip away than deviate from a correct course.*

Delano decided to send his boats after the *Tryal*. At this point, he had about twenty-three men on his ship. He picked twenty of them for the assault, including his clubfooted brother, William, gunner Charles Spence, and midshipman Nathaniel Luther. He put Rufus Low, the officer who presided over the run of floggings, in command.

Before giving the final order to capture the rebel ship, Delano took Cerreño by the arm and stepped him away from his men. He was finally

---

* Other sea captains had fewer qualms in making insurance claims, and not just for lost anchors. The captain of the *Rôdeur*, as discussed earlier, jettisoned blind West Africans, since they were worth more dead as claim payouts than alive as sightless slaves. A more well-known case, mentioned earlier, is the *Zong*, whose owners filed a claim on 132 sick Africans, out of a shipment of 442, thrown overboard by Captain Luke Collingwood.

going to have that word alone. Later, the two would dispute what was said and how it was said, but Delano shortly returned to his men and told them to gather around. When they did, he now began to sound less like a clerk at his counting table and more like a captain possessed.

On the far side of the island, the sun was setting as calmly as it rose, throwing dusky light on the bay. Looking out at the moving *Tryal* with his spyglass from the stern of the *Perseverance*, Amasa could see its remaining sailors climbing high aloft its topgallant masts. Delano pointed to them and reminded his men of the 'suffering conditions of the poor Spaniards' at the hand of the slaves. If the men failed to retake the vessel, 'death must be their fate.' Benito Cerreño, who was on deck listening, 'considered the ship and what was in her as lost,' Delano said. That meant it was a prize for the taking, which he calculated was worth tens of thousands of pesos. 'If we should take her, it should be all our own.'

'God to prosper,' Delano prayed. He told his men that he wished 'never to see their faces again' if they failed. All these encouragements, he later said, were 'pretty powerful stimulants.' The men boarded their boats, gave themselves three huzzahs, and began to row.

Delano's command to capture the *Tryal*, with its double promise of doing good and making money, helped unite a fractured crew. The *Perseverance*'s two boats set off, armed with muskets, pistols, sabers, pikes, and the sharp-edged lances the away men used to skin seals. Rowing fast, the pursuers soon came up along the side of the rebel-held ship, opening musket fire. They directed their shots at the helm, where the leaders of the revolt had gathered. A Spanish sailor whom the West Africans had steering the ship took advantage of the shooting to abandon the wheel and climb up the rigging. But Delano's men mistook him for a rebel and shot him twice. He fell to the deck. A surviving member of Aranda's entourage, a Basque cousin, Joaquín Arabaolaza, who had taken over the steering, was also shot.

The wind had picked up and the *Tryal* began to make headway, but its moss-heavy bow and barnacle-befouled hull slowed it down. Delano's men pulled hard and kept up. They yelled to the Spaniards who had fled up the fore- and mainmasts to cut the sheets holding the sails to the yards, which they did, leaving only the mizzenmast to manage the ship. They kept their firing up for over an hour, wearing the rebels down. There was no one left on board who knew how to steer, and eventually the ship turned round to the wind, allowing the two boats to come up on either side of the bow. Covered by musket fire, their men began to board.

The *Perseverance*'s sailors clambered up the hull. By this point, the sun had set but the nearly three-quarter moon in a cloudless sky lit the deck. On either side of the ship, in each of the boats, a point man held aloft an oil lamp. The West Africans withdrew to the stern, which Delano later described as the 'place of resort for the negros.' Some of the rebels had grabbed empty water casks and bales of yerba maté and erected a makeshift breastwork at amidships, six feet high and running full across its beam. Delano's men, still covered by musket fire from their boats, forced their way over. One West African stabbed Rufus Low with a pike, wounding him badly in the chest. But the barricade was breached. Babo was the first to die. Surrounded by Delano's men, Joaquín, the ship's caulker turned rebel, swung an ax wildly in a circle until he was put down, wounded yet alive.

The West Africans defended themselves with 'desperate courage,' Delano said, but his men used their superior weapons, particularly their lances, with 'extraordinary fury.'

The battle lasted for four hours. At 10 p.m., Delano got word that the *Tryal* was taken. He and Cerreño waited until the next morning to board, bringing with them handcuffs, leg irons, and shackles. They weren't needed.

What they found, Delano said, was 'truly horrid.' Babo's body was among the bales of yerba maté, as were the corpses of six other West Africans: Atufal, Dick, Leobe, Diamelo, Natu, and Quiamobo. The rest were chained tight, hands to feet, through the ring bolts in the deck. They had been tortured. Some had been disemboweled and were writhing in their viscera. Others had had the skin on their backs and thighs shaved off.

This had been done with the *Perseverance*'s skinning knives, which, Delano wrote, 'were always kept exceedingly sharp and as bright as a gentleman's sword.'

23

CONVICTION

The *Tryal* was secured and its slaves 'double ironed.' But Delano didn't trust the ship's surviving crew. Soon after he had boarded, one of Cerreño's mates had slashed the face of a West African with a straight razor. He was going for the man's throat when a hand from the *Perseverance* stopped him. Then, a minute later, a sailor tugged Delano's sleeve and nodded in the direction of Cerreño, who was about to stab a rebel, possibly Mori, with a dirk he had pulled from his belt. Delano grabbed his arm and Cerreño dropped the knife. The American threatened to have the Spaniards flogged if they didn't stand down. It was all he could do to stop Cerreño's men from 'cutting to pieces and killing these poor unfortunate beings.'[1]

Delano felt his authority braced by victory. He ordered the corpses of the six dead rebels, including Babo, to be thrown overboard and then told Cerreño it would be best if he returned with him to the *Perseverance*, placing his second officer, a Mr. Brown, in command of the *Tryal* and asking him to do an inventory of its cargo. Delano had two objectives. He didn't want to be accused of piracy but did want to be rewarded for his services. Brown counted a bag holding nearly a thousand doubloons, another purse with an equal number of dollars, several baskets of watches, and some gold and silver that had belonged to the murdered slaver, Alejandro de Aranda.

Back on the *Perseverance*, Delano started doing the maths. Even with most of its cargo gone, the ship, with its slaves, was surely worth thirty or forty thousand pesos. Divided up proportionally among the mates and midshipmen, the gunner, boatswain, and carpenter, that kind of money might rescue his so-far doomed voyage and buy him some good-will with his disgruntled crew. The question was whether the *Tryal* was a 'prize,' as implied in Cerreño's abandonment of it the day before, in which case they would get it all. Or a 'rescue,' which would yield only a percentage reward. Delano had Low go to Santa María and inform the men there what had happened and the money they could expect if they rejoined the *Perseverance.*

He then made ready to bring the *Tryal* to the nearby town of Talca-huano, which served as the port to the bigger inland city of Concepción, the last major southern outpost of Spanish authority before entering the wilds of Patagonia. Delano wanted to wait for his brother Samuel and the *Pilgrim* to turn up so he used the time to dredge for the anchor the rebels had cut loose from the *Tryal* trying to escape. It was valuable and, in the event the vessel wasn't insured, its loss would be deducted against the ship's worth. When Samuel hadn't arrived by the next day, the two ships set sail.

Talcahuano is tucked inside what seems a sheltered bay protected by a narrow mouth. Its snugness, though, is deceiving, for the seabed is extremely shallow, unable to dilute the force of the tsunamis that hit southern Chile with frequency. The port sits on the Pacific Rim's tec-tonic 'ring of fire' and had been devastated five times already by either a quake or a wave by the time Delano showed up. In his account of his voyages on the *Beagle*, Charles Darwin described arriving at Talcahuano in 1835, just a few days after the town had been struck a sixth time. 'The whole coast,' he wrote, was 'strewed over with timber and furniture as if a thousand ships had been wrecked.' Its storehouses 'had been burst open, and great bags of cotton, yerba, and other valuable merchandise were scattered on the shore.' The shoreline had been raised two or three feet from the violence of the quake. Darwin was equally impressed with the destruction he witnessed along the nine-mile road to Concepción. It was, he said, an 'awful yet interesting spectacle,' giving him some ideas about the elasticity of the earth's crust and the power of the forces that flowed beneath.[2]

Three decades earlier, when the *Perseverance* arrived in the harbour with the *Tryal* following, it was Spain's political authority that was fast shifting. The great edifice of Catholic monarchism that for centuries had ruled over a sprawling world empire was crumbling. In just a few years' time, Chile's revolutionary war for independence would be under way. Delano didn't know it, but the official who would receive him and rule on the fate of the West Africans—Concepción's royal advocate, Juan Martínez de Rozas—was even then imagining an America without Spain.

Rozas was a plotter and a freethinker, later accused by Crown officials of being something worse: an admirer of Napoleon. The jurist was considered one of the best legal minds in the Spanish colonies. It is now known that, by the time the *Tryal*'s rebel leaders were delivered to Talcahuano's port authorities, he was meeting secretly with a small circle of younger students to discuss republican ideas related to self-government. Even as Rozas and his young Voltaire- and Rousseau-reading disciples were conspiring against authority in the New World (one royalist around this time denounced Rousseau's *Social Contract* as the 'Anarchist's Qur'an'), and just a few years before Rozas would begin to gather arms and build a revolutionary army to fight for freedom, he was sitting in judgment of the West Africans for acting on much the same principle on the *Tryal*.[3]

Whatever philosophical problem the case of the *Tryal* might have presented to Rozas, it was for him also personal. His father was among Mendoza's largest slaveholders, and Rozas, born and raised in the Argentine city's close-knit, cousin-marrying community of Spaniards, grew up in a home just a few houses away from his childhood acquaintance, the executed slaver Alejandro de Aranda.[4]

Rozas first deposed the two captains, listening to Cerreño's grizzly description of Aranda's murder and Delano's account of how he saved the *Tryal* and its few surviving crew. When he was finished, he sent a priest to interrogate the slaves, who were being kept in a small holding cell in Talcahuano.

———

Most of the West Africans—the women, children, infants, older men, and young boys—remained on the *Tryal*. Only those surviving leaders of the rebellion had been taken ashore: Mori, Matunqui, Alasan, Yan, Yola, Luis (identified as one of the West Africans, despite a Spanish-sounding name; he perhaps is the same rebel listed elsewhere as Liché), Malpenda, and Samba, or Yambaio, along with the ship's African caulker, Joaquín, and Aranda's servants, José and Francisco.

The priest didn't 'speak their language' so he 'got no information' from the prisoners. He either didn't think of using Mori as an interpreter or Mori wasn't cooperating. The cleric talked more easily with the 'three Christians'—Joaquín, José, and Francisco—who defended themselves by saying that they 'fought against the Spaniards to win their freedom and return to their country.' Unable to do much more, the priest finished his visit by performing the rite of confession on all eleven in Latin.

The captives were provided a public advocate, called the *defensor de los negros*, who argued their case to Rozas. The specifics of his defence are not included in the written summation of the trial. The scribe who recorded the proceedings didn't even bother to mention the advocate's name. The brief description of his defence suggests, however, that he had taken the three most insurgent principles of New World republicanism and tried to extend them to the West Africans: individuals are free, they have a right to revolt against any regime that takes away their freedom, and all men deserve equality before the law.

Even more radically, the *defensor* used a concrete example to flesh out these abstract ideas, comparing their revolt to a recent episode where Spanish prisoners of war murdered their British jailors and escaped: 'The West Africans committed their crime with the intent of winning their liberty and returning to their country, having taken advantage of the negligence of the Spaniards to escape their servitude. Not too long ago, Spanish prisoners did the same . . . and they were called heroes. There is absolutely no difference between that action and this one.'

This summary of the lawyer's argument runs, in its original Spanish, to eighty words. Thirty-five years later, former US president John Quincy Adams would take 135 pages to defend the African rebels on the *Amistad*.

Yet both attorneys based their cases on essentially the same terms: the right of individuals to revolt in defence of their liberty was absolute and universal.

Rozas was unconvinced. Setting aside whatever personal feelings the judge might have had toward the West Africans who murdered Aranda, he had little sympathy for the argument made by their advocate.

Rozas read Roman law for 'moral lessons' and smuggled in French books for political philosophy; France was for lettered Spanish Americans like Rozas what Haiti was for slaves like Mori: a chance to think about alternatives. He was also in regular touch with sailors from New England with news of the American Revolution. William Moulton, the Thomas Paine of the *Onico*, wrote in his diary of conversing while on shore in Talcahuano with a 'learned man' well versed in 'sacred and profane history.' He was probably describing Rozas, who he said assured him that 'the fire of liberty was enkindling thro' all of the Spanish South America.'[5]

Yet Rozas's republicanism had less to do with the inviolability of individual natural rights than with establishing a unified realm of rational public authority that would sweep away all the shadowy spheres of power that existed under Spanish colonialism, such as the privileges enjoyed by the aristocracy and the Catholic Church. Later, Rozas would support the abolition of slavery. But in 1805, slavery was still a legal and public institution, and rebellion against it was a crime against public order.

It took Rozas one week to issue his ruling. Finding sufficient evidence that the actions of the West Africans and their three allies were premeditated, the judge emphasized the brutality of their crimes. He pronounced the eleven slaves guilty of the murder of eighteen men on the day of the revolt and the execution of Alejandro de Aranda and others in the days that followed. He also ruled that their revolt was illegitimate, though he didn't elaborate the reasons why, and that the slaves were guilty of waging unjust 'war' against Delano and his men.[6]

Rozas sentenced Mori, Matunqui, Alasan, Yola, Yan, Malpenda, Luis,

Samba, and Joaquín to death.* He showed leniency to José and Francisco, giving them ten years of labour in the Patagonian prison colony of Valdivia, about 250 miles south of Concepción. At the end of March, the royal court in Santiago ordered the executions to proceed.[7]

The nine condemned men had been transferred from Talcahuano to a jail in Concepción and a gallows built in the town square. On the morning of the day of their execution, soldiers took them out of their cell and chained them one behind the other in a single column, at the head of which was Mori. He then was tied to the tail of a mule. Residents had come out of their houses, and priests, nuns, and monks had gathered in front of churches and convents, and as the procession passed roundabout through the city's streets, the onlookers fell in behind, ringing bells and burning incense. When the parade arrived in the plaza with its gallows, the African women and children who had remained on the *Tryal* were there waiting: Rozas had ordered that they be brought to the city to witness the execution.[8]

Years later, a British consul in Concepción, Henry William Rouse, recounted a story he heard when he first arrived in town: just before the trapdoor sprung and Mori's body fell through, the West African finally spoke. He damned the 'cruel inhumanity of his captors, who, in the complete absence of the law steal men out of their homes.'

The corpses of the nine rebels were cut loose from the gallows and decapitated. Their heads were placed on pikes around the plaza and their bodies burned in a large pyre in its centre. Concepción was then a marshy city, dotted with lagoons and swamps, including one near the main plaza where town authorities disposed of the bodies of men and

---

* When I was in Concepción, Chile, to research this book, I paid a visit to the city's library, whose director, Alejandro Mihovilovich Gratz, is a local historian. From him I heard more of Rozas's prominent role in Chilean history. Rozas was one of the most radical of Chile's founding fathers and, Mihovilovich said, a fierce opponent of slavery. I asked if he thought it ironic that Rozas delivered such an unsparing judgment of the rebels for basically doing what he was conspiring to do at the time. Mihovilovich paused for a second and then asked, 'You're from the United States, no?' I answered yes and knew what was coming. '*Entonces*—well, then—how can you ask such a question?'

women denied Christian burials. That's where the city's executioners scattered the ashes and bones of Mori and his companions. The swamp has long since been filled in and built over, but throughout the rest of the 1800s and into the early twentieth century, Concepción's chroniclers would refer to the lake as the *Laguna de los Negros*—The Lagoon of the Blacks. After the ashes of the 'miserable negros were thrown in the lagoon,' reported one local historian, 'they were converted into *animitas*,' or spirits.[9]

Things had begun to go bad between Amasa Delano and Benito Cerreño even before Mori was hanged. On that first day on dry land upon arriving at Talcahuano, in the initial statement Cerreño gave to Rozas, he had praised the generosity and skill of his friend Masa—as Spaniards tended to pronounce Delano's first name. It was 'divine providence,' he said, 'that sent Masa Delano to repress the Blacks.' Soon, though, the Spaniard realized that the American intended to hold him to the promise he made when, during their brief private conversation on board the *Perseverance*, he offered to compensate Delano for putting down the rebels and returning his ship to him.

Cerreño complained to Spanish authorities that Delano's harassment was 'multiplying his past afflictions.' He was out of his mind when he made the offer, he said. What else could he have done? They had already rowed back to the *Perseverance* and Delano had readied his men for battle. The American, though, refused to give the final order to retake the *Tryal* until he knew 'what part of the prize' he could expect in return. Cerreño said he begged Delano for 'mercy.' He pleaded with the American to help save the 'wretched' sailors who remained on the ship from the 'barbarous, cruel, and bloody hands of the negro slaves.' Yet Delano refused to act until Cerreño said what he wanted to hear.

'Half the ship,' Cerreño said he cried in desperation, but he would have agreed to anything at that moment. 'I just as well could have told him *all of it*, since at that moment my anguish prevented me from reasoning.'

What kind of human being, Cerreño wanted to know, would hold someone to that promise considering the circumstances? He was distraught, terrified, and hardly capable of 'transacting business or negotiating percentages.' The remaining cargo wasn't his to give away. Nor should his misfortunes force him into ruinous debt. Cerreño cited maritime law requiring that property recovered from pirates—as Cerreño considered the West Africans—be returned to its rightful owner. Delano, therefore, was obligated to help a ship in distress. Instead he took advantage of Cerreño's vulnerability to 'bargain.' Cerreño admitted he owed Delano his life. But he insisted he didn't owe him half the value of his ship and his cargo. What the American was calling his due for services rendered was but pirate booty.

Five *Perseverance* crew members who had jumped ship at Santa María only to be taken into custody by Spanish authorities supported Cerreño's allegations. From their jail cells in Talcahuano, they unanimously testified to Delano's calamitous command. The *Perseverance* had been over a year out from Boston, two of them said, and had collected only seven thousand sealskins. John McCain complained that all he had to show for months at sea was a 'jacket, a vest, and two pairs of pants.' Another told of Delano's increasingly frantic captaincy, his meting out floggings for the smallest offence. 'Nothing pleases him,' testified David Brown, who requested permission to stay in Chile. William Brown, 'seeing that the situation was hopeless, resolved not to follow' Delano 'any longer.' Peter Sanson said that 'having wasted the voyage,' the *Perseverance* 'would have to resort to piracy in order to cover its expenses.' This, he claimed, is why he deserted Delano.

These testimonies, Cerreño argued, proved that Delano was little better than a brigand. He asked Rozas to keep Delano away from him. Other 'Anglo-Americans' frequently came into Spanish ports, seeking refuge and testing Spanish 'hospitality,' he said. Delano, with his ingratiating flattery and bad attempts at humour, was something else. With him, the new United States of America had 'produced a monster.'

By early April, Rozas had had enough of both Delano and Cerreño. In general, Rozas liked *bostoneses*. Delano, though, seemed a bit too eager to please and too desperate for praise. As to Cerreño, Rozas had a strong antipathy for most Spanish residents of Lima. Their shipowners monopolized transportation between Concepción and Peru, charging Chileans exorbitant fees to ship their wheat to Lima's market. Moreover, *Limeños* were servile and mannered. 'They were always kneeling and bowing to their viceroys,' he once wrote in a letter to a friend. 'They are obsequious, grovelling before the worst and flattering the inept. They are incapable of either noble or wicked deeds, which would require too much energy or strength of character.'[10]

The judge had tried to negotiate an agreement between the two captains, proposing what he thought a fair compensation of three thousand pesos. Delano rejected the offer with much 'heat and fire,' saying that he had already compromised and was willing to take ten thousand, considerably less than half the ship's worth. Cerreño, he said, knew what he was doing when he promised him recompense but, now that the ship was back in his possession, was trying to renege on a fair offer. Delano argued that he could have claimed possession of all the ship's cargo and the ship itself. Instead he made sure the vessel was 'safely conducted into harbour.' And so he wanted his reward.

Rozas gave up. He granted Cerreño permission to return to Lima and told Delano to take his complaint to Santiago. The *Tryal* left Talcahuano at the end of April, followed shortly by the *Perseverance*. Delano's reputation preceded him: royal authorities in Santiago wouldn't even grant him permission to leave his ship. They told him it would be best if he 'headed for Lima' and spoke directly to the viceroy.[11]

Delano in the past had complained about Spanish legalisms, the endless paperwork, inexplicable double or triple taxes levied on single items, and the complicated and seemingly arbitrary rules and regulations governing trade and navigation. He had trouble with everyday Spanish, but Spanish formalism, with its passive voice and reflexive verbs seemingly intent on confusing subject and object, was a bewildering hall of mirrors.

He had hoped to handle his dispute with Cerreño 'plainly.' In Concepción, he had told Thomas Delphin, an old Irish merchant who had been so long in Chile he called himself Tomás Delfín, that he 'didn't want to pursue a legal dispute of any kind.' It was, Delano said, his most 'fervent desire to avoid a court case.' Now, as he tried to defend himself from charges he only half understood, and fought for compensation he believed he had earned, Delano found himself being passed from one magistrate to another, lost in the twilight world of Spanish colonialism, whose arcane rules and conspiracies grew even more confusing as royal authority faded.

And so Delano went to Lima.

The Machinery of Civilization

Benito Cereno's fictional Amasa Delano reads like a complement to Herman Melville's more famous creation, Captain Ahab, with the men representing two sides of American expansion. One is virtuous, the other vengeful. Amasa is hollowed out, trapped by the superficialities of his own perception of the world. Ahab is profound. He peers into the depths. The first cannot see evil, the second can see only nature's 'intangible malignity.' 'A storm for every calm,' Ahab says in *Moby-Dick*.

The same complementarity applies to Ahab and the historical Amasa Delano. Both men are agents of two of the most predatory industries of their day, their ships lugging the 'machinery of civilization,' as the real Delano put it, to the Pacific, using steel, iron, and fire to kill animals and transform their corpses into value on the spot. Ahab's 'wild egoism' has been read by some as an extension of the individualism born out of American expansion, his rage the rage of a self that refuses to be limited by nature's frontier, an individual supremacy projected into the wide-open ocean, unable to connect with any other human being except, fleetingly, Pip. Amasa too is ego driven. In over five hundred pages of his memoir, he rarely mentions another crew member. You would think he were sailing his ship alone. But his egoism, in contrast to Ahab's, is turned inward, obsessed not so much with mastery of the world, though he does want to succeed, but with mastery of himself.[1]

Ahab is the exception, a rebel who hunts his white whale unto death, against all rational economic logic. He has hijacked the 'machinery,' the

Pequod, and rioted against 'civilization,' pursuing his quixotic chase in violation of the contract he has with his ship's owners. The character today is synonymous with ruin, used to explain everything from George W. Bush's wars to global warming, a planet destroyer embodying man's insatiable quest for more and more resources. But insurgents like Ahab, however dangerous to the people around them, are not the primary drivers of destruction. They are not the ones who will hunt animals to near extinction—or force the world to the brink. Those would be the men who never dissent, who carry out, as Jeremy Harding writes in an essay on *Moby-Dick*, the 'grinding, day-in-day-out extractive process,' men who are 'smitten with the glories of the planet but devoted to their expenditure. Like Amasa Delano.[2]

Delano is the rule. Where the mesmeric Ahab—the 'thunder-cloven old oak'—has been taken as a prototype of the twentieth-century totalitarian, a one-legged Hitler or Stalin, Delano represents a more common form of modern authority. His power is based not on the demagogic pull of charisma but on the everyday pressures involved in controlling labour and converting diminishing natural resources into marketable items. Caught in the pincers of supply and demand and trapped in the vortex of ecological exhaustion, with his own crew on the brink of mutiny because there are no seals left to kill and no money to be made, Delano rallies men to the chase, not of a white whale but of black rebels. Their slide into barbarism, followed by his pursuit, relentless while at the same time mundane, of Benito Cerreño for half the value of his ship and its cargo, happens not because he is dissenting from the laws of commerce and capital but because he faithfully and routinely administers them. He had 'knowledge of his duty,' as he said, and was 'disposed faithfully to obey its dictates.'

PART VII

GENERAL AVERAGE

Average (insurance): A loss to a shipment of goods that is less than a total loss . . . and ultimately comes from the Arabic word *awarijah*, which means 'merchandise damaged by sea water.' . . . A particular average is an insurance loss that affects specific interests only. . . . A general average is an insurance loss that affects all cargo interests on board the vessel as well as the ship herself.

—*DICTIONARY OF INTERNATIONAL TRADE*, 2005

24

LIMA, OR THE LAW OF GENERAL AVERAGE

Nine miles inland and overlooking the Pacific at fifteen hundred feet above the sea, Lima, the City of Kings, the seat of the Inquisition and home of the royal mint, was the grand throne of Spanish Catholicism in South America. Below, on the coast, the port of Callao was impressive in a different sort of way. It was one of the world's busiest global harbours, linking Spanish America to the Philippines, China, Japan, Indonesia, India, and Russia, with a deep anchorage and calm water that gave safe berths to hundreds of ships at a time.[1]

It was also one of the blackest. Over the course of nearly three centuries, about 100,000 Africans had been brought into Peru through Callao. But Callao wasn't just a slave port. It was a slaves' port, the radiating heart of the black Pacific, testimony to the fact that Spain's maritime trade in the Americas, the blood flow of its empire, was largely run by people of colour. One of the first things Amasa Delano would have seen, after entering the harbour and appreciating the spires of Lima in the distance, and after being pulled to the wharf in a ferryboat through flocks of flamingos and then climbing the stairway that ran alongside the breakwater, was a narrow dirt street 'full of sailors and blacks, of all shades of colour, Peruvians and mules.' The streets were busy with African and African American mariners, vendors, craftsmen, teamsters, beggars, and prostitutes, some of them free, others enslaved, all going about their business with a liberty that would have been unthinkable in a US slave harbour (except New Orleans).

The town itself seemed to be 'compressed into the smallest possible dimensions—reduced to its lowest terms,' a tumbledown city of tight alleys and single-story adobe houses, their main rooms with their swinging hammocks open to the street. Delano might have 'wondered at the donkeys, the inconceivable dirt of their drivers, the gay dresses of the women, the extraordinary appearance' of the Quechua soldiers—in small caps and reddish grey uniforms, with 'high cheeks,' their 'eyes . . . burning coal' and a 'volcanic fire raging just under the skin.'

There was a business street of ship chandlers selling rosin, tar, cordage, oakum, axes, and other maritime merchandise, clothing stores filled with Nanking pants, Dutch breeches, and British peacoats, dance halls, and at least one 'wretched' inn and tavern where the men were 'all sharks, the women all black-eyed, and black-faced Susans.' There were Jack Tars on every corner and groups of 'captains sitting in old chairs.'

Despite its dust and dirt, this part of town was considered new in 1805. Old Callao, on the point of a peninsula that jutted out into the harbour, was destroyed in 1746 by a massive tsunami that nearly reached Lima's gates. At least five thousand people were killed in the disaster, almost all of the port's residents, and when Delano visited the ruins he was shocked by the bones that still lay strewn about. Some were from victims who had been trapped in their homes when the quake hit or were the remains of corpses washed up by the tide after the wave subsided. 'The sea vomited bodies for months, the naked cadavers half eaten by fish,' reported a witness from the time. Others were skeletons of those buried in mass graves, 'worked out of the gravel' by erosion.[2]

They were everywhere, scattered on the barren soil and collected in piles in what had been the cellars of the swept-to-sea houses. The most startling scene was a pair of arched vaults, all that was left of a prison building where 'the foreigners as well as the lower order of the Spanish people were confined' when the water hit: 'these arches were filled with human bones, as were also most of the cellars, without any kind of covering over them.' Another visitor described touring the 'arched caverns' and seeing skeletons 'huddled together in the narrow vaults, just high enough to lie down in, and in every variety of posture, in which they yielded to the agonies of dissolution.'[3]

Delano in his memoirs often seems to skim the surface of things, bouncing from event to event, intuiting their importance and even at times offering sharp observations yet never quite comprehending the deep undercurrents of history that churn beneath. But here in Callao, the portal for so many Africans into Lima, itself built over the graves of vanquished Incas, Delano stands amid a vast field of ashen bones and almost grasps the fullness of time. 'The whole of these ruins viewed together,' he writes, 'by a person on the spot, was, I think sufficient to put all the powers of the mind in motion.'[4]

Once in Lima proper, Delano acted something like a New England Yankee in King Carlos's Court. In truth, the royal city better suited Delano than Concepción. That town, for all its Enlightenment radicalism, was prim and provincial. In contrast, Lima, though it still wasn't the dissolute place it would become after independence, was more a melting pot, a place where both inquisitorial Catholicism and prudish Protestantism could find some release. 'The very sound' of the 'word' *Lima*, one English-speaking voyager wrote of the city's name, 'affects me now like some lively, half melancholy Spanish dance.'[5]

The streets were crowded, the stores were stocked, and the city swarmed with 'people of all classes, colours, and professions.' There were more churches than theatres or billiard rooms, and many of them were graceful in their decay. Melville was in the city in 1844 and compared their drooping crosses to the 'canted yards of anchored fleets.'

There were plenty of taverns and inns, too. Delano, who stayed at one favoured by sea captains, describes a practical joke he helped play on a Catholic priest who came to the hotel begging for offerings and urging the Protestant officers to kiss an icon of the Virgin Mary. When the priest momentarily turned his attention away, Delano and his companions hid the Virgin under the sheets of his bed. The cleric became distressed upon not being able to locate the statue until finally one of the sailors pulled back the sheets to reveal Mary underneath. Since the priest was selling her kisses for alms, he said, maybe she decided to go into business for herself and climb straight into bed.

Because officials in Santiago had denied his petition for an audience, brusquely sending him and his ship on their way, Delano thought he would show up unannounced at the viceroy's palace and hope for the best. He arrived early on an autumn Sunday morning, as the viceroy, Gabriel de Avilés Itúrbide y del Fierro, the second marquis of Avilés, readied himself for Mass. It wasn't the most opportune moment to seek an impromptu meeting with the most powerful Spanish official in South America. Madrid's relations with the United States during those months were strained, as negotiations over Thomas Jefferson's purchase of Louisiana from the French, which included large pieces of territory claimed by Carlos IV, were not going well. But Avilés came to enjoy Delano. He gave him permission to come and go as he pleased, when he pleased, so much so that the Duxbury captain became known among palace courtiers as the 'King's favourite.'[6]

Lima's three-story royal palace sat on nearly five acres of land in the centre of the city. The building was famous for its labyrinthine hallways, luscious gardens planted with fig trees and flowers, cavernous halls hung with tapestries and oil paintings, and gallery running along the full length of its second floor. It had been destroyed, rebuilt, and expanded many times since first put up in 1535 by Francisco Pizarro, the conqueror of the Inca empire and the founder of Spanish Peru. By the time Amasa Delano arrived, the royal court was considered 'the best and most sumptuous building in the entire realm, since there has hardly been a viceroy that hasn't added a room or a new wing, adding to the majesty that it represents.'[7]

Amasa visited the palace at least fifty times during his stay in Lima, often losing himself in its 'many turnings and windings.' Having read about the splendour of the court's royal sentinels in *Bank's Geography*, he set out at once to satisfy his curiosity. 'I did not fully believe the account until I saw them myself.'[8] Delano, wearing his coarse wool sailor's coat and cotton pantaloons, inspected the sentries, who were dressed in fine red breeches and gold-laced blue waistcoats, silk stockings, and velvet shoes and were armed with French swords and Swiss halberd pike axes. He also passed a smaller contingent of five ceremonial slaves—*los negros del rey*, the king's blacks—outfitted in expensive Quito-blue cotton shirts with wide velvet collars, ivory buttons, wide-brimmed, high-crowned straw hats, and graceful cotton ponchos. 'The dress of the body guards makes the most elegant and extraordinary appearance of any thing I have seen,' Delano thought.[9]

Delano was as lost trying to figure out the warren of rival commercial interests that seemed to be standing in the way of his receiving his rightful reward, for despite Avilés's affection for Amasa, the viceroy couldn't easily satisfy his complaint. The uprising on the *Tryal*, the loss of much of its cargo, including the exiled, executed, and starved-to-death Africans, affected many powerful interests, including a number of merchants who had financed Cerreño's purchase of his ship. In an economy that ran largely on promissory notes and exchange bills, they weren't likely to pass on a ship full of real monetized wealth in the form of slaves.[10]

When, a few days before Delano arrived, Cerreño had sailed the *Tryal* into Callao's harbour carrying fifty-five masterless slaves, about half of whom were women and children, the investors wanted their share. The West Africans weren't loose fish but, as breathing expressions of debt, credit, and collateral, who they were struck fast to was a matter of dispute.

Now that Aranda was dead, who had the right to sell the surviving *Tryal* rebels? And who would get the profits from their sale? These were two main questions on which the various cases turned. The Buenos Aires rancher turned slaver Juan Nonell, when he heard the news of the uprising and its suppression, gave a Lima lawyer power of attorney to put a lien on the slaves for the value of what Aranda owed him. At the same time, Aranda's father-in-law and wife in Mendoza also filed papers putting a lien on the West Africans. They were looking to recover at least an amount equivalent to the down payment Aranda gave Nonell when he purchased them in April 1804, along with the value of a box of jewels and other property Aranda had been travelling with that had gone missing. Cerreño's many creditors, the men who advanced him loans to purchase the *Tryal*, as well as the merchants who lost cargo during the voyage, also claimed what they said they were owed. And then there was Cerreño himself. He considered the slaves his prize, hoping to sell them to cover his loss, pay his debts, and free himself of Amasa Delano.[11]

To make his case, Cerreño, in his petition to Lima's commercial court, invoked a principle of maritime law known as the law of general average (*avería gruesa* in Spanish). It's an old code, shared by Roman, Islamic, and Christian mariners before specialized cargo insurance became widespread. It was meant to equalize losses resulting from a seafaring disaster. If a crew had to jettison one merchant's cargo to lighten a ship to ride out a storm, then all the merchants with goods on the stricken vessel would be asked to bear some of the loss, based on a percentage of their portion of the total freight. As marine insurance evolved through the 1700s and 1800s, slave ship owners also applied the law of general average to make claims for damages incurred during slave insurrections. They argued that such revolts should be considered comparable to an act of God, a storm, or some other 'peril of the sea,' and hence any resulting damage to the ship or loss of cargo should be distributed among all interested parties (actuaries calculated that there was a one in ten chance that the cargo of any given slaver might revolt and that in a rebellion an eighth of the slaves would be killed). And there is at least one infamous case, that of the *Zong* in 1781, where slave ship owners claimed that the jettisoning of 132 Africans was necessary to save the rest of the slaves and crew because the ship wasn't carrying enough food to cover its journey across the Atlantic.*

---

* The application of general average loss to slave insurrections raised a sticky philosophical problem, for in no other case of cargo loss was the loss caused by the will and actions of the cargo. This issue came to light in a case that reached the Louisiana Supreme Court in 1842, when lawyers for the Merchants' Insurance Company, which had underwritten the slave ship *Creole*, argued that their clients weren't liable to cover damages incurred on that ship as a result of a slave rebellion. Rebellions, they said, were caused not by 'external accidents' but by the 'inherent vices of the subject insured'—that is, the inherent tendency of slaves to rebel. One of the company's lawyers, Judah Benjamin, who later would serve as attorney general for the Confederacy, based his argument on the fundamental humanity of slaves:

Cerreño didn't have insurance but he argued the principle, saying that part of the profit from the sale of the *Tryal*'s slaves should be used to help him offset his debt and rid himself of Delano. His plea was denied on its first hearing but, after months of appeals, he eventually won a partially favourable ruling. A judge ordered the West Africans to be sold to one of Lima's most active slave traders, Jacinto Jimeño, for a price based on their assessed value. Jimeño, in turn, would split his payment among Nonell, Aranda's heirs, and Cerreño. The ruling, though, didn't settle the case. Nonell and Aranda's heirs appealed and Cerreño's creditors continued their demands, as did the merchants whose cargo was tossed to lighten the ship during the storm. The multiple suits and countersuits swirling around the question of how to divide the estimated value of the surviving *Tryal* rebels didn't drag on quite as long as *Bleak House*'s *Jarndyce v. Jarndyce*, but for years no two lawyers could talk about the matter for 'five minutes without coming to a total disagreement as to all the premises.'[12]

Meanwhile, Amasa Delano continued to demand ten thousand pesos from Cerreño. His brother Samuel arrived in Lima in June, telling him that seals were still scarce, confirming without doubt what the brothers already knew: the voyage was a bust.

'What is a slave? He is a human being. He has feelings and passions and intellect. His heart, like the white man's, swells with love, burns with jealousy, aches with sorrow, pines under restraint and discomfort, boils with revenge, and ever cherishes the desire of liberty.' He 'is prone to revolt in the very nature of things. . . . Will any one deny that the bloody and disastrous insurrection of the *Creole* was the result of the inherent qualities of the slaves themselves, roused, not only by their condition of servitude, but stimulated by the removal from their friends and homes . . . and encouraged by the lax discipline of the vessel, the numerical weakness of the whites, and the proximity of a British province?' According to the historian Tim Armstrong, Benjamin argued in another case that 'rebellion is intrinsic to slavery' and that slavery is an 'institution which has since Justinian been described as *contra naturam*, and a result of local conditions rather than of universal application. . . . The more general implication is that the slave's situation is temporary and reversible. The slave can never definitively be treated as an owned thing.' Benjamin's arguments, which won the case for the insurers, in a way parallel those of the Montevideo doctors who invoked the inner emotional lives of slaves to explain the epidemic that swept through the *Joaquín*, an example of how the horrors of slavery were helping to modernize medicine. Here, those horrors were forcing a modernization of law: humans were universal but slavery wasn't, an interesting position for a man who would go on to be the chief lawyer for the Confederate States of America.

For the next couple of months, Delano went before one royal bureaucrat after another. To each, he recited the risk he had put himself and his men in that day in the South Pacific. To each, he pointed out the place in Cerreño's testimony where the Spaniard praised his actions, calling him heroic and generous, and where in another deposition he 'thanked divine providence' for sending 'Masa Delano to repress the Blacks.' To each, he appealed to maritime law and custom regarding rewards and compensation for services rendered. And to each, he reiterated that he could have just kept the whole ship and its cargo, 'every handsome thing.'

Finally, in September, he made one last plea to Avilés. Delano said he understood that the viceroy had many interests to consider. But he begged him to settle the matter once and for all. Since first arriving in Talcahuano, his men had continued to abandon him, often taking valuable equipment from his ship with them. He had been in Lima for months, going deeper in debt trying to feed the men that did stay with him. He was so desperate, he had even tried to sell the *Perseverance* to the Spanish navy, hoping to pay off what he owed and just return home on the *Pilgrim*. The navy declined the offer, thinking it would be too expensive to turn the schooner into a man-of-war. He still had 'nearly thirty men on different islands.' They needed food and other supplies, and if his claim was deferred any longer, it was certain that 'they must suffer.'[13]

Avilés finally told Delano he would rule in his favour, but only if he would lower his demand to eight thousand pesos. Delano had rejected compromising earlier, in Concepción, but now he had little choice but to agree. The viceroy called Cerreño into his office, with Delano present, and told the Spaniard that he would throw him in jail if he didn't pay. Cerreño had yet to receive his share from the sale of the West Africans to Jimeño (it's unknown if he ever did) but on the strength of the decision he was able to mortgage the *Tryal* and borrow the money to pay Delano.

Delano received his reward, eight thousand pesos in gold, but it didn't go far. That was close to the amount he owed various suppliers in Callao for keeping the *Perseverance* afloat and its men fed. It took more than another year, nearly three since he left Boston, for Delano finally to fill its hold with sealskins. In July 1806, he took the *Perseverance* to China, but with the market still glutted he had to wait months before he could sell the fur.

Samuel Delano stayed in the waters off of Chile and Peru for another year, finally leaving in September 1807 with only thirteen thousand skins. On the way to Canton, the *Pilgrim* ran into a northeast gale as it entered the China Sea, turning on its side until its masts were below the waves. Three men were lost and it seemed that the ship would be as well. But then the wind miraculously swung the bow around and righted the vessel before it could fill with water. The *Pilgrim* was saved though nearly all of its skins were ruined.

Back in Lima, Jimeño sold most of the fifty-five West African men, women, children, and infants who came into his possession within a year. Many were purchased individually. They found themselves distributed throughout Lima alone, the solidarity and community they had built up over their long journey shattered. Others were lucky enough to be kept in groups of two or three.

The sociologist Orlando Patterson has written that the essence of slavery was 'social death.' In a way, Patterson describes what the doctors in Montevideo concluded about the *Joaquín* in late 1803, that slavery resulted in *cisma*, or schism, severing humans from their past, from their history, family, and home, and transforming them into 'genealogical isolates.' Nothing illustrates this rupture better than the sales receipts that exist in Lima's archives concerning the *Tryal*'s surviving men, women, and children. The documentation is meagre. At most, the records provide the age and gender of the person being sold, along with the price and credit terms of the transaction. They omit original names and give no indication as to what happened to the babies, whether they were kept with their mothers or sold to different households.[14]

The receipts do provide one bit of information that suggests that the psychic breach wasn't absolute. In a few cases, they reveal the new

Christian names of the West Africans: 'Two new blacks,' purchased by one household for 960 pesos, 'respond to the names Antonio and Manuel and are thirteen years old.' One young boy brought by a merchant 'responds to the name Joaquín.' The phrase 'responds to' is meant to be formalistic and bland. But it jars. It sounds almost like an admission on the part of the masters that these new labels would always be aliases and that the slaves' forfeiture of their recent experiences and past lives would remain incomplete—that the two twelve-year-old girls taken off the *Tryal* and sold to Doña María Daga and Doña María Rivera for 920 pesos might 'respond to the Christian names María and Rosa' but that would never be all they were.

25

THE LUCKY ONE

Though Benito Cerreño had kept the original English name of his ship painted on its hull, he occasionally referred to the *Tryal* as *la Prueba*, a Spanish word that also means a test of faith. It was as common for Catholics in Spanish America to draw on religious themes for the names of their vessels as it was for Protestants in New England, though the former were partial to martyred saints (including San Juan Nepomuceno) while the latter preferred the virtues (like perseverance). In any case, Benito Cerreño, having passed through more trials than Job, decided soon after he had returned to Lima from Concepción to rename his ship. It would now sail as *la Dichosa*—the Lucky One.[1]

Cerreño wouldn't be on it. Vowing never to return to sea, he leased out *la Dichosa* to another merchant captain and dedicated himself to starting a new life on land. A week after his return to Lima, Cerreño married Francisca Murre, a recent widow whose first husband had left her a considerable-size sugar plantation, Hacienda Humaya, about seventy miles north of the city. At the time, the best measure of the value of farmland was not its size but rather the age and height of its crops. When Benito and Francisca moved in, Humaya had twelve fields planted with eighteen-month-old sugarcane upward of twelve feet tall, almost ready to be harvested. All told, with its sugar, fruit orchids, workshops, manor house, and livestock, the plantation was valued at nearly 200,000 pesos.[2]

The assessment included its slaves, since the cane would have been worthless without the hands to cut it. The estate's 236 slaves were assessed at 91,782 pesos, almost half the property's total value. Most of them—129 men and 107 women—had been in America longer than their new master, having been born and raised in Peru and baptized in the Catholic faith. Some were descended from the first Africans present when the estate was founded in 1693. Others might even have had ancestors in Peru earlier than that.

It must have been tempting for Cerreño, as he assumed his gentry life, a life his family back in Andalusia had lost, to believe that he had put all that had happened to him on the *Tryal* behind him. Days removed from the bustle and politics of Lima, Hacienda Humaya sprawled up the mist-shrouded sides of the rolling Huaura Valley. It was an ancient Jesuit estate, connected to the coast by an old, rutted road. When Cerreño took it over, its double-nave chapel still had its original organ, stone-carved baptismal font, and wooden pulpit.

There were no Babos. No Atufals and Moris. No Leobes, Quiamobos, Alasans, Malpendas, or Matunquis. No mass of indistinguishable African women singing death dirges. There were just Humaya's settled sharecropper slaves who lived in small thatched houses along the road connecting the manor house to the plantation's graveyard. Among them was the sixty-three-year-old Juan Capistrano, who ran the grinding mill (he was assessed at three hundred pesos), Domingo de la Nieves (worth one peso for each of his eighty years), and Augustina de la Rosa, a ninety-year-old invalid (ten pesos).

But in 1820, the world once again broke in on Cerreño.

In Spanish America during its wars for independence—which lasted for over a decade, from about 1810 to well into the 1820s—thousands of black slaves in Mexico, Colombia, Venezuela, Argentina, and the Andes quit their fields, workshops, and houses to join insurrectionary armies. In some places, they made up as much as 30 percent of revolutionary forces.

Chile was in the vanguard of independence and emancipation, establishing under the leadership of none other than Juan Martínez de Rozas a self-governing council that in 1811 passed a number of measures limiting slavery. Among them was a 'law of free womb,' which decreed all children born of slave parents to be free, and a ban on the future importation of new slaves into Chilean territory. When Peru's viceroy sent in royal troops to pacify Chile, the Revolutionary Army of the Andes—led by General José de San Martín and made up largely of manumitted slaves from Buenos Aires and Mendoza—crossed into the country from Argentina to defeat them. Many of these slaves-turned-revolutionaries had in effect retraced Babo's and Mori's journey, but under vastly different circumstances: having first arrived in Montevideo as property, they trekked across the pampas as free people, joining San Martín's insurgent forces in Mendoza and then climbing over the Andes to liberate Chile, an important step in achieving the independence of all of Spanish South America.[3]

Numbering in the thousands, these emancipated rebel soldiers, now joined by Chile's free and freed blacks, continued to follow the route of the *Tryal* rebels. They set sail from Valparaiso bound for Lima in August 1820, part of San Martín's expeditionary fleet that vowed to bring down the 'tyrants who believed they could enslave with impunity the sons of liberty.' The flotilla first landed south of Lima. Up and down the crisscrossing valleys that connect the Pacific to the Andes, slaves fled their haciendas to join San Martín, bringing with them food, livestock, and horses pilfered from their plantations. Others simply used the chaos caused by the invasion to escape, joining neither the *patriotas* nor the *realistas*.[4]

On November 9, 1820, San Martín sailed north of Lima, to the Bay of Huacho, at the bottom of the Huaura Valley. Shortly thereafter, his troops marched up the valley with the power to liberate any slave who joined their ranks. On December 27—exactly sixteen years to the day of the *Tryal* revolt—a rebel detachment arrived outside the gates of Humaya. Cerreño, having survived one insurrection, didn't wait around to be caught up in another. He was gone when the soldiers entered the next day, having fled to Lima and abandoned the hacienda to his slaves.[5]

For a while, Lima acted as if what was would always be. Rozas was right about the city's merchants. They were servile. Even as Buenos Aires, Montevideo, Caracas, Bogotá, and Santiago, along with provincial towns like Concepción and Mendoza, were throwing in with independence, 'fortress Lima,' with its surfeit of priests and lords, wealthy merchants tied to the great trading houses of Seville and Cádiz, and well-armed viceregal army, stayed true to Spain. The inhabitants of the city and its surrounding estates, wrote one observer, 'went on in their usual style of splendid luxury, in thoughtless ease and security, till the enemy came and knocked at the "silver gates of the city of kings."'[6]

The knock came in July 1821. San Martín and his army entered Lima and its residents finally realized they were living in new times. 'The consternation was excessive,' wrote the same witness, 'the men were pacing about in fearful doubt what was to be done; the women were flying in all directions to the convents; and the narrow streets were literally choked up with wagons and mules, and mounted horsemen.' Cerreño was likely among those trying to escape the city 'on foot, in carts, on horseback, . . . men, women, and children with horses and mules, and numbers of slaves laden with baggage and other valuables . . . all was outcry and confusion.' Soon, though, the streets were empty, as fear spread that the 'slave population of the city meant to take advantage of the absence of troops, to rise in a body and massacre the whites.'[7]

The lords and ladies of Lima had little to fear. San Martín, after taking Lima, did issue a number of decrees limiting the slave trade and slavery. But, still facing a strong royal army outside of the city, he hoped to win over rural landlords to his cause. He walked a fine line, emancipating slaves who joined his ranks but making clear that runaways still belonged to their owners. Fighting dragged on for years more. It wasn't until December 1824, at the Battle of Ayacucho, that royalist forces were finally driven out.

By that point, the early radical promise of Spanish American independence, which saw the revolutionary armies marching across hacienda lands, freeing slaves by the thousands, had been contained. The legal process of abolition that started in Chile in 1811 would continue. But it did so gradually and conservatively, through measures, laws, and decrees designed to maintain the power of the region's landed elite. Still, by 1855—ten years before the US Civil War ended at Appomattox—the buying, selling, and holding of human beings as chattel was over in all of the American republics that had broken from Spain.

As to Benito Cerreño, he was thrown in jail for a few days on charges of aiding royalist forces shortly after he fled San Martín's troops.[8] But he was soon released and, when life returned to normal, allowed to reclaim Humaya and its people, resuming an aristocratic life now accommodated to republican rule. In 1829, he suffered a hemiplegic seizure that left him paralyzed. He died in 1830. His widow, Francisca, lived until 1853. Abolition was still a year away in Peru, yet on her death she freed all of Humaya's 'large number of slaves' except one, who was left to her daughter.[9]

Cerreño had years earlier lost the vessel previously known as the *Tryal* to his creditors. *La Dichosa,* the Lucky One, was spotted thereafter by Mayhew Folger, the Quaker captain of the *Topaz,* famous for having rescued the survivors of Bligh's *Bounty* from Pitcairn Island. Upon returning to Nantucket in 1810, he told his friend Thomas Coffin that Coffin's old ship was rotting away in the port of Valparaiso, 'stripped, weatherbeaten, and settled in the water.'[10]

26

UNDISTRIBUTED

Schools of porpoises and flocks of seabirds trailed the *Perseverance* as it approached the Cape of Good Hope in May 1807, heading back to New England from China with a hull half filled with porcelain and tea not worth close to enough to cover what Delano owed his men or to pay back his creditors. The vessel was worn down. According to its log, 'all hands' were needed to keep it afloat. 'The ship was very leaky,' and its men were 'obliged to pump her every half an hour.' The weather turned 'gloomy' after it entered the South Atlantic, with flying clouds, baffling winds, and heavy swells from the west. The Fourth of July dawned 'dark and squally.' There was no liquor left on board, but the crew celebrated by dining on lobscouse, a meat stew. On Friday, July 24, 'the highland of Cape Cod' came into sight. A few days later the *Perseverance* was in Boston, having ended a voyage of nearly four years, circling the globe twice and sailing over fifty thousand miles.[1]

Delano had expected something to be waiting for him on his return. 'Many powerful friends' in Lima had told him, he said, that the king of Spain, Carlos IV, would personally send him an additional reward, beyond the gold he had received from Cerreño. It's easy to imagine, as he pleaded his case in one office after another, royal bureaucrats telling him such a thing in the hope he'd move on. As it turned out, there was a gift for him in Boston, though it wasn't what he had hoped. It was a gold medallion embossed with Carlos's profile, along with a letter from Spain's envoy to the United States thanking Delano on the king's behalf for his humane and noble service. Within a few months, Carlos would be dethroned by Napoleon, ending once and for all Delano's hope of receiving, as he put it, 'something essentially to my advantage.'[2]

Delano could have used it. America had changed while he was away. Debt had taken a more central role in the growing nation's economy, and Delano was trapped in its grip, dragged through court and, it seems, thrown into debtors' prison. He had owed significant amounts to various creditors even before the *Perseverance*'s first sail (including to Ezra Weston back in Duxbury). But now he was being sued by people he had never met, by creditors who had bought his debt from earlier creditors or by individuals claiming to be the executors of deceased sailors. He owed thousands of dollars to various people when most of the prisoners in the Boston Gaol were sailors serving time for demands of less than twenty. One George Riley owed about fifty dollars, and he spent six years in the jail. A blind Bostonian was put in for owing six dollars.[3]

Delano continued to run the *Perseverance* for a while more, bringing dried codfish to the Caribbean, his debt, along with the pressure of having to support his family, forcing him to put aside earlier qualms about trading with slave islands. With the help of the Reverend Horace Holley, his pastor at the Hollis Street Unitarian Church, Delano was able to call on some of the city's most prominent residents for help. A young lawyer just starting out, Lemuel Shaw, who would go on to be the chief justice of the Massachusetts Supreme Judicial Court as well as Herman Melville's father-in-law, offered his services pro bono to keep him out of jail. Delano also wrote to Supreme Court justice Joseph Story, later famous for his ruling in favour of the *Amistad* rebels, asking him to intervene on his behalf with a judge presiding over one case. 'Pray befriend an honest man, and oblige,' he begged. Delano defaulted in most of the debt trials. He just didn't show up in court.[4]

Delano sold his ship in late 1810, paying off some of what he owed but not all. He took a job at the Boston Custom House and settled on Summer Street, a short walk from Boston's India Wharf, the broke head of a household of eight, including sisters, nephews, and nieces. It was around this point that, encouraged by Reverend Holley, he began to write his memoirs. His lawyer, Shaw, drew up a contract between Delano and three men, possibly friends but maybe just more creditors, who advanced the money to have the book printed. Sold by subscription, it was meant to reverse Delano's string of 'misfortunes and embarrassments.' 'It is a matter of regret,' Holley wrote in a biographical sketch included in the memoir as an appendix, that a man of Delano's 'generous and disinterested feelings, and who has made such great exertions to secure a handsome living in the world, should be thus unfortunate at this time of his life.'[5]

Delano had high hopes for *A Narrative of Voyages and Travels*. He sent a copy to Secretary of State John Quincy Adams in Washington, asking for a favourable comment that might help sell it and telling Adams that he wrote the book to add to the 'great stock of knowledge already collected by Capt. Cook and others.'* The memoir is filled with extended descriptions of the natural world ('the serpents of Bouro are most remarkable') and useful nautical information, such as the direction of currents, the location of underwater rocks, and which way winds normally blow as one enters this or that harbour. 'The westerly head' of San Félix Island 'is of a different colour from the easterly part.' 'Between the red and black parts is the best place to land.' Delano takes long philosophical detours throughout, considering, for example, the underlying universality of world religions and the similarity between the Greek 'system of dialectics' and Hinduism. 'There is scarcely a notion,' he writes, 'advanced by metaphysicans' that can't be found in 'bramincial writings.'[6]

But as one moves through its pages, *A Narrative* reads less like an encyclopedia of world knowledge than like a long catalogue of botches, fiascos, and debacles testifying to the impossibility of knowledge, or at least the impossibility of doing anything with knowledge once it is collected. Having been catapulted into the world by the great egalitarian thrust of the American Revolution, Delano found it to be one long parade

---

* Adams sent a diplomatic reply, appreciating the gift while avoiding the request for an endorsement: 'I return to you my thanks for the favourable light in which you are disposed to view the opinion I shall no doubt form of this work from the perusal of it.'

of mortifications, a word that comes up often in his memoir. I've described only some of his defeats here. But there were many more. Delano himself described his life, when he was in the Bass Strait thinking he was going to drown, as filled with 'hardships and privations, besides many heartrending scenes of injustice, ingratitude, and disappointment.'

Delano thought his book would help demythologize the world, the way as a young man he thought going to sea would allow him to judge the truth of all the many 'exaggerated accounts' he had read in books and 'false statements' peddled by sailors. He valued seeing the world as it really is, seeing it with, as he put it, 'two eyes.' Perhaps that's why he started his memoir with a story about an effort to trick his crew into reason.

Mariners were a strange 'class of men,' he wrote. They lived their lives charting the movements of the natural world, the expected comings and goings of stars, planets, tides, and currents. But if sailing was a learnable trade, it was also a 'mystery,' as apprentice contracts stipulated. 'Sailors, though usually the boldest men alive, are yet frequently the abject slaves of superstitious fear,' complained Delano. On voyages where gale followed gale in unfathomable succession, mariners, continually exposed to nature's capriciousness, put great stock in the 'traditions which are handed down from generation to generation concerning omens, charms, predictions, and the agency of invisible spirits.' Whistling might summon Satan, drowning a cat would bring a storm, seamen could equally hang a kingfisher by the bill to judge the weather as consult a barometer, and just one word from an astrologer could cause a whole crew to quit a ship.

Delano thought such practices mocked the 'Deity,' as if God would intervene in nature's mechanics for the 'most trifling purposes,' to make, say, the North Star shine in the south. So after overhearing a few of his men on watch one night debating the existence of ghosts, Delano decided he had to do something. He found an old deck mop and outfitted it with white linen to look like a shrouded, slender-waisted woman and hung it from a block above the ship's stern. He intended to gently frighten the night watch and then reveal the hoax, in the hope that reality would 'cure' the men of 'their folly.'[7]

The joke worked too well. A group of men sitting aft upon the quarterdeck were 'struck dumb, fixed immovable with terror, and seemed like so many breathless but gazing petrifactions.' They moved to address the spectre, asking her in the 'name of the Holy God, who are you, and what do you want?' Fearing he had gone too far, Delano took the apparition down and withdrew to his cabin to sleep, planning to reveal the hoax in the morning. But he was woken in the middle of the night by his chief mate, who told him that the crew had gathered on deck 'filled with anxiety and alarm.' Delano tried to calm his men down, but their sufferings were so 'extreme' he couldn't. Afraid to reveal his ploy, he kept quiet. For the rest of the voyage, the affair haunted Delano and caused him a 'great deal of anxiety.' It did not, he admitted, 'accomplish the good that I designed by it.'

It's a fitting prelude to Delano's memoir, foreshadowing deceptions and deceits to come. After such episodes, such as the practical joke played on him by his British mates on Pio Quinto, Delano often lapsed into long passages of brooding and introspection, not unlike Odysseus in Homer's *Odyssey*. But Odysseus was able to use these inner thoughts to his advantage. He plugged his men's ears so they wouldn't succumb to the song of the Sirens and he gulled the Cyclops, allowing him and his men to escape. Delano can only trap himself with his own trick, achieving the opposite of what he intended, confirming to his men the existence of ghosts.

The American Revolution for men like Delano was a great clarifying event, helping to disenchant the world. The Duxbury preachers who supported independence told him that one's fate was not predestined, that man had reason and free will, which gave him the power to make of himself what he would. But for the hapless Delano, faith in reason and free will became its own enchantment, blinding him to the ties that bound men together, that set the limits of who succeeded and who failed, and that decided who was free and who wasn't.*

---

* This is clearest in the section of his memoir when he is talking about his debt problems. Debt was a social scourge—Boston courts sent more than 1,442 debtors to its jail in 1820, some for owing a pittance. Some debtors were new risk takers, investing in various failed

The Age of Revolution tossed Amasa from Haiti to Île de France, Bombay to Lima, returning him home to find nothing waiting other than past-due promissory notes, court summonses, and an America he couldn't get a hold on, a token from a soon-to-be deposed monarch his only medal.[8]

At the end of his last sealing voyage on the *Pilgrim*, after his ship nearly capsized and he had lost all his skins, Samuel Delano recommitted to Christianity. He got caught up in America's Second Great Awakening, a reaction against the intellectualism that had crept into the Christianity of his youth, a return to religion as a sensual, carnal experience. In a letter to his son in New Orleans, Samuel warned him to watch for his soul in that 'sickly place,' reminding him that God had 'sent his only begotten son into the world veiled in humanity to be scourged, buffeted, nailed to the cross, bled and die that we . . . would repent of our sins.' 'Be prepared to die,' he said, for after 'death then comes judgment.' Samuel even had his own prophetic 'night vision,' a confused jumble of 'women,' 'lust,' and 'flesh' that he managed to interpret as a 'confirmation' of the 'sacred scriptures.' He'd come a long way from the exercises in logic that passed as religious sermons in the pews of his childhood church, when ministers like Elijah Brown talked about reason as being the 'guide to bliss.'[9]

---

schemes. Others were wastrels, drinking themselves into penury. But many, like Delano old-time seamen and merchants who thought credit and debt were to be used to support the trade of merchandise, not a trade in and of itself, found themselves pulled down by uncontrollable market forces, including a series of bank failures that ran through New England in the 1810s. There is a suggestion, in a hard-to-read document in Lemuel Shaw's papers, that Delano lost what little savings he had during one such collapse. Yet Delano said the solution to this problem was more personal responsibility. 'It is a duty that every man owes himself to take care of his own earnings,' he wrote, 'and not be outstripped under the operation of any of the foregoing principles.' 'Never let an account lie open with friend or foe, although they may say, "let it all lie just as it does till your return,"' he counsels, for what one thinks will be the 'fair balance' will never be enough to pay 'the demand.' Delano doesn't say who these friends or foes were, but it seems that men whom he trusted were quick to use the courts to multiply his woes. Any sailor who leaves himself open to such legal manipulation will, he writes, find himself 'in his old age penniless and without a friend.' It will 'break his heart, more especially if he possesses a noble mind.'

Amasa went the other way. In his memoir, he displays a toleration and relativism toward other cultures that would become more common later in the nineteenth century, when Melville was writing, but was rare for the early 1800s. Delano is most analytical, most aware of larger social forces, when discussing the impact Europeans had on non-Europeans. In his description of Palau, for example, he is critical of how the arrival of ships full of guns, textiles, jewellrey, and brandy upset the balance between vice and virtue that had existed among the island's residents. Delano appears to be borrowing directly from Jean-Jacques Rousseau's *Discourse on Inequality* when he writes that the merchandise deepened their desires, creating more personal 'wants,' making them more calculating, more instrumental, deceptive even, in pursuing 'dishonest means of gratification.' He also seems to be drawing on Rousseau, as well as the lectures of Duxbury preachers such as Charles Turner and Elijah Brown, writing that civilization is dependent on the creation of a system of virtues to check and balance 'evil . . . base passions.' A rapid increase in 'wants' could make even 'polished nations . . . more miserable than any savages.' It was worse with 'Islanders,' not because of any intrinsic fault but because 'white people' didn't give them time to develop counterweights. 'Europeans' immediately moved in to accelerate the disruption, using their 'arts and force . . . to betray, to kidnap, or to seize openly and violently, the natives for the most selfish and inhuman purposes.' Such actions, he writes, in turn elicited 'reprisals.'

For all its censure, this critique was still grounded in faith, in the Christian optimism Delano took in during his youth. He thought trade, given time and restraint on the part of Europeans, would eventually help 'Islanders' multiply their 'virtues and blessings, and call out a greater variety of talents and sympathies.' But by the 1820s, after yet more misfortunes and embarrassments, probably including jail time, his heart broken and his book not selling, Delano's questioning pluralism evolved into a deeper doubt.

In September 1821, he came across an article in a Boston newspaper, 'Sketches of Indian History,' recounting a meeting between a Seneca warrior named Red-Jacket and Boston missionaries that took place at Buffalo Creek, New York, in November 1805. The encounter ended with Red-Jacket instructing his would-be tutors in the deductive method: 'You say that you are right, and we are lost; how do we know this to be true?' Whether Delano was moved by the suffering of the Indians described by Red-Jacket or impressed with his question, he clipped the article and sent it along with a letter to Samuel in Duxbury.*

'Pray read, and ponder well on every sentence,' Amasa wrote his fundamentalist brother. 'Bring to your mind what you know the Christian race has done to make other people, even one another miserable.' Samuel, too, was struggling with debt, which Amasa here might have been referring to. 'Let me ask you,' he went on, 'who has made you so extremely unhappy in this world but Christians. Consider if any Chinese, Sandwich Islanders, or any other Islanders, has ever done you much wrong, where there was no Christian . . . mixed with it.' In an illegible part of the letter, Amasa seems to say he would not 'abolish Christianity,' as it was the 'religion of our fathers.' But those Christians who took advantage of Indians deserved little respect.[10]

Delano then links this cultural imperialism to his own spiritual unease. After describing himself as unmoored, as 'listing, this way, or that,' he continues:

I will speak one or two words more on the state of my own mind and then

---

* Red-Jacket provided a list of grievances against 'white people': 'We gave them corn and meat; they gave us poison in return. . . . At length their numbers had greatly increased; they wanted more land; they wanted our country.' He went on: 'We understand that your religion is written in a book; if it was intended for us as well as you, why has not the Great Spirit given it to us, and not only to us, but why did he not give to our forefathers the knowledge of that book, with the means of understanding it rightly? We only know what you tell us about it. How shall we know when to believe, being so often deceived by the white people? Brother, you say there is but one way to worship and serve the Great Spirit; if there is but one religion, why do you white people differ so much about it? Why not all agree, as you can all read the book?' The speech continues to this day to be republished and taught in high schools and colleges. Curiously, Red-Jacket had earlier fought against Herman Melville's maternal grandfather, Peter Gansevoort, during the American Revolution.

leave the subject: my mind for many years has been undistributed as to a here-after, as much so it has been for fear the moon would fall down on me and squeeze me to death, I always think when it comes into my mind, that I know nothing about it, and that no other man knows, or ever did know, or ever will know, this till the grave but my Prayer is ever like the soldier who was going into battle—viz—please God, if there is a god, save my soul, if I have a soul.

Your affectionate brother,

Amasa Delano

Amasa died two years later, in 1823, from what seems to have been a heart attack. He wasn't alone. Delano lived with his wife, sisters, and nephews. Judging from his correspondence, though, he felt isolated.

He shouldn't have, not just because of his extended family but because Boston during his last years was something like his hometown, Duxbury, writ large, at least when it came to the triumph of anti-Calvinist Christianity. His brother might have embraced a hellfire Christ, and he himself came close to rejecting Christianity altogether, but the city's religious and intellectual life was dominated by a new generation of Unitarian preachers like Delano's minister, Horace Holley, and the more influential William Ellery Channing, who were even more certain than were Reverends Turner and Brown that men had free will, that both individuals and the world could be governed by reason, that faith could be purged of the gloomy doctrine of predestination, and that Christianity could be reconciled with the Enlightenment. Their theology found expression in reform associations focused on ending slavery, improving the lot of the labouring classes, and women's emancipation, as well as in various secular 'self-improvement' movements popular among a growing middle class. In other ways, too, the American experiment in democracy seemed to be still vital, still dynamic. Throughout New England, for instance, a cultural revival was about to begin, an 'American Renaissance' that would produce philosophers such as Ralph Waldo Emerson and Henry David Thoreau and writers like Herman Melville and Margaret Fuller.[11]

But the contours of the crisis were coming into view. The Missouri Compromise had just divided the nation between free and slave states, turning a moral dispute into a territorial one. Mississippi, Alabama, and Missouri had recently been admitted into the Union and settlers were moving west, taking their slaves with them into Louisiana, the Mississippi Delta, and Texas. A year before Delano's death, over thirty African American slaves, including their reported leader, Denmark Vesey, were hung in Charleston, South Carolina, on charges they were plotting an uprising inspired by the Haitian Revolution.

The republicanism of Delano's youth had begun to fray, pulled one way by radicals who wanted to extend the promise of freedom to all men and the other by preservationists who might be personally opposed to slavery but thought ending it wasn't worth the risk it posed to the country. In Duxbury, Seth Sprague, just a few years older than Amasa, thought slavery was a sin that needed to be extirpated from the land at all costs. But his son, Peleg, who became a US senator, said Jesus Christ himself wouldn't support abolition if it meant 'putting in jeopardy our Government and our Union, under which we have prospered as no people has ever before prospered, and which is shedding upon the nations of the earth a light that no political luminary has ever before shed.'[12]

Amasa started out in the world when it was possible to have that kind of faith in America without needing to openly argue that liberty for some meant slavery for others. He left it thinking he would never know his own mind, nothing about it at all, and that no other man ever could or ever would.

Amasa's total estate comprised one threadbare hammock, assessed at fifty cents, an old pine writing desk, also worth fifty cents, and seven hundred copies of A Narrative of Voyages and Travels—that is, a relic from his sailing life, the hammock, another from his writing life, the desk, and his books, the unsold sum of both.[13]

EPILOGUE: HERMAN MELVILLE'S AMERICA

By the early 1800s, the same fever that had gripped Spanish America had started to spread throughout the southern United States. Just as merchants decades earlier had begun sending more and more slaves over the pampas and then up the Andes, drivers now were moving ever greater numbers of enslaved peoples out of the old slave states of Virginia, North Carolina, Delaware, and Maryland to new sugar and cotton plantations in the Deep South and the Southwest.

Many of them travelled the way Babo, Mori, and untold numbers of other captives did, in single or double columns on foot, their necks shackled together like links in a chain, across flatlands and over mountains. Others went on barges down the Mississippi and Ohio Rivers. And just as Mordeille had unloaded contraband slaves along Río de la Plata's porous beaches, French privateers, most famously Jean Lafitte, worked with merchants in Louisiana, the Mississippi territory, and Texas, dumping slaves they had seized off prize ships on empty stretches along the Gulf Coast, including Galveston Island. When Delano boarded the *Tryal* in early 1805, there were less than a million slaves in the United States, most of them concentrated in the coastal south or just inland, in the states of Tennessee and Kentucky and the Mississippi and the Orleans territories. Four decades later, there were nearly four million, spread from the Atlantic to Missouri and Texas, in total worth over $3 billion, 'more than all the capital invested in railroads and factories in the United States combined.' A trade and a system, slavery in the

United States was also a delirium, a 'fever'—a 'perfect fever' a 'negro-fever,' as newspapers in Georgia described the demand for slaves.[1]

As late as 1850, Herman Melville, along with many others of his generation, could still think that 'to become American is essentially to divest oneself of a past identity, to make a radical break with the past.'[2] 'The past is dead,' he writes in his novel *White-Jacket*. 'The future is both hope and fruition. . . . It is for America to make precedents, and not to obey them.' The remarks come in a lengthy passage advocating for the 'abolition' of flogging on navy ships, a cause Melville uses as a metaphor for other forms of arbitrary, absolute power, including slavery. 'Exempt yourself from the lash,' he tells America's 'captains and commodores.' Later in the passage, Melville imagines the march into the future as a movement across the West to the Pacific: he compares the whole of the American continent to God's covenant with 'Israel of old,' the 'birth-right' of a free people. 'We Americans,' he writes, 'bear the ark of the liberties of the world. . . . We are the pioneers of the world; the advance-guard, sent on through the wilderness of untried things, to break a new path in the New World that is ours.'[3]

But it was enslaved peoples, in the South and Southwest at least, who were beating that 'new path,' cutting down forests, turning America's 'wilderness of untried things' into plantations and marketable real estate and picking the cotton and cutting the sugar that drew more and more territory into a thriving Atlantic economy. Far from quarantining slavery in the South while spreading republican liberties west, expansion revitalized the slave system, allowing southern planters to escape their exhausted soil. Politically as well, by the mid-1840s efforts to realize the nation's manifest destiny, a phrase just then coined, had deepened the predicament caused by slavery. The 1846 annexation of Texas, followed by the invasion of Mexico that same year, had removed the last obstacles to the Pacific. Rather than solving the problems slavery posed to the nation, expansion across the frontier worsened the crisis as slavers, free soilers, and abolitionists fought against losing ground in a growing United States.

Mexico had abolished slavery in 1829, joined by most of the rest of Spanish America by the mid-1850s. But southerners, feeling hemmed in by the North, saw a chance: 'I want Tamaulipas, Potosi, and one or two other Mexican States,' said Mississippi senator Albert Gallatin Brown in 1859, 'and I want them all for the same reason—for the planting or spreading of slavery.' Augusta's *Daily Constitutionalist* was even more ambitious in its call to reestablish slavery in Spanish America. The Georgia paper wanted southerners to build a slave 'empire,' extending from 'San Diego, on the Pacific Ocean, thence southward along the shore line of Mexico and Central America, at low tide, to the Isthmus of Panama; thence South—still South!—along the western shoreline of New Granada and Ecuador, to where the southern boundary of the latter strikes the ocean'—near to the Chilean waters where Amasa Delano's *Perseverance* met Benito Cerreño's *Tryal*. In a way, this vision brings the story full circle, with the nightmare Delano sailed into in 1805 transformed into a dream slavers had five decades later for the whole hemisphere.[4]

For those paying attention, the situation was as alarming as a 'fire bell in the night,' as Thomas Jefferson in 1820 described the division of an expanding republic into competing free and slave camps. Still, through the 1840s, it was possible to believe that abolition would be achieved within the legal and political institutions of the country, by letting the reality of the law catch up with its promise: that *all* men are created equal. This possibility seemed to be confirmed in 1841, when former US president John Quincy Adams invoked the principle of natural rights to successfully defend the African *Amistad* rebels before the US Supreme Court. In a bid to obtain their freedom, fifty-three Africans (forty-nine adults and four children) had risen up, seized the slave ship that was holding them captive, and murdered its captain and some of the crew. Adams argued, among other things, that this act was fully within the 'law of Nature and of Nature's God on which our fathers placed our own national existence.' The rebels were freed and allowed to return to Africa.

But nine years later, Congress passed a law that threw what many thought the natural course of liberalism into reverse. In an effort to appease the southern states, legislators approved the Fugitive Slave Act, which guaranteed that the federal government would return escaped slaves to their owners. It was part of a grand bargain, yet another 'com-promise' worked out by national leaders, men like Boston's own Daniel Webster, who held the protection of property and the preservation of the Union to be higher priorities than the abolition of slavery. Thomas Sims, a seventeen-year-old escaped slave, was among the first caught in the act's net. His arrest on a Boston street in April 1851, on a warrant issued on behalf of his Georgia master, galvanized the city's abolitionist commu-nity, whose lawyers petitioned the chief justice of the Massachusetts Supreme Judicial Court, Lemuel Shaw, Herman Melville's father-in-law, for a writ of habeas corpus.

To grant the writ would be to imply that the Fugitive Slave Act was unconstitutional, confirming the criticisms of southern slavers that Washington wasn't willing to enforce the law. Already, in just the year since the act had been in effect, thousands of escaped slaves living in northern states, including some who had been arrested under the act and had to escape again, had fled to Canada, at least three thousand in the last months of 1850 alone. A large crowd gathered at the Boston courthouse, which was protected by a phalanx of police, marshals, and militiamen. Chains had been wrapped around the building to prevent Sims's escape and Judge Shaw had to bend low to enter: 'the judiciary crawling under his chains,' reported the antislavery press.[5]

Shaw was among the country's most respected jurists. He was per-sonally in favour of emancipation, having over the years creatively inter-preted the law to limit the scope of slavery and expand the definition of free labour. Melville's father-in-law was not what today would be called an originalist. Now, though, believing that the fate of the republic was in his hands, he said that a strict reading of the Constitution limited his ability to contravene federal legislation. At various points, his decision explicitly stated that what he called 'peace,' 'happiness,' and 'prosperity,' made possible by the preservation of 'union,' took precedent over the natural right to freedom. 'Writ refused,' Shaw said.

Then the petition went before Duxbury's Peleg Sprague. Earlier, when he was a US senator, Sprague had said that the 'the Saviour' him-self wouldn't abolish slavery if it meant meddling in a nation's laws. Now as a federal appeals judge he had an opportunity to do as he believed

Jesus would do. Sprague also denied Sims's petition. The prisoner was marched through the streets of Boston to the harbour, put on the *Acorn*, and sailed back to Savannah, where he was publicly whipped and put to work in a rice field.

The Sims case radicalized antislavery reformers, destroying for many of them the legitimacy of the law and legal institutions. Abolitionists compared the chief justice to Pontius Pilate, and Henry David Thoreau apparently had Shaw, and perhaps Sprague, in mind when he said that judges were 'merely the inspectors of a pick-lock and murderer's tools, to tell them whether they are in working order or not.' The rulings 'snapped Ralph Waldo Emerson's equanimity,' leading the philosopher who valued quiet reflection and individual autonomy above all else to call for collective resistance against the law. If judges couldn't figure out how to protect the 'sovereignty of the state' *and* the 'life and freedom of every inhabitant,' then what good was their 'learning or veneration'? Emerson asked. 'They are no more use than idiots.'[6]

Like everything else about Melville's politics, scholars have debated what his opinion was regarding his father-in-law's ruling. For all of Melville's emotional insurgency, his raucous prose celebrating the liberties of the world, his appreciation of the 'tragic graces' of even the 'meanest misfits, castaways, and renegades,' Melville was not an insurrectionist. He feared war and revolution, believing that however justified their cause their consequences would be worse. 'Storms are formed behind the storm we feel,' he later wrote in one of his Civil War poems, titled 'Misgivings.' And he distrusted the zeal of many abolitionists, who were as dangerous, he thought, to the country's 'institutions,' in which were invested the 'great hopes of mankind,' as the Jacobins in Paris had proved to be to the 'promise' of the French Revolution.

What separated Melville from statesmen and judges, like Shaw and Sprague, who designed and upheld the Fugitive Slave Act and other appeasements was that he also knew that the injustices identified by abolitionists and Jacobins were equally destructive of mankind's hopes. He included ship mutinies in many of his stories, starting with his first book, *Typee*. Yet only one of those mutinies is carried forward to completion. Either they are called off at the last moment or the abuse that provoked them is remedied by the intercession or repentance of a higher officer. The sole story where Melville goes ahead with a revolt is *Benito Cereno*, and the resulting disaster is close to total.[7]

Benito Cereno, written four years after the Sims decision, captures the impasse of the 1850s, a sense that the country faced one of two equally unacceptable options: abolish slavery, which might lead to the abolition of the Union, or leave slavery alone and accept the fact that freedom for some required the enslavement of others. The *Tryal*, or as Melville named the ship, the *San Dominick*, not the *Amistad*, was America's metaphor.

Events moved quickly in the years after the Sims case. Kansas 'bled,' John Brown raided, slaves continued to escape, and the Whig Party collapsed, replaced by the antislavery Republicans, who would soon send Abraham Lincoln to the White House.

When the Civil War finally came, Lincoln would sound as severe as Calvin himself, warning Americans that the conflict might be God's retribution for 'all the wealth piled by the bondsman's two hundred and fifty years of unrequited toil.' But earlier, in the 1850s, a cheerier man, Franklin Pierce, led the nation, presiding over a bubble of national confidence and Wall Street profits. Despite the fact that the annexation of Texas and the conquest of nearly half of Mexican territory had worsened the sectional crisis, Pierce told the country to carry on, to cast aside any 'timid forebodings' it might have about the 'evil' of 'expansion.'

The march west wasn't just revitalizing slavery and deepening polarization. It was rendering explicit what had heretofore been implicit, that, as Edmund Morgan wrote, American freedom was 'intertwined and interdependent' with American slavery. Pierce's signature legislation was the Kansas-Nebraska Act, which granted to white settlers the right to decide for themselves if their territory was to be free or slave. Based on a doctrine promoted by northern Democrats called 'popular sovereignty,' the act effectively defined freedom as the freedom of white men to enslave black men, women, and children. In the South, too, defenders of slavery were saying in public what many of them believed in private, that freedom required slavery, that slavery was, in the words of the South Carolinian John Calhoun, a 'positive good,' the foundation of 'free and stable political institutions.'[8]

Melville anticipated his nation's coming catastrophe in *Moby-Dick*, published in late 1851. But that book, despite its apocalyptic ending, was joyful, hinting at possible emotional emancipations, including Pip's ability to draw out Ahab's 'humanities' and the love shared between Ishmael and the islander Queequeg. Who aint a slave? We all are! Four years later, though, midway through Pierce's presidency, Melville might have had that question in mind again when he sat down to rewrite chapter 18 of Amasa Delano's memoir. The answer would have been the same yet the implications grimmer. There were no free people on board the *Tryal*. Obviously not Cerreño, held hostage to the West Africans. Not Babo, Mori, and the rest of the rebels, forced to mimic their own enslavement and humiliation. And not Amasa Delano, locked in the soft cell of his own blindness. Trying to 'break one charm,' Melville wrote of his fictional New Englander, Delano was 'becharmed anew.'

Melville didn't have to make Amasa's kind of oblivion up. Denial was all around him, in his friends and neighbours, people whom he respected. Nathaniel Hawthorne, whom for a while Melville considered the darkest and deepest ponderers of the human condition America had yet produced, wrote with a naïve nostalgia that the southern master and slave 'dwelt together in greater peace and affection . . . than had ever elsewhere existed between the taskmaster and the serf.' Melville's Berkshire neighbour Oliver Wendell Holmes spoke warmly about 'slavery in its best and mildest form'—like the kind the fictional Delano believed existed between Cereno and Babo, until events proved otherwise. And Melville's father-in-law, Lemuel Shaw, later, after he had retired from the bench, continued to believe he made the right decision in sending Thomas Sims back to slavery and spent the last days of his life urging Massachusetts to repeal a law that had nullified the Fugitive Slave Act.[9]

In retelling the story of the *Tryal* uprising and deception, Melville jettisoned Delano's nearly yearlong hounding of Cerreño for half the value of his ship, including the value of its slaves. Instead, he ended his novella with Amasa consoling a dying Benito, a conclusion that I don't think was meant to cast the American captain in a better light. I think it was Melville's way of saying that he no longer believed that his country would, or should even try to, escape history: 'But the past is passed; why moralize upon it?' Melville has Delano advise the Spaniard: 'Forget it. See, yon bright sun has forgotten it all, and the blue sea, and the blue sky; these have turned over new leaves.' Why, Melville's Delano wants to know, can't Cereno do the same and move on? The answer echoes the historical Cerreño's description of the historical Delano as a monster (a description that is not in Delano's memoir and thus that Melville couldn't have been aware of).

'Because they have no memory,' Cereno replies, 'because they are not human.'[10]

Events proved Melville's 'misgivings' wrong. War came, slaves were emancipated, and the Union survived. The United States, it seemed, had broken the paradox of freedom and slavery. Melville was a Union man when the fighting finally did start, calling slavery, in an appendix to his Civil War poems, an 'atheistical iniquity' and joining 'in the exulting chorus of humanity over its downfall.' But he continued to brood, concerned with, among other things, the degeneration of the promise of American freedom into a 'vile liberty,' as he put it in 1876 on the centenary of the American Revolution, with 'reverence' for 'naught'—not for God, not for nature, and not for others.

There's another way of thinking about the relationship between slavery and freedom, beyond simply identifying the paradox, captured in an epigraph Melville used for another one of his short stories: 'Seeking to conquer a larger liberty, man but extends the empire of necessity.' The idea conveys forward motion, hinting that it is not the paradox that defines America but rather the ceaseless bids to escape the paradox, to slip out of the shackles of history, even as such efforts inevitably deepen old entanglements and create new 'necessities'—the way, for example, the opening of the West wound up energizing slavery and accelerating the rush to war. Or the way the rise of free trade promised (and still promises) that if men were set free to pursue their self-interests, an ever more harmonious world would result. Experience has proven otherwise. In the United States, a purer ideal of freedom has come to hold sway, at least among some, based on the principles of liberal democracy and laissez-faire economics but also on a more primal animus, an individual supremacy that not only denies the necessities that bind people together but resents any reminder of those necessities.

The chattel slavery of Africans and African Americans, the historian David Brion Davis writes, had the 'great virtue, as an ideal model, of being clear-cut,' compressing and condensing into an exceptionally grotesque, brutal, and visible institution more diffuse forms of human bondage. The horror was so clear-cut, in fact, that it 'tended to set slavery off from other species of barbarity and oppression,' including both the mechanisms by which former slaves were 'virtually re-enslaved' after the Civil War as well as more subtle 'interpersonal knots and invisible webs of ensnarement.' These invisible traps, Davis writes, are 'so much a part of the psychopathology of our everyday lives that they have been apparent only to a few poets, novelists, and exceptionally perceptive psychiatrists.'

Herman Melville called them 'whale-lines,' and he thought they could hook nations as well as people.[11]

A NOTE ON SOURCES AND OTHER MATTERS

BENITO CERENO

Benito Cereno is a true story but not in the way *Moby-Dick* is a true story. Melville's whale book is based as much on *King Lear* and *Paradise Lost* as it is on the stoving of the *Essex*. *Benito Cereno*, in contrast, is taken almost entirely from chapter 18 of Amasa Delano's *A Narrative of Voyages and Travels in the Northern and Southern Hemispheres: Comprising Three Voyages round the World; Together with a Voyage of Survey and Discovery in the Pacific Ocean and Oriental Islands.* The historian Sterling Stuckey argues that Melville drew on the travel writings of Mungo Park to develop an appreciation of West African culture, and Robert Wallace believes that Melville borrowed imagery from Frederick Douglass, the former slave and abolitionist orator, including for the famous scene in which Melville has Babo terrorize Cereno under the pretense of shaving him. But *Benito Cereno*'s primary source is nearly wholly Delano's memoir, *A Narrative of Voyages.* In his book, Delano reproduces a series of translated Spanish court documents to bolster his claims against Benito Cerreño (whom Delano refers to as Don Bonito throughout). Melville likewise reproduces these documents in his fictional account, with important alterations to support his narrative. The originals are in Chile's Archivo Nacional and Biblioteca Nacional.

Commentary on *Benito Cereno* is extensive. The best interpretations approach the story from opposing perspectives, including Sterling Stuckey, *African Culture and Melville's Art: The Creative Process in* Benito Cereno *and* Moby-Dick, New York: Oxford University Press, 2009; Carolyn Karcher, *Shadow over the Promised Land: Slavery, Race, and Violence in Melville's America,* Baton Rouge: Louisiana State University Press, 1980; Michael Paul Rogin, *Subversive Genealogy: The Politics and Art of Herman Melville,* Berkeley: University of California Press, 1985; Hershel Parker, 'Melville and Politics: A Scrutiny of the Political Milieux of Herman Melville's Life and Works,' PhD dissertation, Northwestern University, 1963; Parker's *Herman Melville: A Biography,* vol. 2: 1851–1891, Baltimore: Johns Hopkins University Press, 2002, pp. 237–42; C. L. R. James, *Mariners, Renegades, and Castaways: The Story of Herman Melville and the World We*

Live In, 1953, Hanover: University Press of New England, 1978; Andrew Delbanco, *Herman Melville: His World and Work*, New York: Knopf, 2005; Eric Sundquist, *To Wake the Nations: Race in the Making of American Literature*, Cambridge: Harvard University Press, 1999; Robert Wallace, *Douglass and Melville: Anchored Together in Neighborly Style*, New Bedford: Spinner Publications, 2005; and Clare Spark, *Hunting Captain Ahab: Psychological Warfare and the Melville Revival*, Kent: Kent State University Press, 2001. See also Christopher Freeburg, *Melville and the Idea of Blackness: Race and Imperialism in Nineteenth-Century America*, Cambridge: Cambridge University Press, 2012, chapter three, and *Critical Essays on Herman Melville's 'Benito Cereno,'* ed. Robert E. Burkholder, New York: G. K. Hall Co., 1992.

MARGINALIA

Over the last hundred years, Melville scholars have doggedly identified not just the sources of his inspiration but the actual copies of books he held in his hands, volumes that he owned, borrowed, or found in public libraries or the collections of family members. One book that has yet to be located is Melville's copy of Delano's *Narrative of Voyages and Travels*. The memoir was widely available shortly after it was published, found as far away as libraries in Canton, China, and the Caribbean, and Melville might have come across it in a ship's library. Or he might have been given a copy by his father-in-law, Justice Lemuel Shaw, who early in his legal career was Delano's lawyer. In the hope of identifying the copy Melville used, I checked a number of first editions (including a second printing in 1818) in libraries and private collections. Melville wrote copious marginalia, annotating Shakespeare, Milton, Emerson, Wordsworth, Arnold, Homer, and others with check marks, underlines, exclamation points, and comments. (For example, alongside the section of the Gospel of Saint John that reads, 'And his disciples asked him, saying, Master, who did sin, this man, or his parents, that he was born blind?' Melville wrote: 'This leading question seems evaded in the following verses.' It is unclear whether the comment refers to the assumption that sin was committed or that blindness is the result of sin.) I imagine, then, that his copy of *A Narrative* was heavily marked up, considering how much detail he took from it to write *Benito Cereno*. Using Worldcat, the old National Union Catalog (with help from Jessica Pigza at the New York Public Library), and online used-book catalogues (like Abebooks and eBay), I've identified about 150 extant first editions in over a hundred libraries and private collections and checked about 75 of them. Alas, no volume indicating that it was owned or used by Melville has yet revealed itself. I'd be happy to share the checklist with anyone who wants to continue the hunt. Contact me at grandin@nyu.edu.

Doctoral dissertations have been written on Melville's marginalia (for example, Walker Cowen, 'Melville's Marginalia,' Harvard, 1965) and there exists a small library of books and articles on Melville's sources, Melville's readings, Melville's Bibles, Melville's Milton, Melville's boredom, and so on. Also, Steven Olsen-Smith, Peter Norberg, and Dennis Marnon edit an extremely useful internet project called 'Melville's Marginalia,' available at http://melvillesmarginalia.org/front.php.

MELVILLE AND AFRICA

Melville didn't know the origins of the slaves on the *Tryal*, other than that some of them were identified as being from Senegal and West Africa. Through the writings of Alexander Falconbridge and Mungo Park, however, he had access to information concerning not just Africa and slavery in general but the region and even the port from which some of the slavers were embarked. Melville's maternal grandfather, Peter Gansevoort, owned a copy of Falconbridge's *Account of the Slave Trade on the Coast of Africa* (London: J. Phillips, 1788), which is now located in the Gansevoort-Lansing Collection at the New York Public Library. Hershel Parker, in an e-mail communication, says that the Falconbridge book probably passed on to the library of Melville's uncle Peter, where, during the summer of 1832, Herman had been 'given free rein to wander.' *An Account* was meant as an exposé, written to stir outrage at the slave trade. As Melville later does, Falconbridge emphasizes similarities between the way black slaves and white sailors were treated, describing in detail the tortures inflicted on both with 'brutal severity' by deck officers. In *Benito Cereno*, Melville writes that, 'like most men of a good, blithe heart, Captain Delano took to negroes, not philanthropically but genially, just as other men took to Newfoundland dogs.' It is true that, as a breed, Newfoundland dogs had a reputation of being good-natured and loyal. But, interestingly, Falconbridge writes that they were also used on slave ships to terrorize: 'Whenever any of the crew were beaten, the Newfoundland dog . . . would generally leap upon them, tear their cloths, and bite them.'

We know that Melville read the traveler Mungo Park, citing him in *Moby-Dick*, *Mardi*, and the serialized original version of *Benito Cereno*. Sterling Stuckey writes that 'Melville found in Park's *Travels in the Interior Districts of Africa* revelations of African humanity so at odds with conceptions of Africa held by whites and free blacks in America that a dramatic shift in his thinking about Africa occurred. However favourably disposed toward Africans he may have been before reading *Interior Districts*, what is revealed there concerning their work skills must have startled him, for the thought that Africans brought any skills into slavery clashed violently with the prevailing thesis that, as a people, they were by nature ignorant, hopelessly inferior to whites' ('The Tambourine in Glory: African Culture and Melville's Art,' in *The Cambridge Companion to Herman Melville*, ed. Robert Levine, Cambridge: Cambridge University Press, 1998, p. 43). Park's account of his travels through Africa was first published in 1799. See also Seymour Gross, 'Mungo Park and Ledyard in Melville's *Benito Cereno*,' *English Language Notes* 3 (December 1965): 122–23.

SLAVERY AND FREEDOM

The literature on the way the conditions of slavery and freedom defined, and depended on, one another is vast and includes nearly all of David Brion Davis's indispensable scholarship. As Davis writes of the gap that existed between the rhetoric of freedom and the reality of slavery: 'Demands for consistency between principles and practice, no matter how sincere, were rather beside the point. Practice was what made the principles possible' (*The Problem of Slavery in the Age of Revolution, Slavery, and Human Progress*, New York: Oxford University Press, 1984, p. 262). The intellectual, philosophical, and religious roots of what we think of as freedom can be traced back to well before the first slave ship sailed for America from West Africa in the early 1500s, or even before the first black-skinned African was sold as a slave in Iberia. But, to borrow from Melville's remarks on Liverpool's Nelson statue, the prosperity of the Atlantic world was indissolubly linked to the prosecution of the slave trade, wealth that in turn helped generalize ideas of freedom, allowing more and more people to understand themselves as free.

In addition to producing the material wealth that made American independence movements possible, there are many ways the idea and practice of slavery shaped the economic and political experience of modern freedom. First, living alongside, and presiding over, black slaves gave white people concrete examples of unfreedom. Second, slavery stood not just as a negative example but as a positive quality of a free man: according to some traditions of political thought, 'one of the characteristics of the free man was to have slaves in his control' (Barry Alan Shain, *The Myth of American Individualism: The Protestant Origins of American Political Thought*, Princeton: Princeton University Press, 1994, p. 300). Third, for slave-owning gentry, treating Africans and African-descended people as commodities helped them escape the commodification of daily life, letting them rise above the grubbing of the marketplace and 'cultivate some of the higher and more ennobling traits of humanity' (Shain, *Myth of American Individualism*, p. 300). Fourth, slaves produced the items of conspicuous consumption, the gold, silver, and leather (and, through sexual reproduction, other slaves) that allowed successful individuals to showcase their 'ennobling traits.' Fifth, the commercialization of society made possible by slavery, and the wealth that came with it, helped democratize these 'ennobling traits,' letting more and more people imagine themselves autonomous and free. Finally, at least as far as this summary is concerned, sentimental depictions of the violence, arbitrariness, and wild abandon of cruel and sensuous passions under slavery helped sharpen the ideal of interiority and self-discipline that stood at the centre of republican and liberal ideals of the self.

See David Brion Davis, *Problem of Slavery*, and *Inhuman Bondage: The Rise and Fall of Slavery in the New World*, New York: Oxford University Press, 2006; Barbara J. Fields, 'Ideology and Race in American History,' in *Region, Race, and Reconstruction: Essays in Honor of C. Vann Woodward*, ed. Morgan J. Koussar and James McPherson (New York: Oxford University Press, 1982) and 'Slavery, Race and Ideology in the United States of America,' *New Left Review* 181 (May–June 1990): 95–118; Shain, *Myth of American Individualism*, especially pp. 288–319; Orlando Patterson, *Slavery and Social Death: A Comparative Study*, Cambridge: Harvard University Press, 1982, and *Freedom: The Making of Western Culture*, New York: Basic Books, 1991; Bernard Bailyn, *The Ideological Origins of the American Revolution*, Cambridge: Harvard University Press, 1967; Eric Foner, *The Story of American Freedom*, New York: Norton, 1999; Robin Einhorn, *American Taxation, American Slavery*, Chicago: University of Chicago Press, 2006; Joan Baum, *Mind-Forg'd Manacles: Slavery and the English Romantic Poets*, North Haven: Archon, 1994; Christine Levecq, *Slavery and Sentiment: The Poli-*

tics of Feeling in Black Atlantic Antislavery Writing, 1770–1850, Lebanon: University of New Hampshire Press, 2008; Debbie Lee, *Slavery and the Romantic Imagination*, Philadelphia: University of Pennsylvania Press, 2004; Jeanne Elders de Waard, '"The Shadow of Law": Sentimental Interiority, Gothic Terror, and the Legal Subject,' *Arizona Quarterly: A Journal of American Literature, Culture, and Theory* 62 (Winter 2006): 1–30; Gillian Brown, *Domestic Individualism: Imagining Self in Nineteenth-Century America*, Berkeley: University of California Press, 1990; Sidney Mintz, *Sweetness and Power: The Place of Sugar in Modern History*, New York: Viking, 1985, and 'Slavery and Emergent Capitalism,' in *Slavery in the New World*, ed. Laura Foner and Eugene D. Genovese, Englewood Cliffs: Prentice-Hall, 1969. For comprehensive treatments of slavery in the Americas that I've relied on throughout this work, see Robin Blackburn, *The Making of New World Slavery: From the Baroque to the Modern, 1492–1800*, London: Verso, 1997, and *The American Crucible: Slavery, Emancipation, and Human Rights*, London: Verso, 2011; Herb Klein, *African Slavery in Latin America and the Caribbean*, New York: Oxford University Press, 1986, and *The Atlantic Slave Trade*, New York: Cambridge University Press, 1999; and David Eltis, *The Rise of African Slavery in the Americas*, Oxford: Oxford University Press, 2000. In Buenos Aires, the work of Alex Borucki and Lyman Johnson, cited throughout, give texture to how the dynamic of freedom and slavery played out on the ground.

MELVILLE AND SLAVERY

Melville's position on slavery has been the subject of much discussion. In considering the question as it relates to *Benito Cereno*, I've drawn from the authors cited below, among others, even though many of them hold opposing opinions, ranging from Hershel Parker, who downplays the importance of slavery and race, to Sterling Stuckey, who insists on the centrality of African and African American culture in Melville's thought and art. Stuckey hears the early notes of jazz in Melville's prose, for instance, speculating that Melville might have picked it up listening to slaves play music on the street corners and in the markets of New York and Albany.

Benito Cereno scrambled the core conceits of both opponents and advocates of slavery. Unlike those religious abolitionists, such as Harriet Beecher Stowe, who portrayed blacks as Christ-like innocents, Melville's Babo unapologetically terrorizes his white captives. To those who defended slavery, like the Virginian George Fitzhugh, by saying that it was founded on 'domestic affection,' that the intellectual feebleness of blacks helps their owners achieve their best selves, that slavery civilizes slave and master alike, Melville's troupe of slave-actors turned such assumptions into a show, using their intellect to perform their expected lack of intellect (see *Sociology for the South, or the Failure of Free Society*, Richmond: Morris, 1984, pp. 37–40, 201). Thus they revealed what southerners said was natural to be artificial, since by definition acting is artifice. It was Babo's 'brain, not body' that 'had schemed and led the revolt.' And for those who believed that the crisis caused by slavery could be solved peacefully, Melville wrote a story that ended in near total destruction (see Rogin, *Subversive Genealogy*, p. 213, for an elaboration of this line of argument).

Melville had read Homer's *Odyssey*, a work that revolves around a character, Odysseus, whom many scholars think of as representing the first 'modern' self, a character not only with interiority but with the cunning to manipulate interiority, to create a schism between what is seen on the outside and what exists on the inside. And while the *Odyssey* is not about slavery, political philosophers, including many around the time Melville was writing, often used chattel slavery, particularly the power masters had over slaves, as a metaphor to represent exactly the kind of ability Odysseus possessed, to use reason and will to master passions and vices. In any case, the deception played out on the *Tryal* is equal to the ruse Odysseus stages to escape Polyphemous in Homer's *Odyssey*. 'I am nobody,' Odysseus says, playing with the subtleties of language to trick the Cyclops, and that's exactly what Mori, Babo, and the rest of the slave-rebel troupe do, act as if they are inconsequential slaves, nobodies hardly worth noticing. Whatever Melville meant *Benito Cereno* to say about slavery, the story is fundamentally about blindness, an inability to see, a persistent theme in Melville's writings. If one compares the story, for example, to Ishmael's discussion in *Moby-Dick* about the 'peculiar sideway position of the whale's eyes,' one realizes that the author had been thinking about the problem Amasa Delano represents for some time.

See Karcher, *Shadow over the Promised Land*; Hershel Parker, 'Melville and Politics'; Eleanor E. Simpson, 'Melville and the Negro: From *Typee* to "Benito Cereno,"' *American Literature* 41 (March 1969): 19–38; Rogin, *Subversive Genealogy*; Stuckey, *African Culture and Melville's Art*; and Spark, *Hunting Captain Ahab*, especially pp. 102–7. See also Wai-chee Dimock, *Empire for Liberty: Melville and the Poetics of Individualism*, Princeton: Princeton University Press, 1989. For Melville's complex engagement with the Civil War, see Stanton Garner, *The Civil War World of Herman Melville*, Lawrence: University of Kansas Press, 1993; Daniel Aaron, *The Unwritten War: American Writers and the Civil War*, New York: Knopf, 1973, pp. 75–90; and Parker, *Melville: A Biography*, vol. 2, pp. 606–25.

THE *NEPTUNE*

The *Neptune* was built by the British East India Company in Bombay, India (hence the teak), to sail as a merchantman under the name *Laurel*. But the French seized and renamed it *Le Neptune*. The British recaptured the ship and auctioned it to John Bolton, who kept its name and outfitted it as a slaver (Merseyside Maritime Museum, Liverpool Register of Merchant Ships, 1793–1802, microfilm reel 23, 70/1799). Had Mordeille not intercepted the ship and its cargo, it might have returned to London with a hold full of dark Caribbean mahogany, used to carve the handsome doors of Bolton's Storrs Hall.

LORD NELSON AND *THE WRONGS OF AFRICA*

Sixteen of the nineteen members of the civic committee established to erect Liverpool's Nelson monument were slavers. The city's mayor, who convened the committee, was John Bridge Aspinall, a prominent slave merchant who, with others in his family, ran over 180 voyages that had carried nearly sixty thousand Africans to the Americas. The committee, though, was chaired by an abolitionist, William Roscoe, a member of Parliament and the author of a number of poems and pamphlets denouncing the slave trade, including *The Wrongs of Africa* and *An Enquiry into the Causes of the Insurrection of the Negroes in the Island of St. Domingo* (1792). Some historians of Liverpool have speculated that Roscoe, in helping to select the monument's design, meant its four enchained prisoners to be a veiled criticism of slavery. Roscoe was also an acquaintance of Herman Melville's father, a fact mentioned by Melville later in his stream-of-consciousness *Redburn* passage: 'And my thoughts reverted to my father's friend, the good and great Roscoe, the intrepid enemy of the trade; who in every way exerted his fine talents toward its suppression; writing a poem ('the Wrongs of Africa'), several pamphlets; and in his place in Parliament, he delivered a speech against it, which, as coming from a member for Liverpool, was supposed to have turned many votes, and had no small share in the triumph of sound policy and humanity that ensued.'

For Aspinall, see Trans-Atlantic Slave Database (http://www.slavevoyages.org /tast/index.faces). For the composition of the monument's subscription committee, see Thomas Baines, *History of the Commerce and Town of Liverpool*, vol. 1, London: Longman, 1852, p. 524. For Roscoe, see Penelope Curtis, *Patronage and Practice: Sculpture on Merseyside*, Liverpool: Tate Gallery Liverpool, 1989, pp. 21–26. For Melville's father's association with Roscoe, see Hershel Parker, *Melville: The Making of the Poet*, Chicago: Northwestern University Press, 2007, p. 46, and Parker, *Melville: A Biography*, vol. 1, p. 9.

THE *TRYAL* AND ITS REBELS

Eric Robert Taylor writes in his very useful survey of hundreds of slave ship rebellions, *If We Must Die in This Way* (Baton Rouge: Louisiana State University Press, 2009), that the *Tryal* rebellion is 'particularly compelling' because of 'the incredible amount of surviving information about it.' This is a startling statement, for by far the most frustrating aspect of doing research for this book was the limited available information concerning the history of the West Africans involved, how they got to America, where they came from, and what they suffered along the way. The scarcity of documentary records underscores the large degree to which New World slavery was an anonymous genocide. There are many memoirs of emancipated slaves, and specific events such as the *Amistad* rebellion and the 1835 Bahia uprising in Brazil produced significant documentary evidence. But the quantity of information pales in comparison with the scale of slavery. See Taylor, p. 139. For the *Amistad*, see Marcus Rediker's magisterial new history, *The Amistad Rebellion: An Atlantic Odyssey of Slavery and Freedom*, New York: Viking, 2012. For examples of memoirs, see Olaudah Equiano's *Interesting Narrative of the Life of Olaudah Equiano; or, Gustavus Vassa, the African*, 1789; James Williams, *A Narrative of Events, since the First of August, 1834*, ed. Diana Paton, Durham: Duke University Press, 2001; and Terry Alford's history of the life of Abd al Rahman Ibrahima, *A Prince among Slaves*, New York: Oxford University Press, 1977.

Of the at least 12,500,000 people taken out of Africa and brought to America, historians have identified only about 100,000 original African names, a figure that gives a sense of the magnitude of the historical silence. Most of these names are listed in the African Origins Project (http://www.african-origins.org/african-data/), which is based on the records of roughly 92,000 enslaved Africans liberated primarily by the British Royal Navy after 1808. While extremely useful, the project is limited. The names are of Africans freed from intercepted slaving vessels after British abolition of the slave trade and might overrepresent ships that embarked slaves in West Africa, from ports running from Senegambia to Biafra. One of the goals of the project is to share the names with African-speaking people so as to identify origin and ethnic group. Respondents have associated the name Mori, or variations, with the Kuranko, who live in what today is Sierra Leone and Guinea, are closely related to the Mandinka, and speak a dialect of Mende. Just under 50 percent of the Kuranko today are Muslim. Most of the other thirteen *Tryal* rebels' names are also associated with embarkations at or around Bonny. It is more likely, though, that the named slave-rebels were embarked somewhere in Senegambia. Correspondence with the Senegalese scholar Boubacar Barry was also very useful in identifying the possible ethnicity and origins of the names. See Alex Borucki, Daniel Domingues da Silva, David Eltis, Paul Lachance, Philip Misevich, and Olatunji Ojo, 'Using Pre-Orthographic African Names to Identify the Origins of Captives in the Transatlantic Slave Trade: The Registers of Liberated Africans, 1808–1862' (forthcoming).

Combing through notary records in Mendoza, Santiago, and Buenos Aires provided information on the sale and transport of 64 Africans by Juan Nonell in April 1804 to the Mendoza merchant Alejandro de Aranda, including the fact that some of them most likely arrived on the *Neptune*. Others in the lot arrived on different ships. Alex Borucki reports that there were regular connections between Senegambia and the Río de la Plata in those years, mostly through US slavers. The *Tryal* rebels all likely came from West Africa but they may not all have been Muslim. Spanish documents alternatively describe them as *guineos, etíopes*, or 'from the coast of Senegal,' a distinction that could mean something or nothing to their owner and overseers. Spanish slavers tended to use *Senegal* to describe the region between the Senegal River and the Gambia River. They might also use *Guinea* to mean that area. More often, though, they meant it to refer to the land south of the Gambia River, running into the part of West Africa that hangs over the Atlantic, including Bonny Island in the vast Niger River delta, where many of the Liverpool prizes captured by Mordeille embarked their captives. *Guinea* and *etiopía* could also just mean all of Africa. Many, perhaps most, slave transactions were illegal and therefore not documented. And since 1804 was the height of 'free trade in blacks' in Montevideo and Buenos Aires, what record keeping there was was often rushed, reflecting the frenzy of the moment. There was information on the *Neptune* in Liverpool and London, but not a manifest or any other paperwork to give information on the four hundred or so Africans the ship embarked at Bonny.

The most important documents, in addition to Delano's memoir, for reconstructing events on the *Tryal* are (for abbreviations, see 'Archives Consulted,' the next section): AGI (Seville), Lima, 731, N.27 ('Carta n° 445 del virrey Marqués de Avilés a Miguel Cayetano Soler, Ministro de Hacienda. Comunica el alzamiento de los negros esclavos de Senegal, conducidos a Lima desde Montevideo y Valparaíso en los navíos "San Juan Nepomuceno" y "Trial," respectivamente,' April 23, 1805); AHN (Madrid), legajo 5543, expediente 5 ('El Capitán Amasu de Eleno presta auxilio en la isla Santa María, a la tripulación de la fragata español Trial, en la que habían sublevado los negros'); BN (Santiago), Sala Medina, MSS, vol. 331, ff. 170–89 ('Informe de Luís de Alva al Presidente Luís Muñoz de Guzmán, Concepción'); ANC (Santiago), Real Audiencia de Santiago, vol. 608, ff. 90–93 ('Libro copiador de sentencias 1802 a 1814'); ANC (Santiago), Tribunal del Consulado, vol. 12, ff. 179–89 ('Informe rebelión de negros en la fragata Trial'); ANC (Santiago), 'Amacio Delano Capitán de la Fragata Perseverancia con el dueño de la Trial sobre el compensativo,' ff. 199–213. Details are also found in uncatalogued bundles of documents related to customs taxes and other paperwork concerning shipping found in Contaduría Mayor, in Santiago's ANC, as well as cited documents describing Delano's subsequent legal conflict with Cerreño found in Chile and Lima. Benjamín Vicuña Mackenna, *Historia de Valparaíso*, vol. 2, Valparaiso: Imprenta Albión de Cox i Taylor, 1869, is also useful, as are Javiera Carmona, 'De Senegal a Talcahuano: Los esclavos de un alzamiento en la costa pacífica (1804),' in *Huellas de África en América. Perspectivas para Chile*, ed. Celia L. Cussen, Santiago: Editorial Universitaria, 2009, pp. 137–58, and Jorge Pinto, 'Una rebelión de negros en las costas del Pacífico Sur: El caso de la fragata Trial en 1804,' *Revista Histórica* 10 (1986): 139–55. For Nonell's sale to Aranda, also see the notary entries for Inocencio Agrelo, April 10, 1805, December 24th, 1806, January 1811, and April 16th, 1839 (marginal notations in the original entry).

HAITI AND FREEDOM

That the Haitian Revolution was a source of hope to enslaved men and women and fear to their enslavers is well known. Less recognized is that it had a direct effect on the course of history. In 1803, Haitians definitively routed Napoleon's invading army, which had orders to retake the island as a French colony. Napoleon had envisioned a restored sugar-producing Saint-Dominique slave island as the anchor of a new French America running up the Mississippi Valley, connecting French Canada to the Caribbean, quarantining the young United States to the east and opening up the west to French settlers. But Haitians forced Napoleon to give up the dream. He sold Louisiana to Thomas Jefferson and turned his attentions to destroying Europe's ancien régime, which, despite his expedient alliances with Madrid's Bourbons, could mean only one thing: deposing those royal houses built on American slavery. After beating the Prussians at the Battle of Jena and checking the Russians at Eylau, Napoleon invaded Portugal and then turned on Spain, deposing the Bourbons and placing his brother Joseph on the throne (thus ending Amasa Delano's expectation that he'd get anything more than a medal for his help retaking the *Tryal*). The combination of a financially draining war against Great Britain followed by France's six-year occupation of Spain and Portugal marked the beginning of the end of Spanish rule in the Americas, paving the way for men like Bolívar and San Martín to launch their wars for independence. There would be many starts and stops, many advances and setbacks, but the continent-wide drive that began with Haiti first to wrest more freedom and then for total freedom was unstoppable. Even as one train of events moved forward in Europe and Spanish America, another accelerated in North America: Haiti's defeat of Napoleon allowed Thomas Jefferson to make his Louisiana Purchase, which set in motion the simultaneous processes of westward expansion and the extension of slavery, leading first to the Mexican-American War and then to the Civil War.

Not too long ago, Haiti barely registered in histories of the Age of Revolution, which focused nearly exclusively on the American, French, and Spanish American Revolutions. Now, due to the work of the following scholars, it is understood to be not just a central event of that age, but, since insurgents insisted on applying the ideal of freedom to really existing slavery, *the* central event: Michel-Rolph Trouillot, Ada Ferrer, Laurent Dubois, Jeremy Popkin, David Patrick Geggus, Sibylle Fischer, Sue Peabody, Julius Scott, Matthew Clavin, and Robin Blackburn.

PABLO NERUDA, JOHN HUSTON, PAUL NEWMAN, AND *I SPY*

In the late 1960s, Pablo Neruda told an interviewer that he couldn't get a handle on the story he wanted to write about the *Tryal* uprising. Where Melville had focused on the deception, Neruda wanted to write about the slaves themselves, calling his screenplay *Babo, the Rebel*. But he found himself 'fighting with shadows,' perhaps meaning the shadow cast by Melville. A fragment of the screenplay that he did finish imagines Melville as the last survivor, like Ishmael, arguing with Neruda over who can best narrate the story:

> NERUDA: *Tell the story.*
> MELVILLE: *Let others tell it.*
> NERUDA: *You are the only witness from that time, your voice is the only one that remains.*

John Huston, who had earlier brought *Moby-Dick* to the screen, wanted *Benito Cereno* to be his last movie and hoped to convince Paul Newman to play Amasa Delano. 'Paul dear,' he wrote on April 8, 1987, 'I hope to make one picture more, this one, . . . and to have you, my favorite actor on Earth, playing it. . . . I would so like our association to end on a note of triumph.' Two months later, the *New York Times* reported that Robert Duvall and Raul Julia had been cast to play Delano and Cereno. Huston died on August 28, 1987, before work on the project could begin.

In the mid-1960s, the poet Robert Lowell produced a stage version of *Benito*

Cereno, starring the actor Roscoe Lee Browne as Babo, or Babu, as Lowell wrote him. The play was broadcast on public TV in 1965, just a few weeks after NBC, having overcome most of the opposition of its southern affiliated stations, premiered the 'first weekly network television show to present a Negro as co-star in an integrated cast,' which was *I Spy*, with Bill Cosby. See '"I Spy" with Negro Is Widely Booked,' *New York Times*, September 19, 1965.

BABO, AFRICAN AMERICAN SCHOLARS AND WRITERS, AND BARACK OBAMA

Neruda might have had difficulty figuring him out, but African American writers recognized Babo. Ralph Ellison used an epigraph from the story for his novel *Invisible Man*, in which the narrator's grandfather reveals on his deathbed that he wasn't an obliging Tom but a stealth Babo, his last advice to his son being to 'overcome' whites 'with yeses, undermine 'em with grins, agree 'em to death and destruction, let 'em swoller you till they vomit or bust wide open.' Sterling Stuckey links Babo to Brer Rabbit, the trickster prominent in African American folktales. Writers from outside the United States, from the decolonizing third world, also saw their struggles in Babo's actions. 'Melville's interest [in *Benito Cereno*] is in a vast section of the modern world,' wrote the Trinidadian C. L. R. James in 1953, 'the backwards peoples, and today, from the continents of Asia and Africa, their doings fill the front pages of our newspapers.' Babo, James thought, was the 'most heroic character in Melville's fiction, . . . a man of unbending will, a natural leader, an organizer of large schemes but a master of detail.' 'What does 'Babo' mean?' asked the Nigerian scholar Charles E. Nnolim in 1974. 'The word "babo" in the Hausa language . . . means "NO"—an expression of strong disagreement. . . . How did Melville know that "Babo" . . . is "NO"?'

More recently, Barack Obama has cited *Benito Cereno* as having influenced him as a young man, perhaps preparing him for the hallucinations of his more feverish critics, who charge him with hijacking the ship of state and fantasize about having his head on a pike.

See Stuckey, *Going through the Storm: The Influence of African American Art in History*, New York: Oxford University Press, 1994; Charles E. Nnolim, *Melville's 'Benito Cereno': A Study in Meaning of Name Symbolism*, New York: New Voices, 1974; Marvin Fisher, *Going Under: Melville's Short Fiction and the American 1850s*, Baton Rouge: Louisiana State University Press, 1977; and James, *Mariners, Renegades, and Castaways*, p. 112.

APES AND ANGELS

Herman Melville read the naturalists and geologists of his day and would consider the implications of what eventually came to be known as Darwinism throughout his whole writing life. He started his literary career joking, a decade before the publication of *On the Origin of the Species*, that man's 'ancestors were kangaroos, not monkeys,' that marsupials were the 'first edition of mankind, since revised and corrected.' Thirty years later, he ended his eighteen-thousand-line poem, *Clarel*, with the question: 'If Luther's day expand to Darwin's year, / Shall that exclude the hope— foreclose the fear? . . . Yea, ape and angel, strife and old debate, / The harps of heaven and the dreary gongs of hell; / Science the feud can only aggravate— / No umpire she betwixt the chimes and knell: / The running battle of the star and clod / Shall run forever—if there be no God.'

Melville purchased a copy of Charles Darwin's *Journal of Researches into the Natural History and Geology of the Countries Visited during the Voyage of H.M.S. Beagle round the World, under the Command of Capt. Fitz Roy, R.N.* in 1847. For Melville's reading of Darwin, see Charles Roberts Anderson, *Melville in the South Seas*, New York: Dover, 1966, p. 265; Merton M. Sealts, *Melville's Reading*, Columbia: University of South Carolina Press, 1988, p. 171; and Mary K. Bercaw, *Melville's Sources*, Chicago: Northwestern University Press, 1987, pp. 2, 74. For the influence of Lyell and Darwin on Melville, see James Robert Corey, 'Herman Melville and the Theory of Evolution,' PhD dissertation, Washington State University, 1968. See also Eric Wilson, 'Melville, Darwin, and the Great Chain of Being,' *Studies in American Fiction* 28 (2000): 131–50. And see the edition of *Moby-Dick* edited by Harrison Hayford, G. Thomas Tanselle, and Hershel Parker, Chicago: Northwestern University Press, 1988, p. 829, for another passage that closely follows Darwin's *Journal of Researches*.

THE REVOLT OF THE *SAN JUAN NEPOMUCENO*

Aside from a brief mention in an article published in a Peruvian history journal, I've found no other scholarly reference to this remarkable uprising. News of the fate of the *San Juan* was carried back to America by three of its passengers, who were taken to Salem, Massachusetts, on the brig *Sukey*, captained by John Edwards, which had been in Senegal trading for hides, gum, peanuts, and palm oil. The first report was published in the *Salem Impartial Register* on July 30, 1801, reprinted in newspapers throughout New England, and translated and published in Buenos Aires in the *Telégrafo Mercantil* on December 16, 1801. For the *Sukey*, see *History of Essex County, Massachusetts: With Biographical Sketches of Many of Its Pioneers and Prominent Men*, vol. 1, ed. Duane Hamilton Hurd, Philadelphia: J. W. Lewis, 1888, p. 92.

AMASA DELANO AND FRANKLIN DELANO ROOSEVELT

Eleanor Roosevelt Seagraves says in an e-mail communication that an old story that her grandfather, FDR, purchased all existing copies of Amasa Delano's memoir is not true. She has no recollection of any family member during her childhood discussing Amasa, though she did wind up editing an abridged edition of *A Narrative* (1994). According to documents found (thanks to Josh Frens-String) in Chile's Ministry of Foreign Relations (Archivo General Histórico del Ministerio de Relaciones

Exteriores, Fondo Histórico, vol. 1404), Roosevelt was made aware of Delano's memoir in 1934, by his undersecretary of state to Latin America, who suggested buying a copy and donating it to Chile's national university as a token of Good Neighbour diplomacy. Roosevelt agreed, apparently inscribing the book thus: 'May the modest part which my kinsman played in the building of Chile encourage further fruitful cooperation between our two peoples who share common ideals of justice, peace and humanity.'

JUAN MARTÍNEZ DE ROZAS, LEMUEL SHAW, AND *BILLY BUDD*

Juan Martínez de Rozas and Lemuel Shaw played similar roles in creating their respective countries' legal systems, helping to turn a mishmash of colonial jurisprudence into coherent bodies of modern republican case law (Shaw's legal decisions, in particular, helped define norms related to commerce, free labour, mental capacity, and free speech). Likewise, Rozas's 1805 ruling in the *Tryal* case is, in a way, comparable to Shaw's 1851 upholding of the Fugitive Slave Act. The two men were personally opposed to slavery yet they both, when forced to adjudicate the struggle between justice and order, chose order (though Shaw's ruling also upheld the nested levels of state sovereignty that is US federalism, a jumble anathema to Rozas).

Melville would take up the question of whether justice was invested in 'lasting institutions' or in natural rights that exist independently of those institutions in his last and posthumously published novel, *Billy Budd*, whose Christlike title character is condemned and executed by Captain Vere, master of a British man-of-war, for unintentionally killing an abusive officer. Some legal scholars believe that Melville based Vere on Shaw. The political theorist Hannah Arendt used *Billy Budd* to argue that since absolute justice can never be represented institutionally, the fight to obtain it leads to perpetual violence, to 'war with the peace of the world and the true welfare of mankind,' as she quotes Melville's summing up of Vere's opinion. Writing in the middle of the insurgent 1960s, Arendt argued that the role of 'virtue' in the institutions of law is 'not to prevent the crime of evil but to punish the violence of absolute innocence,' since the drive to achieve perfection (or 'perfect liberty,' as Amasa Delano saw the benighted goal of French revolutionaries) can destroy society as quickly as, if not quicker than, 'elemental evil.'

For Rozas, see Domingo Amunátegui Solar, *Don Juan Martínez de Rozas*, Santiago: Universo, 1925; Manuel Martínez Lavín, *Biografía de Juan Martínez de Rozas*, Santiago: Imprenta Albion, 1894; Diego Barros Arana, *Historia general de Chile*, vol. 8, Santiago: Editorial Universitaria, 2002, pp. 10–15; and Julio Bañados Espinosa, *Ensayos y bosquejos*, Santiago: Librería Americana, 1884, pp. 255–66. Cristián Gazmuri Riveros, 'Libros e ideas políticas Francesas durante la gestación de la independencia de Chile,' in *América Latina ante la Revolución Francesa*, ed. María del Carmen Borrego Plá and Leopoldo Zea, Mexico: UNAM, 1003, p. 99, describes Rozas as the 'true ideologue of the first steps in the process of Chilean independence.' For Arendt's discussion of *Billy Budd*, see *On Revolution*, New York: Penguin, 1965, p. 84.

Following Arendt, legal theorists continue to debate the meaning of the novel. See Richard Posner, *Law and Literature*, 3rd ed., Cambridge: Harvard University Press, 2009, pp. 211–28; Alfred Konefsky, 'The Accidental Legal Historian: Herman Melville and the History of American Law,' *Buffalo Law Review* 52 (Fall 2004); and Robert Cover, *Justice Accused: Antislavery and the Judicial Process*, New Haven: Yale University Press, 1975.

THE EXECUTION

I'm sure it is reading too much into a mere accident of calligraphy, but it is worth noting, considering that Mori and probably many of the rest of the condemned were Muslims, that Rozas's scribe, when he recorded the part of the execution order that sentenced the prisoners to be paraded through Concepción tied to the tail of a mule, misspelled the al-Andalus-derived *bestia de albarda*, or 'beast of burden.' He split the last word in two and capitalized the article—*bestia Al varda*—which more clearly reveals the word's Arabic origins.

It was standard practice in both Spain and Spanish America to publicly execute and then ritually mutilate the bodies of those convicted of parricide, of rebellion against the authority of king, Church, God, master, or family father, be they white or black. They might be burned alive or hung, like José María de España, a white creole charged with conspiring against Spain in 1799 in Venezuela. After his execution, España's legs and arms were tied to four horses and his body was ripped to pieces; his 'various quarters' were then displayed in prominent locations as a warning. Another style of execution was taken straight from first-century Roman law and entailed whipping the condemned until raw, hanging until dead, and then placing the corpse in a leather sack with the bodies of a dog, snake, cock, and monkey and throwing it into a body of water. The practice decreased in frequency, but it was still occasionally used in Spanish America, including Chile and Louisiana, through the 1700s (though by this time the animals were often symbolically represented through drawings). Later, republican rebels themselves would publicly execute royalists. In 1811, Juan Martínez de Rozas had a traitor to the patriot cause put to death and his bloody body and musket-disfigured face displayed for 'public contemplation.' It is this legal tradition, which held public punishment to be a source of civic virtue, that was invoked in 1841 by the Spanish ambassador to the United States when he petitioned the US government to return the African *Amistad* rebels to Spain so 'public vengeance' could be served.

See Derek Noel Kerr, 'Petty Felony, Slave Defiance, and Frontier Villainy: Crime and Criminal Justice in Spanish Louisiana, 1770–1803,' PhD dissertation, Tulane University, 1983, p. 154. See also Claudia Arancibia Floody, José Tomás Cornejo Cancino, and Carolina González Undurraga, *Pena de muerte en Chile Colonial: Cinco casos de homicidio de la Real Audiencia*, Santiago: Centro de Investigaciones Diego Barros Arana, 2003; José Félix Blanco, ed., *Documentos para la historia de la vida pública del libertador de Colombia, Perú y Bolivia*, Caracas: La Opinión Nacional, 1875, p. 366; V. Lastarria, M. A. Torconal, et al., *Historia jeneral de la República de Chile desde su independencia hasta nuestros dias,* Santiago: Nacional, 1866, p. 310.

MELVILLE AND MANIFEST DESTINY

It is impossible to track a simple movement in Melville's writing from an embrace of the idea of manifest destiny to a more critical stance. His first extended engagement with the notion of the American West's acting as a safety valve was in the novel *Mardi,* published a year before *White-Jacket*'s famous 'ark of liberties' passage. Already in that work, Melville was skeptical: the 'wild western waste' would not be 'overrun in a day,' he wrote, 'yet overrun at last it will be; and then, the recoil must come.' Even earlier, in 1846, in a letter to his brother Gansevoort, Melville was dubious about the US invasion of Mexico. He playfully but cuttingly described the war 'delirium' that had overtaken the country. The gentry were buffing the 'wax red in their coat facings' and the ''prentice boys were running off to the wars by scores.' His generation was twice removed from the American Revolution, but its men longed to live up to their grandfathers' heroics. War with Mexico, Melville feared, would only worsen the craving, increasing the nation's tolerance for militarism. 'Lord, the day is at hand,' he wrote his brother, when the Revolutionary War's 'Battle of Monmouth will be thought child's play.' And he fretted about the consequences, worried that war would beget more war: '"A little spark kindleth a great fire" as the well known author of the Proverbs very justly remarks—and who knows what all this may lead to.' Later, in 1876, Melville would celebrate in verse his navy cousin Guert Gansevoort's heroic actions in the Mexican-American War. But the poem rotates seemingly jingoistic stanzas (with Guert 'dashed splashing through / The blue rollers sunned' to take Veracruz and plant the 'Starry Banner.' 'Hi Santa Anna!') with more skeptical ones, including one that questions the possibility of representing war at all: 'But ah, how to speak of the hurricane unchained.' Interestingly, a decade after the Mexican-American War, Guert Gansevoort (who was the son of Leonard Gansevoort, the first and perhaps main target of Albany's 1793 slave arson) was the commander of the USS *Decatur* when in 1856 it beat back an attack of two thousand Suaquamish and Duwamish peoples trying to retake what today is the Port of Seattle from white settlers.

Like his approach to most other political questions, Melville's opinion of the Jacksonian democracy that drove manifest destiny was ambivalent: *Moby-Dick*'s famous chapter 26, 'Knights and Squires,' seems to celebrate Jackson himself as a prophet of a 'great democratic God' while Melville's next novel, *Pierre,* implies that Jacksonian democracy didn't do away with the old order but merely naturalized inequalities as part of the landscape. Melville consistently criticized the hypocrisy of Christian missionaries and the violence heaped on Native Americans, even at times approaching the level of cynicism that Amasa Delano had reached by the end of his days: 'The Anglo-Saxons—lacking grace / To win the love of any race; / Hated by myriads dispossessed / Of rights—the Indians East and West. / These pirates of the sphere! grave looters— / Grave, canting, Mammonite freebooters, / Who in the name of Christ and

Trade / (Oh, bucklered forehead of the brass!) / Deflower the world's last sylvan glade!' But these are the opinions of one character in a well-populated poem. See Frederick C. Crews's discussion of this passage in 'Melville the Great,' *New York Review of Books*, December 1, 2005. See also the discussion in Parker, 'Politics and Art.' For *Pierre*, see Samuel Otter, 'The Eden of Saddle Meadows: Landscape and Ideology in Melville's *Pierre*,' *American Literature* 66 (March 1994): 55–81.

THE EMPIRE OF NECESSITY

Melville identifies the epigraph he uses for his short story 'The Bell-Tower' ('Seeking to conquer a larger liberty, man but extends the empire of necessity') as coming from a private manuscript, presumably in his possession. Some Melvilleans, though, including Hershel Parker (in an e-mail communication), speculate that he wrote it himself. 'The Bell-Tower,' which Melville published anonymously in *Putnam's Monthly*, starts with two other quotations, both also said to be from the same private manuscript. One of them reads: 'Like negroes, these powers own man sullenly, mindful of their higher master; while serving, plot revenge.' With three commas and a semicolon for sixteen words, it's a wonderfully convoluted phrase, almost as difficult to decipher as the story that follows. 'The Bell-Tower' takes place in Renaissance Italy and concerns a clockmaker who, in the process of casting an enormous bell, kills a worker, whose blood falls into the molten iron, embedding a fatal flaw in the finished bell. When the whole bell-tower apparatus is finished, it includes a cloaked, life-size ringer who moves forward on the hour and strikes the bell with a club, in effect a mechanical robot that Melville explicitly compares to a slave. The story ends with the figure clubbing his maker dead and the tower collapsing. Melville concludes: 'So the blind slave obeyed its blinder lord, but, in obedience, slew him. So the creator was killed by the creature. So the bell was too heavy for the tower. So the bell's main weakness was where man's blood had flawed it. And so pride went before the fall.' The next story Melville published in *Putnam's* was *Benito Cereno*.

Not all societies in the Americas founded on slavery have spent their postabolition history trying to escape the empire of necessity. Latin America's strong social-democratic tradition, which guarantees to its citizens the right to health care, education, and a decent, dignified life, admits that there are limits to individual freedom. These pledges have often fallen short in practice, but the region's rhetorical commitment to social rights at least acknowledges the debt liberty owes necessity. There are many reasons for the divergence between US and Latin American political culture as it relates to social rights and not all of them are related to the history of slavery. But some are: in Spanish America, the fact that the market revolution powered by slavery occurred *before* its break from Spain meant that the movement for political independence and for the abolition of slavery could be seen by many republicans as one and the same thing. Following independence, political disenfranchisement and social domination based on racial categories continued, but *race* was not abstracted into a thing in itself (at least not as much as it would be in the United States). In Latin America, postindependence struggles for political democracy and social rights, for freedom and equality, were less likely to be understood in racial terms, or, if they were, it would be in a good way, with dark-skinned peoples throughout the region fighting for universal social democracy. In the United States, where the slave-driven market revolution occurred *after* the American Revolution, not only was the fight to extend more democratic rights to, and greater freedom for, white men seen as something distinct from the fight for abolition, it was understood by many as dependent on slavery, an understanding that saw its apotheosis in the Kansas-Nebraska Act and John Calhoun's 'positive good' vision of slavery. Then, after abolition, this slavery-forged freedom took new shape on the frontier, which allowed endless opportunities for millions of what Melville called 'sovereign-kings' to flee forward, imagining themselves escaping the master-slave relation, escaping from the empire of necessity.

ARCHIVES CONSULTED

Slavery created the modern world. It's a statement often made, easy to agree with, and hard to process since its truth is lost in its abstraction. But in writing this book, I've come to appreciate the assertion anew, to realize the ways that slavery insinuated itself into the soul and sinews of the West. The research for this history was conducted in archives, libraries, and museums in nine countries, including in Spain (in Madrid, Seville, and Calañas, the Andalusian village where Benito Cerreño was born), Uruguay, Argentina (Buenos Aires and Mendoza, Alejandro de Aranda's hometown), Chile (Santiago, Valparaiso, and Concepción), Peru (Lima and Huacho), Great Britain (Liverpool and London), Senegal (Dakar and Port Saint-Louis), France (Aix-en-Provence), and the United States (Boston, Duxbury—Amasa Delano's birthplace—Albany, New York, Providence, and Washington, D.C., among other places). I've travelled by bus across the pampas and over the Andes, roughly along the route Mori, Babo, and the rest of the West African captives were forced to move by foot and mule, and visited the Huaura Valley in Peru, north of Lima, where Cerreño, having given up sailing after barely surviving his ordeal, took possession of Hacienda Humaya, a sprawling sugar slave plantation. And I've taken an overladened ferry from Lota, Chile, to the Pacific island of Santa María, spending the three-day wait for the return ship with nothing much to do except reread *Benito Cereno* and contemplate the bay where Delano's *Perseverance* met Cerreño's *Tryal* (there wasn't even beer to buy, since most of the island's residents, it seemed, had converted to Pentecostalism).

Some of the locations on this itinerary have only a glancing relationship to slavery, through this particular history. Others, like Seville, Buenos Aires, Port Saint-Louis, Lima, Boston, and Liverpool, were central hubs in a network that financed, administered, and profited from the slave trade, a vast yet surprisingly intimate network, as the story of the *Tryal* illustrates. Along the way, I began to see traces of slavery everywhere, not just in the wealth it left behind, in beautiful Baroque buildings and stately landscaped cities and manicured gardens like the one in Buenos Aires that sits over the old slave market, El Retiro, but in the meaning it created.

Slavery was such an omnipresent institution that it produced its own kind of synchronicity, making chance events seem almost conspiratorial, as if some divine author fit them together into an intentional pattern, like, for just one example, the recurrent influence the Liverpool slaver John Bolton had on Melville's literary production. In addition to dispatching his slave ship, the *Neptune*, to Bonny and raising funds to erect Liverpool's monument to Admiral Nelson, he used his fortune made from slavery to entertain and support some of Britain's greatest Romantic poets, including occasionally William Wordsworth. A friend of the rights of man and an opponent of slavery, Wordsworth had a strong influence on Herman Melville.* According to Hershel Parker (*Melville: A Biography*, vol. 2, p. 165), he taught Melville to find 'the still, sad music of humanity' in nature, to look at a barren landscape and see its social as well as natural history (to look, perhaps, at the 23,000-foot Mount Aconcagua, which separates Argentina from Chile, and realize that a slave road once wound around it). Trying to make sense of some of these connections sent me off on tangents, following history's hyperlinks from one thing to another. I began to feel a bit like Herman Melville himself, who in 1839 looked at Liverpool's 'Lord Nelson expiring in the arms of victory' and saw not a memorial to a man but the slave trade as the key to unlocking history.

Fourteen years passed between Melville's first sight of the Nelson monument and the publication of *Benito Cereno*. But when I visited the statue while in Liverpool, there looking for information on Bolton's *Neptune*, I couldn't help but think Melville had 'Death grim and grasping' in mind when he had Babo lash Aranda's bones to the prow and tell his captives to keep faith with the blacks.

ARCHIVES

Archivo General de la Nación, Buenos Aires, Argentina [AGN (Buenos Aires)]
Archivo General de la Provincia, Mendoza, Argentina [AGP (Mendoza)]
Archivo del Arzobispado, Mendoza, Argentina [AA (Mendoza)]
Archivo General de la Nación, Lima, Peru [AGN (Lima)]
Archivo Arzobispal, Lima, Peru [AA (Lima)]
Archivo General de la Nación, Montevideo, Uruguay [AGN (Montevideo)]
Archivo Nacional de Chile, Santiago [ANC (Santiago)]
Biblioteca Nacional de Chile, Santiago
Archivo Histórico Nacional, Madrid, Spain [AHN (Madrid)]
Archivo General de Indias, Seville, Spain [AGI (Seville)]
Archivo Municipal de Calañas, Calañas, Spain [AMC (Calañas)]
National Archives and Record Administration, College Park, Maryland [NARA (College Park)]

---

* Wordsworth composed a sonnet to Haiti's Toussaint Louverture, who, like Lord Nelson, died at the moment of his triumph: taken prisoner by Napoleon's troops, he perished in a cold French dungeon in the high windy Alps in April 1803, a few months before Haitians drove the French once and for all from their island. 'There's not a breathing of the common wind,' wrote Wordsworth, 'that will forget thee.'

National Archives and Record Administration, Boston [NARA (Boston)]
Duxbury Rural and Historical Society, Massachusetts [DRHS]
Massachusetts Archives, Boston [MA (Boston)]
Houghton Library, Harvard University, Cambridge, Massachusetts
Baker Library, Harvard University, Cambridge, Massachusetts
British National Archives, London [BN (London)]
Maritime Archives and Library at the Merseyside Maritime Museum, Liverpool, UK

OTHER COLLECTIONS

Centro de Estudios Militares del Peru (Lima), Sección Archivos y Catálogos
Franklin D. Roosevelt Presidential Library
New York State Library, Manuscripts and Special Collections
Harvard Law Library, Small Manuscript Collection
Social Law Library (Boston)
New Haven Colony Historical Society
Nantucket Historical Association
Peabody Essex Museum
Library of Congress
Archives Nationales d'Outre Mer (Aix-en-Provence, France)
'Melville's Marginalia Online' (edited by Steven Olsen-Smith, Peter Norberg, and Dennis C. Marnon at http://melvillesmarginalia.org)
The New York Public Library, Gansevoort-Lansing Collection
The New-York Historical Society
John Brown Carter Library, Brown University
Archives Nationales du Sénégal (Dakar, Senegal)

NOTES

INTRODUCTION

1. Amasa Delano, *A Narrative of Voyages and Travels in the Northern and Southern Hemispheres: Comprising Three Voyages round the World; Together with a Voyage of Survey and Discovery in the Pacific Ocean and Oriental Islands*, Boston: E. G. House, 1817.

2. In December 1916, in a magazine called *Pacífico*, the Chilean Joaquín Díaz Garcés wrote a fictional short story, 'El Camino de los Esclavos,' which focused on the overland journey of Mori, Babo, and their companions across the continent. Díaz Garcés had died before the Melville revival of the 1920s and *Benito Cereno* hadn't been translated into Spanish until the 1940s (and wasn't widely available in Latin America until the 1960s), so he must have learned of events on the *Tryal* through the work of the Chilean historian Benjamín Vicuña Mackenna, who wrote about it in *Historia de Valparaíso* (Valparaiso: Imprenta Albión de Cox i Taylor, 1869, vol. 2. In a note to his story, Díaz Garcés said he hoped to open 'indifferent Chilean eyes to the history of African slavery, which, for many years, also sent its sorrowful caravans across our national territory,' a reference that Julio Pinto says, in a personal communication, may refer to the forced deportation of Bolivians and Peruvians. Though he didn't get to it, Díaz Garcés planned to follow up with another story about the 'improbable' events on the *Tryal*. In 1944, two decades after Díaz Garcés's death, the publishing house he helped found, Zig Zag, put out the first Latin American Spanish-language version of *Benito Cereno*. For Neruda, see discussion in appendix.

3. All quotations from *Benito Cereno* are from the version found in *Billy Budd, and Other Stories*, New York: Penguin, 1986. Quotations from the novels *Mardi, Redburn, White-Jacket*, and *Moby-Dick* are from the Library of America editions of Melville's work, New York, 1982 and 1983.

4. Brian Higgins and Hershel Parker, *Herman Melville: The Contemporary Reviews*, Cambridge: Cambridge University Press, 2009, pp. 469–83; Kevin Hayes, *The*

Cambridge Introduction to Herman Melville, Cambridge: Cambridge University Press, p. 79.

5. Hershel Parker, *Herman Melville: A Biography*, vol. 2: 1851–1891, Baltimore: Johns Hopkins University Press, 2002, p. 244 for 'collapsed,' p. 399 for 'cold north.'

6. Edmund Morgan, *American Slavery, American Freedom: The Ordeal of Colonial Virginia*, New York: Norton, 1975, pp. 4–5.

7. 'A mere sea-drudge, a very Guinea slave,' was how a captain of a British naval ship patrolling the coast of Africa and protecting British slavers described himself in 1779. See James G. Basker, ed., *Amazing Grace: An Anthology of Poems about Slavery, 1660–1810*, New Haven: Yale University Press, 2002, p. 283.

8. Based on selected searches done on December 8, 2012, in the Trans-Atlantic Slave Database (http://www.slavevoyages.org/tast/index.faces).

9. At its most basic level, the deception the West Africans managed to pull off on the *Tryal* speaks to debates over slave paternalism, not just to the language the master class used to justify slavery but to questions related to what degree either masters or slaves believed the language. It's a long debate but the place to start, as with most things related to slavery, is with W. E. B. Du Bois, particularly *The Souls of Black Folk* (1903) and *The Negro* (1915). In 1959, Stanley Elkins (*Slavery: A Problem in American Institutional and Intellectual Life*, Chicago: University of Chicago Press), writing in the shadow of the Holocaust, used the phrase 'total institutions' to describe slave plantations, which he compared to concentration camps, as having the same totalitarian power over the enslaved, able to destroy their personalities and force them to internalize their subordination, rendering them into infantile Sambos (as Mori first appeared to Delano). Earl Lewis's 'To Turn on a Pivot: Writing African Americans into a History of Overlapping Diasporas' (in Darlene Clark Hine and Jacqueline McLeod, eds., *Crossing Boundaries: Comparative History of Black People in Diaspora*, Bloomington: Indiana University Press, 1999) discusses the importance of Elkins's essay, along with a generation of scholars, starting in the late 1960s, that 'openly rejected' Elkins's thesis. In the early 1970s, John W. Blassingame (*The Slave Community: Plantation Life in the Antebellum South*, New York: Oxford University Press, 1972) emphasized the ability of slaves to manipulate the roles assigned to them. Eugene Genovese, in turn, spent a career documenting what he, writing with Elizabeth Fox-Genovese, called the 'fatal self-deception' of the master class. In 1971, Genovese, referring to house servants, said that the master class 'had always thought they knew these blacks, loved them, were loved by them, and they considered them part of the family. One day they learned that they had been deceiving themselves and living intimately with people they did not know at all' (*In Red and Black: Marxian Explorations in Southern and Afro-American History*, New York: Pantheon Books, 1971, p. 117).

1. HAWKS ABROAD

1. Clifton Kroeber, *The Growth of the Shipping Industry in the Río de la Plata Region: 1794–1860*, Madison: University of Wisconsin Press, 1957; Carlos Noé Alberto Gue-

vara, *La problemática marítima argentina*, vol. 2, Buenos Aires: Fundación Argentina de Estudios Marítimos, 1981, p. 74; Rubén Naranjo, *Paraná, el pariente del mar*, Rosario: Editorial Biblioteca, 1973, p 180.

2. For the discussion of the *Neptune* in this chapter and subsequent ones, see the following documents in Argentina, Uruguay, and Great Britain: in the AGN (Buenos Aires), in the Tribunales collection, legajo 94, expediente 21; legajo 131, expediente 3288; in the Hacienda collection, legajo 132, expediente 3305, and legajo 120, expediente 3046; and legajo 36 in the collection named División Colonia, Sección Gobierno, Guerra y Marina 9.24.4/1806. In the AGN (Montevideo), in the collection called Protocolos de Marina (1795–1814) for the year 1805, see 'Fianza don Rafael Fernández, don Jaime Illa y don Antonio San Vicente, con don Benito Olazábal.' Also in the AGN (Montevideo), in a collection called Ex. Archivo y Museo Histórico Nacional, in caja (box) 257, carpeta (file) 40, there is a document called 'Obrados de la fragata "Aguila" presa por la fragata "Neptuno."' See also the collection called Escribanía de Gobierno y Hacienda, caja 66, expediente 157 ('Caso de la Hoop'), caja 192 ('Expediente formado sobre ocho rollos de tabaco negro del Brasil hallados en la corbeta Francesa La Ligera su capitán Hipólito Mordell procedente de la costa de África'). See also BN (London) BT 98/63, 229, and ADM 12/110.

3. Description of Bonny is drawn from William Richardson, *A Mariner of England*, London: Murray, 1908, p. 47; Alexander X. Byrd, *Captives and Voyages: Black Migrants across the Eighteenth-Century British Atlantic World*, Baton Rouge: Louisiana State University Press, 2008 (which stresses that the voyage of inland captives to the coast often equalled in time and suffering that of the Atlantic Middle Passage); Alexander Falconbridge, *An Account of the Slave Trade on the Coast of Africa*, London: J. Phillips, 1788; and George Francis Dow, *Slave Ships and Slaving*, Mineola: Dover, 2002.

4. BN (London) T 70/34.

5. Leitch Ritchie, *Travelling Sketches on the Sea-Coasts of France*, London: Longman, 1834. Byrd, *Captives and Voyages*, p. 55, discusses the reputation for fatalism.

6. Mario Falcao Espalter, 'Hipolito Mordeille, Corsario frances al servicio de España,' *Revista del Instituto Histórico y Geográfico del Uruguay* 2 (1922): 473–529. For Mordeille's success at taking US ships, see Greg Williams, *The French Assault on American Shipping, 1793–1813*, Jefferson: McFarland, 2010; for his taking of the *Hope* after a 'desperate resistance' led by its captain, George Astier, see p. 183.

7. Amédée Gréhan, ed., *La France maritime*, vol. 2, Paris: Postel, 1837, p. 157.

8. For Bolton, see Clement Wakefield Jones, *John Bolton of Storrs, 1756–1837*, Kendal: T. Wilson, 1959, p. 51; George Baille, *Interesting Letters Addressed to John Bolton, Esq. of Liverpool, Merchant, and Colonel of a Regiment of Volunteers, to Which Is Annexed Sundry Valuable Documents*, London: J. Gold, 1809, p. 34. For Liverpool and French Revolution, see Cecil Sebag-Montefiore, *A History of the Volunteer Forces from the Earliest Times to the Year 1860*, London: A. Constable, 1908, p. 255;

Historic Society of Lancashire and Cheshire, *Transactions of the Historic Society of Lancashire and Cheshire*, vol. 93, Historic Society of Lancashire and Cheshire, 1942, p. 110; *Patriot*, November 13, 1819. For Wordsworth's friendship with Bolton, including long evenings at Storrs Hall, see Charles Wordsworth, *Annals of My Early Life, 1806–1846*, London: Longmans, Green, 1891, pp. 13, 93; Juliet Barker, *Wordsworth: A Life*, New York: HarperCollins, 2006, p. 392; *George Canning and His Friends*, vol. 2, London: E. P. Dutton, 1909, p. 288; Ian Goodall, 'Storrs Hall, Windermere,' *Georgian Group Journal* 15 (2006–7): 159–214; William Angus Knight, ed., *Letters of the Wordsworth Family from 1787 to 1855*, vol. 2, Boston: Ginn, 1907, p. 129.

9. Manuel Mujica Láinez, *Aquí vivieron: Historias de una quinta de San Isidro, 1583–1924*, Buenos Aires: Sudamérica, 1949, p. 106; Gréhan, *La France maritime*, p. 157.

10. Here's an example of how wars and revolutions could serve as tumbling gears, grabbing men up from one situation and leaving them in another, then again, then again, each time resulting in a change of status. Early in Britain's fight against France, a British merchant ship calling at Cape Coast Castle purchased a cargo of captured Africans. They were considered slaves, locked in the ship's hold, and destined for the West Indies to work on sugar plantations. That ship was captured by the French navy, which took the Africans not as slaves but as conscripts, distributing them among its frigates and men-of-war. The Africans were now sailors. By 1803, however, the British had recaptured sixty-five of them. After some debate within the councils of the Admiralty, the British deemed the Africans to be not slaves but prisoners of war, subjects—or, as the French preferred, citizens—of a legitimate, if rogue, nation. But since the British couldn't get France to live up to its customary obligations and provide for these (or any other, for that matter, white or black) captured sailors, the British had them distributed on ships throughout the Royal Navy. They were sailors once again, as well as, presumably, new British subjects (BN (London) ADM 1/3744). See also John Thompson, *The Life of John Thompson, a Fugitive Slave*, Worcester, 1856, for the memoir of an escaped Maryland slave who found a life of freedom on the high seas.

11. J. Aspinall, *Liverpool a Few Years Since*, London, 1852, p. 8. Emma Christopher, *Slave Ship Sailors and Their Captive Cargoes, 1730–1807*, Cambridge: Cambridge University Press, 2006, p. 11.

12. Marcus Rediker, *Between the Devil and the Deep Blue Sea: Merchant Seamen, Pirates, and the Anglo-American Maritime World, 1700–1750*, New York: Cambridge University Press, 1989. See also Peter Linebaugh and Marcus Rediker, *The Many-Headed Hydra: Sailors, Slaves, Commoners, and the Hidden History of the Revolutionary Atlantic*, New York: Beacon Press, 2001.

2. MORE LIBERTY

1. Samuel Hull Wilcocke, *History of the Viceroyalty of Buenos Ayres*, London: Sherwood, Neely and Jones, 1807, p. 180.

2. Rubén Carámbula, *Negro y tambor: Poemas, pregones, danzas y leyendas sobre motivos del folklore Afro-rioplatense*, Buenos Aires: Editorial Folklórica Americana, 1952, and *Pregones del Montevideo Colonial*, Montevideo: Mosca, 1968. See Lucio V. Mansilla, *Mis memorias: Infancia-Adolescencia*, Paris: Garnier Hermanos, 1904, p. 132, for memories of 'dark skinned hawkers' in Buenos Aires, their baskets filled with bread, milk, fish, peaches, cakes, hot empanadas, 'singing of sweet cider, tripe and giblets.'

3. Domingo Faustino Sarmiento, *Obras completas de Sarmiento*, vol. 42, Buenos Aires: Luz del Día, p. 15.

4. John Purdy, *The Brasilian Navigator; or, Sailing Directory for All the Coasts of Brasil, to Accompany Laurie's New General Chart*, London: R. H. Laurie, 1838, p. 174; Wilcocke, *History of the Viceroyalty of Buenos Ayres*, p. 180.

5. AGN (Montevideo), Archivos Particulares, caja 332, carpeta 4 ('Documentos relativos al Período Colonial. Libro Copiador de correspondencia comercial, a Martín de Alzaga').

6. Lyman Johnson, *Workshop of Revolution: Plebéian Buenos Aires and the Atlantic World, 1776–1810*, Durham: Duke University Press, 2011, pp. 19–20, 299; Jerry Cooney, 'Doing Business in the Smuggling Way: Yankee Contraband in the Río de la Plata,' *American Neptune* 47 (1987): 162–68. Vicente Gesualdo, 'Los Negros en Buenos Aires y el Interior,' *Historia* 2; May 5, 1982: 26–49.

7. George Reid Andrews, *The Afro-Argentines of Buenos Aires, 1800–1900*, Madison: University of Wisconsin Press, 1980, p. 24; Berenice A. Jacobs, 'The *Mary Ann*, an Illicit Adventure,' *Hispanic American Historical Review* 37 (May 1957): 200–12; Charles Lyon Chandler, 'The River Plate Voyages, 1798–1800,' *American Historical Review* 23 (July 1918): 816–26; Ernesto Bassi Arevaol, 'Slaves as Commercial Scapegoats: Smuggling Clothes under the Cover of the Slave Trade in Caribbean New Granada,' paper presented at the American Historical Association Conference, New Orleans, January 5, 2013.

8. See Jeremy Adelman, *Sovereignty and Revolution in the Iberian Atlantic*, Princeton: Princeton University Press, 2006, ch. 2, particularly pp. 58–73. Adelman writes (p. 72) that 'each metropolitan solution, or concession to colonial pressure, yielded to more pressure, and thus accumulated into a sweeping new model of imperial trade: the traffic in slaves was the centerpiece to fuel merchant fortunes and to expand the commercial frontier into imperial hinterlands.' The number of slaves in Spain's American colonies, which had been steadily increasing for a century—needed to mine gold and harvest cacao in Colombia and Venezuela and pick sugar in Peru and Cuba—exploded at the end of the 1700s (Herbert Klein, *The Atlantic Slave Trade: New Approaches to the Americas*, New York: Cambridge University Press, 1999, pp. 38–40). See also for what follows Frank T. Proctor, 'Afro-Mexican Slave Labor in the Obrajes de Paños of New Spain, Seventeenth and Eighteenth Centuries,' *Americas*, 60 (2003): 33–58; Kris Lane, 'Africans and Natives in the Mines of Spanish America,' in *Beyond Black and Red: African-Native Relations in Colonial Latin America*, ed. Matthew Restall, Albuquerque: University of New Mexico Press, 2005, pp. 159–84; Kris

Lane, *Colour of Paradise: The Emerald in the Age of Gunpowder Empires*, New Haven: Yale University Press, 2010, pp. 67–69. For African and Andean interactions in coastal estates, see Rachel O'Toole, *Bound Lives: Africans, Indians, and the Making of Race in Colonial Peru*, Pittsburgh: University of Pittsburgh Press, 2012; Nicholas P. Cushner, *Farm and Factory: The Jesuits and the Development of Agrarian Capitalism in Colonial Quito, 1600–1767*, Albany: State University of New York Press, 1982.

9. For Cuba, see Louis Perez, *Cuba and the United States: Ties of Singular Intimacy*, Atlanta: University of Georgia Press, 2003, p. 5. For discussion of deregulation, see Manuel Lucena Salmoral, *Regulación de la esclavitud negra en las colonias de América Española (1503–1886): Documentos para su studio*, 2005, part 1 (on CD-ROM), pp. 170–75; part 2, pp. 247, 257. See part 1, p. 144, for 'slavers' fever.' For the right 'to buy blacks wherever they were to be found,' see Mario Hernán Baquero, *El Virrey Don Antonio Amar y Borbón*, Bogotá: Banco de la República, 1988, p. 172.

10. Alex Borucki, 'The Slave Trade to the Río de la Plata, 1777–1812: Trans-Imperial Networks and Atlantic Warfare,' *Colonial Latin American Review* 20 (2011): 85.

11. See letter from Thomas White to Messrs. Gardner and Dean, March 17, 1806, Slavery Collection, series II: Gardner and Dean, New-York Historical Society.

12. My understanding of the importance of slavery to South America's market revolution is indebted to Adelman's *Sovereignty and Revolution*. The deregulation of the slave trade was a central component in Spain's efforts to adapt the colonial system to the 'pressures of ramped-up inter-imperial competition.' But, according to Adelman, unlike the large-scale, export-focused plantations found in the US South and the Caribbean, slavery in South America linked together 'ever more diverse and decentralized commercial hubs' throughout the whole of the continent. 'It could be argued,' Adelman writes, 'drawing on Ira Berlin, that South America's expanding hinterlands were slave societies (not simply societies with slaves) where slaves were central to productive processes. Plantations existed, but they were embedded in more diversified social systems,' with smaller establishments and hybrid forms of wage and coerced labour. 'Slavery helped support rapidly commercialized, relatively diffused and adaptive production in the South American hinterlands integrated by the flow of merchant capital. And as it did so, it helped colonies become increasingly autonomous, economically and socially, from metropolitan Spanish and Portuguese command.' In other words, what became American freedom—independence from Spain—was made possible by American slavery (p. 59). Such an approach opens up new ways to compare US and Spanish American slavery and allows for a consideration of the economic importance of slavery without reproducing old debates about whether slavery was capitalist or compatible with capitalism. In the United States, historians have recently returned to an older scholarly tradition emphasizing the importance of slavery to the making of modern capitalism, examining slavery not just as a system of labour or a generator of profit but as a

driver of finance capital and real estate speculation, as well as looking at how plantations served as organizational models for 'innovative business practices that would come to typify modern management,' as Harvard's Sven Beckert and Brown's Seth Rockman write, in 'How Slavery Led to Modern Capitalism,' in *Bloomberg*, January 24, 2012 (http://www.bloomberg.com/news/2012-01-24 /how-slavery-led-to-modern-capitalism-echoes.html). See also Beckert and Rockman's forthcoming edited collection 'Slavery's Capitalism: A New History of American Economic Development,' to be published by University of Pennsylvania Press, as well as earlier work, including Eric Williams, *Capitalism and Slavery*, Chapel Hill: University of North Carolina Press, 1944, and Sidney Mintz, *Sweetness and Power: The Place of Sugar in Modern History*, New York: Viking, 1985; Sidney Mintz, 'Slavery and Emergent Capitalism,' in *Slavery in the New World*, ed. Laura Foner and Eugene D. Genovese, Englewood Cliffs: Prentice-Hall, 1969. See also Walter Johnson's recent *River of Dark Dreams: Slavery and Empire in the Cotton Kingdom*, Cambridge: Harvard University Press, 2013.

13. Slavers, however, who made up a distinct constituency within the guild, complained about this corsair contribution, arguing that it in effect restored a tax on the slave trade that had been earlier abolished by the Crown (José María Mariluz Urquijo, *El virreinato del Río de la Plata en la época del Marqués de Avilés (1799–1801)*, Buenos Aires: Academia Nacional de la Historia, 1964, pp. 78–88).

14. Agustín Beraza, *Los corsarios de Montevideo*, Montevideo: Centro de Estudios Históricos, Navales, y Maritimos, 1978, p. 43; Falcao Espalter, 'Hipolito Mordeille'; Arturo Ariel Bentancur, *El puerto colonial de Montevideo (I). Guerras y apertura comercial: Tres lustros de crecimiento económico (1791–1806)*, Montevideo: Universidad de la Republica, 1997, pp. 322–41.

3. A LION WITHOUT A CROWN

1. See throughout, Marcus Rediker, *The Slave Ship: A Human History*, New York: Penguin, 2008.

2. Andrews, *Afro-Argentines*, p. 31; Johnson, *Workshop*, 38; Susan Migden Socolow, *The Women of Colonial Latin America*, Cambridge: Cambridge University Press, 2000, pp. 84, 132. The *Nymph of the Sea*, a Portuguese bark, had recently delivered 276 Africans from Kilwa, Tanzania. The *Susan*, registered in the United States, came with 90 Gambians. The Spanish *El Retiro de Buenos Aires* had just gotten back with 130 captives from an unnamed place on the 'coast of Africa.' The *San Ignacio*, a brig from Rio de Janeiro, carried honey, rum, coffee, cotton, and slaves. *Semanario de Agricultura, Industria y Comercio*, vols. 1–2 (facsímile), Buenos Aires: Junta de Historia y Numismátic, 1928, p. 151; AGN (Buenos Aires) Sala IX Comercio y padrones de Esclavos; Escribano de la Marina, 49.3.2; Registro de Navios 10.4.7; The Trans-Atlantic Slave Trade Database, http://www.slave voyages.org/tast/index.faces; Elena F. S. de Studer, *La trata de negros en el Río de*

la Plata durante el siglo XVIII, vol. 2, Montevideo: Libros de Hispanoamérica, 1984.

3. María Díaz de Guerra, *Documentación relativa a esclavos en el Departamento de Maldonado, Siglos XVIII y XIX*, Montevideo: Imprenta Cooperativa, 1983, pp. 30–32; AGN (Montevideo), Fondo Archivo General Administrativo, libro 15 A, 'Libro de acuerdos que dio principio en abril de 1800,' Acta del Cabildo, March 28, 1803, f. 87. See also Gesualdo, 'Los negros,' for a rise in master patricides.

4. Johnson, *Workshop of Revolution*, pp. 177–78.

5. *Revista de la Biblioteca Pública de Buenos Aires*, vol. 3, Buenos Aires: Librería de Mayo, 1881, p. 475; AGN (Montevideo), Fondo Archivo General Administrativo, libro 15 A, 'Libro de acuerdos que dio principio en abril de 1800,' Acta del Cabildo, March 28, 1803, ff. 87–89; Carlos Rama, *Historia social del pueblo Uruguayo*, Montevideo: Editorial Comunidad del Sur, 1972, p. 22; Lincoln R. Maiztegui Casas, *Orientales: Una historia política del Uruguay*, vol. 1, Montevideo: Planeta, 2005, p. 28; Oscar D. Montaño, *Umkhonto: Historia del aporte negro-africano en la formación del Uruguay*, Montevideo: Rosebud Ediciones, 1997, p. 151; Agustín Beraza, *Amos y esclavos, Enciclopedia Uruguaya*, vol. 1, Montevideo: Editores Reunidos y Arca, 1968, p. 165–66.

6. W. L. Schurz, *This New World: The Civilization of Latin America*, New York: Dutton, 1954, pp. 180–81; Leslie Rout, *The African Experience in Spanish America: 1502 to the Present Day*, Cambridge: Cambridge University Press, 1976, p. 149; Mariselle Meléndez, 'Visualizing Difference: The Rhetoric of Clothing in Colonial Spanish America,' in *Latin American Fashion Reader*, ed. Regina Root, New York: Berg, 2006, p. 25. The following sources are related to the Albany fire discussed in the footnote: For the fire and the subsequent hanging of accused arsonists, see *Albany Register*, November 25, 1793; *New-York Daily Gazette*, November 25, 1793; *Albany Register*, March 17, 1794; *Albany Register*, January 27, 1894; *Albany Chronicles: A History of the City Arranged Chronologically, from the Earliest Settlement to the Present Time; Illustrated with Many Historical Pictures of Rarity and Reproductions of the Robert C. Pruyn Collection of the Mayors of Albany*, Albany: J. B. Lyon, 1906, p. 384; George Rogers Howell, *Bicentennial History of Albany: History of the County of Albany, N.Y., from 1609 to 1886*, vol. 1, Albany: W. Munsell, 1886, p. 302; 'Examination of Bet Negro Female Slave of Philip S. Van Rensselaer, Esquire,' New York State Library, Manuscripts and Special Collections; Alice Kenney, *The Gansevoorts of Albany: Dutch Patricians in the Upper Hudson Valley*, Syracuse: Syracuse University Press, 1969, pp. 80–107. See also *Oscar Williams, 'Slavery in Albany, New York, 1624–1827,' Afro-Americans in New York Life and History*, vol. 34, 2010 (accessed online July 6, 2012). For the fear that the arsonists were inspired by Haiti, see Henriette Lucie Dillon La Tour du Pin Gouvernet, *Journal d'une femme de cinquante ans*, vol. 2, Paris: Chapelot, 1912, p. 18. For Pomp, see *Collections on the History of Albany*, vol. 2, Albany: J. Munsell, 1867, p. 383. The *Evening Journal* is the undated source given for the description of Pomp, probably the *Albany Evening Journal*.

4. BODY AND SOUL

1. For the king's 'pious mind,' see Ildefonso Pereda Valdés, *El negro en el Uruguay, pasado y presente,* Montevideo Instituto Histórico y Geográfico del Uruguay, 1965, p. 230; Archivo General de la Nación, *Acuerdos del extinguido cabildo de Montevideo,* vol. 17, annex, Montevideo, 1942, pp. 230–31. For descriptions of the 'village,' see Isidoro De-María, *Tradiciones y recuerdos: Montevideo antiguo,* Elzeviriana, 1887; Archivo General de la Nación, *Revista del Archivo General Administrativo,* vol. 6, book 11, Montevideo: El Siglo Lustrado, 1917, p. 78; Karla Chagas, Natalia Stalla, and Alex Borucki, 'Uruguay,' in UNESCO, ed. *Sitios de memoria y culturas vivas de los afrodescendientes en Argentina, Paraguay y Uruguay,* Montevideo: UNESCO, 2011, pp. 112–53. For the treatment of slaves as a problem of the state, see Salmoral, *Regulación,* part 1, pp. 183–207.

2. AGI (Seville), Gobierno, Indiferente 2826, ff. 286–395. Urquijo, in *El virreinato del Río de la Plata,* p. 361, describes the high mortality of the Portuguese slaves. See also Joseph Calder Miller, *Way of Death: Merchant Capitalism and the Angolan Slave Trade, 1730–1830,* Madison: University of Wisconsin Press, 1996.

3. Falconbridge, *Account,* pp. 24–25.

4. In 1798, for example, the Rhode Island slaver, *Ascensión,* purchased 283 slaves in Mozambique, 33 of whom fell ill with smallpox and were quickly unloaded before leaving Africa. Thirty-three died on board. Once in Montevideo, four more died and the remaining healthy ones sold for, on average, over 200 pesos each. Eight 'sickly' ones, though, were disposed of for 90 pesos, a risky investment with a potentially high payoff for the buyer: there was a good chance they wouldn't survive, but if they did, their immunity would make them that much more valuable. See the unsigned, undated account record of trade, Slavery Collection, [1798?], series I: Samuel and William Vernon, New-York Historical Society. That the ship was the *Ascensión* is indicated by other documents in the collection. Regarding the use of slaves to disseminate the smallpox vaccine, see the following documents in the AGI (Seville), Cuba, legajo 1691, December 4, 1806; Indiferente General, legajo 1558-A, June 14, 1804 (for Balmis buying and selling Cuban slaves); Chile, 205 ('Correspondencia de Presidente Luis Muñoz de Guzmán'), November 9, 1805, for transporting the vaccine, 'arm to arm of the blacks.' For the African women who carried the vaccine to Buenos Aires, see Congreso de la Nación, *Diario de sesiones de la Cámara de Diputados,* vol. 1, 1903, p. 398; see also Guillermo Fúrlong Cárdiff, *Historia social y cultural del Río de la Plata, 1536–1810,* vol. 2, Buenos Aires: Tipográfica Editora Argentina, 1969, p. 346; Diego Barros Arana, *Historia general de Chile,* vol. 7, Santiago: Rafael Jover: 1886, pp. 265–71; Gonzalo Vial Correa, *El Africano en el Reino de Chile,* Santiago: Instituto de Investigaciones Históricas, 1957; José G. Rigau-Pérez, 'The Introduction of Smallpox Vaccine in 1803 and the Adoption of Immunization as a Government Function in Puerto Rico,' *Hispanic American Historical Review* 69 (August 1989): 393–423. For Humboldt's observations, see Alexander von Humboldt, *Political Essay on the Kingdom of New Spain,* vol. 1, New York: Riley, 1811, p. 87.

5. For an extensive examination of this in the United States, see Harriet Washington, *Medical Apartheid: The Dark History of Medical Experimentation on Black Americans from Colonial Times to the Present*, New York: Doubleday, 2007; see also Richard Sheridan, *Doctors and Slaves: A Medical and Demographic History of Slavery in the British West Indies, 1680–1834*, London: Cambridge University Press, 2009.

6. For the *Rôdeur*, see Ritchie, *Travelling Sketches on the Sea-Coasts of France*, pp. 76–82, which contains a translation of a firsthand account, and 'Le cri des Africains contre les Européens, leurs oppresseurs; ou Coup-d'oeil sur le commerce homicide appelé Traite des Noirs,' *Journal des voyages, découvertes et navigations modernes; ou Archives géographiques et statistiques du XIX siècle* 36 (October–December 1821): 323–24. Sébastien Guillié's study of the case, 'Observation sur une blépharoblénorrhée contagieuse,' *Bibliothèque ophtalmologique; ou Recueil d'observations sur les maladies des yeux faites à la clinique de l'Institution royale des jeunes aveugles* 1 (1820), was published before these two sources. For Guillié, see Zina Weygand, *The Blind in French Society: From the Middle Ages to the Century of Louis Braille*, Stanford: Stanford University Press, 2009. The case of the *Rôdeur* was cited by abolitionists in France and Great Britain, including Benjamin Constant and William Wilberforce.

7. AGN (Buenos Aires), División Colonial, Sección Gobierno, Tribunales, legajo 94, 26.2.3; also Studer, *La trata*, pp. 311–14.

8. For Alzaga's fear of egalitarianism, see Johnson, *Workshop of Revolution*, pp. 157–78; the quotation is on p. 164.

9. Miguel de la Sierra y Lozano, *Elogios de Cristo y María: Aplicados a quarenta sermones de sus fiestas*, Zaragoza: Pedro Verges, 1646, p. 61; Real Academia Española, *Diccionario de la lengua castellana*, Madrid, 1783; 'On Hypochondriasis,' *Journal of Psychological Medicine and Mental Pathology*, January 1, 1850, p. 3; G. E. Berrios, 'Melancholia and Depression during the 19th Century: A Conceptual History,' *British Journal of Psychiatry* 153 (September 1988): 298–304. Protestants, and at least three of the five surgeons on the *Joaquín* commission were Protestant, might identify Catholics, grimacing and grovelling before their icons, as prone to the condition, betraying the 'low thoughts they had of the divine nature'; see Anthony Ashley Cooper, *Characteristics of Men, Manners, Opinions, Times*, J. J. Tourneisen and J. L. Legrand, 1790, p. 103.

10. Thomas W. Laqueur, 'Bodies, Details, and the Humanitarian Narrative,' in *The New Cultural History*, ed. Lynn Hunt, Berkeley: University of California Press, 1989, pp. 176–77.

11. Manuel Hurtado de Mendoza, Antonio Ballano, and Celedonio Martínez Caballero, *Suplemento al diccionario de medicina y cirugía*, 1823.

12. For Redhead, see José Luis Molinari, 'Manuel Belgrano: Sus enfermedades y sus médicos,' *Historia*, Buenos Aires, 1960, 20 pp. 88–160, p. 130.

13. Johnson, *Workshop of Revolution*, pp. 39–43, 151–54. To compare Montevideo with other urban slave experiences, see, for Mexico City, Herman Bennett, *Africans in Colonial Mexico: Absolutism, Christianity, and Afro-Creole Conscious-*

ness, 1570–1640, Bloomington: Indiana University Press, 2003, and 'Genealogies to a Past: Africa, Ethnicity, and Marriage in Seventeenth-Century Mexico,' in *New Studies in the History of American Slavery*, ed. Edward Baptist and Stephanie Camp, Athens: University of Georgia Press, 2006; for Buenos Aires and Lima, Christine Hünefeldt, *Paying the Price of Freedom: Family and Labor among Lima's Slaves, 1800–1854*, Berkeley: University of California Press, 1994. Emeric Essex Vidal visited Buenos Aires in the early 1800s and observed, in his *Picturesque Illustrations of Buenos Ayres and Monte Video*, London: R. Ackermann, 1820, p. 30, that 'slavery at Buenos Ayres is perfect freedom compared with that among other nations,' a contradiction in terms that, even as it discounted the hardship and suffering of many of the city's residents, still captured their relative autonomy. See Tomás Olivera Chirimini, 'Candombe, African Nations, and the Africanity of Uruguay,' in Sheila Walker, ed., *African Roots / African Cutlure: Africa in the Creation of the Americas*, Lanham: Rowman and Littlefield, 2001, and Mansilla, *Mis memorias*, pp. 132–33. For a comparison with New Orleans, see Ned Sublette, *The World That Made New Orleans: From Spanish Silver to Congo Square*, Chicago: Review Press, 2009; for a comparison with Albany, see Sterling Stuckey, *Going Through the Storm: The Influence of African-American Art in History*, New York: Oxford University Press, 2009, pp. 53–80. For complaints, see Gesualdo, 'Los Negros,' p. 34; also Vicente Rossi, *Cosas de negros: Los orígenes del tango y otros aportes al folklore rioplatense*, Buenos Aires: Aguilar, 1926. For 'sociedad de la nación moro,' along with the many other 'naciones,' see Miguel Rosal, 'Aspectos de la Religiosidad Afroporteña, siglos XVIII–XIX,' available online at http://www.revistaquilombo.com.ar/documentos.htm.

14. Manuel Nuñez de Taboada, *Diccionario de la lengua castellana*, 1825.

5. A CONSPIRACY OF LIFTING AND THROWING

1. Paul Lovejoy, *Trans-Atlantic Dimensions of Ethnicity in the African Diaspora*, London: Continuum, 2003, p. 289; Elizabeth Allo Isichei, *Voices of the Poor in Africa*, Rochester: Boydell and Brewer, 2002, p. 287; Walter Rucker, *The River Flows On: Black Resistance, Culture, and Identity Formation in Early America*, Baton Rouge: Louisiana State University Press, 2006, p. 288; Falconbridge, *Account*, p. 30; Estebán Montejo, and Miguel Barnet, eds., *The Autobiography of a Runaway Slave*, New York: Macmillan, 1993, pp. 63–64. Byrd, *Captives and Voyages*, pp. 20–30, discusses the many meanings of the term *Igbo*.

2. The case of the *Santa Eulalia* is described in the documents cited earlier regarding the *Neptune* and in AGN (Buenos Aires), División Colonia, Sección Gobierno, Guerra y Marina, 9.24.4/1806, legajo 36. See also AGN (Lima), notary record, José Escudero de Sicilia, Escribano del Tribunal del Consulato, 1805. Cristina Mazzeo de Vivó was kind enough to send me a draft of her essay on the voyage, 'Vivir y morir en alta mar: La comercialización del esclavo en Hispanoamérica a fines del siglo XVIII,' which contains additional sources and has been

subsequently published in *Homenaje a José Antonio del Busto Duthurburu*, ed. Margarita Guerra Martinière and Rafael Sánchez-Concha Barrios, 2 vols., Lima: Fondo Editorial PUCP, 2012.

3. Vicente Osvaldo Cutolo, *Nuevo Diccionario Biográfico Argentino (1750–1930)*, vol. 5 (N–Q), Buenos Aires: Editorial Elche, 1978, p. 649; AGN (Montevideo), Protocolos de Marina (1803–4), Registro corriente de Entradas de Marina del año de 1805 ('Fianza: Señor Antonio Pérez por el depósito de los Negros del Bergantín Diana y Polacra Ligera de Mordelle'). One of Mordelle's prizes, the *Diana* was also known as the *Dolores*; see Departamento de Estudios Históricos Navales, *Historia marítima argentina*, vol. 4, Buenos Aires: Departamento de Estudios Históricos Navales, 1993, p. 323.

4. Jacques Duprey, *Voyage aux origines françaises de l'Uruguay: Montevideo et l'Uruguay vus par des voyageurs français entre 1708 et 1850*, Montevideo: Instituto Histórico y Geográfico del Uruguay, 1952, p. 182.

INTERLUDE: I NEVER COULD LOOK AT DEATH WITHOUT A SHUDDER

1. For Thoreau, see his *Political Writings*, ed. Nancy Rosenblum, Cambridge: Cambridge University Press, 1996, pp. 26–27. For Melville's use of slavery as a metaphor for bondage in general, and vice versa, see Carolyn L. Karcher, *Shadow over the Promised Land: Slavery, Race, and Violence in Melville's America*, Baton Rouge: Louisiana State University Press, 1980. For an example of a 'bondman' who 'enjoyed the liberties of the world,' see *White-Jacket*'s Guinea. Hershel Parker, *Herman Melville: A Biography*, vol. 1, 1819–1851, Baltimore: Johns Hopkins University Press, 2005, p. 147.

2. *Moby-Dick*, pp. 798, 1094, 1216–19.

3. John Griscom, *A Year in Europe: Comprising a Journal of Observations in England, Scotland, Ireland, France, Switzerland, the North of Italy, and Holland*, New York: Collins, 1823, p. 30.

4. Herman Melville, *Redburn, White-Jacket, Moby-Dick*, New York: Library of America, 1983, p. 170.

5. Howard Horsford with Lynn Horth, eds., *The Writings of Herman Melville: Journals*, Evanston: Northwestern University Press, 1989, p. 50.

6. A SUITABLE GUIDE TO BLISS

1. Philippe de Lannoy begat Thomas, who begat Jonathan Sr., who begat Jonathan Jr., who begat Samuel, who begat Amasa. See Alicia Crane Williams, ed., Esther Littleford Woodworth-Barnes, comp., *Mayflower Families through Five Generations*, vol. 16, part 1, Plymouth: General Society of Mayflower Descendants, 1999, p. 49; Daniel Delano Jr., *Franklin Roosevelt and the Delano Influence*, Pittsburgh: James Nudi, 1946; Muriel Curtis Cushing, *Philip Delano of the 'Fortune' 1621, and His*

Descendants for Four Generations, Plymouth: General Society of Mayflower Descendants, 2002; *Philip Delano of the 'Fortune' 1621, and His Descendants in the Fifth, Sixth, and Seventh Generations*, parts 1 and 2, Plymouth: General Society of Mayflower Descendants, 2004, 2011.

2. For slavery in Duxbury, see Justin Winsor, *History of the Town of Duxbury, Massachusetts, with Genealogical Registers*, Boston: Crosby and Nichols, 1849, pp. 68, 70–71, 130, 271, 340; for enslavement of Native Americans, see pp. 71, 314. 'Iron-nerved' and able to 'hew down forests and live on crumbs' was how one of the town's founders, Myles Standish, was described in 'Alden Genealogy,' *New England Historical and Genealogical Register*, vol. 51 (October 1897), p. 430. See also George Ethridge, ed., *Copy of the Old Records of the Town of Duxbury, Mas: From 1642 to 1770*, Plymouth: Avery and Doten, 1893, p. 338; Jennifer Turner, 'Almshouse, Workhouse, Outdoor Relief: Responses to the Poor in Southeastern Massachusetts, 1740–1800,' *Historical Journal of Massachusetts* 31 (Summer 2003): 212–14.

3. At times written as: 'The more there is of craft and management in sin, the more it is an abomination to God.' The story of the biblical Amasa's murder is in 2 Samuel, which Herman Melville read closely, judging from the underlinings, checks, and markings in the Bible he was using at the time he wrote *Benito Cereno*. Much appreciation to Clifford Ross for allowing me to consult the book in his private collection. Another Melville family Bible (Philadelphia: Mathew Carey, 1810), now in the New York Public Library's Gansevoort-Lansing collection, in an appendix titled 'Index of Proper Names with Meanings in Original Language,' defines *Amasa* as 'sparing the people.'

4. Amasa came from a line of Indian-killers. In 1637, Philippe de Lanoy had volunteered to fight the Pequots, in a genocidal war that nearly destroyed the Native American group as a people. Survivors were hunted down and either killed or sold to the Spanish as slaves. Philippe volunteered in July 1837, after the infamous Mystic Massacre, where the British surrounded a Pequot roundhouse filled mostly with women, children, and elderly and burned it to the ground, killing hundreds. He might have participated in the July 1837 'swamp engagement,' one of the last battles of the war. Personal communication with Alfred Cave, December 16, 2012. See Alfred Cave, *The Pequot War*, Amherst: University of Massachusetts Press, 1996. For Amasa Delanoe and events surrounding the attack on Saint Francis, see Ian McCulloch and Timothy Todish, eds., *Through So Many Dangers: The Memoirs and Adventures of Robert Kirk, Late of the Royal Highland Regiment*, Fleischmanns: Purple Mountain Press, 3004, pp. 66–67; BN (London), WO 71/68, Marching Regiments (October 1760–July 1761), pp. 147–50; Nicolas Renaud d'Avène des Méloizes, *Journal militaire de Nicolas Renaud d'Avène des Méloizes 1756–1759*, Quebec, 1930, pp. 86–87; Stephen Brumwell, *White Devil: A True Story of War, Savagery, and Vengeance in Colonial America*, Cambridge: Da Capo Press, 2004, pp. 230, 235, 305.

5. Seth Sprague, 'Reminiscences of the Olden Times,' 1845, n.p., in *Hon. Seth Sprague of Duxbury, Plymouth County, Massachusetts; His Descendants down to*

the Sixth Generation and His Reminiscences of the Old Colony Town, comp. William Bradford Weston, n.p., 1915.

6. For the contribution of Duxbury's ministers to the emergence of Unitarianism, see Samuel Atkins Eliot, *Heralds of a Liberal Faith*, Boston: American Unitarian Association, 1910, pp. 122–30, 194–99. For Turner's Election Sermon, see Pauline Maier, *Ratification: The People Debate the Constitution, 1787–1788*, New York: Simon & Schuster, 2011, p. 205, and Charles Turner, *A Sermon Preached before His Excellency Thomas Hutchinson*, Boston: Richard Draper, 1773.

7. For the rebalancing of passions, interests, virtues, and vices, see the discussion in Daniel Walker Howe, *Making the American Self: Jonathan Edwards to Abraham Lincoln*, Cambridge: Harvard University Press, 1997, p. 66, and Albert O. Hirschman, *The Passions and Interests: Political Arguments for Capitalism before Its Triumph*, Princeton: Princeton University Press, 1997.

8. Ira Stoll, *Samuel Adams: A Life*, New York: Simon & Schuster, 2009, pp. 107–8; Harry Stout, *The New England Soul: Preaching and Religious Culture in Colonial New England*, New York: Oxford University Press, 1988, pp. 279, 377.

9. 'The Pence Property,' *Duxbury Clipper*, September 8, 2009.

10. Unitarian Universalist Church at First Parish in Sherborn, http://www.uuac.org /about/roots.pdf, accessed September 5, 2012; Elijah Brown, *A Sermon Preached at the Ordination of . . . Zedeziah* [Zedekiah] *Sanger*, Boston: Fleets, 1776.

11. Winsor, *History of the Town of Duxbury*, p. 144. Roughly a third of Duxbury's male population, about 270 men, pretty much all who weren't needed to keep the town fed, would join the revolutionary militia, and many of them would die at the hands of the British and their allies, including a favourite son scalped by a Seneca warrior. See William Stone, *Life of Joseph Brant (Thayendanegea) including the Border Wars of the American Revolution*, vol. 1, Albany: Munsell, 1865, p. 373. See Kevin Phillips, *1775: A Good Year for Revolution*, New York: Viking, 2012.

12. Sprague, 'Reminiscences of the Olden Times,' n.p., for 'literary attainments.' See also Dorothy Wentworth, *Settlement and Growth of Duxbury*, Duxbury: Duxbury Rural and Historical Society, 2000, p. 108; Weston, *Hon. Seth Sprague of Duxbury*; Patrick T. J. Browne, *King Caesar of Duxbury: Exploring the World of Ezra Weston, Shipbuilder and Merchant*, Duxbury: Duxbury Rural and Historical Society, 2006.

13. 'Old Duxbury Village Once Called Sodom,' *Duxbury Clipper*, June 26, 1996.

14. Turner, 'Almshouse, Workhouse, Outdoor Relief,' pp. 212–14.

15. Gordon Wood, *The Radicalism of the American Revolution*, New York: Vintage, 1993, pp. 230, 246, 305–6. Intellectual historians and political theorists distinguish between republicanism and liberalism in eighteenth- and nineteenth-century America. In broad terms, republicanism emphasized civic responsibility and public virtue while liberalism stressed individual freedom, natural rights, and the pursuit of self-interest. Theoretically, the two ideals are separated in

how they understand the 'common good' to be generated, with the first imaging a virtuous republic transcendent of the individual (Gordon Wood writes that republicanism contained a 'moral dimension, a utopian depth' that valued the 'sacrifice of individual interests to the greater good of the whole'; 'Ideally, republicanism obliterated the individual') and the second arguing that the common good flows out of the private pursuits of the individual. The role of government in the first is to embody or enforce virtue; in the second, it is to protect the plurality of freedoms, rights, interests, and pursuits that generate virtue. Some scholars have seen the tension between republicanism and liberalism as central to American political culture. In practice, there was much slippage and overlap in how both common citizens and politicians and intellectuals experienced these ideals. Men like Amasa Delano, for example, raised in the ethos of what we would call eighteenth-century republicanism, could believe both that morality and responsibility existed above his own personal experience and that leaving him alone to pursue his own interests would add to the public well of virtue. For historians who caution against making too much of the distinctions, see Howe, *Making the American Self*, pp. 10–13; Stephen Macedo, *Liberal Virtues: Citizenship, Virtue, and Community in Liberal Constitutionalism*, Princeton: 1987; Joyce Appleby, *Liberalism and Republicanism in the Historical Imagination*, Cambridge: Harvard University Press, 1992.

16. Or, as a later historian more bluntly translated such sentiments: expansion in postrevolutionary America 'was the only way to honor avarice and morality. The only way to be good *and* wealthy.' William Appleman Williams, *America Confronts a Revolutionary World, 1776–1976*, New York: Morrow, 1976, p. 43. See also Justin Winsor, *The Two Hundred and Fiftieth Anniversary of the Settlement of Duxbury*, Plymouth: Avery and Doten, 1887, p. 47.

17. Howe, *Making the American Self*; Wood, *Radicalism*; Hirschman, *Passions and the Interests*, Princeton: Princeton University Press, 1977.

18. For Delano's quotes, see *Narrative*, pp. 204, 256, 590.

7. THE LEVELLING SYSTEM

1. For Delano's involvement in the opium trade, see DRHS, series 1, box 1, folder 1, 'Amasa Delano to Samuel Delano, Jr., April 23, 1791.'

2. For the quotations here and below, see Delano, *Narrative*, pp. 200–4.

3. Lorenzo Sabine, *Biographical Sketches of Loyalists of the American Revolution*, vol. 2, Bedford: Applewood Books, 2009, pp. 398, 430; Weston, *Hon. Seth Sprague of Duxbury*, p. 73; Winsor, *History of the Town of Duxbury*, p. 138.

4. Meghan Vaughan, *Creating the Creole Island: Slavery in Eighteenth-Century Mauritius*, Durham: Duke University Press, 2005, pp. 231–35.

5. DRHS, series 1, box 1, folder 2, 'Amasa Delano to Samuel Delano, Jr., 1794.'

6. Delano, *Narrative*, pp. 212, 250.

8. SOUTH SEA DREAMS

1. Delano, *Narrative*, pp. 252–53.
2. Delano, *Narrative*, p. 254.
3. DRHS, Bureau of Marine Inspection and Navigation Report, original in NARA (College Park), RG 41.
4. Lorenzo Johnston Greene, *The Negro in Colonial New England*, New York: Athenaeum, 1968, pp. 23–69; William Cahn, *A Matter of Life and Death: The Connecticut Mutual Story*, New York: Random House, 1970; 'Slavery's Fellow Travelers,' *New York Times*, July 13, 2000; 'How Slavery Fueled Business in the North,' *New York Times*, July 24, 2000; 'Slave Policies,' *New York Times*, May 5, 2002; Jay Coughtry, *The Notorious Triangle: Rhode Island and the African Slave Trade, 1700–1807*, Philadelphia: Temple University Press, 1981, pp. 92–95; Sharon Murphy, *Investing in Life: Insurance in Antebellum America*, Baltimore: Johns Hopkins University Press, 2010. See also the Slavery Era Insurance Registry Report, http://www.insurance.ca.gov/0100-consumers/0300-public-programs /0200-slavery-era-insur/slavery-era-report.cfm (accessed December 19, 2012); Ronald Bailey, 'The Slave(ry) Trade and the Development of Capitalism in the United States: The Textile Industry in New England,' *Social Science History* 14 (Autumn 1990): 373–414; Anne Farrow, Joel Lang, and Jennifer Frank, *Complicity: How the North Promoted, Prolonged, and Profited from Slavery*, New York: Ballantine Books, 2006; Richard Hooker, *Aetna Life Insurance Company: Its First Hundred Years*, Hartford: Aetna Life Insurance Co., 1956, pp. 14–15; Gary Simon and Cheryl Chen, 'Actuarial Issues in Insurance on Slaves in the United States South,' *Journal of African American History* 89 (Fall 2004): 348–57. See the review by Shaun Nichols of the conference 'Slavery's Capitalism,' held at Brown and Harvard Universities, H-Net Reviews. May 2011, http://www.h-net.org/reviews /showrev.php?id=33419. See also Beckert and Rockman's summation, 'How Slavery Led to Modern Capitalism,' *Bloomberg*.
5. David Brion Davis, *The Problem of Slavery in the Age of Revolution*, Davis, *Slavery and Human Progress*, New York: Oxford University, Press, 1984; Douglas Egerton, 'The Empire of Liberty Reconsidered,' in James Horn, Jan Ellen Lewis, and Peter Onuf, eds., *The Revolution of 1800: Democracy, Race, and the New Republic*, Charlottesville: University of Virginia Press, 2002, p. 313. p. 262.
6. DRHS, Gamaliel Bradford's Diary. Bradford's daughter, Sarah Alden Bradford Ripley, was an early Concord Transcendentalist and owner of the Old Manse, which she rented to Nathaniel and Sophia Hawthorne. His son, George Partridge Bradford, was a friend of Ralph Waldo Emerson and a Brook Farmer. Bradford himself would found the Society for the Moral Improvement of Seamen in Boston and likely worshiped at the same Unitarian church as did Amasa Delano in the 1810s and early 1820s.
7. Bernard Bailyn, *The Ideological Origins of the American Revolution*, 2nd ed., Cambridge: Harvard University Press, 1992, p. 232; Barry Alan Shain, *The Myth of American Individualism*, Princeton: Princeton University Press, 1994, pp. 288–319.

8. *Patriot Ledger*, posted January 17, 2011, accessed November 9, 2011, at http://www
.patriotledger.com/archive/x2081097545/Add-Duxbury-to-the-list-of-local
-towns-with-historical-ties-to-slavery#ix77ld1nH1SN1. See also *The Sessional
Papers Printed by the House of Lords; Correspondence with Foreign Powers Relat-
ing to the Slave Trade*, London: William Clowes and Sons, 1842, pp. 183–84, for
the British Royal Navy's seizure of the Duxbury brig *Douglas*, bound for Bonny
from Havana, on the charge of having 'on board a suspicious cargo' believed to
be traded for slaves; Browne, *King Caesar of Duxbury*, pp. 94–97, 100–5, 111–12;
Elizabeth Donnan, *Documents Illustrative of the Slave Trade to America*, vol. 3,
New York: Octagon Books, 1965, pp. 102–8; Frederick George Kay, *The Shame-
ful Trade*, London: Muller, 1967, p. 126.

9. 'A Zombie Is a Slave Forever,' *New York Times*, October 30, 2012.

10. Nathaniel Philbrick, *In the Heart of the Sea*: The Tragedy at the Whaleship *Essex*,
New York: Penguin, 2000, p. xi.

11. *Moby-Dick*, p. 1246.

12. Ibid., p. 1239.

13. Colonial Society of Massachusetts, *Publications of the Colonial Society of Massachusetts*, vol. 7, Boston: The Society, 1905, pp. 94–98.

14. Delano, *Narrative*, pp. 49–53, for what follows. The boy was part of the *Panther's* complement of *lascars*, enslaved, bonded, impressed, or otherwise
coerced sailors whom all ships in the Royal Navy and the Bombay Marine
relied on. By this time, *lascar* had come to collectively refer to Burmese, Ben-
gali, Malabar, Malay, Manila, Javanese, Chinese, and other Asian mariners.
The word, originally from either Urdu or Arabic, didn't exactly mean slave but
it generally suggested something quite less than equality. British merchant and
Royal Navy ships often impressed these sailors straight off of Asian vessels.
'Poor lascars,' said one reformer in the British Parliament, British captains
were 'treating them like dogs or slaves, crowding them into forecastles in a
manner compared with which pigs in pig-styes had more accommodation.' See
Anne Bulley, *Free Mariner: John Adolphus Pope in the East Indies, 1786–1821*,
London: British Association for Cemeteries in South Asia, 1992; N. B. Dennys,
ed., *Notes and Queries on China and Japan*, vol. 3, Hong Kong: C. A. Saint,
1869, p. 78; Great Britain, Parliament, *The Parliamentary Debates*, London:
Reuter's Telegram Co., 1895, p. 194; Norma Myers, *Reconstructing the Black
Past: Blacks in Britain, c. 1780–1830*, London: Taylor and Francis (Routledge),
1996, pp. 104–17; Anne Bulley, *The Bombay Country Ships, 1790–1833*, London: Curzon Press, 2000.

15. Davis, *Problem of Slavery*, pp. 558–62. The phrase 'existential impasse' comes from
Alexandre Kojève, *Introduction to the Reading of Hegel*, ed. Raymond Queneau,
Ithaca: Cornell University Press, 1980, p. 46. See discussion in Davis, *Problem of
Slavery* p. 561; G. W. F. Hegel, *The Philosophy of History*, trans. John Sibree, New
York: American Home Library Co., 1902, 511.

INTERLUDE: BLACK WILL ALWAYS HAVE SOMETHING MELANCHOLY IN IT

1. John Freeman, *Herman Melville*, New York: Macmillan, 1926, p. 61; Hugh Hetherington, ed., *Melville's Reviewers: British and American, 1846–1891*, Chapel Hill: University of North Carolina Press, 1961, p. 253.
2. Carl Van Doren, 'A Note of Confession,' *Nation*, December 5, 1928; Adam Hochschild, *King Leopold's Ghost: A Story of Greed, Terror, and Heroism in Colonial Africa*, New York: Houghton Mifflin, 1998, p. 3.
3. Many of these opinions are found in John P. Runden, ed., *Melville's* Benito Cereno: *A Text for Guided Research*, Boston: Heath, 1965. See also Burkholder, ed., *Critical Essays*. For their original sources, see Rosalie Feltenstein, 'Melville's "Benito Cereno,"' *American Literature* 19 (1947): 245–55; Arthur Vogelback, 'Shakespeare and Melville's *Benito Cereno*,' *Modern Language Notes* 67 (1952): 113–16; Newton Arvin, *Herman Melville*, 1950, New York: Grove, 2002, p. 240; Stanley Williams, 'Follow Your Leader: Melville's *Benito Cereno*,' *Virginia Quarterly* 23 (Winter 1947): 65–76; Richard Harter Fogle, *Melville's Shorter Tales*, Norman: University of Oklahoma Press, 1960, p. 137; F. O. Matthiessen, *American Renaissance: Art and Expression in the Age of Emerson and Whitman*, New York: Oxford University Press, 1941, p. 508; Yvor Winters, *In Defense of Reason*, Denver: Allan Swallow, 1947, p. 222. Many of these judgments regarding Babo's moral malignancy were made in the late 1940s, during the transition from World War II to the Cold War. During this period, politics was often presented as metaphysics. That is, the totalitarianism of both the Nazi right and the Stalinist left tended to be understood much as Babo's actions were understood, as motiveless, driven by a hatred of freedom. Scholarship on *Benito Cereno*, and indeed, much of the scholarship on Melville in general, reflected this drift, with Amasa Delano's 'innocence' taken as a metaphor for an America that only reluctantly confronts evil in the world. A good example is Richard Chase's 1950 study of Herman Melville, which uses Melville's skepticism and awareness of evil to criticize Henry Wallace, the Progressive Party, and that section of the New Deal coalition that, after World War II, wanted to return to a focus on remedying economic injustice at home rather on than building up a military to contain the Soviet Union abroad (*Melville: A Critical Study*, New York: Macmillan, 1949). See Clare Spark, *Hunting Captain Ahab: Psychological Warfare and the Melville Revival*, Kent: Kent State University Press, 2001, for the definitive account of Cold War politics and Melville studies. Hershel Parker, in 'Melville and Politics: A Scrutiny of the Political Milieux of Herman Melville's Life and Works,' PhD dissertation, Northwestern University, 1963, p. 222, downplays *Benito Cereno* as a critique of racism: 'Melville made no covert attack on American slavery in *Benito Cereno*.'
4. Sterling Brown, *The Negro in American Fiction*, 1937, Arno Press, 1969, p. 13. Some scholars understood the story to be about slavery yet argued that it upheld, or was trapped in, racial assumptions. See Sidney Kaplan, 'Herman Melville and the American National Sin: The Meaning of *"Benito Cereno,"' Journal of*

Negro History 57 (1957): 12–27. Andrew Delbanco, 'Melville in the '80s,' *American Literary History* 4 (Winter 1992): 709–25, describes post-Vietnam criticism of Melville. See also Marvin Fisher, *Going Under: Melville's Short Fiction and the American 1850s*, Baton Rouge: Louisiana State University Press, 1977. For Sterling Brown's influence, see Anthony Appiah, Henry Louis Gates, Jr., eds. *Africana: Arts and Letters: An A–Z Reference of Writers, Musicians and Artists of the African American Experience*, Philadelphia: Running Press, 2004, p. 114; 'Sterling A. Brown, 87, Poet and Educator, is Dead,' *New York Times*, January 17, 1989.

5. D. H. Lawrence, *Studies in Classic American Literature*, 1923, New York: Penguin, 1990, p. 153. For a description of the fleshy, squint-eyed 'whiteness' on display in Delano's portrait, see Max Putzel, 'The Source and the Symbols of Melville's "Benito Cereno,"' *American Literature* 34 (May 1962): 196.

6. Lewis Mumford, *Herman Melville: A Study of His Life and Vision*, New York: Harcourt, 1962 [1929]; p. 162; Percy Holmes Boynton, *More Contemporary Americans*, 1926, Freeport: Books for Libraries Press, 1967, p. 42.

7. *Moby-Dick*, pp. 993–1001.

8. According to Merton M. Sealts, *Melville's Reading*, Columbia: University of South Carolina Press, p. 160, Melville consulted the following volume, now found in Harvard's Houghton Library: Edmund Burke, *A Philosophical Inquiry into the Origin of Our Ideas of the Sublime and Beautiful, with an Introductory Discourse concerning Taste, and Several Other Additions*, Philadelphia, printed for D. Johnson, Portland, by J. Watts, 1806. Quotations are found on pp. 219, 221, 223, 227–28.

9. THE SKIN TRADE

1. Andrews, *Afro-Argentines*, p. 29; Archivo General de la Nación, *Acuerdos del Extinguido Cabildo de Buenos Aires*, Buenos Aires: Kraft, 1925, p. 212.

2. For the *Susan* and *Louisiana*, see AGN (Buenos Aires) Sala IX 'Comercio y padrones de esclavos, 1777–1808.'

3. For examples of branding marks, see Olga Portuondo Zúñiga, *Entre esclvos y libres de Cuba colonial*, Santiago, Cuba: Editorial Oriente, 2003, pp. 35–43. For the decree, see Salmoral, *Regulación*, part 1, p. 147. For ongoing use of the brand, see Johnson, *Workshop of Revolution*, p. 38.

4. AGN (Lima), notary record, Emeterio Andrés Valenciano, no. 72b, f. 689; AGN (Lima), notary record, Francisco Munarris, no. 449, f. 29. See also the discussion in Kris E. Lane, *Quito 1599: City and Colony in Transition*, Albuquerque: University of New Mexico Press, 2002, p. 65; Alejandro de la Fuente, *Havana and the Atlantic in the Sixteenth Century*, Chapel Hill: University of North Carolina Press, 2008, p. 149.

5. AGN (Buenos Aires), notary record, registro 6, 1803 (Inocencio Agrelo), ff. 244–46; *Documentos del archivo de Belgrano*, vol. 2, Buenos Aires: Coni Hermanos, 1913, p. 334.

6. Dirección General de Estadística, *Registro estadístico de la Provincia de Buenos Aires*,

vol. 11, Buenos Aires: Dirección General de Estadística, 1867, p. 6; Studer, *La trata*, p. 202. Federico Gualberto Garrell, *La Gduana: Su origin, su evolución*, Buenos Aires: Editorial I. A. R. A., 1967, p. 121.

7. John Horace Parry, *The Spanish Seaborne Empire*, Berkeley: University of California Press, 1990, p. 308, writes that the 'first large-scale *saladeros*, salting beef for export, were established at Buenos Aires about 1776.'

8. *Household Words: A Weekly Journal*, January 25, 1851.

9. See Francisco de Solano, *Esclavitud y derechos humanos: La lucha por la libertad del negro en el siglo XIX*, ed. Agustín Guimerá Ravina, Madrid: CSIC, 1990, p. 629; José Pedro Barrán and Benjamín Nahum, *Historia rural del Uruguay moderno: 1851–1885*, 2 vols., Montevideo: Ediciones de la Banda Oriental, 1967; Alex Borucki, Karla Chagas, and Natalia Stalla, *Esclavitud y trabajo: Un estudio sobre los afrodescendientes en la frontera uruguaya (1835–1855)*, Montevideo: Pulmón Ediciones, 2004, pp. 18–22; Andrews, *Afro-Argentines*, p. 31; Alfredo Montoya, *Historia de los saladeros argentinos*, Buenos Aires: Editorial Raigal, 1956, p. 22. For a firsthand description of how slavery spurred the growth of meat salting in Río de la Plata, see the lengthy testimony of the slave trader José Ramón Milá de la Roca, who claimed to have 'perfected' the salting process; AGI (Seville), Buenos Aires, 483 ('Testimonio de Ramón Milá de la Roca,' May 29, 1807).

10. Jonathan Brown, *A Brief History of Argentina*, New York: Facts on File, 2003, p. 111.

11. Benjamín Vicuña Mackenna, *La Argentina en el año 1855*, Buenos Aires: Americana, 1936, p. 131.

12. Lin Widmann, *Twigs of a Tree: A Family Tale*, Bloomington: AuthorHouse, 2012, p. 79.

13. AGI, Buenos Aires, 588, Expedientes de Consulados y Comercio, 1804–06 ('Carta del virrey del Río de la Plata a su Majestad'); AGI, Gobierno, Indiferente 2826, ff. 776–89; Lucía Sala de Tourón, Nelson de la Torre, and Julio C. Rodríguez, *Estructura económico-social de la colonia*, Montevideo: Ediciones Pueblos Unidos, 1967, p. 30. See the 'slavery collection' of the New-York Historical Society for Rhode Island slavers doing such business: letter from Thomas White to Messrs. Gardner and Dean, March 17, 1806, series II: Gardner and Dean; letter from Samuel Chase to Messrs. Vernon and Gardner, August 4, 1798, series I: Samuel and William Vernon; unsigned, undated account record of trade, Slavery Collection, [1798?], series I: Samuel and William Vernon; Messrs. Vernon Gardner & Co. owners of ship *Ascensión* in account current with Samuel Chace, November 17, 1798, series I: Samuel and William Vernon; and Account of Sales of the *Ascensión*'s Cargo of Slaves . . . , March 24, 1798, series I: Samuel and William Vernon.

14. For Milá de la Roca's failure as a slaver, see AGI (Seville), Buenos Aires, 483, 'Testimonio José Ramón Milá de la Roca'; Arturo Ariel Bentancur, *El Puerto Colonial de Montevideo: Guerras y apertura comercial*, Montevideo: Universidad de la Republica, 1997, pp. 255–60. For Romero's success, see AGI (Seville),

Buenos Aires, 592, 'Expedientos sobre permiso para la introducción de negros, 1798–1805'; AGN (Buenos Aires), División Colonia, Sección Gobierno, Tribunales, legajo 91, expediente 17, IX-36-7-3 ('Autos sobre la participación de Tomás Antonio Romero en el contrabando'); La revista de Buenos Aires 18 (1869): 177; AGI (Seville), Gobierno, Indiferente 2826, ff. 369–423; AGN (Buenos Aires), Navíos, Topografía, 10-4-7 ('Valor de los frutos extraídas de cuenta de don Tomás Antonio Romero como producto de esclavatura'); Borucki, 'Slave Trade,' p. 99; Jeremy Adelman, *Republic of Capital: Buenos Aires and the Legal Transformation of the Atlantic World*, Stanford: Stanford University Press, 1999, pp. 44, 74; Eduardo R. Saguier, *Genealogía de la Tragedia Argentina (1600–1900)*, vol. 1, 'La cultura como espacio de lucha,' available at http://www.er-saguier.org/obras/gta/indice.php accessed July 26, 2011; Germán O. E. Tjarks, *El Consulado de Buenos Aires y sus proyecciones en la historia del Río de la Plata*, vol. 2, Buenos Aires: Universidad de Buenos Aires, Facultad de Filosofía y Letras, 1962, p. 569; Susan Migden Socolow, *The Bureaucrats of Buenos Aires, 1769–1810: Amor al Real Servicio*, Durham: Duke University Press, 1987, pp. 236–41; Sigfrido Augusto Radaelli, *Memorias de los Virreyes del Río de la Plata*, Buenos Aires: Editorial Bajel, 1945, p. 393; Studer, *La trata*, p. 288; AGI (Seville), Buenos Aires, 592, 1798 ('Testimonio de expediente promovido por Don Tomás Antonio Romero'); Berenice Jacobs, 'The *Mary Ann*, an Illicit Adventure,' *Hispanic American Historical Review* 37 (May 1957): 200–12; John Brown Carter Library, Brown and Ives Papers, Sub-Series L: Schooner *Eliza*, and Sub-Series FF: Ship *Mary Ann*. For shortage of currency, see David Rock, *Argentina, 1516–1987*, Berkeley: University of California Press, 1985, p. 71.

15. For Aranda's debt and his involvement with the Mendoza merchant guild, see Saguier, *Genealogía de la Tragedia Argentina*, especially vol. 2, 'Derrumbe del orden imperial-absolutista y crisis del estado colonial (Río de la Plata-siglo XVIII),' and appendix B-XI. For Aranda's previous slave purchases, see the document dated April 18, 1801, in AGN (Buenos Aires) Sala IX 'Comercio y padrones de esclavos, 1777–1808.'

10. FALLING MAN

1. Jean de Milleret, *Entrevistas con Jorge Luis Borges*, Caracas: Monte Avila Editores, 1971, p. 27. For the Llavallol family, see *Obras completas de Sarmiento*, vol. 42, Buenos Aires: Luz del Día, p. 15; Stelio Cro, *Jorge Luis Borges: Poeta, saggista e narratore*, Milan: Mursia, 1971, p. 246; Jorge Luis Borges and Fernando Mateo, *El otro Borges: Entrevistas (1960–1986)*, Buenos Aires: Equis Editores, 1997, p. 98; Roberto Alifano, *Diálogos esenciales con Jorge Luís Borges*, vol. 3, Buenos Aires: Alloni/Proa, 2007, p. 63.

2. For information on the Aranda brothers, see the following documents: In the AA (Mendoza): Libro de bautismo (matriz), no. 6, f. 272; Libro defunciones

(matriz), no. 3A, f. 215; Libro matrimonios (matriz), no. 4, ff. 133–133v; Censo Parroquial (April 1, 1802). In the AGP (Mendoza), the notary records of Francisco de Videla, no. 89, ff. 81–86v ('Testamento de Manuel Fernández de Aranda'); José de Porto y Mariño, February 14, 1800; and Santiago Garnay, 41v. In the same archive, see also Libro Mayor, Real Caja de Mendoza, folders 37, 39, 40. For the political importance of Aranda's stepfather, José Clemente Benegas, see *Revista del Instituto de Historia del Derecho* 9 (1958): 101–4; Damián Hudson, *Recuerdos históricos sobre la provincia de Cuyo: 1824–1851*, vol. 2, Buenos Aires: Alsina, 1898; and Jorge Comadrán Ruiz, *Los Subdelegados de Real Hacienda y Guerra de Mendoza (1784–1810)*, Mendoza: Universidad, 1959. Benegas was in charge of tax collection in Mendoza when Aranda would have transported the *Tryal*'s slaves through the town. See AGP (Mendoza), folder 86, document 64. For the 'aristocratic' standing of Aranda's future father-in-law, Isidro Sáinz de la Maza, see Leoncio Gianello, *Historia del Congreso de Tucumán*, Buenos Aires: Academia Nacional de la Historia, 1966.

3. Julian Mellet, *Viajes pro el interior de la América Meridional, 1808–1820*, Santiago: Editorial del Pacifico, 1959.

4. AGP (Mendoza), folder 74, document 29 ('listas militares'); AGN (Buenos Aires), Licencias y Pasaportes, libro 6, f. 198 ('Pide permiso para regresar a Mendoza'); AGN (Buenos Aires), Criminales, legajo 50, expediente 5 ('El alcalde ordinario de la ciudad de Mendoza, Juan de la Cruz Vargas, sobre haberse ausentado ésta y otras personas hacia Chile, sin el correspondiente permiso de ese juzgado'); AGN (Buenos Aires), Despachos Militares y Cédulas de Premio, libro 2, f. 85 ('Nicolás Aranda es nombrado alférez del Regimiento de voluntarios de caballería de Mendoza').

5. For María Carmen's birth, see AA (Mendoza), Libro de bautismos (matriz), no. 8, f. 23; For her marriage to Aranda, see AA (Mendoza), Libro de matrimonios (matriz), no. 4, ff. 113–13v.

6. For the Puebla vineyard, see Pablo Lacoste, *La mujer y el vino: Emociones, vida privada, emancipación económica (entre el reino de Chile y el virreinato del Río de La Plata, 1561–1810)*, Mendoza: Caviar Bleu, 2008, and 'Viticultura y movilidad social: Provincia de Cuyo, Reino de Chile, siglo XVIII,' *Colonial Latin American Historical Review* 13 (2004): 230.

7. AA (Mendoza), Libro de bautismos, no. 11, f. 174.

8. José Mariluz Urquijo, 'El horizonte femenino porteño de mediados del setecientos,' *Investigaciones y ensayos* 36 (July–December 1987): 83; AA (Mendoza), Libro de matrimonios (matriz), no. 11, f. 9v; AGP (Mendoza), Censo parroquial 1777, folder 28, document 2.

9. Pablo Lacoste, 'El arriero y el transporte terrestre en el Cono Sur (Mendoza, 1780–1800),' *Revista de Indias* 68 (2008): 35–68.

10. Luis César Caballero, *Los negros esclavos en Mendoza, algunas genealogías*, Mendoza: Cuadernos de Genealogía, 2010, p. 233.

11. Gesualdo, 'Los negros'; Mansilla, *Mis memorias*, p. 133.

11. THE CROSSING

1. Mellet, *Viajes*; Concolorcorvo, *El lazarillo de ciegos caminantes desde Buenos Aires hasta Lima, 1773*, Buenos Aires: Compañía Sud-Americana de Billetes de Banco, 1908; D. J. Robinson, 'Trade and Trading Links in Western Argentina during the Viceroyality,' *Geographical Journal* 135 (March 1970): 24–41; Alonso de Ovalle, *Histórica relación del Reino de Chile y de la misiones y ministerios que ejercita en él la Compañía de Jesús*, Santiago: Instituto de Literatura Chilena, 1969.
2. Robert Proctor, *Narrative of a Journey across the Cordillera of the Andes*, London: Constable and Co., 1825, p. 7; Max Wolffsohn, 'Across the Cordillera, from Chili to Buenos Ayres,' *Gentleman's Magazine* 268 (1890): 589; Charles Samuel Stewart, *Brazil and La Plata: The Personal Record of a Cruise*, New York: Putnam, 1856, p. 325. For earlier slave caravans, see Gesualdo, 'Los negros,' p. 28.
3. Victoria Ocampo, *338171 T. E. Lawrence of Arabia*, Buenos Aires: Editoriales Sur, 1942, p. 12; David Garnett, ed., *The Letters of T. E. Lawrence*, Garden City: Doubleday, Doran, 1939, p. 56.
4. Proctor, *Narrative of a Journey*, p. 17.
5. 'Sheep Husbandry in South America,' *Cultivator and Country Gentleman*, May 3, 1866.
6. Edmund Burke, *A Philosophical Inquiry into the Origin of Our Ideas of the Sublime and Beautiful, with an Introductory Discourse concerning Taste, and Several Other Additions*, Philadelphia: J. Watts, 1806, p. 81, 140; Corey Robin, *The Reactionary Mind*, New York: Oxford University Press, 2011, pp. 147–48.

12. DIAMONDS ON THE SOLES OF THEIR FEET

1. Reginaldo de Lizárraga, *Descripción breve de toda la tierra del Perú, Tucumán, Río de la Plata y Chile*, Madrid: Ediciones Atlas, 1968, p. 375.
2. Ricardo Rodríguez Molas, *Los sometidos de la conquista: Argentina, Bolivia, Paraguay*, Buenos Aires: Bibliotecas Universitarias, 1985, pp. 200, 254.
3. AGP (Mendoza), notary record, Juan de Herrera, no. 5, March 24, 1601, ff. 96–98v; Caballero, *Los negros esclavos en Mendoza*, Mendoza, 2010, p. 20.
4. Rolando Mellafe, *La introducción de la esclavitud negra en Chile: Trafico y rutas*, Santiago: Universidad de Chile, 1959, pp. 250–51; Vial Correa, *El Africano en el Reino de Chile*, pp. 85–86. For later attempts to tax this overland slave route, see ANC (Santiago), Contaduría Mayor, 2nd ser., vol. 645 ('Alcabala entrada por cordillera esclavos 1777'), and vol. 812 ('Almojarifazgo, 1778'). See also ANC (Santiago), Contaduría Mayor, 1st ser., vols. 1881–991 and 1992–99, for goods, including slaves, coming over the Andes to be shipped out of Valparaiso to Lima during the years 1803 and 1804.
5. ANC (Santiago), Contaduría Mayor, 1998; Pedro Santos Martínez, *Las comunicaciones entre el Virreinato del Río de la Plata y Chile por Uspallata (1776–1810)*, Santiago: Universidad Católica, 1963.

6. Edward Arthur Fitzgerald et al., *The Highest Andes: A Record of the First Ascent of Aconcagua and Tupungato in Argentina, and the Exploration of the Surrounding Valleys*, London: Methuen, 1899, pp. 173–74; Peter Schmidtmeyer, *Travels into Chile, over the Andes, in the Years 1820 and 1821*, London: Longman, 1824, p. 315.

7. 'José Espinoza y Felipe Bauza Vieje de Santiago a Mendoza,' in *La Expedición Malaspina en la frontera del imperio español*, ed. Rafael Sagrado Baeza and José Ignacio González Leiva, Santiago: Editorial Universitaria, 2004, pp. 875–83; Jerónimo de Vivar, *Crónica y relación copiosa y verdadera de los reinos de Chile*, Santiago: Colloquium Verlag, 1979, p. 187.

8. Quotations come from the edition Melville consulted, Darwin's *Journal of Researches into the Natural History and Geology of the Countries Visited during the Voyage of H.M.S. Beagle round the World, under the Command of Capt. Fitz Roy, R.N.*, 2 vols., New York: Harper and Brothers, 1846, vol. 2, pp. 76–77.

9. Concolorcorvo, *El lazarillo de ciegos caminantes*, p. 150; Francisco Le Dantec, *Cronicas del viejo Valparaíso*, Valparaíso: Ediciones Universitarias, 1984, pp. 68–72; Vial Correa, *El Africano en el Reino de Chile*, p. 90.

INTERLUDE: HEAVEN'S SENSE

1. *Moby-Dick*, pp. 1233–37.
2. Sandra A. Zagarell. 'Reenvisioning America: Melville's "Benito Cereno"' in Burkholder, ed., *Critical Essays*, p. 58.
3. In 1847, Herman Melville purchased a copy of Charles Darwin's *Journal of Researches*. See Sealts, *Melville's Reading*, p. 171. The passage quoted here is in vol. 2, p. 86. For 'Lot's wife,' see *More Letters of Charles Darwin: A Record of His Work in a Series of Hitherto Unpublished Letters*, vol. 1, New York: Appleton, 1903, p. 23 (April 18, 1835).

13. KILLING SEALS

1. Richard Ellis, *The Empty Ocean: Plundering the World's Marine Life*, Washington, D.C.: Island Press, 2003, p. 155.
2. Robert McNab, *Murihiku and the Southern Islands: A History of the West Coast Sounds, Foveaux Strait, Stewart Island, the Snares, Bounty, Antipodes, Auckland, Campbell and Macquarie Islands, from 1770 to 1829*, Invercargill: W. Smith, 1907, p. 221.
3. James Kirker, *Adventures to China: Americans in the Southern Oceans, 1792–1812*, New York: Oxford University Press, 1970, p. 78.
4. John Byron et al., *An Account of the Voyages Undertaken by the Order of His Present Majesty for Making Discoveries in the Southern Hemisphere*, London: W. Strahan, 1785, p. 44.
5. Kirker, *Adventures to China*, p. 73.

6. Edward Cooke, *A Voyage to the South Sea and around the World in the Years 1708 to 1711*, 1712, New York: Da Capo Press, 1969; Woodes Rogers, *A Cruising Voyage round the World: First to the South-Seas*, London: A. Bell and B. Lintot, 1712.

7. Augustus Earle, *A Narrative of a Nine Months' Residence in New Zealand in 1827: Together with a Journal of a Residence in Tristan D'Acunha, an Island Situated between South America and the Cape of Good Hope*, London: Longman, 1832, p. 344.

8. Samuel Johnson et al., *The World Displayed; or, A Curious Collection of Voyages and Travels, Selected from the Writers of All Nations*, vol. 8, London: J. Newbery, 1760, p. 39; William Dowling, *A Popular Natural History of Quadrupeds and Birds*, London: James Burns, 1849, pp. 103–4.

9. Robert K. Headland, *The Island of South Georgia*, Victoria: Cambridge University Press, 1992, p. 52.

10. Delano, *Narrative*, p. 306.

11. George Little, *Life on the Ocean; or, Twenty Years at Sea*, Boston: Waite, Peirce, 1844, pp. 106–7.

12. George Staunton, *An Authentic Account of an Embassy from the King of Great Britain to the Emperor of China: Including Cursory Observations Made, and Information Obtained in Travelling through That Ancient Empire, and a Small Part of Chinese Tartary*, London: G. Nicol, 1797, p. 236.

13. William Jardine, *The Naturalist's Library*, vol. 8, Edinburgh: W. H. Lizars, 1839, p. 222; Richard Phillips, *A Million of Facts, of Correct Data, and Elementary Constants in the Entire Circle of the Sciences and on All Subjects of Speculation and Practice*, London: Darton and Clark, 1840, pp. 172–73; *Gentleman's Magazine, and Historical Chronicle* 83 (1813): 339.

14. Antoine-Joseph Pernety, *The History of a Voyage to the Malouine (or Falkland) Islands: Made in 1763 and 1764, under the Command of M. de Bougainville*, London: T. Jefferys, 1771, p. 203.

15. *Papers of the New Haven Colony Historical Society* 3 (1882): 148.

16. Edmund Fanning, *Voyages round the World: With Selected Sketches*, New York: Collins and Hamay, 1833, p. 26.

17. 'Narrative of a Sealing and Trading Voyage in the Ship *Huron*, from New Haven, around the World, September, 1802, to October, 1806, by Joel Root, the Supercargo,' *Papers of the New Haven Colony Historical Society* 5 (1894): 160.

18. William Moulton, *A Concise Extract, from the Sea Journal of William Moulton*, Utica: n.p., 1804, p. 62.

19. *The Voyage of the Neptune: 1796–1799*, exhibit pamphlet, New Haven Colony Historical Society, October 1996–June 1997; Edouard Stackpole, *The Sea-Hunters: The New England Whalemen during Two Centuries, 1635–1835*, New York: J. B. Lippincott, 1953, p. 192; Diary of David Forbes, New Haven Colony Historical Society, MSS 22, box 1, folder L; Francis Bacon Trowbridge, *The Trowbridge Genealogy: History of the Trowbridge Family in America*, New Haven: n.p., 1908, p. 76.

20. 'Letters of Sullivan Dorr,' *Proceedings of the Massachusetts Historical Society* 67 (October 1941–May 1944): 297–302.

21. Kirker, *Adventures to China*, p. 70.

22. Richard J. Cleveland, *Voyages and Commercial Enterprises, of the Sons of New England*, New York: Leavitt and Allen, 1857, p. 9; Briton Cooper Busch, *The War against the Seals: A History of the North American Seal Fishery*, Montreal: McGill–Queen's University Press, 1985, p. 36.

14. ISOLATOS

1. *Moby-Dick*, p. 916.

2. Kirker, *Adventures to China*, p. 70.

3. Stackpole, *Sea-Hunters*, p. 192.

4. Kirker, *Adventures to China*, p. 77; Diary of David Forbes, May 2 and May 4, 1799.

5. Diary of David Forbes, April 13, 1799.

6. Rediker, *Between the Devil*, p. 218.

7. Samuel Eliot Morison, *Maritime History of Massachusetts, 1783–1860*, Boston: Houghton Mifflin, 1921, pp. 319–24.

8. Kirker, *Adventures to China*, p. 75; Eugenio Pereira Salas, *Los primeros contactos entre Chile y los Estados Unidos, 1778–1809*, Santiago: Editorial Andrés Bello, 1971, pp. 146–47; ANC (Santiago), Capitanía General, vol. 375 ('Caso de la Venta del Bergantín Mentor,' June 14, 1804); 'Letters of Sullivan Dorr,' *Proceedings*, p. 352. For *Strike*, see *Economic Review* 5 (April 1895): 216; see also Rediker, *Between the Devil*, p. 205.

9. Tim Severin, *In Search of Robinson Crusoe*, New York: Basic, 2002, p. 52. There is some uncertainty as to who the captain of the *Nancy* was during this incident. Most accounts suggest it was J. Crocker out of either Boston or New London. But Russian sealers, according to Glynn Barratt, *Russia and the South Pacific, 1696–1840: Southern and Eastern Polynesia*, vol. 2, Vancouver: University of British Columbia Press, 1988, p. 244, believed it was a captain named Adams. And Richard Cleveland, in *Voyages and Commercial Enterprises*, p. 212, lists the identity as 'Captain H——.' There is also a discrepancy regarding the date, with some accounts saying the incident took place in 1805 and others in 1808. For the quotations, see Otto von Kotzebue, *A Voyage of Discovery, into the South Sea and Beering's Straits*, vol. 1, London: Spottiswoode, 1821, p. 143.

10. Ralph Paine, *The Ships and Sailors of Old Salem: The Record of a Brilliant Era of American Achievement*, New York: Outing Publishing Co., 1908, pp. 323–24.

11. 'Letters of Sullivan Dorr,' p. 361.

12. Ibid., p. 352.

13. 'The Voyage of the Neptune,' *Papers of the New Haven Colony Historical Society* 4 (1888): 48.

15. A TERRIFIC SOVEREIGNTY

1. Moulton, *Concise Extract*, 1804.
2. Rediker, *Between the Devil*, pp. 208, 218; Falconbridge, *Account*, p. 39.
3. *Niles' Weekly Register* 48 (1835): 67; Cyrene M. Clark, *Glances at Life Upon the Sea, or Journal of a Voyage to the Antarctic Ocean: In the Brig Parana, of Sag Harbor, L.I., in the Years '53 '54; Description of Sea-Elephant Hunting among the Icy Islands of South Shetland, Capture of Whales, Scenery in the Polar Regions, &c.*, Middletown: Charles H. Pelton, 1855, p. 49.
4. Delano, *Narrative*, p. 291.
5. 'Narrative of a Sealing and Trading Voyage in the Ship *Huron*,' p. 163; Busch, *War against the Seals*, pp. 15–16. Nantucket Historical Association, Ships Logs Collection, *Topaz*.

16. SLAVERY HAS GRADES

1. Anna Davis Hallowell, *James and Lucretia Mott: Life and Letters*, Boston: Houghton Mifflin, 1881, p. 32; Otelia Cromwell, *Lucretia Mott*, New York: Russell and Russell, 1958, p. 9. For the *Tryal*, see NARA (College Park), RG 76, Spain, Disallowed Claims, vol. 55, *Trial or Tryal*; ANC (Santiago), Capitanía General, vols. 789 and 908; see also ANC (Santiago), notary records, José María Sánchez, Valparaíso, May 18, 1802, and Escribanos de Valparaíso, vol. 24, April 29, 1802, and December 16, 1803. See Rogers, *Cruising Voyage*, pp. 140–80, for a firsthand account of a series of privateering raids in 1709 launched from Pacific islands on Spanish commercial ships, including two vessels carrying fifty African slaves en route from Panama to Lima. Carol Faulkner, *Lucretica Motts' Heresy: Abolition and Women's Rights in Nineteenth Century America*, Philadelphia: University of Pennsylvania Press, 2011, p. 22.
2. Peabody Essex Museum, 1800 Mashpee Census, miscellaneous bound documents, MSS 48, box 2, folder 16 ('Levi Mye the son of Newport half blood, has a numerous family by his first, of full blood and by his second wife, partly Negroe, has two or three children').
3. Jack Campisi, *The Mashpee Indians: Tribe on Trial*, Syracuse: Syracuse University Press, 1991, p. 88; Peabody Essex Museum, 1800 Mashpee Census. For presettlement epidemics, as well as a more detailed discussion of the historiography on New England Native Americans during this period, see Nathaniel Philbrick, *Mayflower: A Story of Courage, Community, and War*, New York: Penguin, 2006, pp. 48–49; 372–73.
4. Jean Hankins, 'Solomon Briant and Joseph Johnson: Indian Teachers and Preachers in Colonial New England,' *Connecticut History* 33 (1992): 49; Mark Nicholas, 'Mashpee Wampanoags of Cape Cod, the Whalefishery, and Seafaring's Impact on Community Development,' *American Indian Quarterly* 26 (Spring 2002): 165–97. For Amos Haskins, see Daniel Vickers, 'Nantucket Whalemen in the Deep-Sea Fishery: The Changing Anatomy of an Early American Labor Force,' *Journal of American History* 72 (1985): 277–96.

5. 'Stephen Hall and Another versus Paul Gardner, Jun., & al.,' October term, 1804, *Reports of Cases Argued and Determined in the Supreme Judicial Court of the Commonwealth of Massachusetts*, vol. 1, Boston: Little, Brown, 1851, pp. 172–80.

6. James D. Schmidt, '"Restless Movements Characteristic of Childhood": The Legal Construction of Child Labor in Nineteenth-Century Massachusetts,' *Law and History Review* 23 (Summer 2005): 323. For the phrase 'boundless license of removal'—that is, the right of masters to send their apprentices anywhere, see the case Commonwealth v. Edwards (which cites Hall et al. v. Gardner et al.) in Pennsylvania Supreme Court, *Reports of Cases . . . 1754–1845*, vol. 6, Philadelphia: Kay and Brothers, 1891, p. 204. Hall et al. v. Gardner et al. would be cited or mentioned in at least nineteen subsequent cases, in both northern and southern states (as well as Hawaii): Weeks v. Holmes (Mass. 1853); Randall v. Rotch (Mass. 1831); Coffin v. Bassett (Mass. 1824); Mason v. Waite (Mass. 1823); Davis v. Coburn (Mass. 1811); Brooks v. Byam (Mass. 1843); J. Nott & Co. v. Kanahele (Hawaii King. Jul Term 1877); In re Gip Ah Chan (Hawaii King. Aug Term 1870); W. B. Conkey Co. v. Goldman (Ill. App. 1 Dist. Dec 04, 1905); Vickere v. Pierce (Me. 1835); Futrell v. Vann (N.C. Jun Term 1848); Dyer v. Hunt (N.H. 1831); Overseers of Town of Guilderland v. Overseers of Town of Knox (N.Y. Sup. 1826); Commonwealth v. Edwards (Pa. 1813); Lobdell v. Allen (Mass. Oct Term 1857); Lord v. Pierce (Me. 1851); and Gill v. Ferris (Mo. Apr Term 1884). Thanks to Ron Brown, associate director for Collection Services at New York University School of Law Library, for providing these citations. Claiming that chattel slaves were really indentured servants was one way slave owners moving from a slave state to a free one tried to keep their property. One of the cases above, Commonwealth v. Edwards, citing Hall et al. v. Gardner et al., helped limit that practice. See Paul Finkelman, *An Imperfect Union: Slavery, Federalism, and Comity*, Clark: Lawbook Exchange, 2000, p. 58.

7. *Decisions at Chambers by Single Justices of the Supreme Court of the Hawaiian Islands*, Honolulu: Hawaiian Gazette Co., 1889, pp. 25–41.

8. Despite his loss, Coffin continued to warmly defend Spanish Americans and taught many Spanish phrases to his daughter Lucretia, who would go on to be a prominent abolitionist and suffragist. See Faulkner, *Lucrecia Mott's Heresy*.

9. AGN (Lima), notary records, Vicente de Aizcorbe, no. 72; 1802–3, ff. 642v–44.

INTERLUDE: A MERRY REPAST

1. In *Billy Budd and Other Stories*, pp. 73, 78–79.

17. NIGHT OF POWER

1. Evelyn Underhill, *Mysticism: A Study in the Nature and Development of Man's Spiritual Consciousness*, London: Jack Books, 1980, pp. 81, 86; Reynold Alleyne Nicholson, *The Mystics of Islam*, London: George Bell, 1914, p. 20; Samar Attar, *Debunking the Myths of Colonization: The Arabs and Europe*, Lanham: University

Press of America, 2010, p. 62; Cheikh Anta Mbacké Babou, *Fighting the Greater Jihad: Amadu Bamba and the Founding of the Muridiyya of Senegal, 1853–1913*, Athens: Ohio University Press, 2007; Nile Green, *Sufism: A Global History*, Hoboken: John Wiley, 2012. E. E. Evans Pritchard, *Witchcraft, Oracles and Magic among the Azande*, London: Oxford University Press, 1937, p. 2.

2. Ousman Murzik Kobo, *Unveiling Modernity in Twentieth-Century West African Islamic Reforms*, Leiden: Brill, 2012, p. 134; Lansiné Kapa, *The Wahhabiyya: Islamic Reform and Politics in French West Africa*, Evanston: Northwestern University Press, 1974, p. 49.

3. There is only one Arabic version of the Qur'an, with many English editions. I've used the translation by Abdullah Yusuf Ali, *The Qur'an: Text, Translation and Commentary*, Singapore: Muslim Converts' Association, 1946. Court records differ on whether the rebellion occurred early in the morning of December 27 or December 28, 1804. Likewise there are two-day discrepancies between Delano's dating of the rebellion and Cerreño's. But Laylat al-Qadr can fall on the last ten odd-numbered days in Ramadan; December 28, 1804, converts in the Islamic calendar to the 25th of Ramadan, 1219. See Reis, *Slave Rebellion*, pp. 118–19, for a comparison with the Bahian Malê revolt. Port and tax documents found in ANC (Santiago), Contaduría Mayor, 1st ser., vols. 1993, 1998, 2335, 2338, and 2339, give the itinerary of the *Tryal* for 1804: July, Lima to Valparaiso and ports south; September, Valparaiso to Lima, carrying, among other cargo, an unnamed African male slave and an unnamed female slave brought overland from Buenos Aires to be sold in Lima; October 3, Lima to ports south, including Concepción; November 20, return from Concepción to ports north, carrying wheat, lard, cypress and pine planks, bottles and casks of wine, butter, cheese, oregano, pine nuts, chickens, and *fresadas*, or biscuits; December 2, arrival in Valparaiso. For the description of the early nineteenth-century traveler, see Schmidtmeyer, *Travels into Chile*, p. 208.

4. W. Jeffrey Bolster, *Black Tars: African American Seamen in the Age of Sail*, Cambridge: Harvard University Press, 1998.

5. Concolorcorva, *El lazarillo*, pp. 250–51.

6. For information on the Cerreños of Calañas, see the following documents in AMC (Calañas, Spain): legajo 252 (assorted resolutions 1827–94); legajos 202–3 (militia lists, 1771–1830); legajo 559 (asset holders, A–L); legajo 560 (ecclesiastical and other holdings); legajo 561 (tax lists covering years 1760–1850); legajo 562 (the *Unica Contribución* tax of 1771); legajo 1134 (sundry records of estate partitions and inheritance distribution); legajos 1129–30 (estate partitions and inheritance distribution, 1762–72); legajos 1092–95; 1099–1100 (notary records, 1757–1804). See also Antonio Ramírez Borrero, *Calañas en la segunda mitad del s. XVIII*, Huelva: Diputación Provincial, 1995; José de la Puente, *Historia marítima del Perú: La independencia de 1790–1826*, part 5, vol. 2, Lima: Editorial Ausonis, 1972, p. 168. For Cerreño's ongoing indebtedness to his Peruvian creditors, see AGN (Lima), notary record, Francisco Munárriz, no. 453, f. 432 ('Obligación a

Don Juan Ignacio Rotalde'). Cerreño's cousin, Ramón Marques, was also involved in the financing of the *Tryal*; see AGN (Lima), notary record, Vicente de Aizcorbe, no. 72, ff. 642v–644r. For his cousin's coming to Cerreño's aid, see AGN (Lima), notary record, José Escudero de Sicilia, no. 214, ff. 980r–981v and 1048r–1049r. For Cerreño serving as guardian of Marques's daughters after Marques's death, see AGN (Lima), notary record, Francisco Munárriz, no. 453, f. 428r.

7. Henriette Lucie Dillon La Tour du Pin Gouvernet, *Journal d'une femme de cinquante ans*, vol. 2, Paris: Chapelot, 1912, p. 18; Alice Kenney, *The Gansevoorts of Albany: Dutch Patricians in the Upper Hudson Valley*, Syracuse: Syracuse University Press, 1969, pp. 80–107; *Albany Gazette*, November 25, 1793, reprinted in the *New-York Daily Gazette*, November 25, 1793; 'Examination of Bet Negro Female Slave of Philip S. Van Rensselaer, Esquire,' New York State Library, Manuscripts and Special Collections; *Albany Chronicles: A History of the City Arranged Chronologically, from the Earliest Settlement to the Present Time; Illustrated with Many Historical Pictures of Rarity and Reproductions of the Robert C. Pruyn Collection of the Mayors of Albany*, Albany: J. B. Lyon, 1906, p. 384.

8. Cristina Soriano, 'Rumors of Change: Repercussions of Caribbean Turmoil and Social Conflicts in Venezuela (1790–1810),' PhD dissertation, New York University, 2011, p. 151.

9. Ada Ferrer, 'Haiti, Free Soil, and Antislavery in the Revolutionary Atlantic,' *American Historical Review* 117 (2012): 40–66.

10. *Letters on West Africa and the Slave Trade: Paul Erdmann Isert's Journey to Guinea and the Caribbean Islands in Columbia (1788)*, trans. and ed. Selena Axelrod Winsnes, Oxford: Oxford University Press, 1992, p. 180.

11. I thank Jennifer Lofkrantz, who in a personal communication provided information on slavery and Islamic law in West Africa.

18. THE STORY OF THE *SAN JUAN*

1. María Luisa Laviana Cuetos, *Guayaquil en el siglo XVIII: Recursos naturales y desarrollo económico*, Seville: CSIC, 1987, p. 292. For the free and enslaved people of colour in Guayaquil's shipyards, see Lawrence Clayton, *Caulkers and Carpenters in a New World: The Shipyards of Colonial Guayaquil*, Athens: Center for International Studies, Ohio University, 1980. The *San Juan*'s West Africans might have arrived in Montevideo on one of the following two ships: the *Rainbow*, which arrived in August 1800 carrying ninety-one slaves (AGN-A, Sala IX, 18-8-11; thanks to Alex Borucki for the citation), or the *Astigarraga*, owned by the Montevidean merchant José Ramón Milá de la Roca, which came into Montevideo on June 15, 1800, carrying fifty-eight Senegalese. See AGI (Seville), Buenos Aires, 483 ('Testimonio de Ramón Milá de la Roca,' May 29, 1807), f. 11. For the *San Juan*'s cargo, as well as its alias, *God's Blessing*, see the 'Derechos de Alcaldía' and 'Derechos de Almojarifazgo' documents in AGN (Buenos Aires),

Sala XIII, 39-9-3, Aduana Montevideo, for the months September through November 1800. For Rotalde, see Patricia Marks, *Deconstructing Legitimacy: Viceroys, Merchants, and the Military in Late Colonial Peru*, University Park: Penn State University Press, 2007, p. 32. For Ullague, see Ronald Escobedo Mans illa, Ana de Zaballa Beascoechea, and Óscar Álvarez Gila, eds., *Comerciantes, mineros y nautas: Los vascos en la economía americana*, Bilbao: Servicio Editorial, Universidad del País Vasco, 1996, p. 86.

2. *Telégrafo Mercantil*, December 16, 1801. The French colonial archives contain nine documents related to this revolt, dated from 1816, when the ship's Peruvian owner took advantage of the fall of Napoleon (and the 'return of the august House of Bourbon to the throne of its ancestors, which restored the ancient relationship between the monarchies of Spain and France') to win compensation for its loss. See Archives nationales d'outre mer (Aix-en-Provence, France), Fonds Ministeriel, Series Geographique, Senegal Papers, series 6, dossier 3. Mention of the event is also found in 'Correspondance du gouverneur Blanchot (François Emilie de Verly), gouverneur de Gorée et du Sénégal de 1786 á 1807, avec le ministre (an X/1808),' located in Fonds Ministerial, in the subcategory Sénégal et Côtes d'Afrique—Sous-série C^6 1588/1810.

3. Eric Robert Taylor, *If We Must Die in This Way*, Baton Rouge: Louisiana State University Press, 2002, p. 172; see also David Richardson, 'Shipboard Revolts, African Authority, and the Atlantic Slave Trade,' *William and Mary Quarterly* 58 (January 2001): 69–92.

4. *Letters on West Africa*, p. 176; Taylor, *If We Must Die*, p. 110. Johannes Postma, *The Dutch in the Atlantic Slave Trade, 1600–1815*, New York: Cambridge University Press, 2008, p. 167, writes that the explosion was caused by a cannon blast from a hostile ship.

5. For Saint-Louis around this time, see Howard Brown, 'The Search for Stability,' in *Taking Liberties: Problems of a New Order from the French Revolution to Napoleon*, ed. Howard Brown and Judith Miller, Manchester: Manchester University Press, 2002, p. 37. See also George Brooks, *Yankee Traders, Old Coasters, and African Middlemen: A History of American Legitimate Trade with West Africa in the Nineteenth Century*, Boston: Boston University Press, 1970; Lucie Gallistel Colvin, *Historical Dictionary of Senegal*, Scarecrow Press / Metuchen, 1981, pp. 81–98. For Charbonnier, see Sylvain Sankalé, *À la mode du pays: Chroniques saint-lousiennes d'Antoine François Feuiltaine, Saint-Louis du Sénégal, 1788–1835*, Paris: Riveneuve, 2007; Léon Diouf, *Église locale et crise africaine: Le diocèse de Dakar*, Paris: Karthala, 2001; Joseph-Roger de Benoist, *Histoire de l'Eglise catholique au Sénégal du milieu du XVe siècle à l'aube du troisième millénaire*, Paris: Karthala, 2008; Martin Klein, 'Slaves, Gum, and Peanuts: Adaptation to the End of the Slave Trade in Senegal, 1817–48,' *William and Mary Quarterly* 66 (October 1999): 895–914; Philip Curtin, *Economic Change in Precolonial Africa: Senegambia in the Era of the Slave Trade*, Madison: University of Wisconsin Press, 1975; James Searing, *West African Slavery and Atlantic Commerce: The Senegal River Valley, 1700–1860*,

Cambridge: Cambridge University Press, 1993. For Spaniards' still taking slaves out of Saint-Louis despite abolition, at least prior to the tenure of Charbonnier, see AGI (Seville), Buenos Aires, 483 ('Testimonio de Ramón Mila, de la Roca,' May 29, 1807). For Charbonnier's troubled administration, see Archives du Sénégal, Dakar, Sous-Série 3 B 1 'Correspondance depart du Gourverneur du Sénégal à toutes personnes autres que le Ministre (1788–1893)' 3 B 1, documents 91 to 104.

6. AGI (Seville), Lima, 731, ('Carta n° 445 del virrey Marqués de Avilés a Miguel Cayetano Soler, ministro de Hacienda,' April 23, 1805).

19. MOHAMMED'S CURSED SECT

1. Herb Klein, *The Atlantic Slave Trade*, New York: Cambridge University Press, 1999, pp. 5–6; Robin Blackburn, *The Making of New World Slavery: From the Baroque to the Modern, 1492–1800*, London: Verso, 1997, pp. 67–80; Stuart Schwartz, ed., *Tropical Babylons: Sugar and the Making of the Atlantic World, 1450–1680*, Chapel Hill: University of North Carolina Press, 2004.

2. John Esposito, *The Oxford Encyclopedia of the Modern Islamic World*, New York: Oxford University Press, 1995, p. 134. Aurelia Martín Casares, *La esclavitud en la Granada del siglo XVI: Género, raza, y religion*, Granada: Universidad de Granada, 2000, p. 435.

3. Federico Corriente, *Dictionary of Arabic and Allied Loanwords: Spanish, Portuguese, Catalan, Galician and Kindred Dialects*, Leiden: Brill, 2008, p. 36.

4. James Muldoon, *The Americas in the Spanish World Order: The Justification for Conquest in the Seventeenth Century*, Philadelphia: University of Pennsylvania Press, p. 24. See James Carroll, *Jerusalem, Jerusalem: How the Ancient City Ignited Our Modern World*, Boston: Houghton Mifflin Harcourt, 2011, 152–53; Karoline Cook, 'Forbidden Crossings: Morisco Emigration to Spanish America, 1492–1650,' PhD dissertation, Princeton University, 2008, pp. 84–87; Barbara Fuchs, *Mimesis and Empire: The New World, Islam, and European Identities*, Cambridge: Cambridge University Press, 2004, p. 74; Frank Graziano, *The Millennial New World*, New York: Oxford University Press, 1999, p. 25. The quotation in the previous paragraph is from Francisco López de Gomara, *Histórica General de las Indias*, Caracas: Fundación Biblioteca Ayacuch, 1979, p. 31.

5. Vincent Barletta, *Covert Gestures: Crypto-Islamic Literature as Cultural Practice in Early Modern Spain*, Minneapolis: University of Minnesota Press, 2005, p. 3.

6. Cook, 'Forbidden Crossings,' p. 40.

7. See the discussion in Rudolph T. Ware, 'The Longue Durée of Qur'anic Schooling, Society, and State in Senegambia,' in *New Perspectives on Islam in Senegal: Conversion, Migration, Wealth, Power, and Femininity*, ed. Mamadou Diouf and Mara Leichtman, New York: Palgrave Macmillan, 2009, pp. 22–23. Mungo Park, traveling among Muslim Fulbe in the 1790s, wrote that 'in the exercise of their faith, however, they are not very intolerant towards such of their countrymen as still retain their ancient superstitions' (*Travels in the Interior Districts of Africa*, New York: E. Duyckinck, 1813, p. 57). See also Paul Lovejoy, 'Slavery, the Bilād

al-Sūdān, and the Frontiers of the African Diaspora,' in *Slavery on the Frontiers of Islam*, ed. Paul Lovejoy, Princeton: Markus Wiener, 2004, p. 16. For 'lesser spirits,' see Lansiné Kapa, 'The Pen, the Sword, and the Crown: Islam and Revolution in Songhay Reconsidered,' *Journal of African History*, vol. 25, no. 3 (1984): 241–56. See also William Desborough Cooley, *The Negroland of the Arabs Examined and Explained: Or, An Inquiry into the Early History and Geography of Central Africa*, London: J. Arrowsmith, 1841, a fascinating interpretation by a nineteenth-century British geographer of centuries-old classical Arabic manuscripts describing relations between Arab traders and sub-Saharan Africans, including patterns of commerce, slavery, and religious conversion.

8. Joan Cameron Bristol, *Christians, Blasphemers, and Witches: Afro-Mexican Ritual Practice in the Seventeenth Century*, Albuquerque: University of New Mexico Press, 2007, p. 29. *The Christian Traveller: Western Africa: Being an Account of the Country and Its Products, of the People and Their Conditions, and of the Measures Taken for Their Religious and Social Benefit*, London: Charles Knight, 1841, p. 73.

9. André Alvares de Almada, *Brief Treatise on the Rivers of Guinea*, translated and edited by Paul Edward Hedley Hair, Liverpool: Department of History, University of Liverpool, 1984 [c. 1594], pp. 19; 46. See also a nineteenth-century Portuguese edition of Alvares de Almada, *Tratado breve dos Rios de Guine' do Cabo-Verde . . .*, Porto: Commercial Portuense, 1841.

10. Balthasar Barreira, 'Achievements on the Coast of Guinea and Sierra Leone,' in *Jesuit Documents on the Guinea of Cape Verde and the Cape Verde Islands, 1585–1617*, ed. and trans. P. E. H. Hair, Liverpool: University of Liverpool, 1989, sect. 29, ch. 2, p. 6. For how literacy was spread along the Gambia River valley by itinerant Islamic clerics shortly after the beginning of the Atlantic slave trade, see André Alvares de Almada, *Brief Treatise on the Rivers of Guinea*, c. 1594, ed. and trans. P. E. H. Hair, Liverpool: University of Liverpool, 1984, p. 46; Theodore Canot, *Adventures of an African Slaver*, Mineola: Courier Dover, 2002, p. 180.

11. Terry Alford, *Prince among Slaves: The True Story of an African Prince Sold into Slavery in the American South*, New York: Oxford University Press, 1977.

12. Sandoval's treatise was published in Spain in two editions during his life, first in 1627 and then a second, expanded version in 1646. Quotations come from an edition translated by Nicole von Germeten: Alonso de Sandoval, *Treatise on Slavery: Selections from De instauranda Aethiopum salute*, Indianapolis: Hackett Publishing, 2008. Quotations and relevant passages are found on pp. 33, 56, 68, 113, 120, and 136.

13. Manuel Barcia, '"An Islamic Atlantic Revolution": Dan Fodio's Jihād and Slave Rebellion in Bahia and Cuba, 1904–1844,' *Journal of African Diaspora, Archaeology, and Heritage* 2, no. 1 (May 2013): 6–17. There is debate over the degree to which Sufism can be considered a 'reform' movement. See Bernd Radtke and F. S. O'Fahey, 'Neo-Sufism Reconsidered,' *Der Islam* 70 (1993): 52–87; W. G. Clarence-Smith, *Islam and the Abolition of Slavery*, New York: Oxford University Press, 2006, p. 153; Lovejoy, 'Slavery, the Bilād al-Sūdān, and the Frontiers of the African

Diaspora,' p. 15. In *Benito Cereno*, Melville writes that Babo in Africa was a 'black man's slave,' a fact not given in Delano's account or found in other historical records, suggesting that he was aware of inter-African slavery.

14. Thomas Ewbank, *Life in Brazil; or, A Journal of a Visit to the Land of the Cocoa and the Palm*, New York: Harper and Brothers, 1956, p. 439.

15. Rout, *African Experience*, p. 24; Charles Christian and Sari Bennett, *Black Saga: The African American Experience. A Chronology*, New York: Basic Civitas Books, 1998, p. 4; Jane Landers, and Barry Robinson, eds., *Slaves, Subjects, and Subversives: Blacks in Colonial Latin America*, Albuquerque: University of New Mexico Press, 2006, p. 49.

16. For the presence of Islam in American slavery, see the following important work: Paul Lovejoy, 'Muslim Freedman in the Atlantic World: Images of Manumission and Self-Redemption,' in Lovejoy, ed., *Slavery on the Frontiers of Islam*, Princeton: Markus Wiener Publishers, 2004; Allan Austin, *African Muslims in Antebellum America: A Source Book*, New York: Garland, 1984; Edward Curtis, *Encyclopedia of Muslim-American History*, vol. 1, Infobase Publishing, 2010; Rout, *The African Experience in Spanish America*; Michael A. Gomez, *Exchanging Our Country Marks: The Transformation of African Identities in the Colonial and Antebellum South*, Chapel Hill: University of North Carolina Press, 1998, and *The Black Crescent: The Experience and Legacy of African Muslims in the Americas*, Cambridge: Cambridge University Press, 2005; Sylviane Diouf, *Servants of Allah: African Muslims Enslaved in the Americas*, New York: New York University Press, 1997; and Vincent Thompson, *Africans of the Diaspora: Evolution of Leadership, 18th Century to 20th Century*, Lawrenceville: Red Sea Press, 2000. For the ideological threat of Islam to Catholicism, see Cook, 'Forbidden Crossings: Morisco Emigration to Spanish America, 1492–1650,' and Fuchs, *Mimesis and Empire*, p. 74. For firsthand perceptions of this threat, see, in addition to the work already cited, António Galvão, *Tratado dos descobrimentos antigos, e modernos . . .*, Lisbon: Officina Ferreiriana, 1731, and Gomes Eannes de Azurara (Gomes Eanes de Zurara), *Chronica do descobrimento e conquisita de Guiné*, Paris: Aillaud, 1841; for the role slavery played in Islamic theology, especially in West Africa during the epoch of jihads, see Lovejoy, 'Slavery, the Bilād al-Sūdān, and the Frontiers of the African Diaspora'; Radtke and O'Fahey, 'Neo-Sufism Reconsidered,' *Der islam* 70 (1993): 52–87; W. G. Clarence-Smith, *Islam and the Abolition of Slavery*, New York: Oxford University Press, 2006; Babou, *Fighting the Greater Jihad*, and David Robinson, *The Holy War of Umar Tal: The Western Sudan in the Mid-Nineteenth Century*, Oxford: Clarendon Press, 1985; for possible Islamic influence in a series of powerful slave revolts in Cuba throughout the first decades of the 1800s, see Manuel Barcia, *Seeds of Insurrection: Domination and Slave Resistance on Cuban Plantations*, Baton Rouge: Louisiana State University Press, 2008. João José Reis's study of the 1835 Bahia rebellion is the key study of the largest urban slave revolt in American history: *Slave Rebellion in Brazil: The Muslim Uprising of 1835 in Bahia*, trans. Arthur Brakel, Baltimore: Johns Hopkins University Press, 1997. Reis has slightly

revised his earlier position regarding the centrality of Islam in the Bahia rebellion: Muslims were undoubtedly leaders of the rebels, but he now emphasizes 'an
ethnic rationale guiding their collective action.' After the rebellion was suppressed, Brazilian authorities singled out Muslims for punishment: 'Muslims
had been badly hit by repression in 1835, the religion became strictly prohibited, while hundreds of Muslim slaves were sold to the South, freed Muslims
were deported or left spontaneously to Africa, while others migrated to Rio de
Janeiro and other southern cities. Although a few Muslims in Bahia were still
active in the second half of the century, Islam was unable to recruit among cre-
oles, and eventually disappeared as an organized religion . . . ;' Reis, 'American
Counterpoint: New Approaches to Slavery and Abolition in Brazil,' paper presented at the Annual Gilder Lehrman Center International Conference at Yale
University, October 29–30, 2010, available at http://www.yale.edu/glc/brazil
/papers/reis-paper.pdf.

INTERLUDE: ABOMINABLE, CONTEMPTIBLE HAYTI

1. Eric Foner, *The Fiery Trial: Abraham Lincoln and American Slavery*, New York:
   Norton, 2010.
2. Patrick Geggus and Norman Fiering, *The World of the Haitian Revolution*, Bloom-
   ington: Indiana University Press, 2009, p. 320; David S. Reynolds, *Mightier Than the
   Sword*: Uncle Tom's Cabin *and the Battle for America*, New York: Norton, 2011. p. 75;
   Matthew Clavin, *Toussaint Louverture and the American Civil War: The Promise
   and Peril of a Second Haitian Revolution*, Philadelphia: University of Pennsylvania
   Press, 2009, pp. 41–43.
3. See 'At the First Performance of Lamartine's Play in Paris,' *North Star*, June 13, 1850.
   See also 'Toussaint L'Ouverture,' *North Star*, June 13, 1850; 'Toussaint L'Ouverture,'
   Frederick Douglass' Paper, September 4, 1851; 'Isaac Toussaint L'Ouverture, Son of
   the Haitian Negro General,' *Frederick Douglass' Paper*, November 25, 1854. Douglass himself wouldn't discuss Haiti and its revolution in detail until after his 1861
   visit to the country. Prior to this, he reserved the topic for 'certain audiences to avoid
   conjuring images of a race war.' See Clavin, *Toussaint Louverture*, p. 218; *Frederick
   Douglass: Selected Speeches and Writings*, ed. Philip Foner and Yval Taylor, Chicago:
   Chicago Review Press, 2000. The scholar Robert Wallace has recently made a strong
   case for the covert but important influence Douglass had on Melville, who incorporated ideas and images from the speeches of the former slave and abolitionist into
   his writing. See *Douglass and Melville: Anchored Together in Neighborly Style*, New
   Bedford: Spinner Publications, 2005, pp. 110–18, for the comparison between Douglass's and Melville's uses of the volcano metaphor, as well as other influences Douglass might have had on *Benito Cereno*.
4. Eric J. Sundquist, *To Wake the Nations: Race in the Making of American Literature*, Cambridge: Belknap, 1998, p. 170.
5. In a personal communication, Hershel Parker says he believes Melville was at
   his home in Pittsfield, Massachusetts, on February 26, 1855. Elliott (sometimes

spelled Elliot) didn't explicitly compare Haiti to the South. But the *Times* did in its review of the lecture: 'Your men, your slaves, chattels—have the old, human, inextinguishable passion for Liberty within them'; slave discontent 'does not show itself now' and neither did it for a long time in 'St. Domingo.' The paper even recycled Frederick Douglass's metaphor to warn slavers about 'the volcano on which you dwell' ('Toussaint L'Ouverture—Lecture by C. W. Elliott,' *New York Times*, February 27, 1855). See also 'The Danger to the South,' *New York Times*, May 9, 1855 and C. W. Elliott, *Heroes Are Historic Men: St. Domingo, Its Revolution, and Its Hero, Toussaint Louverture. An Historical Discourse Condensed for the New York Library Association, February 26, 1855*, New York: J. A. Dix, 1855. Elliott was a friend and colleague of Frederick Law Olmsted—the two men would soon begin to work together to lay out New York's Central Park—and it was Olmsted who proofread *Benito Cereno* for *Putnam's Monthly*.

20. DESPERATION

1. Delano, *Narrative*, pp. 277, 299.
2. Mention of William's clubfoot comes from the Hoyt Papers, in DRHS. Thanks to Carolyn Ravenscroft.
3. Delano, *Narrative*, pp. 420–21.
4. François Péron, *King Island and the Sealing Trade, 1802*, Canberra: Roebuck Society, 1971, p. 14.
5. Marjorie Tipping, *Convicts Unbound: The Story of the Calcutta Convicts and Their Settlement in Australia*, Ringwood Penguin Books Australia, 1988; Robert Knopwood, *The Diary of the Reverend Robert Knopwood, 1803-1838*, Hobart: Historical Research Association, 1977, p. 47; F. M. Bladen, ed., *Historical Records of New South Wales*, vol. 5, Sidney: N.S.W. Government, 1895, pp. 172–77, 186–97, 225, 263, 813–15, William Joy, *The Exiles*, Sydney: Shakespeare Head Press, p. 52; James Backhouse Walker, *Early Tasmania: Papers Read before the Royal Society of Tasmania during the Years 1888 to 1899*, Hobart: The Society, 1902, p. 45.
6. Delano, *Narrative*, p. 430; C. H. Gill, 'Notes on the Sealing Industry of Early Australia,' *Journal of the Royal Historical Society of Queensland* 8 (1967): 234; Patsy Adam Smith, *Moonbird People*, Sydney: Rigby Limited, 1965, p. 41.
7. Walker, *Early Tasmania*, pp. 41–42.
8. *Sydney Gazette*, August 19, 1804.
9. Ibid., April 22, 1804; August 19, 1804; August 26, 1804; September 2, 1804; and October 7, 1804, tracked the movement of the *Perseverance* and the *Pilgrim* in New South Wales.
10. Juan Fernández was used as a prison colony and, as Delano and his men were arriving in the middle of a series of escapes, the Spaniards didn't want any foreigners on the island. See Benjamín Vicuña Mackenna, *Juan Fernández, historia verdadera de la isla de Robinson Crusoe*, Santiago: R. Jover, 1883, p. 308; Ralph Lee Woodward, *Robinson Crusoe's Island: A History of the Juan Fernández*

Islands, Chapel Hill: University of North Carolina Press, 1969; José Toribio Medina, *Cosas de la colonia: Apuntes para la cronica del siglo XVIII en Chile*, Santiago: Fondo Histórico y Bibliográfico José Toribio Medina, 1952, pp. 100, 266–67.

11. Delano, *Narrative*, pp. 467–68. For a moment, it seemed as if neither Amasa nor his 'hurl-footed' brother would survive. Looking behind him, Amasa saw William weighed down with a heavy peacoat 'struggling very hard' to stay afloat on a brace of wood 'with his lame feet and confined arms.' He then turned away, toward the far-off *Pilgrim*, to see his other brother, Samuel, running back and forth from one mast to the other. In that moment of horse-market panic, Delano calmed himself by thinking of whales. 'As the female species of whale when her young is struck stays braving all the harpoons and lances that can be used for her destruction, until her offspring has breathed its last, and not till then the mother disappears,' so Delano knew that as long as his brother before him kept a frantic watch, the 'brother behind' him was still afloat. If Samuel were to withdraw from the deck, then William 'should be drowned.' Amasa then serenely reflected on what would happen to him should he die, brushing off his world of woe: 'For myself I could not perceive that life was of such great importance as I had already suffered a great many hardships and privations, besides many heartrending scenes of injustices, ingratitude, and disappointments.' The scene is faintly similar to one of *Moby-Dick*'s most moving passages, in a chapter called 'The Grand Armada,' where, in the middle of a frantic hunt, Ishmael, on the *Pequod*'s whaleboat, finds himself suddenly in the middle of a pod of nursing whales: 'Far beneath this wondrous world upon the surface, another and still stranger world met our eyes as we gazed over the side. For, suspended in those watery vaults, floated the forms of the nursing mothers of the whales, and those that by their enormous girth seemed shortly to become mothers. The lake, as I have hinted, was to a considerable depth exceedingly transparent; and as human infants while suckling will calmly and fixedly gaze away from the breast, as if leading two different lives at the same time; and while yet drawing mortal nourishment, be still spiritually feasting upon some unearthly reminiscence;—even so did the young of these whales seem looking up towards us, but not at us, as if we were but a bit of Gulfweed in their new-born sight. Floating on their sides, the mothers also seemed quietly eyeing us.' The scene soothes Ishmael, just as thoughts of a whale and her cub soothed Amasa: 'And thus, though surrounded by circle upon circle of consternations and affrights, did these inscrutable creatures at the centre freely and fearlessly indulge in all peaceful concernments; yes, serenely revelled in dalliance and delight. But even so, amid the tornadoed Atlantic of my being, do I myself still for ever centrally disport in mute calm; and while ponderous planets of unwaning woe revolve round me, deep down and deep inland there I still bathe me in eternal mildness of joy.'

12. For Rufus Low on the *Essex*, see Library of Congress, 'Sailing Master Rufus Low's Journal,' Edward Preble Papers; George Henry Preble, *The First Cruise*

of the United States Frigate Essex, Salem: Essex Institute, 1870, p. 43; Christopher McKee, *Edward Preble: A Naval Biography, 1761–1807*, Annapolis: Naval Institute Press, 1996, p. 81.

21. DECEPTION

1. Rogers, *Cruising Voyage*, p. 145.
2. Ibid., p. 146.
3. For Santa María Island, see ANC (Santiago), Capitanía General, vol. 772, no. 5 (1804); Capitanía General, vol. 522, no. 22 (1757); Real Audiencia, vol. 3000, no. 279 (1665); Real Audiencia, vol. 3030, no. 36 (1637). Also in AGI (Seville), in Chile 25 and 221, correspondencia, there are documents describing Spain's fear, in 1804, of losing the island to British pirates and smugglers.
4. Melville, *Benito Cereno,* p. 161.
5. Scholars have celebrated the trickster tradition among African Americans, who kept alive oral fables about wily humans and crafty animals such as Brer Rabbit, who use their wits to outfox the powerful. The tales, told at night around the hearth, could be traced back to peasant and pastoralist communities in Africa and not only allowed slaves to laugh at their masters but to pass on survival strategies, how to use guile as a weapon, to the next generation. See Larry E. Hudson, *Walking toward Freedom: Slave Society and Domestic Economy in the American South*, Rochester: University of Rochester Press, 1994, pp. 150–52; Lawrence Levine, *Black Culture and Black Consciousness: Afro-American Folk Thought from Slavery to Freedom*, New York: Oxford University Press, 1978, p. 125. Sterling Stuckey explicitly links *Benito Cereno*'s Babo to Brer Rabbit: 'The play of irony that informs Babo's activities . . . is precisely that adopted by Brer Rabbit in his African American expression. . . . What is certain is that Babo is so much like Brer Rabbit that it is perfectly logical that he should have come from Senegal, a thriving center of tales of the African hare, Brer Rabbit's ancestral model.' Both Brer Rabbit and Babo are 'linked to a shared sense of moral righteousness, which leads them to become forces of retribution that unsentimentally punish the purveyors of greed and cruelty' (*Going through the Storm: The Influence of African American Art in History*, New York: Oxford University Press, 1994, pp. 165, 167). Babacar M'Baye, in *The Trickster Comes West: Pan-African Influence in Early Black Diasporan Narratives*, Jackson: University Press of Mississippi, 2009, examines the influence of Senegalese folklore, particularly that associated with the Wolof, on African American culture.
6. For Islam and ideas of slavery and freedom, see William Gervase Clarence-Smith, *Islam and the Abolition of Slavery*, London: Hurst and Co., 1988, pp. 1–4, 19–25, 152–54, 223–29; Franz Rosenthal, *The Muslim Concept of Freedom prior to the Nineteenth Century*, Leiden: Brill, 1960, pp. 32, 110–12; Paul Lovejoy, 'The Context of Enslavement in West Africa: Ahmad Baba and the Ethics

of Slavery,' *Slaves, Subjects, and Subversives*, ed. Landers and Robinson, pp. 9–38.
7. Delano, *Narrative*, pp. 324–25.

22. RETRIBUTION

1. Quotations for this chapter are found in Delano, *Narrative*, pp. 325–28. For the evolution of maritime insurance, see Jonathan Levy, *Freaks of Fortune: The Emerging World of Capitalism and Risk in America*, Cambridge: Harvard University Press, 2012. For the *Zong*, see Jane Webster, 'The *Zong*, in the Context of the Eighteenth-Century Slave Trade,' and James Oldham, 'Insurance Litigation Involving the *Zong* and Other British Slave Ships, 1780–1807,' both in *Journal of Legal History* 28 (December 2007): 285–98 and 299–318. See also Ian Baucom, *Specters of the Atlantic: Finance Capital, Slavery, and the Philosophy of History*, Durham: Duke University Press, 2005.

23. CONVICTION

1. Delano, *Narrative*, p. 328.
2. Darwin, *Journal of Researches*, vol. 2, pp. 46–47.
3. Guillermo I. Castillo-Feliú, *Culture and Customs of Chile*, Westport: Greenwood, 2000, p. 27; Sergio Villalobos, *Tradición y reforma en 1810*, Santiago: RIL Editores, 2006, p. 199; Diego Barros Arana, *Historia general de Chile*, Santiago: Editorial Universitaria, 2002, vol. 8, p. 15; 'Observaciones sobre los serviles anarquistas de Córdova de la Plata,' *Década Araucana*, July 12, 1825, p. 5.
4. AGP (Mendoza), Censo parroquial mes de setiembre de 1777, folder 28, document 2.
5. Moulton, *Concise Extract*, p. 83. Rozas would later befriend another American, Procopio Pollock, a freemason from Philadelphia and ship surgeon on the *Warren* who spread republicanism through his clandestine *Gazeta de Procopio*, which translated revolutionary news and propaganda into Spanish.
6. Here, 'war' is translated from '*hicieron armas contra los Americanos.*'
7. The most common crimes that would get a convict sent to Valdivia were desertion, theft, murder, and vagrancy, with the prison population split roughly between Spaniards and mestizos, with a few Indians. In early 1804, there were no Africans or African descendants among the population. See ANC (Santiago), Real Audiencia, vol. 2470 ('Relación que manifiesta los desterrados que se hallan en las obras de plaza, y presidio de Valdivia').
8. AGC (Santiago), Capitanía General, vol. 873 ('Expediente formado ante la Intendencia de Concepción relativo a la construcción de un tabladillo en el Cuartel de Dragones de Concepción').
9. Hernán San Martín, *Nosotros los Chilenos*, Santiago: Editora Austral, 1970, p. 251.
10. Barros Arana, *Historia general*, vol. 8, p. 78, for *Bostonés*.
11. ANC (Santiago), Contaduría Mayor, 1st ser., vol. 1634, ff. 334–335.

INTERLUDE: THE MACHINERY OF CIVILIZATION

1. Newton Arvin, *Melville*, New York: Sloane, 1950, p. 180, for 'wild egoism.'
2. Jeremy Harding, 'Call Me Ahab,' *London Review of Books*, October 31, 2002.

24. LIMA, OR THE LAW OF GENERAL AVERAGE

1. For the descriptions of Callao, see George Peck, *Melbourne, and the Chincha Islands, with Sketches of Lima, and a Voyage Round the World*, New York: Scribner, 1854, pp. 142–145; Gilbert Farquhar Mathison, *Narrative of a Visit to Brazil, Chile, Peru, and the Sandwich Islands*, London: Bentley, 1825; Proctor, *Narrative of a Journey*, William Bennet Stevenson, *Historical and Descriptive Narrative of Twenty Years' Residence in South America*, London: Longman, 1829.
2. Charles Walker, *Shaky Colonialism: The 1746 Earthquake-Tsunami in Lima, Peru, and Its Long Aftermath*, Durham: Duke University Press, 2008, p. 10.
3. Hugh Salvin, *Journal Written on Board of His Majesty's Ship Cambridge, from January, 1824, to May, 1827*, Newcastle: Walker, 1829, p. 30. Salvin here perhaps mistakenly attributes the skeletons as belonging to recent victims of royalist forces during the war for independence, since what he describes is nearly identical to what Delano witnessed years before that war.
4. Delano, *Narrative*, pp. 487–88.
5. Peck, *Melbourne*, p. 150.
6. Delano, *Narrative*, p. 494.
7. Bernabé Cobo, *Historia de la fundación de Lima*, Lima: Imprenta Liberal, 1882, p. 56.
8. Delano, *Narrative*, p. 494.
9. AGN (Lima), Real Hacienda Caja Real, legajo 1931, cuaderno 1630, for the dress of *los negros del rey*.
10. For months, Cerreño had been presumed dead and his ship lost; his creditors had filed papers to recover their investment through a sort of royal insurance policy. See AGN (Lima), signatura GO-BI 2, legajo 91, expediente 775.
11. For claims made on Aranda's cargo by his father-in-law, Isidro Maza, and his wife, Carmen Maza, see AGP (Mendoza), notary records, José de Porto y Mariño, no. 152, ff. 46–47 ('Transcripción del poder de don Isidro Sainz de la Maza'), and ff. 91v–92v ('Transcripción del poder del 27 de julio de 1805 de doña María del Carmen Maza'). For Nonell, see AGN (Buenos Aires), notary records, Inocencio Agrelo, no. 6, ff. 387–88 ('Poder de Don Juan de Nonell a favor de Don Antonio de Estapar'); AGN (Lima), notary records, José Escudero de Sicilia, no. 214, ff. 660–63, 715v–719, 1177v, 1182. For Cerreño's debt, see AGN (Lima), notary records, José Escudero de Sicilia, no. 214, ff. 660–63, 715v–719, 1048r–1949r, 1177v; AGN (Lima) TC-GO 2, legajo 13, expediente 612 ('José Escudero de Sicilia, escribano mayor del Real Tribunal del Consulado de Lima solicita la cancelación de cantidad de pesos por las costas obradas en los autos de la avería gruesa que sufrió la fragata Trial, por la sublevación de una partida de negros'); and AGN

(Lima), TC-JU, legajo 182, expediente 519 ('Ante el Real Tribunal del Consulado de Lima').

12. Michael Lobban, 'Slavery, Insurance, and the Law,' *Journal of Legal History* 28 (December 2007): 320–22; Tim Armstrong, 'Slavery, Insurance, and Sacrifice in the Black Atlantic,' in *Sea Changes: Historicizing the Ocean*, ed. Bernhard Klein and Gesa Mackenthun, New York: Routledge, 2004.

13. AGN (Lima), Real Hacienda, legajo 1033, cuaderno 1632 1805.

14. Orlando Patterson, *Slavery and Social Death: A Comparative Study*, Cambridge: Harvard University Press, 1982, pp. 5, 331. Many of these sales are in AGN (Lima), notary records, Manuel Malarin, no. 390. See especially ff. 555, 571, 574, 620, 667, 673. See also AGN (Lima), Cabildo-Causas Civiles (CA-JO 1), legajo 158, expediente 2994; legajo 153, expediente 280; and legajo 154, expediente 2848.

25. THE LUCKY ONE

1. AGN (Lima), TC-JU 1, legajo 182, expediente 519 ('Autos seguidos por Miguel de Monrreal, capitán y ex maestre de la fragata "Trial"') September 25, 1806; AGN (Lima), Real Hacienda, legajo 1036, expediente 1635.

2. AGN (Lima), Real Audiencia, Tierras y Haciendas, legajo 21, cuaderno 133, f. 44 ('Testimonio del Inventario de la Hacienda de Humaya'), and AGN (Lima), signatura C-13, legajo 25, expediente 31 ('La Administración e Intendencia de Temporalidades con Benito Cerreño'). See also AA (Lima), Parroquia del Sagrario (Catedral): Libros de Matrimonios, no. 11 (1785–1846) f. 125; AA (Lima), Parroquia del Sagrario, Indice de Pliegos Matrimoniales, no. 4 (1791–1814), April 21, 1805, f. 1v.

3. In 1823, the Senate of an independent Chile voted unanimously to immediately abolish slavery, with no apprenticeship period or compensation paid to slaveholders. The move, writes Robin Blackburn, was 'more radical' than the gradual, court-brokered abolition that had by then taken place in the states north of the Mason-Dixon Line in the United States (Blackburn, *The Overthrow of Colonial Slavery, 1776–1848*, London: Verso, 1988, p. 358). Chattel slavery in Chile was not as deeply rooted an institution as it was in Peru, Brazil, or even Argentina, where it took longer to abolish. There were between ten and twelve thousand Africans or people of African descent in Chile around this time, about half of whom were slaves; most lived in and around Santiago or farther north. In a southern city like Concepción, it was Indians who tended to be enslaved. See Simon Collier and William F. Slater, *A History of Chile, 1808–2002*, Cambridge: Cambridge University Press, 2004, p. 42. For Rozas's importance as a jurist, see Fernando Campos Harriet, 'Don Juan Martínez de Rozas, jurista de los finales del periodo indiano,' *VII Congreso del Instituto Internacional de Historia del Derecho Indiano, Buenos Aires, 1 al 6 de agosto de 1983*, Buenos Aires: Pontifica Universidad Católica, 1984.

4. Peter Blanchard, *Under the Flag of Freedom: Slave Soldiers and the Wars of Independence in Spanish South America*, Pittsburgh: University of Pittsburgh Press, 2008, pp. 92–97, 103.

5. Diego Barros Arana, *Historia general de Chile*, vol. 9, Santiago: Editorial Universitaria, 2002, pp. 85–88; *Memorias, Diarios y Crónicas*, vol. 2, ed. Felix Denegri Luna, Lima: Comisión nacional del sesquicentenario de la Independencia del Peru, 1975, p. 589. 'James Paroissien, anotaciones para un diario' (August 18, 1820–March 19, 1821), *Colección de obras y documentos para la historia argentina: Guerra de la independencia*, vol. 17, part 1, Buenos Aires: Senado de la Nación, 1963, p. 32.

6. Basil Hall, *Extracts from a Journal Written on the Coasts of Chili, Peru, and Mexico, in the Years 1820, 1821, 1822*, vol. 1, London: Constable and Co., 1824, p. 90.

7. Hall, *Extracts*, pp. 219–20.

8. Centro de Estudios Militares del Perú, Sección Archivos y Catálogos, tomo 1: 1821–23, legajo 2, document 6; legajo 17, document 274; *Gaceta de Gobierno de Lima*, January 22, 1817.

9. Robert Maclean y Estenós, *Sociologia Peruana*, Lima: Librería Gil, 1942, p. 154; AGN (Lima), notary records, Pedro Seminario, no. 776, f. 181 (April 17, 1852).

10. William Edward Gardner, *The Coffin Saga: Nantucket's Story, from Settlement to Summer Visitors*, Cambridge: Riverside Press, 1949, p. 168.

26. UNDISTRIBUTED

1. Houghton Library, Harvard University, 'Perseverance (Ship). Logbook, 27 Jan–24 Jul 1807' (MS Am 465.5).

2. Notice of the commendation was reprinted in newspapers throughout the Northeast. See, for example, the *Portsmouth Oracle*, August 22, 1807, and the *United States Gazette*, August 21, 1807.

3. Records in the Massachusetts Supreme Judicial Court in MA (Boston) show that Delano began defaulting on his debt in 1797. He owed at least $500 to three men. See Turner V. Delano, Supreme Judicial Court for Plymouth Counter, May term 1799, Record Book Summary. See also DRHS, Delano Papers, series 3, box 2, folder 2, 'Summons for Amasa Delano to appear in Plymouth Court of Common Pleas,' February 9, 1799; 'Summons for Amasa Delano to appear in Plymouth Court of Common Pleas,' July 7, 1799; 'Martin Bicker and Others Recover Damages from Amasa Delano,' April 3, 1798; 'Bond of Arbitration between Amasa Delano and Timothy Parsons to Settle Dispute,' February 25, 1798. One debt suit involved Sally Rutter, a woman whom he had never met who claimed to be the rightful executrix of a will of James Blake, who had sailed on the *Perseverance*'s second voyage. Blake died before returning to the United States but Rutter said she had in her possession a receipt Delano had given him in Canton for the amount of $1,608. Blake and his bosom mate, Phineas Trowbridge, had been exceptionally troublesome to the Delano brothers. They were 'ever plotting,' according to testimony given by Delano's first mate. Left on Más Afuera to hunt seals, they lived 'only

them two together' and conspired to rob Delano out of thousands of dollars' worth of skins. Rutter also alleged that, before sailing, Delano had borrowed from Blake $1,400 as seed money for the voyage, promising a return of $28,000 upon completion of the trip. The Court of Common Pleas ordered Delano to pay Rutter $2,198.05, plus court fees of $32.60, and the decision was upheld by the Supreme Court on appeal. There is no evidence that Delano satisfied the judgment; that he failed to appear at the final hearing meant he was likely arrested. See MA (Boston), Judicial Archives, 'Supreme Judicial Court for Suffolk County, Amaso Delano, in Review v. John & Sally Rutter, Executors of the Estate of James Blake,' file papers, docket no. 348. For debt in Boston, see Port Society of Boston and Its Vicinity, *Report of the Managers of the Port Society of the City of Boston and Its Vicinity*, Boston: H. Eastburn, 1836, p. 13; Charles Sellers, *The Market Revolution*, New York: Oxford University Press, 1992, p. 87.

4. Harvard Law Library, Small Manuscript Collection, Judge Story Papers.
5. Information on this phase of Delano's life comes from various sources: 1810 Census, Boston, Ward 11, Suffolk, p. 107, line 33; National Archives micropublications, M 252, roll 21; *The Boston Directory; Containing the Names of the Inhabitants*, Boston: Edward Cotton, 1809, p. 47 (also see 1810 ed., p. 63). Delano's father died in 1814, leaving his house, land, and livestock, along with two meetinghouse pews, to the younger William, who was then starting a family. Childless Amasa inherited $200 but it immediately went to his creditors. Samuel received $500 and each of the three Delano sisters, Irene, Abigail, and Elizabeth, inherited $100. Information from Probate no. 6321, Estate of Samuel Delano, d. 6 Nov. 1814, and from Plymouth County Registry of Deeds, book 70, p. 148, summarized in notes available at the DRHS. See also DRHS, Delano Papers, box 8, folders 17 and 18 for Delano's 'accounts' with Weston.
6. Franklin D. Roosevelt Presidential Library, Hyde Park, New York, Frederic Delano Papers, exchange of letters between Amasa Delano and Secretary of State John Quincy Adams, December 1817.
7. For 'most trifling purpose,' see Perry Miller, *Errand into the Wilderness*, Cambridge: Harvard University Press, 1984, pp. 66–67.
8. Sellers, *Market Revolution*, p. 87; Bruce Mann, *Republic of Debtors: Bankruptcy in the Age of American Independence*, Cambridge: Harvard University Press, 2009. The progress of Delano's life, as he tells it in *A Narrative*, reads much like Melville's *Israel Potter*, published just before *Benito Cereno*, which tells the story of a life that starts out 'gloriously' but leads 'nowhere,' that of a Revolutionary War veteran who 'proves to have little flexibility, little resilience (after a series of defeats), but an almost infinite capacity for suffering and enduring.' The story begins with Potter leaving his farm to fight at the Battle of Bunker Hill, a battle Melville describes in ignoble terms: Potter is bewildered by the battlefield's 'dense crowd and confusion' and begins to swing his rifle butt wildly, like the way 'seal-hunters on the beach' swing their clubs. He looks down and thinks he sees a sword being thrust up at him. But the weapon is in a hand attached to a severed arm. After the battle, Potter is catapulted into the world of

high politics. He conspires with Benjamin Franklin in France, fights at the side of John Paul Jones, tries to help Ethan Allen escape from jail, and even meets King George. But he is as lost in the mazes of history as Amasa was in Lima's royal palace. Melville ends his story by bringing Potter, after half a century of exile, back to Bunker Hill on July 4, 1826, where a crowd has gathered to view the now completed monument. But instead of being recognized as a Son of Liberty, Potter is nearly run down by a 'patriotic triumphal car' flying a gilt-embroidered banner celebrating veterans of the battle. He returns to his father's homestead, but no one recognizes him there either. Unable to convince the government to give him a pension, he dies broke; 'his scars proved his only medal.' For the descriptions of *Israel Potter*, see Andrew Delbanco, *Herman Melville: His World and Work*, New York: Knopf, 2005, p. 226; Parker, *Herman Melville: A Biography*, vol. 2, p. 224.

9. DRHS, Delano Papers, ser. 1, box 1, folder 5, Samuel Delano Jr. to Samuel Delano III, March 21, 1820; DRHS, Delano Papers, ser. 1, box 1, folder 5, Samuel Delano, Jr. to Captain Henry Chandler, December 11, 1832.

10. DRHS, Delano Papers, ser. 1, box 8, folder 14, Amasa to Samuel Delano, Jr., September 7, 1821. For Samuel's finances, see DRHS, Delano Papers, ser. 3, box 2, folder 2, 'Attachment of Goods and Estate of Samuel Delano, Jr.,' July 22, 1822, and 'Settlement of Grievance between Samuel Delano, Jr. and G. W. Martin,' April 21, 1823.

11. Daniel Walker Howe, *What Hath God Wrought: The Transformation of America, 1815–1848*, New York: Oxford University Press, 2009, p. 617.

12. *Speeches and Address of Peleg Sprague*, Boston: Phillips, Samson, 1858, p. 452.

13. MA (Boston), Judicial Archives, docket no. 27093, vols. 121 (pp. 300 and 464); 121-1 (p. 37); 172 (p. 104); 193 (p. 226); 207 (p. 170).

EPILOGUE: HERMAN MELVILLE'S AMERICA

1. Daniel Johnson and Rex Campbell, *Black Migration in America: A Social Demographic Hisory*, Durham: Duke University Press, 1981; John Russell Rickford, *Spoken Soul: The Story of Black English*, Hoboken: John Wiley, 2002, p. 138; Walter Johnson, 'King Cotton's Long Shadow,' *New York Times*, March 30, 2013; Frederic Bancroft, *Slave Trading in the Old South*, 1931, New York: Frederick Ungar, 1959, p. 363, for fever quotes. See also Johnson, *River of Dark Dreams*, pp. 374–78; John Craig Hammond, *Slavery, Freedom, and Expansion in the Early American West*, Charlottesville: University of Virginia Press, 2007; Matthew Mason, *Slavery and Politics in the Early American Republic*, Chapel Hill: University of North Carolina Press, 2006; Adam Rothman, *Slave Country: American Expansion and the Origins of the Deep South*, Cambridge: Harvard University Press, 2007, p. 193.

2. Stephen Matterson, 'Introduction,' in Herman Melville, *The Confidence-Man*, New York: Penguin, 1990, p. xxiv. At the same time, Melville was also questioning this belief; see Hershel Parker, 'Politics and Art.'

3. *White-Jacket*, pp. 505–6; For Melville's 'radical' break with the past, Matterson, 'Introduction,' *The Confidence-Man*, p. xxiv. For Melville's use of naval discipline and the arbitrary power of officers as a metaphor for slavery, and one southern reviewer's recognition of the metaphor, see Karcher, *Shadow over the Promised Land*, pp. 44–47.

4. Robert May, *The Southern Dream of a Caribbean Empire*, Baton Rouge: Louisiana State University Press, 1973, p. 164.

5. John M. Murrin, Paul E. Johnson, James M. McPherson, Alice Fahs, and Gary Gerstle, *Liberty, Equality, Power: A History of the American People*, Independence Cengage Learning, 2012, p. 463; *Liberator*, May 23, 1851.

6. Robert Cover, *Justice Accused: Antislavery and the Judicial Process*, New Haven: Yale University Press, 1975, p. 251; *The Writings of Henry David Thoreau: Cape Cod and Miscellanies*, New York: Houghton Mifflin, 1906, p. 396; Jeannine DeLombard, 'Advocacy "in the Name of Charity" or Barratry, Champerty, and Maintenance? Legal Rhetoric and the Debate over Slavery in Antebellum Print Culture,' in *Law and Literature*, ed. Brook Thomas; Turbinger: Gunter Narr Verlag, 2002, p. 271, Robert D. Richardson Jr., *Emerson: The Mind on Fire*, Berkeley: University of California Press, 1995, p. 496; Louis Menand, *The Metaphysical Club: A Story of Ideas in America*, New York: Farrar, Straus and Giroux, 2001, p. 21; Len Gougeon, *Virtue's Hero: Emerson, Antislavery, and Reform*, Athens: University of Georgia Press, 2010, p. 244; William Nelson, 'The Impact of the Antislavery Movement upon Styles of Judicial Reasoning in Nineteenth-Century America,' *Harvard Law Review* 87 (1974): 513–66; Anthony Sebok, *Legal Positivism in American Jurisprudence*, New York: Cambridge University Press, 1998, p. 69; *Reports of Cases Argued and Determined in the Supreme Judicial Court of the Commonwealth of Massachusetts, 1851*, vol. 61, Boston: Little, Brown, 1853, p. 310; Don Fehrenbacher, *The Slaveholding Republic: An Account of the United States Government's Relations to Slavery*, New York: Oxford University Press, 2002, p. 234. For Shaw's previous antislavery rulings, see Cover, *Justice Accused*. In 1844, for instance, Shaw freed Robert Lucas, who arrived in Boston on the USS *United States* (the same ship that carried Herman Melville home from his soon-to-be famous Pacific voyages). Shaw's ruling in the Lucas case was in a way similar to the earlier one issued by the state's Supreme Judicial Court in the suit brought by James Mye's would-be masters, who had signed him up as a hand on the *Tryal* with the expectation that they would receive a percentage of his shares. With Lucas, his owner had enlisted him in the navy and collected his pay, but once docked in Massachusetts, the slave petitioned the court for his freedom and Shaw granted it. 'None but a free person can enter a contract,' Shaw wrote.

7. Parker, *Herman Melville: A Biography*, vol. 2, p. 454.

8. For 'popular sovereignty' as 'white supremacy,' see Pamela Brandwein, *Reconstructing Reconstruction: The Supreme Court and the Production of Historical Truth*, Durham: Duke University Press, 1999, p. 38; Ashraf H. A. Rushdy, *American Lynching*, New Haven: Yale University Press, 2012, p. 143; Kristen Tegtmeier

Oertel, *Bleeding Borders: Race, Gender, and Violence in Pre-Civil War Kansas*, Baton Rouge: Louisiana State University Press, 2009, p. 4.

9. Delbanco, *Melville*, pp. 153–54; Parker, *Melville and Politics*, p. 234.

10. *Benito Cereno*, p. 257.

11. Davis, *Problem of Slavery*, p. 563; Douglas Blackmon, *Slavery by Another Name: The Re-Enslavement of Black Americans from the Civil War to World War II*, New York: Anchor Books, 2008.

ACKNOWLEDGMENTS

In the early 1920s, the British war journalist and novelist H. M. Tomlinson let Americans in on a secret. There existed an obscure book that certain people used as an 'artful test' to identify like-minded souls. If they gave it to you to read, Tomlinson wrote in the *Christian Science Monitor*, and you 'showed no surprise,' you'd be deemed 'no good.' But, being that they 'were half afraid of the intensity of their own conviction,' they wouldn't tell you you were no good. They'd keep quiet. If, however, Herman Melville's *Moby-Dick* possessed you, you would have proved yourself worthy, able to 'dwell in safety with fiends or angels and rest poised with a quiet mind between the stars and the bottomless pit.' Ninety years later, I felt that I had my own password into a knowing world of fiends and angels. When asked what I was working on, I'd say I was researching events that inspired a Herman Melville story. 'Not *Moby-Dick*,' I'd say, 'another one.' Less than half had heard of *Benito Cereno* and fewer still had read it. Those who had, though, knew it was different. It was Corey Robin who first let me in on the secret and I owe the idea of this book to him.

Over the years, I've kept a running list of people who helped in large and small ways move this work along, and if I've left anyone out, I apologize. Though I cite their scholarship throughout, special credit is due to the historians Alex Borucki and Lyman Johnson. They have been extremely generous taking time to respond to my questions and read the manuscript. I also want to thank the friends and colleagues, at NYU and elsewhere, who listened, suggested, corrected, and indulged, including Barbara Weinstein, Ada Ferrer, Sinclair Thomson, Michael Ralph, Gary

Wilder, Laurent Dubois, Donna Murch, Chuck Walker, Mark Healey, Karen Spalding, Gerardo Rénique, Jennifer Adair, Debbie Poole, Kristin Ross, Harry Harootunian, Eric Foner, Emilia da Costa, Ned Sublette, Constance Ash-Sublette, Walter Johnson, Fred Cooper, Ernesto Semán, Bob Wheeler, Julio Pinto, Peter Winn, Gil Joseph, Stuart Schwartz, Tom Bender, Matt Hausmann, Amy Hausmann, Robert Perkinson, Christian Parenti, Laura Brahm, Jack Wilson, Gordon Lafer, Josh Frens-String, Christy Thornton, Aldo Marchesi, Ervand Abrahamian, Carlota McAllister, Marilyn Young, Deborah Levenson, Liz Oglesby, Molly Nolan, Lauren Benton, Cristina Mazzeo de Vivó, Henry Hughes, Jorge Ortiz-Sotelo, and Chris Maxworthy. Jean Stein graciously read the manuscript and offered constant encouragement. Eleanor Roosevelt Seagraves kindly took the time to discuss Delano's memoir. Susan Rabiner has helped guide the work along since the beginning. In the middle of the project, between the archival research and the writing, I fell into a Melville obsession, from the depths of which one thing kept me going: knowing that Richard Kim would understand.

Many, many people assisted in the research of this book, including Roberto Pizarro, Seth Palmer, Liz Fink, Kyle Francis, Matthew Hovious, Flor Maribet Pantoja Diaz, Emiliano Andrés Mussi, Yobani Gonzales Jauregui, Andrés Azpiroz, Christy Mobley, and Adam Rathge. Rachel Nolan put her many skills, including an unanticipated knowledge of Catholic saints, to proofreading and fact-checking. In Mendoza, Luis César Caballeros conducted key research and Diego Escolar was a gracious host. Boubacar Barry helped me speculate about the origins of the names of the *Tryal* rebels; Al Cave passed on information about the Pequot War; Clifford Ross allowed me to look at one of Melville's family Bibles; at the NYPL, David Rosado facilitated the reproduction of a number of illustrations and Jessica Pigza put together a list of extant first editions of Delano's memoir; BJ Gooch, the archivist at Transylvania University Library, confirmed that Horace Holley was indeed the author of Amasa Delano's biographical sketch; Michael Dyer, at the New Bedford Whaling Museum, identified illustrations; Jennifer Lofkrantz cleared up certain points of Islamic law; in Concepción, Alejandro Mihovilovich Gratz shared his deep knowledge of the region's history, as did

Manuel Loyola and Magdelana Varas, members of a dance and theatre troupe, Teatro del Oráculo, dedicated to the recuperation of popular, or 'people's' history: after happening on a reference to the 1805 execution of Mori and the other West Africans, they began to research the events of the *Tryal*, staging, in 2006, *La Laguna de los Negros*. Information on this and other productions can be found on the group's website: http://www.teatrodeloraculo.cl/. Elizabeth Bouvier, head of the archives of the Massachusetts Supreme Court, passed on and helped interpret documents related to Amasa Delano's various debt cases; Ron Brown, at the New York University School of Law Library, compiled a list of legal cases that cited *Hall et al. v. Gardner et al*. I'd also like to thank Ibrahama Thioub and Ibra Sene for sharing their knowledge of Dakar's archives with me.

Carolyn Ravenscroft, the archivist at the Duxbury Rural and Historical Society, deserves special mention. Carolyn was with this project from nearly its beginning and though there are only so many times one can use the word *generous* in acknowledgments, that she was, and more so. Hershel Parker was once kind enough to respond to an unsolicited e-mail inquiry and I hope he doesn't regret it! Ever since, he has been exceptionally charitable in answering questions and sharing his unmatched knowledge of Herman Melville's life and work.

I was privileged to be able to finish a final draft of the manuscript while a Gilder Lehrman Fellow in American History at the New York Public Library's Cullman Center for Scholars and Writers. As if time to write and access to the library's collections weren't benefit enough, the year also allowed the rare opportunity to discuss all sorts of things with the wonderful people who keep the Center and Library running, especially Jean Strouse, Marie d'Orginy, Paul Delaverdac, Caitlin Kean, and Maira Liriano, and a terrific cohort of fellow fellows: Mae Ngai, Betsy Blackmar, Philip Gourevitch, Said Sayrafiezadeh, Valentina Izmirlieva, Gary Panter, Jamie Ryerson, John Wray, Luc Sante, Shimon Dotan, Katie Morgan, Tony Gottlieb, Ruth Franklin, and Daniel Margocsy.

I owe an enormous debt of gratitude to all the people at Metropolitan Books, including Rick Pracher, and Kelly Too but especially Riva Hocherman and Connor Guy. They helped in more ways than can be counted here. Again, it has been a pleasure to work with Roslyn Schloss. And Sara Bershtel: whenever I'm asked to compare the differences between having a manuscript reviewed by a university publisher and having one reviewed by a trade press, my thoughts revert to Sara. There's no comparison. She brings a formidable commitment, precision, and intelligence to thinking about the content and form of a book, beginning with the first conversation and not ending until the acknowledgments are being written. I'm lucky to have her as an editor and even more so as a friend. Thank you.

In the past, I've thanked Tannia Goswami, Toshi Goswami, and, of course, Manu Goswami. I get to again, but this time also Eleanor Goswami Grandin, born on, depending on what calendar one is using, either the 20th of Rabi-al-thani 1435 or the 23rd of Ventôse 220, but in any case starting the world anew.

ILLUSTRATIONS CREDITS

I'm indebted to the following individuals and institutions for permission to publish images from their collections: Carolyn Ravenscroft and Erin McGough of the Duxbury Rural and Historical Society (for the painting of the *Perseverance*, image 15); Schomburg Center for Research in Black Culture, of the NYPL (image 5); the Print Collection, Miriam and Ira D. Wallach Division of Art, Prints and Photographs of the NYPL (images 9, 10, 11, and 20); the General Research Division of the NYPL (images 21, 25, 27, 28, 31); the Picture Collection of the NYPL (image 36); Michael Dyer of the New Bedford Whaling Museum (for images 30 and 34); The British Library (image 32); and Garrick Palmer, who graciously allowed me to produce two of his wonderful wood engravings (images 33 and 37), which illustrate a 1972 edition of *Benito Cereno*.

FIRST INSERT:

Image 1:   'Capturant le Gustave Adolphe,' Ange-Joseph-Antoine Roux, 1806.

Image 2:   René Geoffroy de Villeneuve, *L'Afrique, ou histoire, moeurs, usages et coutumes des africains: le Sénégal* (1814).

Image 3:   Engraving by T. H. Birch, 1837, original in the National Maritime Museum (Greenwich, London).

Image 4:   'Slaves on the West Coast of Africa,' Auguste-François Biard, c. 1833.

Image 5:   Johann Moritz Rugenda, *Voyage pittoresque dans le Brésil* . . . (1835).

Image 6:   'View of Montevideo from the Bay,' Fernando Brambila, c. 1794.

Image 7:   Charles Darwin, *Journal of Researches* . . . (Thomas Nelson, 1890).

Images 8, 12,
  and 13:   César Hipólito Bacle, *Trages y costumbres de la Provincia de Buenos Aires* (1833[1947]).

Images 9, 10,
  and 11:   Jean-Baptiste Debret, *Voyage pittoresque et historique au Brésil* (1834).

Image 14:   Amasa Delano's *A Narrative . . .* (1816).

Image 15:   From the Collection of the Duxbury Rural and Historical Society; photograph by Norman Forgit.

Image 16:   Nelson's Monument, Liverpool, drawn by G. and C. Pyne, engraved by Thomas Dixon, in *Lancashire Illustrated: From Original Drawings* (1831).

SECOND INSERT:

Image 18:   *C. H. Pellegrini: Su Obra, su vida, su tiempo*, compiled by Elena Sansinea de Elizalde (1946).

Image 19:   César Hipólito Bacle, *Trages y costumbres de la Provincia de Buenos Aires* (1833[1947]).

Image 20:   Jean-Baptiste Debret, *Voyage pittoresque et historique au Brésil* (1834).

Images 21
  and 25:   Alexander Caldcleugh, *Travels in South America* (1825).

Images 23
  and 24:   Charles Darwin, *Journal of Researches . . .* (Thomas Nelson, 1890).

Image 26:   Charles Darwin, *Journal of Researches . . .* (Ward Lock, 1890).

Image 27:   George Anson, *A Voyage Round the World* (1748).

Image 28:   *The Boy's Own Paper*, December 10, 1887.

Image 29:   Map by Alexander Hogg, in G. A. Anderson, *A New, Authentic, and Complete Collection of Voyages Round the World* (1784).

Image 30:   'Ann Alexander,' Guiseppi Fedi, 1807.

Image 31:   P. D. Boilat, *Esquisses Sénégalaises* (1853).

Image 32:   'Plano de la Isla Santa María en la costa del reyno de Chile,' 1804.

Image 35:   'View of Talcahuano,' Fernando Brambila, c. 1794.

INDEX

Page numbers in *italics* refer to illustrations.

ABOUT THE AUTHOR

GREG GRANDIN is the author of *Fordlandia*, a finalist for the Pulitzer Prize, the National Book Award, the National Book Critics Circle Award, and the James Tate Black Prize, as well as *Empire's Workshop* and *The Last Colonial Massacre*. A professor of history at New York University and a member of the American Academy of Arts and Sciencs, he has been a recipient of fellowships from the Guggenheim Foundation and, most recently, the New York Public Library's Cullman Center, where he was the Gilder Lehrman Fellow in American History. Grandin has served on the UN Truth Commission investigating the Guatemalan civil war and has written for the *London Review of Books*, *New Statesman*, the *Los Angeles Times*, the *Nation*, and the *New York Times*.